BLUEPRINT FOR VICTORY
BRITAIN'S FIRST WORLD WAR BLITZKRIEG AIR FORCE

BLUEPRINT FOR VICTORY
BRITAIN'S FIRST WORLD WAR BLITZKRIEG AIR FORCE

GREG BAUGHEN

FONTHILL

Fonthill Media Limited
Fonthill Media LLC
www.fonthillmedia.com
office@fonthillmedia.com

First published in the United Kingdom and the United States of America 2014

Copyright © Greg Baughen 2014

ISBN 978-1-78155-392-3

The right of Greg Baughen to be identified as the author of this work has been asserted by him in accordance with the Copyright, Designs and Patents Act 1988

All rights reserved. No part of this publication may be reproduced, stored in a retrieval system or transmitted in any form or by any means, electronic, mechanical, photocopying, recording or otherwise, without prior permission in writing from Fonthill Media Limited

Typeset in 10pt on 13pt Sabon LT Std

Printed and bound by CPI Group (UK) Ltd, Croydon, CR0 4YY

Contents

	Acknowledgements	7
	Preface	8
1	Cities in the Front Line	11
2	The Tactical Vision	32
3	Early Success and Stalemate	48
4	Fading Promise and Fokkers	67
5	Naval Help and Flying Dreadnoughts	79
6	Ascendancy and the Seeds of Disaster	88
7	RFC in Crisis	96
8	The Brave New World of Strategic Bombing	117
9	A Modern Tactical Air Force	138
10	The Government Opts for the Bomber	150
11	New Options on the Battlefield	160
12	Tactical Air Support Comes of Age	166
13	A Glimpse into the Future	179
14	Strategic Bombing in Retreat	191
15	Last Gasp for the Long-Range Bomber	210
	Conclusion	227
	Endnotes	232
	Sources and Bibliography	250
	Index	252

Acknowledgements

My thanks to the staff of the National Archives, the RAF Museum, the Imperial War Museum and the Liddell Hart Centre for their assistance. My apologies to the security officers at the National Archives for always being so reluctant to leave at closing time. An enormous thank you to Phil Butler, Paul Hare and Phil Carradice for their help with the illustrations. Thanks also to the Canada Aviation and Space Museum for their generous assistance. Thanks to my family for their support and in particular my son for passing on his IT skills.

Preface

This book is a response to a myth and a flawed policy. The myth was that the fighting over the battlefields of France in the First World War could teach nothing about how air power should be used in future wars. The flawed policy was long-range bombing. The myth had its genesis in the years that followed the First World War. The Air Staff were anxious to draw a line under the experience of that conflict and start afresh. During the First World War, the air arm had heroically supported the Army, but it was not a role that satisfied air force ambitions. The leaders of the newly independent RAF did not want to be 'ancillary' or 'auxiliary' ever again. The air force wanted to be the equal of the Army and Navy, and that meant having its own independent war-winning strategy. To the visionaries of the time, it all seemed logical enough. Armies could win wars on land and navies could defeat nations at sea. There seemed no reason why an air force should not win a war in the air.

There was a superficial logic about it. Armies and navies, however, operate in two entirely different domains, connected only by coastlines. They perhaps had some justification for developing their own independent strategies and fighting their own wars. The air is not a self-contained environment and it is connected to sea and land. The air force could not avoid interacting with armies and navies. It was not so easy for the air force to go its own way. However, the post-war Air Ministry was determined to find a way. It declared armies and navies obsolete. In future wars, tactical air power would have nothing to support, and battles would be decided by fleets of long-range bombers.

Some reinterpretation of history would be required to sustain the theory. The official history, *The War in the Air*, written between 1922 and 1937 under the guidance of the Air Ministry, had little choice but to describe in detail the considerable support the air force had provided the Army, but it also managed to give the impression that the air force was the product of some bygone era, as relevant to modern warfare as Napoleonic infantry squares or lance-wielding cavalry. Politicians were quick to support the bomber cause. They quickly understood that the bomber was a weapon that affected them directly. They had a duty to protect their own citizens and feared the consequences if they did not. Internal revolution was just as great a danger as having to submit to the will of some foreign power. Politicians needed the security a bomber deterrent provided.

In the decades that followed the First World War, the myth took root that early planes were far too primitive for any useful lessons to be learned. The extraordinary changes in the appearance of the aeroplane supported this idea. Within twenty years, sleek monoplanes were almost unrecognisable from the open-cockpit biplanes of the First World War. Another twenty years and swept wing jets made the planes of the First World War seem even quainter. No other weapons were evolving so dramatically and quickly. The aeroplanes of the First World War looked as if they belonged to a bygone era. What had been the cutting-edge technological marvels of their age became frail, almost comical contraptions.

The myth and the flawed policy fed off each other. Histories celebrated the formation of the independent Air Ministry and Royal Air Force as a victory of progressive thinking over the conservative military. Britain won the Second World War because the Germans, with their out-dated blitzkrieg-orientated Luftwaffe, did not understand how to use air power. The Russians did not understand either. It was just as well that the British, and indeed their American allies, did, otherwise the Russian Army would not have been able to advance 1,400 miles from Stalingrad to Berlin, or so the argument went.

The air war of 1914–1918 became a romantic irrelevance. Both sides had wasted huge amounts of money putting planes into the air that served no purpose, apart from satisfying the desire of some egocentric individuals to return to an era of gallant jousts. The personalities attracted more attention than the battles, tactics or machines. It was, of course, nonsense. The aeroplanes were not fragile. They might look quaint but they were extremely tough war machines; they had to be if they were to withstand the enormous physical forces involved in flying and manoeuvring at high speeds. The missions they flew were vital. Armies do not waste money on weapons they do not want or need. Most significantly of all, the lessons learned in the First World War were priceless.

Tentatively and almost apologetically, historians began to reassess, but the myth and the flawed strategic bombing argument had gained a seemingly irreversible momentum. One hundred years later, the machines of the First World War are still often dismissed as flimsy contraptions. The Army is still condemned, even ridiculed, for wanting the air force to be at its 'beck and call'. Many still believe strategic bombing works.

In fact, air forces today, as a matter of course, provide armies with precisely the sort of air support developed in the First World War. All the tactical applications of air power that are now standard were not just pioneered during the First World War, they were used operationally, and by the end of the war had become a normal part of Army operations. The air capability the British Army would require in future conflicts was defined in the battles of the First World War. All the problems that would beset long-range bombing in the decades to come were also becoming very apparent. It was not just the technology. The problems were intrinsic to the method.

All these lessons were there to be learned. They were lessons learned the hard way. Many mistakes were made, many false paths trodden. The lessons came at the price of the lives of many brave aircrews. These were the lessons that the post-war Air Staff wiped from the slate. They were not carelessly forgotten or casually overlooked. They were deliberately discarded.

This book examines the lost lessons of the First World War.

CHAPTER 1

Cities in the Front Line

In 1670, Francesco Lana, an Italian priest, came up with an ingenious proposal for a ship that could fly. Vacuum-filled copper spheres would lift the ship into the air and sails would propel it forward. It was not even remotely practicable. The copper spheres could not possibly be strong enough to contain a vacuum and light enough to benefit from the lift generated, but the idea set Lana thinking about the possible military applications of such an invention. The imaginative priest conjured up a frightening picture of future wars with flying machines destroying ships, military fortifications and defenceless cities with 'iron weights', 'fireballs and bombs', which could be 'hurled from a vast height … with the certainty that the aerial ship could come to no harm'. It was a frightening prospect, but Lana consoled himself with the thought that God would surely never allow such a terrifying machine to be invented.[1]

In 1783, the Montgolfier brothers rose 100 feet into the air in a hot air balloon, essentially using the same buoyancy principles Lana had been relying on. Eleven years later in the Battle of Fleurus, the French Army was using a hydrogen-filled balloon to observe the Austrian Army. Whereas the non-military Lana had dwelt on the death and destruction his aerial ships might wreak, the more pragmatic military were far more interested in the less dramatic but hugely useful intelligence gathering capability. From the very beginning of military aviation, what civilians feared and what the military found useful tended to be very different.

By the end of the nineteenth century, streamlined airships were navigating the skies; Lana's nightmare was becoming a reality and his description of the dangers posed was setting the agenda for future air theorists. The Italian priest had identified the two key targets aerial craft might be used against: a country's armed forces, either on land or sea, or non-military targets such as cities where civilians would bear the brunt of the attack. Whether air power should be used primarily to support military and naval forces in conventional battles, or independently to attack homes and factories, intimidate civilians and destroy the capability to wage war, remains controversial to the present day.

In the late nineteenth century, fears of the future capabilities of flying machines were fuelled by an explosion of interest in popular science fiction. Adventure stories described flying machines cruising through the atmosphere like ships at sea, inspiring an interest in aviation among future aeronautical pioneers such as John Dunne, Geoffrey de Havilland and Claude Grahame-White. The stories also exposed a darker side to the aeronautic adventure with countries or renegade individuals terrorising innocent civilians with the air weapon.[2] The stories tapped into an ancient fear of violent assault from the heavens with gods wreaking retribution on the defenceless below. By the turn of the century, the seeds of fear for the new air weapon had been well and truly sown in the public consciousness. So concerned were politicians about this new threat, they were already drawing up international agreements to ban weapons that had not yet been developed. The 1899 Hague Peace Conference outlawed the launching of explosives or projectiles by balloons or 'by other new methods of a similar nature', but the restriction was only binding for a five-year period.[3] Governments seemed anxious to keep their options open.

The politicians might have been concerned, but to Britain's military leaders, the potential aerial threat seemed no more than science fiction. The mighty British Empire was at its peak. Britain seemed invincible. On the European mainland, however, Germany was becoming increasingly hostile and the expansion of her Navy was causing concern. Britain prided herself on the supremacy of her Royal Navy, which for centuries had guaranteed the country security and influence. Confidence in the country's naval supremacy, however, was about to be disturbed by the possibility that potential enemies might be able to attack or even invade Britain without the Royal Navy being able to do anything about it. On 2 July 1900, Count Von Zeppelin's LZ-1, a hydrogen-filled rigid airship, made its first flight, and by 1908, the more advanced LZ-4 was capable of staying in the air for twelve hours and flying 240 miles.

Less awe inspiring, and indeed scarcely noticed at the time, was the first controlled flight by a heavier-than-air machine—a short 120-foot hop in 1903 by the Wright brothers in their Flyer. The significance of this breakthrough was not appreciated in Europe until 1908 when the Wright brothers brought their latest Flyer across the Atlantic. The plane, capable of flying up to 50 miles, caused a sensation at various public displays. Among those impressed was the press magnate Lord Northcliffe, who immediately set about alerting his readers to the dangers that Britain now faced.

The airship rather than the aeroplane seemed the more obvious menace. The enormous Zeppelins had captured the imagination of the German public and wild theories abounded about how they might be used in time of war. Rudolf Martin, a self-styled expert on military matters, talked of how 200,000 troops might be transported to Britain by a fleet of 10,000 airships. Martin was convinced that this new weapon would make the mighty British Navy an irrelevance.

Just as sea power had enabled the British Empire to dominate the world in the nineteenth century, so in the new century, air power would enable Germany to dominate.[4]

These claims were reported in full in Northcliffe's newspapers. They were greeted in Britain, and indeed Germany, with a scepticism that was entirely justified. Airships were extremely expensive to build. A fleet of 10,000 Zeppelins would cost as much as 150 dreadnought-class battleships, well beyond any nation's military budget. Northcliffe's newspapers were as sceptical as anyone, but continued to focus public attention on the potential danger of less formidable armadas. To encourage interest in aeronautics, Northcliffe's *Daily Mail* offered prizes for achieving various aeronautical feats, including a £500 prize for the first pilot to cross the English Channel in an aeroplane.

The War Office was initially less than awestruck by the new weapon. General Sir William Nicholson, the Army's Chief of the Imperial Staff (CIGS), could not see how either the airship or the aeroplane could possibly be of any military value. Even simple reconnaissance would be beyond them. Aeroplanes could not stay in the air unless they were flying at more than 30 mph and a cavalryman hurtling along at such a speed on his new mechanical 'horse', totally incapable of slowing down, never mind stopping, would not be able to observe anything. Airships could hover and therefore might be more useful, he conceded, but they were huge objects. If they flew low they would be shot down and if they flew high they would not be able to see anything.[5]

Colonel Capper, in charge of the Farnborough Balloon Factory, was doing his best to generate some interest in the potential of military aviation, but his Factory did not have much to show for its efforts. The Factory-designed British Army Airship No. 1 successfully flew in 1907, but after a year of testing was declared unsafe to fly and abandoned.[6] Capper acquired the services of Samuel Cody, an eccentric American entertainer, and Lieutenant John Dunne, a war invalid, both of whom had been experimenting with gliders and man-lifting kites. Neither had an engineering background, rather epitomising the amateur approach to aeronautics common at the time, but this would not prevent both developing successful aeroplanes. Cody is credited with the first flight in Britain. In September 1908, his British Army Aeroplane No. 1 just about got off the ground, and the following month managed to fly 1,400 feet, which would eventually be considered far enough to constitute the first official aeroplane flight in Britain, even though the flight ended in a crash landing. Indeed, the following day, *The Times* reported the event as an accident rather than a triumphant first for the country.[7] It was not the most auspicious of starts. While the armed forces of other European nations were experimenting with aeroplanes and airships, neither the British Army nor Navy possessed a single flyable example of either.

The politicians continued to show more interest than the military. At a second peace conference held at The Hague in 1907, Germany rather ominously did not renew the 1899 restriction on launching projectiles from aircraft. It was agreed that undefended towns should not be bombarded 'by any means whatsoever', although what exactly constituted 'undefended' was not clearly defined.[8] The British Government was sufficiently concerned by the threat to set up a subcommittee of the Committee of Imperial Defence (CID), the political and military body that co-ordinated British defence policy, which, under the chairmanship of Lord Esher, was to examine how the airship and aeroplane might be used by or against Britain.

The members included Haldane (Secretary of State for War), McKenna (the First Lord of the Admiralty), Lloyd George (the Chancellor) and various military and naval figures, including the Army chief Nicholson. The lack of any practical experience of flight did not inhibit the experts called before the committee. At least two agreed that an aerial invasion using thousands of Wright Flyers was feasible. One of them, Sir Hiram Maxim—whose inventions included the fully automatic machine gun—pointed out that if such a fleet carried bombs instead of troops, 1,000 tons of nitroglycerin could be dropped in a single night, leaving London looking like 'last year's buzzard's nest'. Lloyd George asked another witness, Charles Rolls, co-founder of Rolls-Royce, if it was true airships could 'set towns on fire'; he was assured that they could.[9] For the future Prime Minister, it was a grim foretaste of the horrors future wars might entail.

The committee tended to focus on the more extravagant predications of how aircraft might threaten targets in Britain, rather than more mundane military applications on the battlefield. It concluded an enemy might be able to drop bombs on or land raiding parties close to military establishments in the British Isles, but that it would be many years before large-scale bombing or the airlifting of troops would be practical operations of war.[10] Aeroplanes in particular were only at a very early stage of development and were, Haldane insisted, 'a long way from being the slightest practical use in war'.[11] Nicholson did not think anyone would be foolish or brave enough to fly and fight in the air,[12] and given the horrors that faced future airmen, trapped in crippled, blazing aircraft miles above the ground with no means of escape, it was not an entirely unreasonable prophecy.

Haldane insisted there was no need to hurry. As an island nation, Britain had little to gain and everything to lose by the development of air power. Britain could not stop its development, but there seemed little point spending money encouraging it. If progress was made abroad, the very nature of flight would make it difficult to conceal. Rather than buy in foreign technology, as many were urging, he believed there was time for Britain to adopt a more systematic approach with British engineers and scientists establishing a sound foundation of knowledge by working through the problems of aeronautics from first principles. Haldane was not in the least impressed by 'clever empiricists' like Capper, Cody and Dunne.[13]

Haldane decided that the Farnborough Balloon Factory could continue working on the *Mayfly* airship for the Navy, but the development of aeroplanes could be left safely in the hands of the private sector. All experiments with aeroplanes taking place at the Balloon Factory were to end and Dunne and Cody were summarily dismissed, although Cody managed to get himself reinstated to help develop the *Mayfly*. Dunne and Cody continued working on their respective aeroplanes and by 1910, both had machines flying successfully. Indeed, Dunne's remarkably stable tailless flying wing was perhaps the first machine to fly that did not require the constant attention of the pilot to prevent it careering out of control.[14] These efforts seemed to be the sort of private enterprise Haldane was anticipating, but they did not attract any orders, financial support or much official interest.

Meanwhile, in line with Haldane's desire for a more systematic and scientific approach to aeronautical research, the enthusiastic but unqualified Colonel Capper was replaced by a civilian engineer, Mervyn O'Gorman. O'Gorman was an imposing figure who did not underestimate his own importance. He was never happy with what he considered to be the rather demeaning superintendent title, and made determined but unsuccessful efforts to get it changed to something that reflected more accurately the power and influence he felt he should have.

To keep the government informed on developments at home and abroad, an Advisory Committee for Aeronautics, comprising leading scientists and members of the armed services, was set up in the spring of 1909. In the meantime, the emphasis in Britain would be on basic research rather than practical experimentation. To many politicians and public figures, this scarcely seemed an adequate response. In January 1909, an Aerial League of the British Empire had been created to draw attention to the danger facing the nation. In a speech to the National Defence Association, a founder-member of this league, Lord Montagu, described how easily enemy airships would be able to bypass Britain's land and sea defences, and deliver a crippling blow to key political and communication targets. He warned that no defence whatsoever existed to such an attack. He was one of the first—and by no means the last—to point out that due to its geographical position, London was particularly vulnerable. No other major power had its capital so close to its frontier and, indeed, so close to a likely enemy. He asked his listeners to imagine the effects a couple of hundred explosive and gas shells would have on nerve centres such as government offices, telephone exchanges, railway stations, the stock exchange, royal palaces, the Houses of Parliament, 'and the most crowded streets and most thickly inhabited portions of the Metropolis'.[15]

It was the sort of talk that could only increase public nervousness. In the spring and early summer of 1909, there were countless reports of mysterious airships flying over the British Isles. These stories received plenty of press coverage and Haldane was quizzed in parliament about the origin of the mysterious visitors.[16]

Northcliffe was also alarmed, although not by the threat these airships appeared to pose to the country's security. His concern was the embarrassing state of panic Britain seemed to be descending into and feared Britain was becoming an international laughing stock.[17]

Bleriot's cross-Channel flight in July 1909 gave the press more opportunity to focus public attention on Britain's vulnerability and government inaction. The flight did not represent any great leap forward in aircraft performance. Aeroplanes had already flown considerably further and two months earlier the latest Zeppelin had reportedly stayed in the air for nearly thirty-eight hours and flown some 500 miles.[18] The notion that Britain's insularity offered any protection in the new aerial age had long since disappeared. Nor perhaps should the sight of the insignificant looking Bleriot monoplane, struggling across the Channel with its lone pilot, have struck fear into the hearts of the British public. It was, nevertheless, a dramatic act of showmanship that shook the country, all the more so because the prize for the crossing had been put up by a British newspaper and a foreigner had won it. This embarrassment ensured Britain's backwardness in aeronautical matters continued to receive full coverage, especially in Northcliffe's group of newspapers.

Science-fiction writers did nothing to ease public concerns. In 1908, H. G. Wells' *War in the Air* was published, in which London, Paris, Berlin and New York were destroyed by airships. In 1909, cinema goers in Britain were treated to a vision of the future by the short silent movie *Airship Destroyer* where a fleet of airships attack Britain and intercepting fighters are shot out of the sky. The special effects of the day might have made the individual exploding bombs look rather comical, but there was nothing comical about the blazing city the film shows the airships leaving behind.[19]

In the first parliamentary debate on aeronautics in August 1909, Haldane was severely criticised for ignoring the threat the airship posed. There was talk of the demoralising effect the random dropping of explosives by airships 'at the very commencement—indeed almost before war is declared' would have on defenceless citizens. One speaker did not wish to associate himself with such sensational and alarmist claims, but even he felt 'we could no longer shut our eyes to the fact that aerial fleets are being created on a large and comprehensive scale by foreign countries'.[20] One member of parliament, the Liberal Alfred Mond, was less sure that such fleets could ever be a decisive weapon of war. 'With civilised nations, warfare is not conducted by simply destroying property and killing civilians, or by dropping dynamite about London, Paris or Berlin,' he suggested. 'Such a proceeding would have no effect at all on the ending of the war. No nation would make peace because the enemy was killing its civilians.'[21] It was a valid point. There was nothing logical about a country surrendering so readily to a merciless enemy who had shown no compunction about killing women and children. Accepting occupation and servitude to such a cruel aggressor scarcely seemed the lesser of the two evils on offer. Crucially, as Mond pointed out, naval and military forces would be completely unaffected by any such acts of terror and would carry on fighting until one side prevailed. It was, however, a lone voice. The majority did not expect an enemy to be so logical or civilised. Whether Mond was right or not would be at the crux of a debate that would rumble on into the thermonuclear age.

Meanwhile, the War Office was keeping an eye on what other countries, in particular Germany, were up to. Their first report in November 1909 observed that airships had flown for over twelve hours and the latest Zeppelins carried enough fuel to stay in the air for nearly two days. Bomb-dropping trials had also taken place and it was also noted that the Zeppelin base near Cologne was menacingly situated at just about the closest point on German soil to Great Britain.[22] By the following year, Zeppelins were reported to have flown 820 miles with eight people aboard, a lifting capability that could easily be turned into a bomb-carrying capability and a range that was sufficient to fly from Cologne to London and back.[23] Further alarm was caused by proposals put forward by the German delegation at the first International Conference on Aerial Navigation in Paris in 1910. The Germans were very anxious to establish the right of any aircraft to fly over the airspace of any nation. It would mean in wartime, Zeppelins would no longer have to fly around neutral countries like Holland or Belgium to reach Britain. The Zeppelin base at Cologne took on an even more sinister significance.

The low-level British delegation had not expected anything so significant to be on the agenda and wired home for advice. The CID dispatched Captain Maurice Hankey, an assistant secretary of the committee, to deal with the problem. Hankey alerted the French, secured their support, and the German suggestion was rejected,[24] but even the conservative British Army General Staff was forced to concede the Germans were apparently planning to use their Zeppelins aggressively and preparation had to be made for a battle to control the skies over Britain.[25] Hankey, who would assume an increasingly influential position in government planning in the decades to come, was left in no doubt that Germany had every intention of making maximum use of what he considered to be a dangerous and highly significant new factor in warfare.

The Admiralty too were becoming increasingly concerned about the potentially catastrophic consequences even a few bombs dropped on their sprawling stores of ammunition might have; as their responsibilities ended at the coast, they wanted to know what the War Office planned to do about defending their stores. Rear Admiral Ottley, the secretary of the CID and president of the committee investigating these naval concerns, was also alarmed. He prepared a paper for the CID in which he suggested that the rapid progress being made in aviation meant the conclusions of the Esher Committee were already out of date. Esher agreed. In October 1910, he sent a note to the CID pointing out that much had happened since he had written his report and suggested aeroplanes should be developed for the British Army and operated by a 'British Air Corps'.[26] Esher's intervention was viewing the air menace from a significantly different perspective. While Ottley, Hankey, the politicians and the Admiralty were concerned about the implications for civilians, cities and installations in Britain, Esher's first concern was that the British Army should get the air support other nations were already developing for their armies. Britain was already well behind her continental neighbours. Observers at the annual French Army manoeuvres in September 1910 were impressed by the extensive use made of aircraft; it was this, rather than the alarmist talk of mass destruction from the air, that inspired Esher to write to the CID. During its own manoeuvres, all the British Army could muster was a couple of planes acquired out of their own pocket by some artillery officers interested in finding out if aeroplanes could be used instead of balloons for directing artillery fire. These were used with mixed fortunes, but for the enthusiasts the potential was clear.[27]

It was the need for a tactical air force, rather than any desire to defend the British Isles, that inspired a reversal in War Office policy and a decision in October 1910 to get the Balloon Factory at Farnborough involved again in testing aeroplanes and training pilots to fly them.[28] From this point on, the pace of military aviation development in Britain would begin to accelerate. In April 1911, the first experimental air force units were created when the Farnborough Balloon School became an Air Battalion with two companies, one operating balloons and the other aeroplanes. Their commander, Sir Alex Bannerman, did not appear to be the most inspired choice to lead this fledgling air force. He was a Royal Engineer, the branch of the Army responsible for balloons, and could not even fly a plane. He had also caused outrage within aeronautical circles just a few months before by suggesting no progress had been made in developing aeroplanes for military purposes since the Wright brothers' first flight.[29] Understandably, aeroplane pilots were not the least bit impressed by their new commander.[30] Nevertheless, under his leadership, good progress was made. In the spring of 1911, specifications were drawn up for the sort of aeroplane that the company would need. It would have to be able to operate from near the front line and Army headquarters, so it was expected to be capable of taking off from and landing on 'ploughed fields, clover, thick grass or stubble'. It would have to carry an observer and pilot, who would both need to be 'protected from wind, cold and oil' and have a good view above and below. It should be capable of flying as slowly as 38 mph and as fast as 55 mph. Silencers were to be considered so the engine and propeller could operate 'with as little whirring as possible'.[31] The rather odd speed requirement equates approximately to 60–90 kph and was no doubt lifted from a continental requirement. The higher speed was required to ensure the aeroplane could make reasonable progress against a strong wind. The lower speed was necessary because it was felt the slower the plane flew, the easier it would be to observe from and the smaller the field it could take off from and land in. The need for slow speed to observe was the more controversial issue. Many shared Nicholson's concerns about the practicality of observing anything from such a fast moving platform, a major disadvantage of the aeroplane when compared to the balloon. It took the experience of flying to appreciate how little height has to be gained before the ground below is not hurtling past at impossibly high speeds, and indeed how much can be seen from high altitudes. Those who flew soon appreciated that the higher you go, the clearer the atmosphere becomes. A lot more can be seen looking one mile vertically down than one mile horizontally at ground level.[32]

While this specification was being formulated, the War Office ordered its first planes—four Boxkites from Bristol, or the British and Colonial Aircraft Company, as it was known then. The plane was no more than a copy of a French Maurice Farman with a few small improvements. Indeed, Bristol only narrowly avoided being sued by the French company.[33] These were delivered during the summer, which gave Bannerman very little time to get his aeroplane company ready for the autumn 1911 Army manoeuvres, the first big test for his air units. Bannerman was soon anxious to acquire something better than the Boxkites. These were fine for introducing inexperienced pilots to military aviation, but the plane was so slow that a strong headwind could almost bring forward progress to a halt. Bannerman, showing more drive than he is often credited with, was anxious to get the search for the Boxkite replacement going as soon as possible so his crews would not find themselves in the same position again the following year, struggling to master new equipment just weeks before manoeuvres were due to begin.[34] Indeed, Bannerman seemed to have experienced a dramatic conversion. Seven months after declaring the military aeroplane had made no progress, Bannerman was suggesting that enough was now known about the capabilities of the aeroplane to justify the formation of a fully operational permanent air unit. Aerial reconnaissance would be the principal role, not because that was all the aeroplane could do, but because it was so important—commanders would probably not dare risk losing valuable machines on other less profitable missions.[35]

Bannerman did not rule out the possibility of attacking targets on the ground, but he doubted a small target could be hit from a safe altitude and with a larger target like a town, Bannerman observed that indiscriminate bombardments for months on end by traditional ground-based heavy artillery often brought little reward and he saw no reason why aircraft would bring more success. On the battlefield, bombing might be useful to eliminate a particularly troublesome strongpoint, but given the current state of development, bombing was unlikely to be the best use of air power. Aerial reconnaissance would be far more important. The conversion of the sceptical Bannerman into an aeroplane enthusiast was a reflection of how seriously military aviation was now being taken. Not that there was much actual evidence for this confidence. The annual manoeuvres Bannerman had been preparing for were supposed to be held in the Cambridge area, but when they were cancelled, plans for the involvement of the Air Company became a simple cross-country exercise to see if the planes were capable of reaching Cambridge in one piece. Even this proved too challenging—six planes took off, but only two eventually made it, the other four crashing on the way.[36] British aviation still had a long way to go before it could prove it would be 'of some practical use in war', but the foundations were being laid. The first detailed specification had been drawn up and it was no longer a question of whether aeroplanes would be useful, but how they would be used.

To find out, the Army needed more aeroplanes to experiment with. France was the leading aeronautical nation and a few French planes were acquired, but very few British-built planes joined them. Haldane's emphasis was on basic research and most of the increased air budget was spent on improving facilities at the Balloon Factory.[37] The ambitious O'Gorman was able to build a substantial and impressively well-equipped research establishment which, he hoped, would become the hub of all British aeronautical effort. Much to O'Gorman's frustration, aeroplane design was not one of the Factory's responsibilities, but an administrative sleight of hand enabled O'Gorman to get round this restriction. The Factory was responsible for repairing damaged aeroplanes and they soon found themselves having to repair a rather troublesome Bleriot monoplane. O'Gorman rather craftily managed to get authorisation to reconstruct rather than just repair the machine.[38] It was not uncommon at the time for designers to reconstruct crashed planes with substantial modifications to ensure the plane did not crash again for the same reason, but O'Gorman took the idea to the limit. He used the Santos-Dumont 14bis, the first European plane to fly, as his inspiration for the reconstruction—this was a pusher where the engine was at the rear of the plane pushing it. O'Gorman turned the monoplane Bleriot tractor, with an engine at the front pulling the plane, into a biplane pusher. The result was a machine that bore no resemblance whatsoever to the original Bleriot. Reconstruction became no more than an administrative euphemism for aircraft design and construction where often the only surviving feature of the original damaged plane was its engine. O'Gorman, with the tacit approval of Seely, Haldane's more proactive deputy, would use this ruse to develop a whole range of original designs.[39]

Farnborough adopted the practice of naming their reconstructed aeroplanes after the configuration of the design that had inspired them, so the reconstructed Bleriot monoplane became the Santos Experimental 1 (S.E.1). In December 1910, the Factory acquired the services of Geoffrey de Havilland, who brought with him his own aeroplane. This was also a pusher and resembled the French Farman designs, so de Havilland's plane became the F.E.1 (Farman Experimental 1). Tractor designs were referred to as B.E.s, Bleriot Experimentals. The first, the B.E.1, started life as a French Voisin pusher before being 'repaired' into a tractor.⁴⁰ The first planes the Factory produced did not have any particular combat role; O'Gorman's aim was simply to build a plane that was safe and easy to fly, and this, rather than War Office combat requirements, dictated the design. The Bleriot Experimentals were two-seaters, with the passenger over the plane's centre of gravity and the pilot behind, which had the advantage that the plane could be flown with or without the passenger. The disadvantage in a tractor design of this arrangement was that it put the passenger between the pilot and the propeller, with a wing above and a fuselage and another wing below, making it difficult for the passenger to see anything. It certainly did not provide the excellent all-round view for the observer required by the War Office military aeroplane specification.

Meanwhile, it was the ability of planes to drop bombs, not simply observe, that was attracting public attention. In April 1911, Claude Grahame-White, who had won celebrity status for various aeronautical exploits, predicted that the Navy's much vaunted dreadnought-class battleships would be vulnerable to air attack and proposed a public demonstration at his own Hendon aerodrome to prove it. Prime Minister Asquith, McKenna, Haldane, Seely, Winston Churchill, and many Army and Navy officers joined a large crowd that witnessed Grahame-White dropping bombs from a low altitude on the outline of a battleship. According to *Flight* magazine journalists present, Grahame-White got within two feet of a bull's-eye with small bombs and then dropped a 100-lb sandbag from 'a reasonable height' with 'equal success'.⁴¹ Allowing for a little enthusiasm with the reporting, and even if the bombs were not dropped from 2,000 feet as sometimes claimed, it was a spectacular display, but one that impressed the civilians present, including Churchill, more than the hard-nosed generals and admirals.⁴²

Up to this point, the Navy had been slower than the Army to see the possibilities of the aeroplane. At the beginning of 1911, members of the Royal Aero Club had lent the Navy two planes and provided free instruction for four pilots, including a Lieutenant Samson, but this was as far as the Navy had got. In September 1911, the Navy's airship, the *Mayfly*, after several unsuccessful attempts to get into the air, broke her back. By this time, Samson had completed his training and was experimenting with airbags that would enable aeroplanes to take off and land on water, and launching ramps that would enable them to take off from warships. Samson's enthusiasm and drive, coupled with the accident to the *Mayfly*, convinced the Admiralty that the aeroplane, not the airship, was the way forward. Churchill's appointment as McKenna's replacement as First Lord of the Admiralty in October 1911 gave naval aeronautics another boost. Late in 1911, the Navy set up its own flying school and research centre at Eastchurch run by Samson.

At around this time, the international situation was beginning to look more worrying. The Agadir Crisis in the summer of 1911, when Germany briefly threatened to challenge French control of Morocco, demonstrated to the British Government just how real the threat of war with Germany was becoming. With the loss of the only British airship in existence, the *Mayfly*—or the 'Won't fly' as Churchill rechristened it[43]—it was also very clear just how far Britain was behind her potential enemy in military aeronautics. In parliament, Seely was being asked why it was planned to increase the number of military planes from ten to just sixteen when the French already had 200.[44] Britain had some catching up to do. With some fanfare, the War Office released the details of the military aeroplane specification it had drawn up and announced a competition would take place in August 1912, open to British and foreign companies, to find the best plane meeting these requirements. It was not the time frame Bannerman had in mind and whether a public competition was the best way to go about selecting air force equipment was debatable. It was certainly not necessary as excellent planes like the Avro 500 would fly and win small orders before the competition even took place.[45]

The debate about the role of the air force was also very public. In December 1911, the future of military aviation was the subject of two meetings organised by the Aeronautical Society. The meetings were high-profile events, attended by aircraft designers and various military, naval and political figures; Seely, Bannerman and O'Gorman were all present at the second meeting, along with General Henderson, the Director of Military Training at the War Office. Those expressing views included serving officers and members of the Air Battalion. The views stated at these meetings were not supposed to represent or shape official thinking, but the conclusions became the basis for future policy. The meeting concluded that two main types of plane were required: a short-range tactical reconnaissance machine and a long-range high-speed strategic reconnaissance scout. The former would essentially be the two-seater required by the War Office aeroplane competition. The scout only needed to be a single-seater as the information required would be of a very general nature rather than the detailed battlefield dispositions the tactical machine was to record. Its high speed would enable it to evade the enemy and get the information back to base as quickly as possible.

There was also a very distinct third role, which was just as important, but would not necessarily require a different type of plane. No one was in any doubt that the information the scouts and reconnaissance planes were seeking would have to be fought for. The high-speed scout might get away with being unarmed, but the short-range tactical machine would have to defend itself, so the observer would need to carry a weapon. Indeed, such an armed plane could also be used offensively against enemy reconnaissance planes. It would have to be as stable as possible to ensure a steady platform for the gunner and there were suggestions that a three-seater with two gunners would be even better. It was accepted that the armed two/three-seater would never be able to catch lighter and faster single-seater scouts, which seemed a rather fundamental disadvantage, although some held out hope that large numbers of these planes would be able to block the path of the approaching scout by sheer weight of numbers.

One lone voice saw a different way. Colonel F. Stone, a regular commentator and speaker on military aviation issues, suggested the high-speed scout rather than the slower two-seater would be a better option for shooting down enemy planes. A 'one-man machine' with 'manoeuvring power ... speed, rapidity of ascent and descent, and power to turn sharply' corresponding 'more to the torpedo-boat than to the armoured cruiser' would be able to 'outpace and outmanoeuvre its enemy'. It was a fairly accurate description of the air superiority fighter of the future. Unfortunately, the only weapon the colonel could come up with for the lone pilot was a hand grenade. The colonel's ideas did not seem to get any support and the meeting concluded that two and three-seaters were the way forward for fighting machines, but in essence, the colonel had the right idea.[46]

Meanwhile, the growing political instability in Europe and the criticisms of inaction was forcing the government to act. Asquith set up another subcommittee of the CID to consider the organisation of a future British air force. Bannerman was not included, a snub for the Air Battalion commander, who had still not learnt to fly and does not appear to have won over the pilots under his command. Ottley and Hankey would be secretaries of the committee and members included Churchill, Seely, O'Gorman and Samson. It also included one of the first Army officers to learn to fly—General Henderson, who was one of the interested observers at the recent Aeronautical Society meetings.

Henderson had led a distinguished career in Army intelligence and was one of the Army's leading experts on reconnaissance. He first became aware of the military possibilities of aircraft while recuperating from an operation in a Harrogate hotel. A plane happened to land in a nearby field and after talking to the pilot, he came to realise how significant this invention was for his particular field of interest. At the age of forty-nine, he learned to fly and obtained his pilot's licence on the second attempt.[47]

Another future grandee of the air force to make a significant contribution to the subcommittee, in a support capacity at least, was a certain Captain Sykes. Sykes had first become interested in military aeronautics when he was attached to the Balloon Section of the Royal Engineers in 1904. During a trip to Italy, he had been impressed by the use the Italian Army was already making of aircraft and became convinced that aviation would play a decisive part in future wars. Sykes anticipated a whole range of military applications, including photo-reconnaissance, air combat and bombing—initially, he believed reconnaissance would be the most important application. Aircraft would be able to carry out strategic reconnaissance in a fraction of the time required by traditional cavalry and on the battlefield they would be able to report on enemy dispositions, identify targets for the artillery, direct its fire and observe the way the battle was progressing.[48]

The make-up of the subcommittee guaranteed the positive result Asquith wanted and it did not take its members long to produce it. In February 1912, the committee recommended the creation of a Flying Corps as an independent formation with a Naval Wing and a Military Wing, and a Central Flying School providing aircrews for both. The two wings were supposed to be complementary, capable of reinforcing each other should Britain only be involved in a conflict on sea or land. In April, the King formally approved the formation of the Royal Flying Corps (RFC) and at the same time the Factory at Farnborough became the Royal Aircraft Factory. It was supposed to serve both the military and naval wings, although its remit on aeroplanes still went no further than 'repairs and reconstruction'.[49] The Military Wing would consist of one airship and seven aeroplane squadrons—the balloon squadron and the first three aeroplane squadrons had been formed by the spring of 1913. Funds were released for the purchase of 131 planes. While the Air Battalion had been little more than a temporary and experimental training unit, the new force would be maintained on a permanent war footing.[50]

Naval aviation was to be run by Captain Murray Sueter, who had been involved in the failed *Mayfly* project, but had seen enough to be convinced that aircraft had huge potential. The War Office Air Department, which would be part of Henderson's Training Directorate, was initially run by Captain Ellington, a future Chief of Air Staff, with Lieutenant-Colonel Brancker as his second in command. Ellington would soon be returning to his artillery regiment and it was Brancker who would play the more significant role in the immediate future of the air force. Brancker had seen what observation balloons were capable of while serving in South Africa,[51] and later, in India, he had flown in a Boxkite as an observer during cavalry manoeuvres. The obvious potential of aerial reconnaissance impressed Brancker and the Army officers who watched his flight, a certain Lieutenant-General Douglas Haig among them. When Brancker returned to Britain in 1912, he was posted to the 43rd Battery of the Royal Field Artillery where he was involved in early experiments with aeroplane-directed artillery fire. After a period in Germany, he was posted to Henderson's department and found himself in its Air Department as Ellington's deputy.

To co-ordinate the two wings of the RFC, Seely formed an Air Committee with Henderson, Sykes, Samson and Sueter among its members, which Seely saw as a stepping stone towards a fully-fledged Air Ministry with the same powers as the Admiralty and War Office.[52] In practice, this first attempt to create a single unified air service came to nothing with endless squabbles about which wing should control which types of aircraft. It was left to a despairing Captain Paine, the Royal Navy commander of the joint Army/Navy Central Flying School, to point out that it was supposed to be a united air service where such matters were irrelevant.[53] It would be many decades before such noble aspirations as these came anywhere near realisation. Indeed, there seemed very little the two services could agree on. Both had very different attitudes on aeroplane procurement, with the Admiralty quite happy to use private firms, while Henderson worried about security and preferred to use the Aircraft Factory to develop the planes the Army required.[54] The Admiralty's willingness to deal with the private sector led to the Navy establishing close links with companies like Short and Sopwith, which would be a source of much future friction between the two services. The Admiralty was soon disassociating itself from the Royal Aircraft Factory and the Navy continued to use its own Eastchurch flying school, even though a naval officer had been put in charge of the joint services Central Flying School. The Naval Wing was also soon unofficially referring to itself as the Naval Air Service and the name stuck, although technically the two air services were still wings of a joint Army/Navy Royal Flying Corps.[55]

The Navy was soon showing more interest than the Army in using aircraft to attack targets on the ground. Samson set about investigating the problems of flying with and dropping bombs of various sizes.[56] Trials revealed it was just about possible to attack a submarine on the surface before it had time to submerge.[57] The Admiralty asked the Woolwich Arsenal to develop appropriate anti-submarine bombs[58] and set about designing a bombsight that would ensure they hit their target.[59] The Navy also wanted to launch torpedoes from the air. The standard naval 14-inch torpedo weighed some 812 lbs, an enormous weight for aeroplanes of the time. Nevertheless, in 1913, a Sopwith seaplane struggled into the air with one.[60] In July 1914, with some prodding from Churchill, a torpedo was dropped, although it was little more than a stunt; with the weight of the torpedo, the plane could barely carry enough fuel to get into the air.[61] Other hefty items the Navy considered essential operational equipment included wireless sets and, if the plane was to take off from water, it would also have to haul floats into the air. All these requirements meant naval planes needed more power. While the War Office could not imagine ever wanting much more than 150 hp, the Admiralty issued a requirement for engines capable of at least 200 hp.

With all Admiralty requirements pointing to the need for high-lifting capability, the development of planes with the potential for long-range bombing was inevitable. If a plane could carry a torpedo, it could carry a smaller bomb load much further. Sueter was soon speculating about how such planes might be used to bomb distant enemy ports. Indeed, if airships were used, targets even further afield such as rail communications and government offices might be targeted.[62] The Navy was already showing an interest in attacking targets that were not particularly naval in character.

There was no official Admiralty policy to develop an independent long-range bombing strategy at this time, but it was a concept that sat very comfortably in the naval mind. Covering great distances to take on an enemy was the Navy's normal mode of operation and the bomber provided another way of doing this.

The navigational equipment and skills required were a natural extension of the skills that had been developed for navigating the seas. Trials took place with bombs as heavy as 200 lbs,[63] and specialist torpedo-bombers like the Short 184 floatplane were ordered to carry them. There was not so much enthusiasm in naval circles for meeting more basic naval requirements. The shore-based planes the Navy was acquiring were a start, but first and foremost, a Navy needed planes for its fleet. Despite Samson's early experiments and some trials with a seaplane carrier, these ideas were not pursued. On the outbreak of war, the Navy had no means of taking any of its warplanes to sea.

The War Office was more determined to get more basic requirements such as air reconnaissance sorted out. Reconnaissance was by no means the only role aeroplanes were expected to perform. RFC squadrons were expected to be multi-purpose, all capable of any role the Army might require and that included bombing. Henderson and General Sir John French, who took over from Nicholson as CIGS in 1912, had doubts about the bomber as an efficient way of attacking troops, but they did believe it would be a very useful way of destroying enemy equipment and supplies.[64] However, there was no desire to bomb targets beyond the immediate tactical zone and there would be no need to carry anything as heavy as a torpedo or fly as far as a distant German port. Special planes would not be required. Even in the tactical zone, where bombing would be competing with conventional artillery, it was difficult to imagine bombs could achieve anything particularly significant. While the Admiralty had the prospect of a torpedo sinking a ship or a single bomb disabling a submarine to encourage them, a bomb dropped on the battlefield could not be expected to achieve anything so dramatic or useful. Bombing was not ignored but it was not a War Office priority. Henderson was quite happy to leave bomb-dropping development in naval hands with the Royal Aircraft Factory providing input on Military Wing requirements.[65]

As far as Henderson was concerned, the two crucial roles for military aeroplanes would be those outlined at the Aeronautical Society meetings he attended; air combat and reconnaissance, with the latter catered for by a single-seater for strategic reconnaissance and the two-seater for tactical reconnaissance. The two-seater was covered by the Bleriot Experimentals O'Gorman was developing, while for the high-speed scout, O'Gorman began work on a scaled-down version of the Bleriot Experimental, the B.S.1 (Bleriot Scout 1). Equally important was a means of shooting down enemy aircraft. Henderson wanted O'Gorman to develop two distinct capabilities—a plane armed with a light machine gun for dealing with aeroplanes and a second type armed with a heavy machine gun or cannon for shooting down airships.[66] The explosive shell of a cannon seemed ideal for engaging airships, but these were very heavy weapons. The 1868 St Petersburg's declaration had banned the use of explosives in shells smaller than 400 grams, about 1 lb, which approximated to a 37-mm calibre gun. The Vickers one-pounder quick-firing cannon was an early contender for aerial use, but it weighed 230 lb, nearly ten times more than a standard Army Vickers machine gun, which was already heavy for the aeroplanes of the day.

There was no doubting the urgency in getting planes armed. In May 1912, the Air Department told O'Gorman to get trials underway with anything to hand, dummy guns if necessary, if only to test possible mountings.[67] O'Gorman assumed that a fighting plane would need a second crewmember to fire the weapon. A pilot pointing his aeroplane at the target and firing with a fixed weapon was not considered possible, not because the propeller got in the way—a pusher solved that problem—but because it was simply not thought possible to control an aeroplane with a sufficient degree of dexterity. The best position for a specialist gunner was the nose of a pusher, with its excellent view and field of fire forward. French Henri Farmans and Factory Farman Experimentals were aircraft of the pusher variety and both were used in early gun firing experiments. The second in the Farman Experimental series, the F.E.2, had flown in 1911. In July 1912, it was fitted with an early model Vickers Maxim machine gun and from this point on the 'F.E.' would stand for 'Fighting Experimental' rather than 'Farman Experimental'. Early experiments with the gun-carrying F.E.2 got some enthusiastic press coverage,[68] which may have reassured those worried by the Zeppelin threat, but aiming the weapon from an unstable platform proved immensely difficult.[69] Shooting down aircraft was not going to be easy.

The F.E.2 was not the only Factory design getting publicity. The press was full of stories about the Army's latest 'secret weapon', the 'silent' B.E.1, which was fitted with silencers and designed by Farnborough and clearly was not very secret. Private companies were less than impressed that the Factory did not seem to be complying with Haldane's decision to leave the development of aeroplanes in the hands of the private sector. The military aeroplane competition, however, was to give them an opportunity to demonstrate what they were capable of.[70] With Henderson having expressed a preference for Factory designs, and indeed their Bleriot Experimental already being pencilled in for production,[71] the cards were more heavily stacked against private designers than they imagined.

Twenty-four entries turned up for the competition, but so did O'Gorman's B.E.2, the second version of the Bleriot Experimental. O'Gorman insisted it was there purely for comparison purposes. As a government design, the Factory plane was not allowed to take part, but as far as the private companies were concerned, it seemed like the main contender, especially when the plane started to get glowing reviews from journalists invited to fly in the plane as passengers.[72] Somehow, the competition's complicated scoring system managed to come up with Cody's entry as the winner. Even by the standards of 1912, his biplane, with its Wright Flyer-style forward elevator, looked hopelessly obsolete. Cody's victory earned him an order for two machines, but when they were delivered, Sykes declared them to be useless for military purposes. One crashed, killing the pilot, and the other,

Sykes suggested, being the 'last representative of a type of considerable historical interest', should be donated to the Science Museum where it still resides.[73] Other prize-winning entries were the Coanda design from Bristol and various versions of the French Deperdussin, all very modern-looking monoplanes. Two examples of each of the participating Coandas and Deperdussins were bought, but within days, one of each had crashed. This, following problems with other monoplanes, resulted in all Military Wing monoplanes being grounded.

The competition was a disaster for private enterprise. Far from winning orders, the best private companies could offer had been condemned as unsafe to fly. The non-participating Factory B.E.2 was quietly assessed using the same points system the private entries had been judged by and came out as by far the best design, even though the limited view of the poorly positioned passenger can scarcely have won it many points. Instead of building its own Coanda monoplane, Bristol ended up building B.E.2s under licence. As O'Gorman and Henderson had wanted, the Factory was becoming the principal source of RFC equipment.

It was not just the plane's state-funded origins that were controversial. To many, the B.E.2 looked almost as old fashioned as Cody's effort. Whenever Seely presented strength or production figures in parliament, the first question was always how many were monoplanes. It was the litmus test of a modern design. O'Gorman's preference for the biplane was greeted in some quarters with derision, but he was right. Structurally, the square shape formed by the two wings of a biplane and joining struts was much stronger than monoplane wings supported by the fuselage. At the speeds these planes flew, the extra drag of the struts was not a significant factor. In the early days of aviation, the biplane was the way forward, not the monoplane, and private companies were soon following the Factory example.[74]

The monoplane ban had swept aside most of the opposition the B.E.2 might have had, but not all. One surviving challenger was the biplane Avro 500, a small number of which had already been ordered. There was little to choose between the two machines but O'Gorman effectively had the entire aircraft industry, for what it was worth, at his disposal, and it was his plane that was built in much greater numbers. Four more Avros were ordered in December 1912,[75] but other companies were given contracts to build B.E.2s. It was a triumph for O'Gorman. The money invested in the Factory and the scientific approach of the designers and technicians working there was paying off. It seemed that Factory designs were best and his establishment was becoming the centre of aeronautical excellence O'Gorman wanted it to be. Any private design had to meet with Farnborough's approval if it was to be ordered. Not many were.

The Factory set up its own development programme that would meet all future RFC requirements. It included development of the S.E. single-seater, high-speed scouts and the R.E. Reconnaissance Experimentals, the definitive production version of the B.E. series. There would be specialised versions to operate from particularly small front line airstrips (R.E.4) and a more powerful high-lift version (R.E.7) with extended wings. The Factory was also developing a range of F.E. series fighting planes. Seely, who had taken over from Haldane in the summer of 1912, was quite happy to encourage this reliance on the Factory, although in public, he refused to concede there had been any change in government policy. The Factory was, however, taking on a huge task. Each category of aeroplane was a major development programme, and, in addition, the Factory was conducting weapons trials, developing aeroplane equipment, and pursuing various aeronautical research programmes. Despite the resources that were being invested in the Factory, the organisation was seriously overstretched. Meanwhile, the rest of the British aircraft industry was underemployed and given no inkling of what the Army wanted beyond the basic two-seater required by the military aeroplane competition.

Soon after the military aeroplane competition, the annual autumn Army manoeuvres took place, the first in which there would be a major effort to involve aviation. With all their monoplanes grounded, trainers and planes involved in trials and experimental work at Farnborough had to be drafted in to make up the numbers, and even then only seventeen aeroplanes and three airships could be mustered for the two opposing forces.[76] The exercises involved a force, led by Lieutenant-General Haig, advancing towards London, and another, led by Lieutenant-General Grierson, blocking its path in the Cambridge area. Both sides were soon putting the handful of airships and aeroplanes they had been allocated to good use, and both commanders were impressed with the information they provided. Grierson was particularly impressed with his wireless-equipped *Gamma* airship, which was able to transmit a stream of up-to-date information to his headquarters. Developing wireless equipment light enough for Army planes to carry became an urgent priority.[77] The exercises convinced Grierson that aviation had transformed warfare. The first task in any future war, he believed, would be to 'get rid of' the enemy reconnaissance planes. The side with the 'last aeroplane afloat' would win the battle.[78] Haig was perhaps a little more circumspect, having been caught out by his planes' failure to spot an important element of Grierson's forces. Haig had learned the hard way that an aircraft not seeing something does not mean it is not there. Even so, Haig was impressed by the contribution aircraft had made and was convinced that in future conflicts the air and Army commanders would have to work side by side at the same headquarters.

It was realised that it would not be so easy for aircraft in future. Troops could be expected to make more effort to conceal their presence. Also, it was felt insufficient account had been taken of planes being lost to ground fire, and in the future there would inevitably be resistance in the air to contend with. Not all planes were going to make it back with their vital information.[79] Sykes, in his summary of the manoeuvres, emphasised the importance of ensuring planes did make it back by developing fighters that would gain 'command of the air' from the very beginning of a battle.[80]

Following the 1912 manoeuvres, an appreciation of the value of military aviation was no longer confined to a few enthusiastic aviators. No one was in any doubt that military aviation had a major role to play in future wars, and indeed, within Army circles there was an enthusiasm for developing it.[81] This was not always apparent in the post-war reminiscences of some air force officers. Sykes liked to ridicule Army conservatism and the soldier's love of the horse, and was particularly harsh on Haig. In 1911, according to Sykes, Haig let it be known that he believed Sykes was wasting his time with aeroplanes. His comment to officers at the Army Staff College on the eve of war, 'I hope none of you gentlemen is so foolish as to think the aeroplanes will be able to be usefully employed for reconnaissance,' is often used as evidence, although this too seems to have originated with Sykes.[82] Haig was a cavalryman and for him and many of his generation, the horse was a central and much loved aspect of Army life. Any threat to it might have prompted the odd ill-considered remark, but the advantages of seeing what the enemy was doing from the air were so obvious, no one could doubt the value of the aeroplane. Even while Haig was in India long before the 1912 manoeuvres and before he even met Sykes, he had been sufficiently impressed by the potential of aviation to send officers to Britain to learn to fly in order to set up an Air Corps in India.[83]

The new Army chief, Field Marshal French, another cavalry officer, set the tone by declaring, 'Aviation is one of the most important subjects to which the modern officer can pay attention at the present day.'[84] Air support would in future be an integral part of all Army operations. There was, however, an equally strong belief within the Army that the bombing of cities that so many feared would and could never be decisive in war. In years to come this would often be misinterpreted as a failure to accept the importance of air power. The Army had no doubts about the importance of air power, but only when it was used in conjunction with ground forces on the battlefield.

Another officer excited by the potential aviation had displayed at the 1912 Army manoeuvres was a certain Hugh Trenchard. Trenchard had been one of the first pupils to arrive at the Central Flying School. After being wounded in the Boer War, the thirty-nine-year-old major possessed only one good lung, but was desperate to become a fully qualified pilot before reaching the age of forty, the newly established cut-off age for pilots. Trenchard achieved his aim despite, by all accounts, having no natural talent as a pilot. For Trenchard, a military career that was going nowhere suddenly had a purpose. Trenchard stayed at the Central Flying School as an instructor, impressing Captain Paine with his stern disciplinarian approach and organisational skills, and was soon appointed as Paine's deputy. Trenchard was not someone who found it easy to express his views succinctly, either verbally or in writing, which perhaps explains why there is no record of his early thinking on the future of military aviation. In truth, Trenchard was a pragmatist rather than a theorist, someone who used theories and ideas to achieve his own ends rather than someone who generated new ideas. For the time being, Trenchard would remain very much on the side lines, helping to run the training programme, but the war that would propel him to the highest level of command was fast approaching.

For all the War Office's new enthusiasm for aviation, Britain was still way behind the major continental powers in terms of the tactical development of the aeroplane, aeronautical manufacturing capability, and front line air force strength. Nevertheless, the importance of the aeroplane had been established. The Army, however, was not getting carried away. The aeroplane was revolutionary but it was not going to revolutionise warfare. As Sykes emphasised, 'The main principles of war have been the same for centuries and will probably remain so for several more.'[85] Four years later, he would not be so sure.

CHAPTER 2

The Tactical Vision

With the Army manoeuvres over and the borrowed planes returned, Farnborough could get back to the task of developing a fighting plane that would be capable of providing the 'mastery of the air' Sykes and Grierson required, and O'Gorman was instructed to push these trials through as quickly as possible. By November 1912, the new Lewis machine gun was being used to fire through the floor of an F.E.2 at approximately aircraft-sized targets on the ground from altitudes of 500 and 1,000 feet, but even in this simplified scenario, only a small number of hits were achieved. The gun worked well. The drum feed avoided the jamming problem that would be inevitable with conventional belt-fed machine guns, which ideally needed a second person to feed the belt squarely into the gun. The overall design was the most compact on offer and the weapon was light.[1]

The Ordnance Department were not going to be hurried into placing an order. They were looking for a weapon that could serve the whole Army, and in normal Army usage, the Lewis tended to overheat and mud and grass tended to clog the ammunition drum. Neither of these problems would affect their use in aeroplanes in a cooling slipstream well above any grass or mud, but the Ordnance Department was not going to make any decisions until alternatives, including the latest version of the Vickers, had also been trialled. Henderson told O'Gorman to get these trials completed as quickly as possible; he was none too impressed when months later O'Gorman finally got round to telling the Air Department that the latest Vickers gun, dispatched months before, had not yet arrived. He was even less impressed when O'Gorman then discovered it had arrived after all, but 'had carefully been kept secret from me by an assistant'.[2]

Frustrated with the pace at which the Factory was moving, Henderson decided responsibility for weapons trials should be taken away from O'Gorman and passed to the squadrons.[3] In each squadron, 'officers in charge of experiments' were appointed, with their efforts co-ordinated at Sykes' headquarters by Major Musgrave, an aviation enthusiast ever since he had witnessed Bleriot's arrival on the cliff tops at Dover. A list was drawn up of the areas of research these officers were expected to organise and the squadrons set to work investigating the equipment and methods that would be needed for tasks such as artillery observation, reconnaissance and attacking targets on the ground and in the air. The appointed officers were expected to read up on the areas of research assigned to them, organise trials within the squadrons, and report back to Musgrave and Sykes every week with the results of their squadron's efforts. They were to 'avoid the tendency to expect that civilian inventors or foreign governments will supply us with the ideas and apparatus we need all ready-made'. 'Civilian inventors' was perhaps a reference to O'Gorman.[4]

The official history, using post-war reminiscences, likes to play up the haphazard, casual and amateurish approach of these early efforts with officers buying their own equipment because 'government funds were scanty',[5] but this does not reflect the sense of genuine urgency that existed at the time. The idea of getting the squadrons involved was to speed things up by bypassing the sophisticated and systematic but rather laborious approach adopted by Farnborough. The new emphasis was on practical improvisation rather than careful and theoretical scientific analysis, but it was expecting a lot of service personnel. No. 3 Squadron's tasks included investigating techniques for photo-reconnaissance. The advantages of studying a print at leisure on the ground and at any required magnification rather than struggling to make notes in the air were obvious enough and developing appropriate equipment and techniques had a high priority. The squadron was promised purpose-built equipment was being developed by the Aircraft Factory, but in the meantime they were told to do the best they could with whatever was available. They did indeed use their own cameras but requests for reimbursement were instantly approved. Funds were not that 'scanty', nor was the squadron's research the casual and freelance effort it is sometimes portrayed. The efforts of all the squadrons were monitored very closely.[6]

The purpose-built photographic equipment No. 3 Squadron had been promised was a semi-automatic system with the camera mounted in the base of the rear fuselage of a B.E.2, cushioned in horse hair and operated by levers. The system automatically replaced photographic plates so that overlapping images of the ground could be taken and stored for processing. It was a very ambitious project. Trials were supposed to have been completed by May 1913, but the apparatus proved more difficult to perfect than anticipated and development dragged on into the winter of 1913–14; indeed, it would be many years before anything as sophisticated as this became available.[7] It was another example of why Sykes and Henderson were keen to get more improvised trials going at squadron level rather than wait for what the scientists and engineers at Farnborough might eventually come up with. Ideally though, something between the ultra-sophistication of the Farnborough approach and the makeshift efforts of squadron aircrews was needed.

Over-reliance on the Factory was also slowing down deliveries of the aeroplanes the squadrons needed to conduct these experiments. The problem was not funding. The sums of money devoted to aviation were not huge compared to France and Germany, but given the British Army was not as large as continental conscript armies, funding was adequate and enough to equip the three aeroplane squadrons due to be formed before the spring of 1913. The problem was that not enough planes were ordered. Private designs had been discredited and the perfectionist O'Gorman was determined to produce the perfect plane before recommending large-scale production of any of his designs. In this search for perfection, the B.E.2 was followed in quick succession by the B.E.3, B.E.4, B.E.5 and B.E.6, but only the B.E.2 was ordered and only in very small numbers.

Critics of the government were soon pointing out that there was not much sign of the money invested in aviation being translated into front line strength. Seely blamed problems beyond his control, like the grounding of the monoplanes, but even including these, very few planes had been delivered to the Army. This did not stop Seely insisting in parliament in April 1913 that the RFC already possessed no less than 101 planes. In fact, the front line Military Wing squadrons had twenty-four planes between them, of which only twelve were serviceable.[8] Rather deviously, Seely, who, as Secretary of State for War was only responsible for the Military Wing, made sure he was referring to the Royal Flying Corps. With the Navy referring to their wing as the Naval Air Service, the term 'Royal Flying Corps' was already beginning to be associated with the Army's Military Wing, but technically it still included both Army and Navy wings. Seely's figure included all naval aircraft, training planes, grounded monoplanes, and indeed just about anything the Army had that looked as if it might have once flown, including planes officially described as 'wrecked' or 'destroyed by fire' about which 'decisions are pending'.[9]

When disbelieving MPs threatened to visit the airfields and count the planes, Seely ordered the newly arrived Brancker to go round the training schools and buy as many machines as he could with money that Brancker freely admitted was about to be returned to the Treasury unspent.[10] The funds to buy more planes clearly existed. The planes Brancker bought were perhaps good enough to impress spying MPs, but were quite useless for military purposes and most were soon scrapped. Meanwhile, orders for planes such as the excellent Avro 500 were increased to a mere dozen and contracts to various companies to build the B.E.2 under licence never exceeded half a dozen.

While the equipment crisis deepened, Henderson was trying to consolidate his Air Department. Henderson had decided that air issues could not be dealt with by the War Office in the same way as other Army matters. The machine gun was an example of where Army and air force requirements did not coincide. The air force had to have more control over its own development. Henderson persuaded the War Council to create a new semi-autonomous Directorate of Military Aeronautics, which came into being in September 1913. It had three departments responsible for general policy and training (M.A.1), design and procurement

(M.A.2), and finance (M.A.3). Henderson, suspecting the new position was not a particularly good career move, became a somewhat reluctant director of the new organisation. Ellington ran the M.A.1 department, effectively becoming second-in-command.

The creation of the Directorate seemed to be the end of Brancker's involvement in aviation. The ability to fly was a requirement for working in the new Directorate, but Brancker's poor eyesight seemed to rule this out. Fate, however, seemed to be constantly drawing him back to aviation, so he decided to throw caution to the wind and enrol on a pilot training course. Brancker was told at his medical that he was so short-sighted that if he flew, he would be a 'danger to himself and everybody else'. However, he managed to convince the authorities to make an exception and passed the course to become part of the new Directorate as a fully-fledged member of the RFC.[11] Soon after, Ellington returned to his artillery regiment and Brancker replaced him, becoming Henderson's second-in-command.

The new Directorate had acquired considerable powers. According to Brancker, it dealt with all air force matters, except 'actually feeding the men!'[12] It had a unique status within the War Office with Henderson having direct access to the Secretary-of-State for War. The existence of the Directorate encouraged the idea of aviation being not just a specialist area but a specialist career. This was not initially how even the strongest advocates viewed military aviation. Henderson was excited by the military potential of aviation, but he also wanted to command troops in the field and climb as high as possible up the Army promotion ladder. There was nothing so strange about Ellington leaving his post in the Air Directorate, going to the Central Flying School to complete his training as a military pilot, and then joining his artillery regiment. For these officers, aviation was important, just as artillery or infantry tactics or any other aspect of Army operations are important. Seeing aviation as just another aspect of Army operations helped keep the advantages of military aviation in perspective and encouraged a more integrated air policy.

Having an independent Directorate of Military Aeronautics did not encourage such a mentality. The Directorate inevitably became, administratively and psychologically, very much a self-contained department within a department, just as the RFC was becoming a service within a service. Recruits joined the RFC, not the Army, and the service was beginning to acquire its own internal structure and ethos. The air arm was beginning to detach itself from the Army and the seeds for future problems were being sown. The Admiralty, in contrast, continued to treat aircraft and aviation like any other aspect of naval equipment with the relevant policy, training and procurement departments picking up responsibility. This had its disadvantages but helped ensure knowledge of aviation was more diffuse within the service.[13]

At this stage, there was no tactical or doctrinal rift within the Army. Ironically, while the less self-contained Naval Air Service was harbouring thoughts of an entirely independent long-range bombing role for aviation, the Military Wing was not trying to go beyond the immediate tactical needs of the Army. For all its independence, the Directorate of Military Aeronautics and the RFC understood they were there to serve the Army; however, the new Directorate did not seem to make best use of the independence and power it had won. The Army air budget was doubled in 1913, had a 50 per cent supplementary increase early in 1914, and was doubled again for the subsequent financial year.[14] These funds were supposed to facilitate an acceleration in the formation of the planned eight squadrons. Despite this, the number of planes being ordered was inadequate and it seems the funds allocated were still not being spent. In 1914, the 50 per cent supplementary increase included an allocation from the Admiralty budget as compensation for the transfer of the airships of No. 1 Squadron to the RNAS; this was supposed to pay for the re-equipment of No. 1 Squadron with aeroplanes. Indeed, twenty-four R.E.5s were ordered from the Aircraft Factory for this purpose, but according to Brancker, the naval money ended up being returned to the Treasury because the Directorate already had ample spare funds to cover the cost.[15]

The heart of the problem was O'Gorman's desire to build the perfect plane. He seems to have persuaded Seely, Henderson and Brancker that it was not worth wasting money on anything that did not meet his high standards. Seely also seems to have been persuaded there was no particular urgency. A plane could be built 'in a matter of a few weeks or less' he told his critics in parliament, and 'arrangements could easily be made to manufacture a great number, far more than we should ever require and far more than is in the possession of any other country.'[16] It was rather a rash claim. In the meantime, O'Gorman continued his quest for perfection, which meant a perfectly stable plane. Stability was a hugely important issue. Most early planes were inherently unstable, which meant they required constant attention if the pilot was not to lose control. By the summer of 1913, O'Gorman's Bleriot Experimental programme had reached the B.E.8. The definitive operational version was supposed to be the Reconnaissance Experimental series, the first of which was the scaled down R.E.1 version of the Bleriot Experimental. This went some way towards achieving O'Gorman's goal of inherent stability, but this in turn spawned a series of R.E. adaptations and improvements.

Still, O'Gorman was not happy, and in the autumn of 1913, he wanted to start afresh; but his request for funding to develop a new plane was refused, perhaps more an indication of War Office frustration with the delays than a desire to save money. O'Gorman was not to be denied and simply labelled his redesign the B.E.2c, which, although it looked like previous B.E.2a/b models, had a completely new wing and was effectively a new plane.[17] Meanwhile, perfectly good privately developed planes were not getting the orders they deserved. Sykes rated the Avro 500 a tough and capable plane,[18] but only twelve were ordered. The Avro 504 that followed in the summer of 1913 was even better. It was stable, fitted with ailerons for controlling direction—while Factory Bleriot Experimental designs were still relying on wing warping—and could fly faster and higher than the latest B.E.8. Nonetheless, while the Factory plane was ordered before the prototype had even flown, the Avro 504 would have to wait until April 1914 for an order.

The lack of substantial orders for either Factory or privately developed planes had serious long-term implications for the British aircraft industry. The tiny numbers ordered meant it was not worth setting up production lines. Planes were built individually and the aircraft industry did not develop a capability to mass produce. The first substantial contract was for the twenty-four R.E.5 reconnaissance planes ordered to re-equip the ex-airship No. 1 Squadron, and these were to be built by the Factory. For private companies it was the last straw. It seemed the Royal Aircraft Factory was responsible for deciding which planes the RFC should be equipped with, choosing their own and awarding themselves the contracts to build them.

The prototype of O'Gorman's latest definitive B.E.2c finally flew in May 1914, and with it he achieved his goal of fully stable flight. Brancker describes how he flew the prototype from Farnborough to Netheravon, only needing to use the controls to take off and land, and wrote a reconnaissance report on the way.[19] The plane was a triumph for O'Gorman and his Royal Aircraft Factory. Arguably though, it was not superior to the Avro 504, which had flown the year before and was easy enough to fly to remain the RAF's standard basic trainer well into the 1930s, long after the B.E.2s had been consigned to the scrapheap. Brooke-Popham, c/o No. 3 Sqn., was not even convinced the B.E.2c was better than the French Henri Farman pusher. The Farman was slower and more difficult to fly, but at least its observer could observe and fire a weapon.[20] The 'ideal' definitive B.E.2c still had the observer in an impossible position in front of the pilot. It might have been an easy plane to fly, but it was far from being the ideal warplane.

In addition to a stable reconnaissance plane, the Factory was also supposed to be developing a fighting plane. Although work continued on the Farman style F.E. Fighting Experimental pushers, O'Gorman realised that a machine handicapped by the un-aerodynamic pusher framework and the need to carry a second crewmember would always have a problem trying to intercept a plane that was not handicapped by either. A specialist fighting plane was required. O'Gorman initially hoped to get round the aerodynamic problems of the pusher with his F.E.3 design, a cannon-armed two-seater. It still had a pusher engine, but instead of the tail being connected to the fuselage by un-aerodynamic framing that passed round the propeller, there would be a single boom that passed through the centre of the propeller and engine. It was another typically imaginative and ambitious Farnborough project that soon encountered problems. The plane was flown, but the tail boom proved to be too weak; trials were suspended and work began on an improved F.E.6 using the same principle.[21]

Even if these technical problems could be overcome, it was still one engine pushing an aircrew of two. Either the number of aircrew had to be reduced or the number of engines increased, and if a specialist gunner was required, there was no choice. Two engines mounted in the wings would provide more power, eliminate the need for the un-aerodynamic framework of the pusher, and still leave the nose free for the gunner. The F.E.2 and F.E.3 were to be followed by the twin-engine, two-seater F.E.4, the three-engine, four-seater F.E.5, and the cannon-armed, twin-engine, two-seater F.E.7.[22] Fighting planes would follow the pattern of fighting ships: the bigger the better. Developing twin and multi-engine planes, however, introduced a whole new range of problems for Factory staff to solve, and there was no prospect of any of these proposals flying in the immediate future. With hindsight, it is clear the Factory was hurtling down the wrong path. The solution was to be found in smaller, not bigger planes.

Progress with the basic two-seater pusher was slow. A second F.E.2 had been built in 1913 but crashed in February 1914. A fresh start was made with the F.E.2a, but this was still under construction in the summer of 1914. With the F.E.3 being reworked as the F.E.6 and the construction of the larger twin-engine planes in the project stage, the Factory could not even offer a prototype fighting plane to experiment with. An increasingly frustrated Directorate felt obliged to look beyond the Factory; an example of the Admiralty's Vickers Experimental Fighting Biplane series, the future Gunbus, another two-seater pusher, was ordered.

While waiting for something better, squadrons experimented as best they could with Henri Farman pushers, but machine guns were in desperately short supply—squadrons would get hold of one then almost immediately be told someone else needed it.[23] Aircrews found themselves in the hopeless position of developing air combat techniques and tactics with pistols and rifles, and no realistic aerial targets to aim at. Sykes and Musgrave were demanding more effort, but in the circumstances, there must have seemed little point in even trying.[24] Sykes tried to get things moving by getting a flight from No. 3 Squadron on the Salisbury Plain gun ranges where it was hoped they might get some practice by attacking balloons towed by cars, but finding a free slot seemed impossible. The proposed trials were put off until after the 1913 Army manoeuvres and then Sykes decided to switch them to the Hythe School of Musketry where the coastal location would enable balloons to be towed by high-speed boats.[25] They finally got going in January 1914 and were supposed to last several months. Unfortunately, poor weather restricted the work done and at the beginning of February, the War Office ordered the trials to end, much to Musgrave's annoyance. There was time to decide that the Lewis was the best machine gun available, but this was merely a confirmation of what had been known for some time. Firing practice got no further than a few attempts at hitting targets on the ground and did little more than underline the problems pilots had at hitting anything, moving or stationary.

None of the air combat exercises involved any sort of mock air-to-air combat between two aircraft, which might have provided more of a feel for the problems and possible alternative ways of tackling them. The Army manoeuvres were perhaps opportunities for such experiments. These tended to be seen as a hindrance to the development of a fighting plane with trials stopped or postponed until they were over. They should perhaps have been seen as an opportunity for mock combat in something approaching realistic conditions. This would also have met the Army criticism that these manoeuvres ignored the possibility that reconnaissance planes might be intercepted and shot down. During the 1913 manoeuvres, the *Delta* airship was 'attacked' by two aeroplanes who claimed its destruction, but the umpires, not unreasonably, decided that as the aeroplanes were unarmed, their 'victory' did not count. However, it did occur to at least one participant that there ought to be more of this sort of mock combat.[26] Everybody was assuming a fighting aircraft had to have a second crew member to aim the weapon, and all efforts were being focused on how this could be done. More realistic mock air-to-air combats might have set the RFC off on a different path a little sooner.

There were no doubts about the importance of air combat. Brancker was already talking about the need to band specialist fighting squadrons together in brigades 'for the purpose of achieving command of the skies'[27] and Musgrave and Sykes believed the failure to develop an efficient fighter was the most serious problem facing the air arm.[28] Nor was it just an issue of establishing air superiority over the battlefield. Musgrave was already worrying about the effect the massive aerial attack everyone was expecting would have on Army mobilisation. He feared much 'confusion and dislocation' would be caused by attacks on telephone exchanges, wireless stations, railway stations and ships, not to mention the War Office and Admiralty.[29] Such fears prompted the question of whether it was time for the Army to consider how it might make more use of bombers. A specialist bomber had not been a War Office requirement, but the Royal Aircraft Factory was developing a 3-cwt (336-lb) bomb and adapting the R.E.5 to carry it. With a longer upper wing to lift the bomb and extra fuel, this became the R.E.7.

Sykes and Musgrave believed even larger, high endurance machines were required, capable of carrying heavy loads relatively slowly, planes which would need 'consorts' to protect them.[30] Sykes had begun to talk about the possibility of attacking troops, ammunition dumps and supply trains with 'a low-flying-armoured destroyer', and more distant 'enemy arteries of supply' with large twin-engine planes with a range of 700 miles.[31] The targets would still be tactical, but tactical in a much broader sense. The bombing experiments conducted by the squadrons were scarcely encouraging such ideas. In May 1913, No. 3 Squadron was involved in trials with flour bombs dropped on imaginary targets, but without any bomb aiming equipment, observers simply dropped the bombs over the side of the plane as accurately as they could. Unsurprisingly, the results were not particularly impressive. From 200 feet, pilots got within 20 feet of the target, but from 1,800 feet, the best effort missed by 400 yards.[32] The results were at odds with Grahame-White's claims that he had hit targets accurately from 2,000 feet at his 1911 Hendon demonstration. Had he really been flying so high, his admiring spectators would probably have been in more danger than the mock battleship. Musgrave, with the Artillery Ordnance College, and the Royal Aircraft Factory with their Mark 1 bombsight, were both working on the bomb-aiming problem. Perhaps somewhat optimistically, a bomb-aiming system was ordered from Germany.[33]

However, it was not just bombs that could be used against ground targets. Musgrave speculated that the machine guns and cannon carried by fighters might be used for much more than interception. On the battlefield, they could be used to attack targets like reserves assembling in the rear. Planes armed with machine guns would, he suggested, bring columns of troops marching to the front to an immediate halt, while similar attacks on trains packed with troops would not be 'a pleasant subject for contemplation'.[34] It was, however, the lack of an effective means of engaging the enemy in the air that worried Musgrave most. The time had come, he insisted, to decide on the best gun, the best mounting, and the best available aeroplane to carry it, and this should be ordered in large numbers as soon as possible. Musgrave suggested the School of Musketry should offer courses on air-to-air firing, or perhaps even a new school of aerial musketry specialising in air-to-air combat should be opened. Most important of all, it was vital to get something into service in numbers, even if it was only Henri Farman pushers. 'Under existing conditions, the Military Wing would find themselves somewhat helpless if opposed by foreign armed aircraft.'[35]

However, Musgrave's ideas on the ideal fighting plane were very typical of the time. Speed was not important, heavy armament and long range were: 'The function of the gun ship is to hit hard, not fly fast.'[36] There was a very clear consensus about taking fighter development in the wrong direction and without any meaningful trials it was difficult to come to an alternative conclusion. Although the means of achieving the desired results might be suspect, there was no doubting the vision. Long-range bombing and low-level ground attack were now being considered in addition to observation, reconnaissance and air combat. Musgrave was already anticipating all air force roles performed by day would eventually also have to be performed by night, and pilots would have to start getting used to night flying. With round the clock air operations, the possibilities were limitless. With control of the skies, a seaborne invasion of Britain would be impossible and, in an ironic inversion of what was to occur nearly thirty years later with the German Afrika Corps trapped in Tunisia, Musgrave suggested that the channel between Tunisia and Sicily would be impossible to navigate if the Italian air force controlled the skies above.[37]

Unlike the approach of the Admiralty, this boldness was not at the expense of basic reconnaissance. This was by far the most developed RFC application of aeronautics and the most immediately useful. Extensive trials with aeroplane directed artillery fire took place. Signalling was primitive with lamps and Very pistols, but by the spring of 1914, wireless sets were becoming available which were light enough to be carried by the R.E.5 and, if flown as a single-seater, even the B.E.2. For photo-reconnaissance, the squadrons were still making do with hand-held cameras and there was a chronic shortage of these. Nevertheless, extensive trials had been conducted with the equipment that was available, and the results, achieved in various light conditions, altitudes and angles, and with different photographic processes, were all compared.[38]

Technically, British aeroplane design was closing the gap with foreign designs; in high-speed single-seater scouts, Britain was beginning to set the pace. Since these were essentially the same as the privately produced high-speed racers, this was one area where private companies could compete with the Factory. The basic formula was simple—fit the most powerful available engine to the smallest possible airframe. This was also the design philosophy behind many future fighter designs. The designers of the scouts and racers did not know it at the time, but they were effectively designing the first genuine single-seater fighters.

These planes had very different characteristics to the stable, pilot-friendly B.E.2s. High maximum speeds brought with them high landing speeds and tricky handling characteristics, as demonstrated by the Factory's first scout, the 100-hp 92-mph Bleriot Scout 1 (B.S.1). This advanced plane, with its moulded plywood monocoque fuselage, flew for the first time in March 1913 but crashed within weeks. For the rebuilt version, the 'Bleriot' part of the name was dropped and the plane became the 'Scout Experimental 2', the S.E.2, the first in a series of designs that would eventually culminate in the illustrious S.E.5a. With a less powerful 80-hp engine, the S.E.2 flew again in November 1913 and achieved a reasonably impressive 85 mph. The newly created No. 5 Squadron, based at Farnborough, tried the plane and did not find it too hot to handle.[39]

November 1913 also saw the arrival at Farnborough of Tom Sopwith's latest racer, the Tabloid. This used a standard fabric-covered fuselage but still managed to exceed 90 mph with a passenger. It also had a lower landing speed than the S.E.2. Higgins, the commander of No. 5 Squadron, rated the Factory's S.E.2 as the easier plane to fly,[40] but the Tabloid's conventional structure and low landing speed gave the Sopwith plane an edge.[41] The plane was good enough to loosen the Factory stranglehold on production contracts and a dozen were ordered.[42] Another privately developed racer, Barnwell's excellent Bristol Scout biplane, was also challenging O'Gorman's claimed superiority. Its top speed of 97.5 mph had Seely's opponents in parliament pouring scorn on his insistence that Factory designs were best.[43] The Bristol single-seater was precisely the sort of privately developed plane the government should be ordering, they insisted, but the only order Bristol got was for more B.E.2s.

O'Gorman's Factory, however, was fighting back. With the S.E.4 biplane, Folland took aerodynamic finesse to new heights. The plane was designed to break the world airspeed record and with its streamlined engine cowling, contoured fuselage and enclosed cockpit, it would not have looked out of place in the late 1930s. No one could be persuaded to fly the plane inside its claustrophobic celluloid bubble, but minus its enclosed cockpit, it smashed the world record held by the Deperdussin monoplane with a remarkable 135 mph— more proof that the biplane need not necessarily be slower than a monoplane. Its 150-hp Gnome engine was far too unreliable for anything other than short record breaking dashes, but re-engined with a more trustworthy 100-hp Gnome, it still managed a respectable 90 mph,[44] although this was no more impressive than the less refined Sopwith racer, and significantly less impressive than the Bristol Scout.

O'Gorman certainly believed his Factory, with its meticulous, systematic and scientific approach, ought to be developing the best designs, but planes such as the Avro 504, Sopwith Tabloid and Bristol Scout were denting this theory. Nevertheless, in many respects the Royal Aircraft Factory was leading the way. The methods of many early designers were casual to say the least. Tom Sopwith, one of the best in Britain, was not particularly analytical in his approach to aeroplane design. He simply went by what looked right—an approach that needed a degree of luck or inspiration, depending on your point of view.[45] The Factory was establishing standards for the rest of the aircraft industry that helped encourage a more rigorous approach to aeroplane design. It is also worth noting that Bristol had been inspired to abandon the monoplane and adopt the biplane format for their Scout by the Factory B.E.2s they were building under licence.

With designers of the calibre of Folland and de Havilland, one would expect Factory designs to be of the highest quality, but they were not necessarily going to be any better than those produced by the likes of A. V. Roe, Tom Sopwith or Frank Barnwell. Indeed, there was a disadvantage to the Factory's meticulous attention to detail. O'Gorman might consider the industry approach somewhat rough and ready, but they could get an equivalent design in the air faster, and their planes were not dropping out of the sky any more regularly than Factory designs.

Both Henderson and Brancker seemed well aware of O'Gorman's faults and were perhaps a little irritated by his arrogance. Brancker described him as 'volatile, artistic and imaginative', but it was 'hard to hold his attention to the practical facts of the moment'.[46] Nevertheless, Brancker and the War Office would appear to have been mesmerised by O'Gorman's boundless confidence. Brancker trusted his judgement and seems to have been persuaded that there really were no planes in the country worth ordering, apart from the ones the Factory was working on. On the eve of war, Brancker was lamenting that no decision could yet be reached about what the standard RFC reconnaissance machine should be, although the sole reason, it would seem, was that O'Gorman had not yet finished tinkering with his definitive B.E.2c. The first Avro 504s were already being delivered, but Brancker was still 'awaiting reports on their efficiency'.[47] It seemed there had been plenty of time to establish this, given that the prototype had flown in July 1913. The plane seemed to do everything expected of it and Sykes had spoken highly of its lower-powered predecessor. The new version was easy to fly and faster than the B.E.2c. In February 1914, it broke the altitude record held by the B.E.2, all of which might perhaps be considered sufficient proof of its efficiency.

The prevailing lack of urgency did not help. In the spring of 1914, Brancker, like many, did not believe war was particularly imminent and thought the Directorate still had plenty of time to make decisions about which aeroplanes should be ordered.[48] The doubling of the air budget in April 1914 brought no acceleration in production. Asquith, who was now Prime Minister and Secretary of State for War, was more concerned by the internal threat posed by the controversial Ireland Home Rule issue than preparing the Army to deal with any external threat. It would seem the right time for Henderson and Brancker to assert their authority and take the initiative. They had their own department and budget, and could to some extent control their own supply, but with Seely's departure, the orders dried up completely. Sykes was constantly complaining there were insufficient planes to equip the squadrons that he had been instructed to create. His appeal in mid-June to know how many aeroplanes were on order brought the response that since the twelve Avro 504s ordered on 1 April, the day after Seely resigned, just thirteen planes had been ordered—two B.E.8s and eleven Farmans, to be built under licence in Britain.[49]

The aero-engine situation was even more alarming. Excellent British aeroplane designs were emerging and limited production was underway, but all these designs relied on French engines. The government had tried to get aero-engine development going by offering cash prizes for successful designs. Companies with car engine experience like Sunbeam and Rolls-Royce were encouraged to take part, but the Sunbeam offering was heavier and less efficient than French designs, and Rolls-Royce preferred not to get involved. The only British aero engine ready for production in the summer of 1914 was the Factory R.A.F.1, a derivative of a French Renault design. The only complete engines delivered were ten 80-hp Gnome rotaries built under licence by Sopwith.[50] The Army was not short on ideas about how air power might be used; some advanced aeroplanes had been developed and RFC aircrews were acquiring considerable tactical expertise. Even the funding was not lacking, but the hardware required had simply not been ordered in sufficient quantities and the aircraft industry remained hopelessly underdeveloped.

Pressure from the industry and growing frustration with O'Gorman's Factory resulted in British aircraft companies finally being allowed to know exactly what the War Office wanted. In the spring of 1914, details were released of the speed, climb, range, and lifting capability necessary for the five categories of plane required by the Army. It was essentially O'Gorman's development programme made public. The five types specified were a high-speed single-seater scout (85 mph), a short and long-range two-seater reconnaissance plane, and two fighting planes.

While the RFC was waiting for the aeroplanes that would control the skies above the battlefield, the British public wanted to know who was going to defend them from the Zeppelins. The danger had been brought sharply back into focus by an incident on the night of 14 October 1912, when many believed they had heard an airship prowling over the naval base at Sheerness. The incursion happened to coincide with a lengthy trial flight by a Zeppelin, which made the reports that much more credible.[51] Once again, the British press focused its attention on the vulnerability of the country to air attack, and there was more alarmist talk about the destruction that would be wrought by airships capable of carrying up to ten tons of bombs. *Aeroplane* magazine, which, under the editorship of the ever belligerent C. G. Grey, was never afraid to play up the danger, melodramatically described how following a German air attack on the capital, '...the disorganised and panic-stricken survivors of the population of London will have the sole, although sorry, satisfaction before passing under German domination, of hanging the guilty ministers'.[52]

In parliament, both the War Office and Admiralty were criticised for not taking the threat more seriously. There was overwhelming support for providing the Army with air support, but there were objections to the War Office air requirement being built solely around the needs of the Army. Seely was adamant that by day the Zeppelins would be too vulnerable to anti-aircraft fire and by night they would not be able to find their targets. He also ventured the thought that the best way of countering an air attack was not to attempt to shoot down the bombers, but to build a retaliatory force that would deter such an attack. On this matter, Seely was happy to defer to the Admiralty with whom he apparently believed responsibility for such matters rested.[53] The concept of the counter deterrent as a means of defence was born, and it seemed the War Office believed it was the Admiralty's job to develop it—a responsibility Churchill, a close friend of Seely's, would have no objection taking on.

Air defence over mainland Britain was supposed to be the responsibility of the War Office, but following the Sheerness incident, the Admiralty no longer intended to wait and see what the War Office might do to protect their naval bases. In November 1912, the Admiralty placed a contract with Vickers for a specialist land-based Zeppelin interceptor, and the company set to work on what would become the Gunbus. The Navy had established flights of land and seaplanes around the British coast, primarily for reconnaissance, anti-submarine patrols, and to warn of invasion, but to these roles was now added the air defence of targets of particular interest to the Navy. The War Office resented this encroachment on what they still considered their responsibility, but with no plans of their own, they were in no position to object. How successful these naval flights might be, with only pistols or rifles for armament, was another matter. It was not even clear if aeroplanes had the performance to get within firing range of a Zeppelin. Planes were not that much faster than airships, and while they could climb faster at lower altitudes, the airship could climb to altitudes beyond the reach of an aeroplane. Furthermore, the lifting capacity of the airship was far greater than an aeroplane—the former could accommodate numerous defensive machine gun positions without seriously affecting performance, while the weight of even a single gun had a substantial effect on the performance of an aeroplane.

If the aeroplane reached the airship, it was also far from obvious that even machine-gun fire would bring one down. Rifle-calibre bullets would pass straight through the hydrogen gas bags, probably only causing small leaks. Even if incendiary or explosive shells were used, it was assumed that the Germans would take the basic precaution of surrounding the hydrogen gas bags with an inert gas—easily provided by the exhaust from its engines—which would deny the hydrogen the contact with oxygen it would need to burn. In fact, the Germans had not done this, but the fear that they had taken this precaution encouraged the development of more exotic alternatives to cannon and machine guns. These included dropping bombs on the airship from a higher altitude and, even more ambitious, the 'Fiery Grapple', which consisted of grappling hooks trailed by an aircraft over the airship to rip open the skin. The escaping gas would then be ignited with an explosive charge—a method which seemed as dangerous for the intercepting pilot as the Zeppelin being attacked.[54] In public, Churchill remained upbeat and, in typically good form, claimed in parliament: 'Any hostile aircraft, airships or aeroplanes which reached our coast during the coming year would be promptly attacked in superior force by a swarm of very formidable hornets.'[55] In reality the defences were virtually non-existent.

A lecture given to the Royal United Service institution by a Colonel Jackson caught the mood of public alarm. The colonel speculated on the consequences of attacks on the Admiralty or the War Office and how the population might react if water supplies were cut off or ships bringing in food were sunk in the Thames. He warned Londoners not to expect any protection from the Hague Conventions:

> This is the age of the 'knock out' blow in everything. Would any ruler harden his heart to such an action? Who can say? If it seemed probable that such panic and riot would be caused as to force the Home Government to accept an unfavourable peace, then perhaps it might be done.[56]

Seely, freed from his ministerial responsibilities but still chairman of the Air Committee, joined the clamour for better air defence. He was horrified when he was told that the only way of bringing down a Zeppelin might be suicide ramming attacks. Seely warned Asquith of the extreme danger facing the country, and Hankey urged the Prime Minister to set up an enquiry into the state of the country's defences. Asquith, however, was far too concerned about the prospect of civil war in Ireland to worry about Zeppelins.[57]

For the War Office, the prospect of the Admiralty taking over their responsibilities was a greater incentive to act than the Zeppelin threat itself. In response to the coastal defence flights set up by the Navy, Henderson came up with his own plan for a force of 162 planes to be based on the coast to provide air support for local Army units dealing with raids or invasion, and to provide a defence against air attack. However, the Army had to have priority. These coastal squadrons would not be created until after the eight squadrons required by the Expeditionary Force had been established.[58] By the time Henderson made this proposal, Britain was already on the brink of war.

On 25 July 1914, Major-General Wilson, the Director of Military Operations, burst into Brancker's office with the news that war was imminent. Brancker was taken completely by surprise.[59] Suddenly and far too late, orders began to flow; the entire £1 million annual budget disappeared in a week. To his horror, Brancker discovered that British companies were not ready for bulk production and were only capable of assembling planes individually by hand. It was hardly surprising given that the War Office had not placed any bulk orders. With British companies unable to respond, War Office officials were dispatched to France with instructions to acquire as many Farman aircraft and French engines they could lay their hands on.[60]

Air defence of Britain was now the least of the War Office's problems. The entire Military Wing would be dispatched to France with the Expeditionary Force, taking with it every available useful plane. The location and movements of the German Army would be far more important than shooting down Zeppelins heading for London. Sykes mobilised his RFC and gathered his squadrons in the south of England. Sufficient resources existed for just four of the seven squadrons to be deployed operationally. Henri Farman pushers were still the only aircraft capable of carrying a machine gun. In July, the RFC tested the Admiralty's Vickers Gunbus. Brooke-Popham considered it an improvement over the Henri Farman as a gun carrier[61] and more were ordered, but for the time being, the RFC would have to make do with Farmans. There were only a handful of machine guns of any description and squadrons had to be hurriedly issued with a dozen rifles as substitutes.[62]

On 28 July, the Austro-Hungarian Empire declared war on Serbia. Europe was hurtling towards war. There was doubt, even at this stage, about whether the British would restrict their efforts to supporting Belgium, or if they would co-operate with the French. To the bitter end, the Admiralty opposed any large-scale intervention on the continent. The handful of divisions the British could put in the field, the Admiralty argued, would make an insignificant contribution in a battle that would be dominated by the large conscript continental armies. Instead, Britain should rely on her traditional strategy of using British supremacy at sea to blockade Germany. The government was tempted, but politically, a commitment on the ground was needed. The Army would support the French.

Henderson took the opportunity to abandon his post at the War Office to become the operational commander of the RFC in France, with Sykes demoted to his chief of staff. Henderson still retained his position as Director of Military Aeronautics, but the junior Brancker was effectively left in charge. Trenchard took over from Sykes as commander of what was left of the RFC in Britain. This changeover was, according to Trenchard, a frosty affair with neither in the best of moods. Trenchard resented not being given an operational command in France, while Sykes had even more reason to feel disgruntled as he believed he had been promised he would retain command of the RFC when it moved to France. The two were soon at loggerheads over whether Trenchard's priority should be building new squadrons or replacing casualties.[63] Sykes, following the official line that the war would be brief, insisted reinforcements were the priority, but Trenchard would have none of it. The course of events would prove Trenchard right, but one suspects it was sheer bloody-mindedness rather than inspired reasoning that shaped his views. The bitterness of the altercation set the tone for the relationship between the two men, and their mutual dislike and distrust would rapidly escalate into something little short of a mutual loathing. Trenchard felt Sykes was conceited and indecisive while Sykes apparently claimed Trenchard's 'loud voice betrayed a vacant mind'.[64] For the time being, the English Channel would keep them at arm's length of each other. Trenchard was left with scarcely anything to get a training programme going, but these were the circumstances in which Trenchard would always thrive. Not for the last time he would get the best out of what little he had.

Naval forces were also mobilising. On 27 July, the fifty-odd planes available to the RNAS were ordered to concentrate at Felixstowe, Great Yarmouth, and on the Isle of Grain (Kent), principally to provide defence for naval bases, but also as some sort of defensive shield for London. Indeed, on 29 July, Churchill issued instructions that the primary purpose of all RNAS aircraft was to provide air defence for Great Britain—an interesting priority for the air arm created to support the Navy. Amid rumours of an immediate Zeppelin attack, the RFC was persuaded to reassign one of its four squadrons to air defence. Sykes disapproved, but the Army Council reluctantly ordered No. 4 Squadron to move to Eastchurch.

On 1 August, Germany declared war on Russia, and followed it two days later with a declaration of war on France. A German invasion of Belgium seemed inevitable; Britain was on the brink of war. Londoners were about to find out how real the Zeppelin threat was.

CHAPTER 3

Early Success and Stalemate

On 4 August 1914 Britain declared war on Germany following the invasion of Belgium by German troops. Tension in London grew as the government and people braced themselves for the anticipated Zeppelins. An article in the ever alarmist *Aeroplane* magazine speculated whether British nerve would stand the test or if bombardment from the air 'would result in a panic stricken mob rushing to Buckingham Palace clamouring for peace'.[1]

The Times attempted to reassure its readers as best it could. The Germans had no more than thirteen airships and would not be able to attack by day. By night, darkness would only protect the raiders for eight hours, which, at a leisurely 30–40 mph did not give them very long to find their targets and make their escape. If they were still in the vicinity of the British Isles as dawn broke, the faster aeroplanes would 'be after them'. By night or day, they would be vulnerable to rifle fire if they flew below 4,000 feet. Cloud might conceal their whereabouts, but it would also prevent the Zeppelin crews from finding their targets. They might conceivably do some damage, but only if their bombs were dropped with 'unexpected accuracy', which might have left readers wondering about the fate of the innocent bystander who happened to be under bombs dropped with expected inaccuracy. Readers were assured that if the Zeppelin evaded the aircraft and anti-aircraft fire, 'she will indeed be fortunate'. Even though the article was clearly intended to play down the danger, it still managed to overstate the scale of the threat. There were in fact only four German airships deployed in the West. While exaggerating the effectiveness of the available defences, the efforts to maximise the difficulties the Zeppelin crews would face were more accurate than the writer perhaps realised or intended.[2]

When war was declared, all available naval planes were on alert, ready to deal with airships or aeroplanes. From 8 August, the patrol zone covering East Anglia and Kent was extended northwards to protect the entire North Sea coastline, a huge and a rather hopeless undertaking for a force consisting of just fifty planes. Meanwhile, all four available RFC squadrons, including No. 4 Squadron previously diverted to Eastchurch for air defence duties, were heading for Dover, en route for France. The RFC were asked to support the naval air defence effort by covering the northern and southern ends of the enormous front the Admiralty had committed itself to defend. Kitchener, who had just taken over from Asquith as Secretary of State for War, agreed to this without fully understanding what was involved. Brancker was horrified and explained to Kitchener that Henderson was taking to France just about every operational plane the RFC had. A flight from No. 4 Squadron was retained at Dover to meet the RFC commitment to the southern end of the line. A single plane was all that could be mustered to meet the RFC's promise to cover the Scottish coast.[3] There were numerous reports of Zeppelins flying over Britain. On many occasions, planes were scrambled to search for the illusive intruders, but these reports all proved to be false alarms. It was just as well. The available equipment was so inadequate for the task that startled naval pilots were told suicide ramming attacks might really be the only option.[4]

While naval planes scoured the skies over Britain for intruders, the sole German Navy airship was being used for reconnaissance over the North Sea, and the three German Army airships, with a fourth that joined them on 10 August, were used for reconnaissance and bombing in support of the German ground forces. On 6 August, a Zeppelin raid killed nine civilians in Liege, and another ten died in Antwerp on 25 August. Liege was under attack at the time and was therefore a legitimate target, but Antwerp was being bypassed by the westward advancing German Army, and this raid seemed more like an act of deliberate terror. Photos of the damage were soon appearing in newspapers and all raids on Belgian towns were quickly condemned as barbarous atrocities in Britain and countries sympathetic to the anti-German coalition. Churchill, in typically flamboyant mood, ordered the RNAS to hunt down and destroy the Zeppelin responsible.[5]

First-hand reports coming out of the bombed cities emphasised that far from hastening victory on the ground, the outrage provoked was tending to stiffen the determination of the citizens to resist. This was no doubt the line the authorities were encouraging journalists to take, but at the very least, the civilian casualties were a gift for the anti-German propaganda machine. There was no sign of the panic and riots predicted by some, and no demands that the Belgian Government give in to this intimidation by surrendering. Newspaper reports of the raids in the United States roused sympathy for the unfortunate Belgians, reinforcing the image of Germany as a barbaric aggressor and increasing popular support for the nations opposing her.

The relatively low civilian casualties should perhaps have eased fears in Britain. Instead, it was taken as a warning that far worse lay round the corner. After the Antwerp raid, the Admiralty rather melodramatically warned Kitchener that enormous quantities of explosives might soon be falling on London, and wanted to know what the War Office planned to do about it.[6] Churchill may not have approved of such alarmist talk, but even he was worried about naval bases in the firing line.

Brancker did not believe any sort of effective aerial defence was really possible, but nor did he think it was necessary. He considered the scale of the threat had been grossly exaggerated,[7] and it was not going to deter the War Office from sending every possible plane to France to support the BEF. The War Office could scarcely claim to be making any contribution to the air defence of Great Britain, and on 3 September, Kitchener accepted the logic of the situation by formally asking the Admiralty to take over full responsibility. The RFC offered to continue to do what it could to assist the Navy with any aircraft it happened to have in the country, but the priority for the War Office was the battle in Belgium where German forces were now advancing rapidly.

The Admiralty was as concerned as the War Office by this rapid advance, although mainly because German occupation of bases on the Channel coast would put aeroplanes as well as Zeppelins within range of targets in Britain.

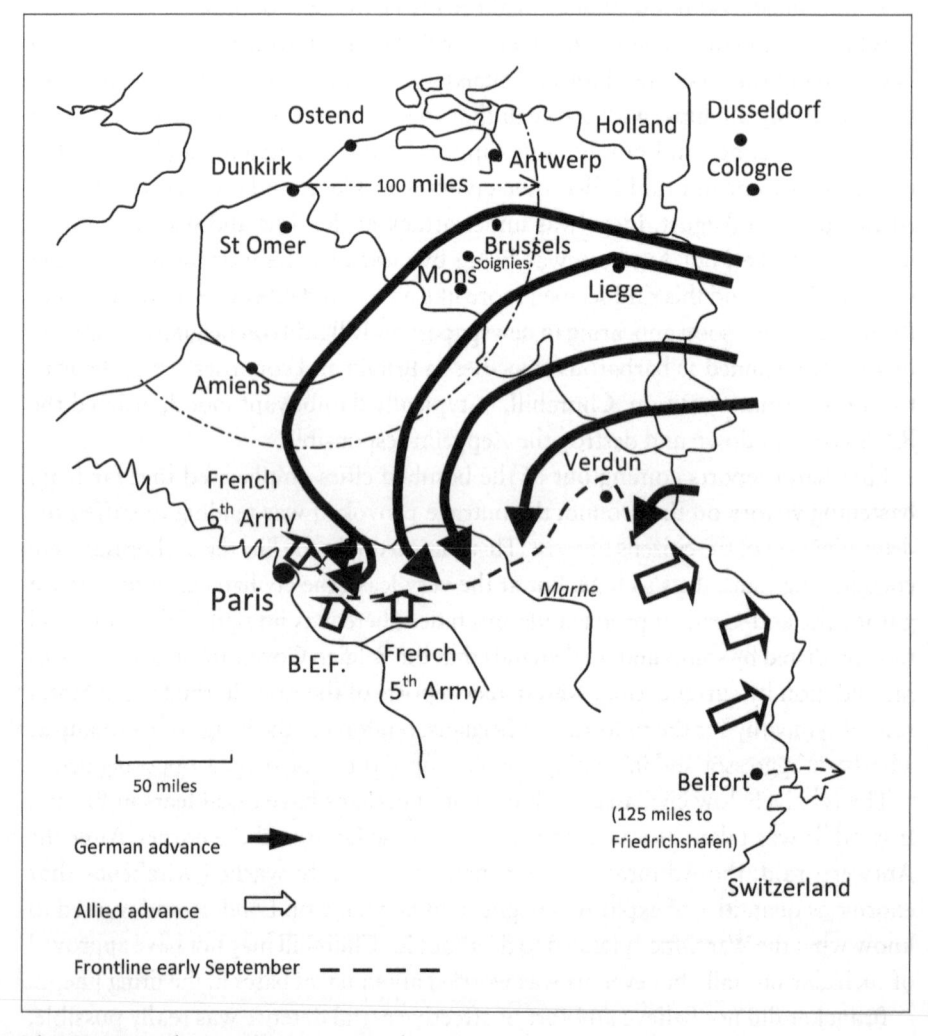

The German advance: August-September 1914.

On 27 August, a force of Royal Marines, accompanied by a RNAS squadron with nine assorted planes under the command of Samson, arrived in Ostend to assist the Belgian defences. When it became clear the Belgians had made no preparations to defend the town, the force was ordered home with the aeroplanes flying via Dunkirk, but mist forced the planes to land there. Samson, anxious to get involved in the fight, managed to delay the continuation of the flight home and was rewarded by the arrival of new orders. His RNAS squadron would now be the first line of defence against the Zeppelin. Churchill instructed the squadron to stay put and ensure no Zeppelin bases were established within 100 miles of Dunkirk. Mobile units equipped with armoured cars and supported by RNAS reconnaissance planes using advance airfields up to 50 miles inland were to patrol and control the area around Dunkirk, which was effectively a huge no man's land on the right flank of the advancing German Army.[8]

However, Churchill had promised that the Zeppelin responsible for the Antwerp raid would be hunted down. Samson was also expected to accomplish this, even if it meant operating much further than 100 miles from Dunkirk. Despite his public confidence in the RNAS defence flights, privately Churchill had few illusions about their capabilities. A more aggressive role seemed likely to bring more reward. The favoured anti-Zeppelin weapon was the 20-lb Hale bomb; if it really could destroy a Zeppelin, it seemed far easier to drop one on a stationary Zeppelin on the ground rather than in flight.[9] In fact, three Zeppelins had already been destroyed by ground fire in daylight tactical operations, a role the huge airships were clearly not suited to.[10] By the time Churchill made his promise, the Zeppelin that had bombed Antwerp, Z9, was the only surviving member of the original fleet. British intelligence had identified two main Zeppelin bases threatening Britain—Düsseldorf and Cologne, both 200 miles from Dunkirk—and a miscellaneous collection of planes was sent to Antwerp to attack them. Even from Antwerp, the Zeppelin bases were out of range; a forward refuelling base had to be organised east of Antwerp, rather precariously located in no man's land and defended by an armoured car detachment. Following an unsuccessful attempt on 22 September, poor weather prevented a further attempt until 13 October, by which time Antwerp was about to fall. No forward refuelling stop was now possible, so an extra fuel tank was fitted to two Sopwith Tabloids, and on 13 October, these set off with a handful of 20-lb Hale bombs for the Cologne and Düsseldorf Zeppelin sheds. One of the planes found the Düsseldorf shed and dropped its bombs from a height of 500 feet, successfully destroying a brand new Zeppelin Z9. In a dramatic vindication of his offensive policy, Churchill had got his Zeppelin.[11]

This success encouraged the Admiralty to plan more long-range raids. With the fall of Antwerp, all RNAS planes were forced to pull back to Dunkirk, putting targets in Germany out of range. Instead, the force focused its efforts on Belgian ports U-boats might be using. The Admiralty saw no reason why the naval bombers should be restricted to operations from coastal bases. On

21 November, three naval Avro 504s, under the command of Flight Lieutenant Pemberton-Billing, were transported to Belfort in eastern France from where they bombed the Zeppelin factory at Friedrichshafen on the Swiss border. The raid represented a significant widening of the RNAS role. This was not an attack on a purely tactical target like a Zeppelin at its operational base, it was an attempt to cut off the supply of Zeppelins at source. It therefore constituted the first British attempt at strategic bombing. According to the official history, the raid 'wrought havoc on the Zeppelin works destroying the gas works, which exploded, and sent up gigantic sheets of flames'.[12] Other accounts suggested that only a few windows were blown in.[13] The raid made a bigger impression on those taking part than their intended target. The reports of the returning pilots certainly impressed Pemberton-Billing, encouraging his belief that future wars would be decided by air forces operating independently of armies and navies.[14]

But there was little sign of this in 1914. The year came to an end and still no Zeppelin had attempted to drop any bombs on Britain. Nevertheless, the Zeppelin threat had by no means been a figment of the British imagination. There was no shortage of enthusiasts among German naval, diplomatic and industrial circles for a Zeppelin campaign against Britain.

It was on 21 December 1914, nearly five months after the outbreak of war, that the first attack was made on the British Isles, and this by a seaplane that harmlessly dropped a couple of small bombs close to Dover pier.[15] However, the British people would not have long to wait before the Zeppelins started dropping far more deadly loads.

Meanwhile, it was the land battle in Belgium and northern France that had become the focal point of the conflict. Apart from the single flight of No. 4 Squadron retained at Dover, all available RFC operational squadrons moved to France with the BEF. On departure, the four squadrons possessed thirty-seven Bleriot Experimentals, three Avro 504 reconnaissance planes, twelve Farman pushers, seven Bleriots, and four Sopwith Tabloids. Some flew direct to France, while others were shipped. By 15 August, forty-four planes of Nos 2, 3, 4, and 5 Squadrons had gathered at Amiens. It was a force instilled with aggressive intent. The bombs were often just grenades, and rifles were often the best air-to-air weapon, but the intention and expectation was clear. Pilots were to attack the enemy at every opportunity, in the air and on the ground, whatever their mission. It was an aggressive mind-set that British aircrews would maintain throughout the war.

The BEF was assigned the secondary role of helping to cover the left flank of the main French offensive across her eastern frontier. This soon collapsed and the British forces found themselves in the path of the main German drive, which was supposed to swing round to the east and west of Paris, encircling and destroying the French armies south-east of the French capital. The British Army was instructed to advance into Belgium through Mons to Soignies on the left flank of the French 5th Army.

On 16 August, even before it had flown its first operational sortie, the RFC suffered its first fatal casualty when a B.E.8 stalled on take-off.[16] It was the first of the many accidents that were responsible for a large proportion of RFC casualties throughout the war. On 19 August, the RFC flew its first operational sorties. Two planes were sent off, without observers, to determine the extent of the German advance, but operating in an alien environment proved too much for the lone pilots; both got lost and had to land to ask the way.[17] It was not the best of starts, but lessons had been learnt. Future missions would be flown with observers, and planes stopped getting lost and started providing Army commanders with useful information, not just on German movements, but equally importantly, on the movements of their French allies on their right flank. During the Battle of Mons, RFC planes kept Field Marshal French and his commanders informed of German units advancing towards the town, the retreat of the French 5th Army on his right, and German columns advancing in the direction of his exposed left flank. The British Army fended off German attacks on 23 August and then pulled back in a retreat that was to end behind the River Marne early in September. The squadrons were constantly moving to new bases as the Army retreated, but continued flying over the front. For such an inexperienced force, it was a brilliant display of mobility and improvisation in extremely difficult circumstances. The RFC had come a long way since the autumn 1911 Army manoeuvres when it lost two-thirds of its planes trying to fly to Cambridge. The information RFC planes provided on German movements was at the very least useful and helped ensure the BEF survived as a coherent fighting force.[18]

The scene was set for the 'Miracle on the Marne'. In the first days of September, British and French reconnaissance planes reported a significant change in the direction of the northernmost German advance, with enemy forces swinging round to the south and heading towards the River Marne. Feeling victory was close, the commander of the German Army, Von Moltke, had decided to abandon the sweep to the west of Paris and roll up the left flank of the Allied armies east of the capital. This decision exposed the right flank of the German Army to the reserve French 6th Army gathering east of Paris; on 6 September, the French counterattacked. Air reconnaissance followed the German efforts to counter this threat and spotted the gaps opening up in front of British forces. The BEF and the French 5th Army advanced and the German Army was soon in general retreat. The counterattack on the Marne ended the German chance of a quick victory in the west and brought to an end what had been a spectacularly successful three weeks of operations. Information on the German change of plan was a crucial factor in the Allied victory. Aerial reconnaissance was by no means the sole source of intelligence, but Allied planes had spotted the change, and it was a clear and dramatic example of the value of aerial reconnaissance.

As far as the Army was concerned, the first month of the war had entirely vindicated their decision to deploy all available air resources tactically. The predicted aerial assault on the British Isles had not materialised and attacks on civilian targets in Belgium had not had any significant effect on the course of the fighting. Meanwhile, a critical campaign had been fought on the battlefields of France and aerial reconnaissance had played its part in denying victory to the German Army by a narrow margin. The RFC had done its best to attack ground targets and had even attempted to engage enemy aircraft, but these activities paled into insignificance when compared to what aerial reconnaissance had achieved. It was the priceless information gathered that justified the RFC's existence.

Initially, the highly fluid situation made information on German strategic intentions the top priority, and RFC squadrons were attached to the BEF headquarters rather than individual Army units. There was a shift in priorities during the Battle of the Marne when a squadron was placed at the disposal of each of the two advancing British corps for tactical reconnaissance. As the British Army expanded, it became standard practice for each corps to be given its own short-range tactical reconnaissance/artillery observation squadron.[19]

The war would not be over by Christmas and Kitchener set about creating a massive volunteer Army to match the conscript armies of France and Germany. Once Britain and France was fully mobilised, their combined might would overwhelm a German Army that had to divide its efforts between a Western and an Eastern Front. The concurrent expansion of the RFC created the need for more air commanders and gave a frustrated Trenchard the opportunity to test his leadership skills at the front. As was often to be the case with appointments involving Trenchard, this would not pass off without an element of controversy.

In November, the BEF was divided into two armies, each supported by its own RFC wing. Henderson offered Trenchard command of the First Wing, supporting Haig's 1st Army. Trenchard accepted, but while he was en route to France, Henderson accepted an offer to take command of an infantry division. His sudden departure from the RFC left Trenchard's arch-enemy, Sykes, as Henderson's natural successor. When Trenchard discovered Sykes was to be his commander, he claimed it would be quite impossible to serve under him, and asked to leave the RFC and be transferred back to his regiment.[20] Whether this played any part in Kitchener's subsequent decision to order Henderson back to the RFC is debatable, but it says much about Trenchard that he should unashamedly rejoice in being responsible for such an extraordinarily ill-disciplined outburst. When he finally made it to Haig's headquarters, Trenchard described how he was delighted to find the Army commander so attentive to his ideas on how air support could be developed. However, the grilling received by Trenchard was perhaps more a case of Haig wanting to make sure he was up to the task of providing the air support he already knew he required.[21]

Henderson's return meant demotion for Sykes, leaving both extremely disgruntled. Sykes was determined to regain the prize that he now believed had been plucked from his grasp twice by airing the view that Henderson could not possibly command the RFC and carry out his functions as Director of Military Aeronautics.[22] It was not an unreasonable view, but it was hardly likely to endear Sykes to his commanding officer. Relations between Sykes and Henderson, never good, were soon in terminal decline.[23] When, in May 1915, the Admiralty approached the War Office about the possibility of having Sykes advise on RNAS operations in support of the Dardanelles landings, Henderson jumped at the opportunity to be rid of his ambitious chief of staff. For Sykes, it was not a good career move. The Dardanelles campaign would prove to be a disaster and following it, Sykes' career seemed to be in limbo. Henderson refused to have him back in the air service in any capacity. Trenchard, by this time occupying the top post Sykes had wanted, rather condescendingly and no doubt with some relish, agreed to have him back as a wing commander, provided he did exactly as he was told—scarcely a palatable prospect for Trenchard's former superior. For the time being, Sykes would pursue his career outside the air service, although he would eventually return and outrank both Trenchard and Henderson.

Meanwhile, back in early 1915, the Western Front had descended into stalemate. Following their retreat from the Marne, the Germans had focused their efforts on securing the Channel ports; when the fighting died down, both sides found themselves facing powerful defences that stretched from the Channel coast to Switzerland. With no flanks to turn, the only option was for the artillery to blast a hole through the defences of barbed wire and machine gun emplacements. Naturally, the best way of stopping the enemy from doing this was to eliminate his artillery. The war was becoming a duel between the opposing artillery arms; to succeed, the guns needed to know where the enemy trench systems and gun positions were. Tactical reconnaissance became the key to success. Aerial photographic reconnaissance was essential to locate the targets, and only aerial observation could ensure the accuracy of the guns.

Techniques for correcting artillery fire evolved rapidly. Clock coordinates were introduced so that the fall of a shell relative to the target could be described more neatly and precisely in terms of distance and angle. Wireless sets were in use for directing artillery fire as early as September 1914, although for some time into 1915, a shortage of sets meant some aircrews were relying on visual signalling. Artillery observation was initially always pre-planned with close co-ordination between airmen and artillery officers before each mission. However, standard grids of the immediate battle area were created, which enabled aircrews to pass information on the precise location of new targets spotted during the course of a sortie to artillery batteries.[24] The ability to hit fleeting targets of opportunity would, after much trial and error, become a standard capability for specific batteries on permanent standby.[25]

Bombing operations were slower to develop. From the very beginning, reconnaissance crews took a supply of small bombs or grenades on reconnaissance missions to attack targets of opportunity.[26] There were plenty of potential targets in and around the battlefield, especially during the opening stages of the war when there was more movement and anti-aircraft defences were less well developed. Some, like Lieutenant-Colonel Strange, who was soon devising his own petrol bombs to supplement official ordnance, needed little encouragement. To Strange, the potential was clear and he was surprised attacks on enemy troops were not organised on a grander scale as they were the 'only way of helping the hard-pressed soldiers'.[27] The time for such support would come, but these early exploratory efforts achieved little. On occasion, German units caught in the open were taken by surprise, but the impact on the course of the fighting was negligible and the attacks became even less effective once both sides were well ensconced in their trench fortifications. Some argued reconnaissance and artillery observation were too important to allow scarce planes and aircrews to be risked on low-level attacks of dubious value, but most commanders continued to encourage reconnaissance crews to carry bombs, more for morale than any military advantage. It was all part of the aggressive ethos commanders were seeking to nurture within the RFC. Bomb loads were soon moving from hand grenades to simple 20/25-lb bombs and eventually to 100/112-lb bombs. The B.E.2 could struggle into the air with a couple of these, provided the plane was flown as a single-seater. One flight in every squadron was supposed to specialise in bombing operations, but squadrons had to decide for themselves on the best bombing technique. With no bombsights, the only advice squadrons got was that they might have to fly very low to achieve any useful results.

Despite the many problems that had to be overcome, the early months of the war were a time of enormous optimism about the future of military aviation. In November 1914, Field Marshal French described this sense of optimism:

...almost every day new methods for employing them [aeroplanes], both strategically and tactically, are discovered. The development of their use and employment has indeed been quite extraordinary, and I feel no effort should be spared to increase their numbers and perfect their equipment and efficiency.[28]

Pre-war plans had called for the creation of eight squadrons to support an Army of six divisions. Kitchener had ambitious plans for a BEF with no less than six armies, each with three corps with three divisions each. Working on a basis of one squadron for every corps, one for each Army headquarters, and six squadrons at GHQ, Brancker arrived at a required front line strength of thirty squadrons. Kitchener dismissed this as timid and, rather arbitrarily, told Brancker to double it,[29] but a tenfold increase in front line strength was entirely beyond the means of the underdeveloped British aircraft industry. The home command had difficulty maintaining the existing RFC squadrons at full strength, even though the only significant losses in these early months were the result of accidents.

Industry was slow to adapt to the new circumstances. Initially, firms like Rolls-Royce assumed peace and their lucrative luxury car market would soon return. Only when it became clear the war would not be over by Christmas did companies begin to realise war contracts were the only way of surviving. After initially refusing to get involved, Rolls-Royce agreed to build air-cooled Renault engines under licence. They were also asked to develop an air-cooled engine of their own design, but as the company only had experience of water-cooled engines, they decided to develop one of these instead. The result would be the Eagle and a scaled-down version, the Falcon, two of the best engines developed in the First World War.[30]

In the last four months of 1914, the entire British aircraft industry only built ninety-nine engines. A total of 144 aircraft were delivered to the RFC in France in this period. It was the spring of 1915, eight months after the outbreak of war, before the eighth of the pre-war planned squadrons began to form, and rather than the eighteen aircraft per squadron planned before the war, the establishment of each squadron had to be limited to twelve. In the spring of 1915, front line strength stood at just eighty-five planes.[31]

The Neuve Chapelle offensive was the first major British effort of 1915. It was a small-scale tactical operation with the limited aim of eliminating a potentially dangerous German salient. If the first stage proceeded satisfactorily, an effort might be made to gain the slightly higher ground around Aubers, which in turn would merely be a preparatory step for a possible major assault on Lille. In the build up to the offensive, lavish use was made of aerial photography. The front under attack was photographed to a depth of between 700 and 1,500 yards, providing commanders with detailed maps of the defences that faced them.[32]

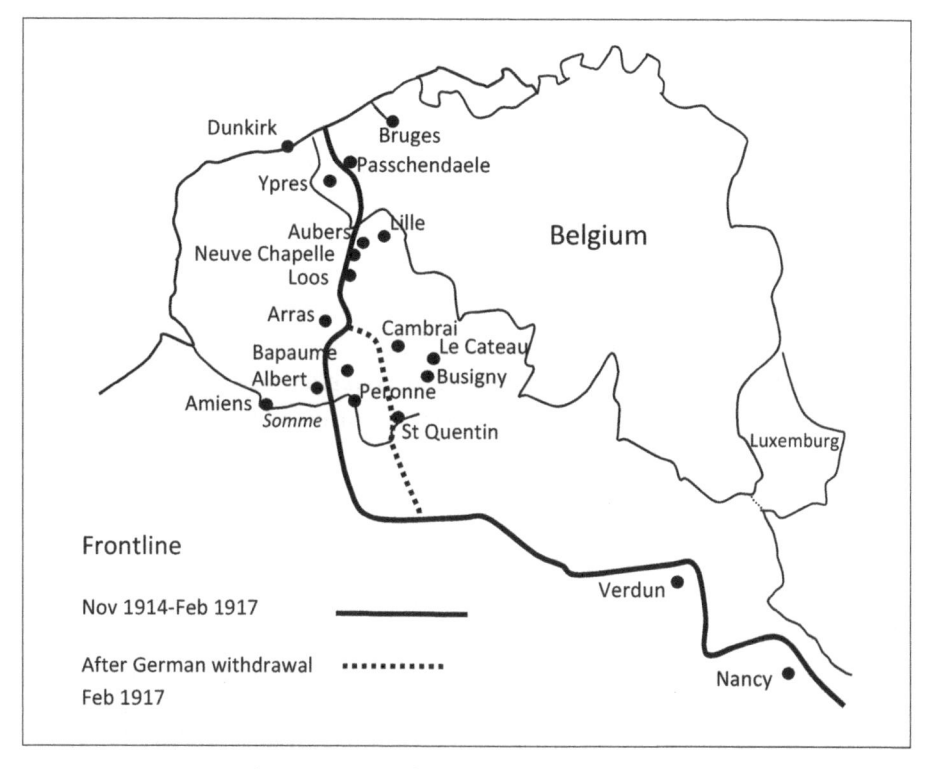

Western Front: November 1915–March 1918.

It was anticipated that as soon as the attack was launched, the Germans would switch reserves from quieter sectors of the front; to prevent this, planes would be used to seal off the battle zone. This was the first time RFC bombers would be involved in a pre-planned and co-ordinated bombing operation. From the afternoon of the first day of the offensive, air units from the 2nd and 3rd Wings attached to neighbouring armies not directly involved in the operation would bomb railway lines and stations behind the German front. The initial assault on 10 March was preceded by a short thirty-five-minute artillery barrage provided by nearly 350 guns. The bombardment proved effective and the village of Neuve Chapelle was quickly captured. In the afternoon, the RFC implemented its plans to attack railway stations, but this only involved single aircraft bombing five railway stations and junctions with 25-lb and 100-lb bombs. In at least two of these attacks, spectacular results were apparently achieved. Even a lone aircraft dropping its bombs from a couple of hundred feet would inevitably cause temporary mayhem. Agents enthusiastically reported delays of up to three days,[33] but the bombers did not prevent or even delay the movement of German reserves. It would not be the last time that far too much was expected of far too few planes. Later and far more substantial efforts at battlefield interdiction in this and future conflicts would prove to be equally unrewarding.

Attempts to renew the advance on 10 March proved a costly failure, partly because of a shortage of artillery ammunition. Poor weather also robbed the reconnaissance squadrons of the opportunity to direct artillery, and communications between the front and command centres deteriorated rapidly with the destruction of telephone lines by enemy fire. Knowing exactly how far friendly forces had advanced and therefore where to place supporting artillery fire was becoming a major problem. Wireless equipment was still far too bulky for advancing infantry to carry into battle, but planes could carry it. Therefore, for the follow-up attack on Aubers Ridge in May 1915, wireless-equipped Maurice Farmans patrolled above the advancing infantry to report their position, marking the debut of the so called 'contact patrols'. The attack towards Aubers Ridge was due to be launched on 7 May, but when misty weather, which would rule out effective air observation, was forecast, it was postponed until 9 May. It was a measure of how important aerial reconnaissance had become that poor weather was enough to call off an operation. This time, the short pre-assault barrage did not have the desired result, and the attack was repulsed with heavy losses. The Farman 'contact patrols' were a failure. The infantry did not reach the points where it had been decided they would lay out the identifying white strips, and the Farmans were not flying low enough to identify where the infantry were. Further to the rear, bombers made another effort to interdict the battle zone, but it was a total failure with no aircraft even claiming success. Artillery direction was more successful with aircraft mostly being used to direct fire towards known German batteries in pre-arranged shoots, but troop concentrations spotted during the course of missions were also shelled.[34]

The failure of this attack led to calls for more substantial artillery support. The attempt to capture the village of Festubert on 15 May was preceded by four days of shelling. The infantry attacked under the cover of darkness, some progress was made and a number of enemy trenches were captured; however, some of the advancing infantry were hit by friendly artillery fire, which would discourage using darkness for cover in future attacks. Aircraft could only observe in daylight, so the infantry had to attack in daylight. Each new engagement reinforced the importance of aerial artillery observation to the point where the weather, and the ability of aircraft to fly, became the determining factors in whether an offensive should go ahead or not. During the initial stages of a local counter-attack at Hooge in August 1915, air observations enabled friendly artillery to suppress enemy fire, but when the weather suddenly deteriorated and the aircraft were grounded, the scale of enemy artillery increased noticeably.[35] The persistent shortage of shells was another reason why aircraft-directed fire was preferred to indiscriminate blanket barrages; efficiency had become a critical aspect. British Army commanders began designing their tactics around the need for aerial observation.

The Neuve Chapelle and Aubers Ridge offensives had sent mixed signals about the value of short, sharp artillery barrages. Rather prematurely, the advantages of surprise would be forsaken for the apparent certainty that given sufficient time, artillery would destroy all the defences that lay in the path of the infantry. Lengthy pre-offensive artillery barrages became the norm, even though they inevitably gave the enemy all the warning they needed about where the attack was coming, and plenty of time to organise reserves.

While aircraft were demonstrating their ability to direct artillery, the bombing of communication targets in the rear was not producing such noteworthy results. A report on RFC bombing operations between 1 March and 20 June 1915 concluded that the results were 'in no way commensurate with the efforts made' and 'it may well be as well to eliminate bomb dropping altogether from their role, and to confine them to reconnaissance, observation and fighting in the air, in which they have proved their value and for which the Allies cannot have too many aeroplanes'. The report claimed that of 141 attacks on railway stations, only three had been successful. It was particularly scathing of attacks on 'enemy billets', which usually meant the random bombing of French and Belgian villages and towns in which, inevitably, 'the wrong people get killed'.[36] The report went on to suggest that better results might be achieved if bombing was carried out by specialist bomber squadrons and disorganised individual attacks were replaced by operations in which aircraft bombed simultaneously and in strength. Most crucially, it emphasised that if the tactical bombing of targets in the rear was to have any effect, it had to be very closely related to ongoing operations at the front, simply because any disruption caused was likely to be very short lived. A small delay during a crucial phase of a battle might be important, while a small delay when there were no ongoing operations served no purpose. The report stated that following these principles ought to result in tactical bombing making a more useful contribution, but it warned it would be unrealistic to ever expect decisive results. It was a report that could have been describing any number of future air interdiction programmes in the First World War and many subsequent conflicts. The report on bombing also referred to the importance of 'fighting in the air', an aspect of air warfare that it rated just as important as observation and reconnaissance. In the early stages of the war, there had been relatively little air combat. As the report suggested, in 1915, this was beginning to change.

Developing an efficient fighting plane had been one of the RFC's top pre-war priorities and the failure to do so was its biggest disappointment. The only consolation was that no other nation had been any more successful. But the lack of suitable equipment was not going to stop RFC pilots from trying. Just days after the RFC arrived in France, a couple of B.E.2s armed with handguns and a Henri Farman, piloted by Flight Lieutenant Strange, with a gunner armed with one of few available Lewis machine guns, attempted to take-off and intercept an aircraft approaching their airfield. From a standing start, it proved quite impossible to get anywhere near the intruder.[37] The handicap of the relatively light Lewis gun was so great that Farman crews preferred to make do with a rifle, which at least made it more likely they would get within range of the opponent. The first victory was gained on 25 August when three B.E.2s assailed a German Taube with pistols, startling the German pilot to such a degree that he put his plane down in the nearest field.[38] A couple of days later, an unarmed Sopwith Tabloid achieved the same result by aggressive feint attacks.[39] It was hardly a method that could be relied on.

A few days later, Henderson was signalling home: 'There are no aeroplanes with the Royal Flying Corps that are really suitable for carrying machine guns … Request you endeavour to supply efficient fighting machines as soon as possible.'[40] It would prove to be a long and tortuous path before these 'efficient fighting machines' emerged, and it would take even longer before the correct tactics for their employment were developed. Initially, so serious were the problems both sides were having in engaging enemy planes that aircrews stopped bothering to carry defensive armament. Even unarmed, the early RFC reconnaissance planes sometimes struggled to make their way back to their bases against the prevailing westerly winds. Any unnecessary weight could reduce their progress to a crawl, increasing the time they were exposed to pot shots from troops below. Well into 1915, most RFC reconnaissance planes were still flying unarmed. It was hardly surprising crews took to waving at their enemy rather than firing at them whenever their paths crossed.[41]

Specialist fighters were being developed. Vickers and the Factory were working on their two-seater pushers. Delays were put down to technical problems with the engines, but the real issue was that tried and trusted engines were not powerful enough to push the un-aerodynamic pusher and its crew of two fast enough. Turning to more powerful but less well-developed and reliable engines inevitably led to problems. The Vickers Gunbus eventually managed just 70 mph, which was enough to intercept a Zeppelin, but was far too slow to catch an aeroplane.[42] Nevertheless, deliveries to the Western Front began in February 1915. The plane created a place for itself in aviation history by equipping the first specialist fighter squadron, No. 11 Squadron, which arrived in France in July 1915 equipped entirely with the Gunbus, although in practice it was used as a multi-purpose squadron like any other.[43] The appearance of the plane did not go unnoticed by German pilots, and all future RFC pushers would be known to the enemy as 'Vickers'. Quite sensibly, German pilots tended to give the armed but lumbering pusher a wide berth. It was a source of frustration to RFC aircrews that German pilots would not stand their ground and fight, and this certainly gave the RFC an illusion of superiority, but it was more a psychological than a meaningful superiority. Since the Gunbus lacked the speed to give chase, it posed very little real danger to German pilots.[44]

The F.E.2 had the same problem. The outbreak of war induced the Directorate to order a batch of twelve of the latest version, the F.E.2a, with a 100-hp Green engine, even though the prototype had yet to fly. When it did get into the air in January 1915, it struggled to reach 6,000 feet and managed just 75 mph. A few were sent to the front, but further deliveries were held back until a more powerful 120-hp Beardmore engine was available. Even with this engine, it barely managed 80 mph—an improvement on the Gunbus, but still considered far too slow by the pilots who flew them.[45] Despite this, large numbers were ordered. The production version, the F.E.2b, had a simplified structure to make it easier for companies with no previous experience of building aircraft to be brought into the production programme, but redesigning the plane and setting up production lines took time, and the first F.E.2b did not arrive in France until early 1916.

While the designers back home worked on their two-seater pushers, the pilots at the front were coming to the conclusion it was pointless persevering with the pusher or two-seater as a fighter if the extra aerodynamic drag and weight meant the plane could never be fast enough to catch up with the planes it was supposed to shoot down. The fastest planes available to the RFC were the high-speed, single-seater reconnaissance scouts. There were only a handful—a few Tabloids and Martinsyde S1s, a couple of requisitioned Bristol Scouts, and the S.E.2 prototype. Both the Martinsyde and Bristol scouts were in production, but there was little demand for them in France as reconnaissance planes. In the static siege warfare on the Western Front, there was not much need for long-range strategic reconnaissance, and two-seaters were better for tactical reconnaissance. The single-seater scouts were a handful to fly and those in France tended not to be used much.

The one quality they did have was speed, and pilots interested in taking on the enemy were soon eying them up as an alternative to the two-seater pushers. Using the scout for air combat solved the speed problem, but it meant the gun had to be mounted so the pilot could fly with one hand and aim and fire with the other. Flying and aiming a gun at the same time was not easy, and several pilots saw the advantage of fixing the gun and manoeuvring the plane to aim. Initially, guns were fixed to the side of the fuselage and angled to miss the propeller, but it was not easy to aim in one direction and fly in another. Nor were there enough machine guns, and rifles were often used instead.[46] It was hardly surprising there were few successes, but pilots believed that a single-seater with just a rifle fixed at an angle was better than struggling into the air with a specialist gunner.

Naval pilots were coming to the same conclusions. Some had gone one step further and fixed a machine gun to fire through the propeller arc with tape on the propeller to provide extra protection. The advantages of firing straight ahead were so great that pilots were willing to risk shooting off their own propeller. However, neither naval nor military commanders seemed impressed by fixed-gun single-seaters. Longmore, commanding RNAS squadrons at Dunkirk, told his RFC colleagues that there was a debate among his pilots about the relative advantage of 'fast handy' single-seaters and planes 'with one or more gunners'. However, Longmore emphasised the difficulty lone pilots had aiming their weapons and how he had been impressed by the German 'double fuselage tractors that can fire in all directions' which his pilots were encountering in combat. He felt this was the sort of plane more likely to bring success.[47] RFC commanders tended to agree. When Strange was passing through RFC HQ in St Omer and was asked which planes he considered best for the fighting role, he had no hesitation in choosing the single-seater Bristol Scout. His response, however, did not impress his inquisitors and he was asked to choose between the Vickers Gunbus and the F.E.2.[48]

The pilots who had to do the fighting might be convinced the single-seater was the way forward, but there were only a few suitable planes to experiment with and few opportunities to prove the point. Nor had the enthusiasm of the pilots been rewarded with any significant success. There was no evidence the single-seater tractor was better than the two-seater pusher.

In the absence of any substantial numbers of single-seater tractor scouts or two-seater pushers, any plane capable of carrying a gun continued to be used for air combat, but at least the arrival of more powerful two-seaters like the B.E.2c and French Morane-Saulnier Parasol meant carrying a machine gun was less of a handicap. An assault on Hill 60 in the Ypres salient in April 1915 saw the first British systematic deployment of fighters and the first organised attempt to establish air superiority in a defined space. No. 1 Squadron's mixed bag of Parasols, B.E.8s and Avro two-seaters were given the task of denying German reconnaissance planes access to that sector of the front by flying continuous patrols along and beyond the front line.[49] Air fighting was becoming a regular element of operations and the development of an efficient fighting plane more urgent.

In Britain, designers continued to work on ever larger two and multi-seater designs. The Factory's ingenious single-engine two-seater F.E.6 proved impractical and had to be abandoned, but there was confidence the extra power of twin or multi-engine designs ought to provide the necessary speed. The Factory was working on their F.E.4, F.E.5 and F.E.7, and Vickers had responded to the 1914 cannon-fighter requirement with their twin-engine E.F.B.7 (Experimental Fighting Biplane 7).[50]

Meanwhile, a Frenchman, Roland Garros, had solved the aiming problem by fixing his machine gun to fire directly ahead through the propeller arc with metal deflectors on the propeller blades to prevent damage. The system was used operationally for the first time in April 1915, and in the first eighteen days of April, Garros, flying alone in a two-seater Morane-Saulnier Parasol, claimed no less than three enemy aircraft destroyed. The French adopted the system as standard armament on the monoplane Morane-Saulnier N single-seater fighter and the RFC in France were sufficiently impressed to order three Morane-Saulnier Ns for trials.

Word of the success of the Morane deflector had also reached the War Office, and on 27 June, RFC HQ in France was asked to arrange for an example to be sent to Britain for testing. Henderson also seemed anxious to get trials going, asking the War Office to use the 'S.E.4 or some other scout' to measure the loss in performance the deflectors on the propeller caused.[51] The S.E.4 had crashed in August 1914, but its successor, the entirely new S.E.4a, was an equally suitable candidate for the deflector system, but the trials never took place. Mysteriously, three different sets of the French deflectors all managed to go missing crossing the Channel,[52] and no attempt was made to reproduce what was fundamentally a very simple idea. A moveable gun was still thought to be the better approach.

The Germans were showing far more interest in the French idea. On 18 April, Garros had been shot down in his specially modified Parasol and the deflector system fell into German hands. It was not so much the deflector that interested his captors—it was the fixed gun firing directly ahead that was the crucial revelation. German engineers were working on a synchronised gun that did not need deflectors, but without much urgency as there were doubts it would be possible to aim a fixed weapon. The French had now proven it was possible and development of the synchronisation system was given maximum priority. In July, a synchronised gun fitted to a Fokker E1 monoplane shot down its first victim, ironically a French two-seater Morane-Saulnier Parasol. The Germans had gone from no fixed guns to a fixed forward-firing synchronised gun in one step. Even so, the scale of the breakthrough was still not appreciated. The German air force still saw their new armed C-class two-seater reconnaissance planes as their main fighter.

On the British side there were glimpses of what single-seaters might achieve. In June 1915, Lanoe George Hawker was assigned one of the few available Bristol

Scouts and fitted it with a Lewis machine gun to fire at an angle outwards past the propeller. Hawker was, by all accounts, a brilliant marksman, and he needed to be to hit anything with the arrangement. He managed to claim a victory on 20 June, and on 25 July, he was involved in three separate combats in a single sortie, claiming three victories and earning the Victoria Cross.

Meanwhile, even before the Fokker arrived, the latest German planes, particularly the Aviatik C-Class two-seaters, were causing enough problems for RFC pilots. German planes seemed capable of flying faster and higher than anything the RFC had, and German pilots were becoming noticeably more confident and aggressive. Twenty-six encounters with enemy planes in May became thirty-two in June and forty-seven in July. In the future, information would have to be fought for. The 'real struggle for air supremacy' was finally beginning, warned Brooke-Popham, Sykes' successor at RFC HQ, and losing it might have serious consequences.[53] The RFC needed an air superiority fighter.

The solution the Directorate came up did not involve a tractor scout like the S.E.4a or the French deflector system. It was not even originally intended primarily as a fighting plane. It was the brainchild of de Havilland, who had left the Factory and become chief designer at Airco, the 'Aircraft (Manufacturing) Company'. His first design was the two-seater D.H.1 pusher, which was essentially a smaller and lighter version of his F.E.2. This was followed by an even smaller single-seater version, the D.H.2, which flew in July 1915. It was not in response to any direct requirement from the RFC command in France, nor was it an attempt to revolutionise the fighting plane. It was simply intended to fill the high-speed reconnaissance scout role. For the specialist fighting role, de Havilland was working on his twin-engine three-seater D.H.3, which was much more in line with official thinking on what fighting planes should look like, and was indeed effectively no more than a smaller version of the F.E.4. The armament of the single-seater D.H.2 was very much an afterthought. The prototype had a machine gun mounted on the side of the cockpit, which the pilot could aim sideways as he was flying. There was no intention at this stage of having a fixed forward-firing gun. Although handicapped by its pusher configuration, thanks to its 100-hp engine, it was as fast as the Bristol Scout.

The prototype was sent to France in July 1915 for operational trials. The 2nd Wing had been encountering a high number of enemy aircraft, so it was decided that Captain Maxwell Pike of No. 5 Squadron should try out the 'armed scout'. Pike was very impressed. No German plane could equal the de Havilland design for speed and climbing power he proclaimed, and the view from the cockpit was better than any plane he had previously flown. De Havilland was to fly out personally to France to discuss with Pike any improvements that might be required,[54] but their meeting never happened. On 9 August, Pike was engaging a German reconnaissance plane near Ypres when he was hit in the head by defensive fire. He managed to land, but died soon after. The Germans had captured an intact example of the RFC's latest combat plane before it had even gone into production. Significantly, the

Germans did not rush to copy the single-seater pusher format. Garros' Morane-Saulnier Parasol had been a much more interesting find. De Havilland may never have got to hear Pike's suggested improvements, but the prototype had done enough to prove its worth and the 'armed scout' was ordered into production, more now for its air combat qualities than scouting capabilities. On the production version, the gun was mounted centrally in the nose, but it was still moveable. Following the same formula, the Royal Aircraft Factory began work on the F.E.8 pusher, their first 'Fighting Experimental' single-seater, also with a moveable gun.

Meanwhile, Henderson and his wing commanders were meeting to discuss the future types they wanted developed for their squadrons. Although the Fokker had not yet appeared on the British front, RFC commanders were well aware of the success the single-seater tractor was having further south against the French, but this did not seem to influence their thinking. The French deflector system was discussed and rejected partly because of the reported 10 mph speed handicap it imposed, although this was no more than the handicap imposed by the pusher layout. Moveable guns were preferred to fixed guns, either forward firing with a pusher or backwards with a tractor.[55] Only Burke, commander of the 2nd Wing where the D.H.2 had been tested, was in favour of a single-seater, but it had to be a pusher—no single-seater tractors were required. Unhampered field of fire, stability and endurance were the most sought after qualities. The two-seater fighters were expected to have an endurance of four hours and the single-seater six hours.[56] The endurance requirements were daunting. The D.H.2 could not even manage three hours and Brancker feared the requirements could only be met by large twin-engine planes.[57] Everything was pointing to the need for larger combat planes. The RFC requirements justified the work the Factory and companies like Vickers and Airco were doing on twin-engine fighting planes. The Vickers E.F.B.7 had just flown and a dozen were ordered, while work also began on the smaller and lighter twin-engine E.F.B.8 armed with a machine gun instead of a cannon.[58]

The Bristol team under Frank Barnwell, responsible for the single-seater Bristol Scout, was also set to work on a twin-engine fighter. Barnwell had enlisted in the RFC at the outbreak of war and was about to depart for France with No. 12 Squadron when he was ordered back to Bristol to help develop the planes Henderson and his commanders wanted. The design he came up with, the Bristol Twin Tractor A (TTA), was a twin-engine fighting machine with a gunner in the nose armed with two machine guns and the pilot behind expected to operate a rearward-firing gun.[59] Ironically, design of this plane went ahead while unarmed Bristol Scouts were rolling off the adjacent production lines.

Three days before RFC commanders decided no single-seater tractors were required, a B.E.2c of No. 2 Squadron reported an inconclusive combat with a German single-seater tractor monoplane. The Fokker E1 had arrived on the British front. The Germans, however, had still not realised the significance of their breakthrough and like the British, they still believed the two-seater was the more effective combat plane.

The Fokkers were spread around the German reconnaissance squadrons for escort duties. On the British side, the significance of the Fokker E series was initially lost in the generally more aggressive approach all German aircraft were displaying. Losses in air combat were scarcely frequent occurrences—just six planes were lost in July and this dropped to only three in August. Despite these relatively light casualties, the RFC felt it was on the defensive.[60]

The threat was considered sufficient for escorts to be organised for reconnaissance planes. These would be any plane capable of carrying a gun that was available, often another two-seater reconnaissance plane. However, the high speeds of the tractor scouts made them particularly attractive escorts, despite the problems arming them. Their extra speed allowed them to manoeuvre around the plane they were escorting, chasing off aggressors if required without necessarily falling hopelessly behind. It became standard to attach one or two scouts to each squadron specifically for escort duties just as the German air force was doing with its Fokkers. It provided a useful role for the handful of Bristol Scouts that were trickling across the Channel. They were still arriving unarmed and all modifications necessary to enable them to carry a weapon had to be made by the squadrons in the field.

To add to the RFC's problems, as well as being technically outclassed by its opponents, it was also finding itself seriously under strength for the wide variety of tasks it was now expected to perform. When the war broke out, there had been four squadrons out of a planned eight to support the four divisions sent to France, and they had been used primarily for reconnaissance. The air force was now expected to co-operate with artillery, monitor the progress of advancing friendly forces, photograph enemy lines, bomb and increasingly engage in air combat, and the recent need for escorts was a further strain on resources. Yet in the summer of 1915, while the Army had expanded to thirty divisions, there were still only eleven RFC squadrons available.[61]

Expanding Britain's small pre-war aircraft industry inevitably took time. The training programme also needed time to adjust. Initially, many of the pilots the schools were turning out had to be used as instructors to meet the huge numbers of pilots the future air force would require. Even though personnel and material losses were still relatively light after a year of war, little progress had been made in increasing front line strength. As Sykes had pointed out, it did not help that Henderson, the Director of Military Aeronautics, was in France commanding the RFC instead of organising expansion in London. His junior second-in-command, Brancker, complained he was at a severe disadvantage when it came to competing for the available resources with other departments, both inside and outside the War Office. If Henderson wanted a more rapid expansion of the RFC, he had to return to London and take up his director's post full-time. Henderson was forced to bow to the logic of Brancker's arguments. In August 1915, Henderson surrendered command of the RFC and returned to London. There was never any doubt who would replace Henderson at St Omer. Hugh Montague Trenchard was waiting to fulfil his destiny.

CHAPTER 4

Fading Promise and Fokkers

The blunt and uncompromising Trenchard had established his credentials for the top job while commanding the First Wing attached to Haig's 1st Army. He was a man of strong, if not always entirely consistent views, who throughout his career would need an 'English merchant', as he called them, to turn his incoherent speech and, some would say, thoughts into well-reasoned and presentable arguments.

Like most officers of his generation, Trenchard believed in the power of the offensive. On the ground after a year of stalemate and costly unsuccessful offensives, there seemed good reason to conclude that attack was not always the best option; however, in the air, there seemed more justification for maintaining the offence. Trench warfare seemed to have no equivalent in the air. Like many, Trenchard saw aerial warfare as analogous to naval warfare, where the seas could not be occupied but had to be dominated by offensive patrolling. He laid great store on superior morale to achieve this domination. By attacking, you maintained the morale of your own forces at a high pitch. Going on the defensive or avoiding the enemy smacked of defeatism and would inevitably lead to lower morale and fighting efficiency. There was nothing revolutionary or unusual about Trenchard's offensive instincts. Sykes and Henderson had similar philosophies and at squadron level, pilots like Hawker and Strange were imbued with the offensive spirit. This attitude was already well established within the RFC Trenchard was taking over. It was, nevertheless, a philosophy that, taken to extremes, would lead to enormous and unnecessary losses.

Trenchard showed no desire to go beyond the requirements laid down by his predecessor Henderson with a squadron for each corps, one for each Army and one for his headquarters, which for three armies each with three corps, amounted to a modest thirteen squadrons. Trenchard suggested as more squadrons became available, each Army should get a second squadron for bombing duties, raising the eventual requirement to just sixteen squadrons. This was less than Brancker's proposal which Kitchener had dismissed as feeble, and a very small proportion of the sixty squadrons Kitchener had suggested as a target overall strength.[1] It was a modest demand, but talk of sixty squadrons was rather meaningless if, after a year of war, only seven new squadrons had arrived.

There were differences of opinion between St Omer and London about how the available resources should be organised and deployed. Trenchard wanted his squadrons to remain multi-purpose. He feared removing bomber and fighting duties from observation/reconnaissance squadrons would result in squadrons losing their offensive spirit. Brancker preferred a more centralised air force with bomber squadrons concentrated at GHQ level and specialist fighter squadrons. The War Office had been setting the pace on the squadron specialisation issue. Brancker had already presented Henderson and his commanders with a fait accompli in July 1915 by sending No. 11 Squadron equipped entirely with the Vickers Gunbus. In August, he was promising the delivery of 'a certain number of squadrons composed of fighting aeroplanes,' equipped with the two-seater F.E.2 and single-seater D.H.2, and in September, Hawker was recalled from France to help form and command the first D.H.2 squadron. Trenchard, however, still insisted air fighting and bombing should be the responsibility of all squadrons and performed by all aircraft types.

These were the principles the RFC continued to apply in Trenchard's first major operation as RFC commander: the September 1915 Loos offensive. Together with a French offensive further south, this was the first serious effort to achieve a decisive breakthrough of strategic proportions. The attack was launched on 25 September by Haig's 1st Army. Air defence was provided by the unemployed squadrons of the neighbouring 2nd Army, mostly B.E.2cs, but also a sprinkling of Vickers Gunbuses, Bristol Scouts, F.E.2bs, Avro 504s, Morane Parasols, R.E.5s and a Caudron. Since all the Fokkers were grounded at the time because of structural problems, and poor weather prevented much flying, scarcely any air combats occurred, so few conclusions could be drawn about the effectiveness of these planes as fighters.

2nd and 3rd Army squadrons were also used for bombing. Communication targets in the rear were attacked whenever weather allowed, and again brought some individually spectacular results which impressed at the time, although post-war German accounts indicate that despite some disruption, no troop reinforcements arrived late as the result of aerial bombing.[2] On the battlefield, artillery was again seen as the key to success. Much smaller and lighter wireless sets were becoming available, which meant planes such as the B.E.2 could carry one as well as an observer, a welcome development given the increased likelihood of encountering armed enemy planes. For photo-reconnaissance, there was still no sign of anything as sophisticated as the totally automatic internally mounted camera the Factory had been working on before the war, but cameras were now rather crudely fixed to the side of the fuselage rather than handheld.[3]

Again, planes pinpointed enemy artillery before and, when weather allowed, during the course of the attack, but low cloud and poor visibility hindered observation and reconnaissance. An attempt was made to report the location of enemy positions holding up the advance to the planes above, so artillery could be called in. Strips displayed on the ground were supposed to indicate the distance and direction of potential targets, but in the heat and stress of battle, troops found little time for such complications. Similarly, signals indicating the position of advancing infantry were rarely used and the contact patrols were not flying low enough to spot those that were.[4] The offensive on the ground was another dismal failure with 60,000 casualties for a gain of just one mile.

The Loos offensive brought an end to the campaigning season for 1915. For the RFC, it was a disappointing end to a year that had started with such high hopes. There were doubts about the effectiveness of bombing behind the front line, contact patrols had proven to be a failure, and while air observation was directing artillery reasonably efficiently, efforts to make it more responsive to the needs of the advancing infantry had failed. Most significantly of all, the efforts of the RFC were not bringing success on the battlefield any closer.

Disillusion with tactical air power was just one element of a more general disillusion with the way the war was being conducted. A second Christmas was approaching with no end to the fighting in sight. A change of personnel was required and French gave way to Haig, bringing Trenchard back into partnership with his former Army commander. Haig had absolute confidence in Trenchard and was quite happy to leave the development of the RFC in his hands. Whenever Trenchard required it, he would get Haig's unquestioning support. The commander had the complete freedom of action his powerful personality required, and his air force would become a little more detached from the rest of the Army.[5]

Haig shared his predecessor's faith in the power of the offence, but was determined not to renew the ground offensive until the supply problems with ammunition were resolved and sufficient infantry was in place to make victory certain. This, he estimated, would not be until the summer of 1916, which gave Trenchard time to build up the strength of his air units. Brancker had reworked and expanded Trenchard's modest request for reinforcements into a twenty-seven squadron scheme to provide air support for three armies. Each Army would now have a corps wing with the short-range reconnaissance squadrons assigned to each corps and an Army wing with three squadrons equipped with longer-range reconnaissance, bomber and fighter planes. Another wing with six squadrons would be attached to GHQ. This comfortably exceeded Trenchard's requirements.

With Henderson in London, the Directorate was in a better position to ensure the resources were made available to create these squadrons. Freed from the day-to-day command at the front, Henderson also had more time to consider a much broader and ambitious role for the air force, one that went beyond the Army's immediate tactical needs. While in France, he had encouraged the development of tactical bombing, and in his summer 1915 list of requirements, had included a specialist bomber with a range of 500 miles. It was the first time a bomber had been a specific RFC requirement.[6]

Back in London, Henderson began to expand his ideas. He explained to the Chief of the Imperial General Staff, Archibald Murray, that the RFC would soon have the front line strength to do much more than just support the Army. He was confident the aeroplane production and crew training problems were a thing of the past, and was anticipating a period of rapid expansion. By the end of March, he believed Trenchard would have the twenty-seven squadrons he had been promised with twenty-four more squadrons in reserve or available for duties overseas. With squadrons being created at one a week, there would soon be a substantial surplus and Henderson suggested that this be used to launch an 'aerial offensive on a considerable scale' against targets in Germany. This was not possible immediately as Germany was too far from the front line and Henderson saw no point in attacking targets in occupied territories. However, if British armies could advance to within 150 miles of targets in '...Germany proper, we now have the means to inflict serious damage, both material and moral, on places of military importance'.[7]

Henderson suggested that once the first thirty-six squadrons had been created, subsequent squadrons 'should be equipped chiefly with aircraft of long-range and weight carrying capacity'. Henderson was anxious to get an immediate decision so long-term planning could begin.[8] Henderson's proposal was audacious and a remarkable vote of confidence in the capabilities of the bomber, especially given the scathing conclusions of the June RFC report, but these conclusions were soon being forgotten. An RFC HQ report in December 1915 accepted that there was still much to learn about bombing but results ought to be much better now that the 'go as you please' attitude had been eradicated and the tactic of concentrated mass attacks carried out by 'swarms of aircraft' adopted. The attacks on communication targets during the Loos raid were judged 'certainly most effective' and it was believed 'the enemy's traffic was considerably disorganised'.[9] It was a somewhat embellished description of bombing operations that reflected the enthusiasm of returning aircrews far more accurately than the results they were achieving.

For Henderson, long-range bombing was not a revolutionary new approach to war. The bomber was merely a way of extending Army firepower to targets up to 150 miles away. Instead of long-range artillery targeting ammunition dumps, long-range bombers would target ammunition factories. It was, nevertheless, a policy that involved attacks on distant targets that could not have any immediate effect at the front. He had also mentioned enemy morale as a target, which added a new dimension to the assault. Henderson was moving towards the Admiralty's naval blockade strategy of slow strangulation, and the air force was taking its first steps towards an independent bombing strategy.

Crucially, there was no question of diverting resources from Trenchard's tactical air force. The new force was only going to be created with squadrons over and above those required by the RFC at the front. It seemed a perfectly sensible experiment to conduct with resources that would not be required for anything else. Henderson's proposal, however, did not take into account Kitchener's plans for the further expansion of the Army. Trenchard and Henderson were basing their requirements on the needs of the three armies in the field, but Kitchener was planning on creating six. A fourth Army was being formed and Trenchard was already asking for another five squadrons for this. To complicate matters further, Henderson's optimistic predictions for the creation of squadrons were based on the extremely low combat losses so far suffered. Up to the end of August 1915, less than 100 planes had been lost since the outbreak of war. This was about to change as air combat became more frequent and losses more common.

While Henderson speculated about what a future long-range bomber force might achieve, it was the battle for air superiority over the front that was the more immediate concern for his Directorate. The War Office seemed more aware of how the battle might be won than the RFC commanders in France. It was Brancker who had taken the lead with the creation of specialist fighter squadrons; the need for more fighting squadrons was one of the reasons why Brancker's expansion plan was so much more ambitious than Trenchard's. Indeed, Trenchard would need some convincing that the resources Brancker was putting at his disposal were really necessary. Brancker and Henderson wanted bomber/reconnaissance squadrons equipped with a mixture of R.E.7 and F.E.2s, and specialist fighter squadrons, some with the F.E.2 two-seater and others with the D.H.2 single-seater.[10] Trenchard agreed with the greater emphasis on bomber and fighter planes and he wanted as many F.E.2 'fighting planes' as possible, but he was puzzled by the D.H.2 scout squadrons. He still saw armed scouts as having a relatively minor role, providing close escort for other squadrons. Trenchard could not see any point in equipping an entire squadron solely with scouts as 'most days there would be nothing for them to do'. If he had to have scouts, he wanted them distributed among the F.E.2 squadrons. However, he could not have enough 'fighting aircraft' and was rather surprised and disappointed that there were no plans to include the Vickers Gunbus, even though he freely admitted the performance of existing models of the pusher was second-rate. Planes like this were Trenchard's idea of a real fighter. As Henderson gently pointed out, 'I think our difference of opinion is that you look upon them (D.H.2s) as scouts whereas I look on them as single-seater fighters.' Henderson insisted scouts would be very effective if used in large formations, but Trenchard's idea of a fighting plane was not a single-seater.[11]

As Henderson was suggesting, the meaning of the term 'scout' was in transition, and the changing meaning of the word would leave plenty of scope for misunderstanding, confusion and mistakes. Scouts had been developed for high-speed reconnaissance and were often small and fast, which coincidentally made them potentially excellent fighters, but this was by no means true for all scouts. Martinsyde, for example, had developed a rather bulky successor to their

S1 scout, the long-range Martinsyde G100, which soon earned the nickname 'Elephant'. The Factory was developing the B.E.12, a single-seater scout version of the B.E.2 for photo-reconnaissance and bombing, which was nearly as large as the Martinsyde Elephant. Neither was manoeuvrable enough for the fighter role Henderson was envisaging for scouts. The same was true for the latest 'Fighting Experimental' from the Factory. In December 1915, O'Gorman informed Trenchard he was sending out the prototype F.E.8 pusher for service trials, crediting it with a top speed of 97.8 mph and boasting of its excellent stability.[12] O'Gorman, and indeed Trenchard, had yet to realise that this was not a quality that was sought after in a fighter.[13]

Meanwhile, naval pilots were getting their hands on a scout that had all the qualities needed for air-to-air combat. In May 1915, the first example of the French Nieuport 10 began to reach the RNAS. The plane had started life as a two-seater reconnaissance aircraft, but French pilots had started using it as a single-seater with a gun fixed to the upper wing firing over the propeller. So successful was this arrangement, the plane went into production as a single-seater. The Nieuport 10 was far superior in terms of flying characteristics and armament to the monoplane Morane-Saulnier N, and it became the standard French fighter. A scaled-down version—the Nieuport 11 Bébé—was lighter, faster and more manoeuvrable. The Nieuport soon became the RNAS fighter of choice.

The Nieuport 10 was not so dissimilar to the Bristol Scout and there was no reason why the Bristol plane could not have been used as the French were using the Nieuport. Towards the end of 1915, Nos 12 and 4 Squadrons tried out the French-style wing-mounted guns on their Bristol Scouts. A pilot at No. 12 Squadron flew the plane for over two hours and reported no difficulties, but at No. 4 Squadron, the pilot felt that the single gun upset the centre of gravity and claimed the plane tended to go into a nosedive every time he tried to bank. No. 4 Squadron's wing commander happened to be Brancker, who had been rewarded for his unstinting efforts on the home front with a brief spell in France commanding the 3rd Wing. Brancker rated the pilot first class and to be relied on, and no doubt took his negative view of the fixed gun single-seater scout back to the War Office when he returned to London.[14] Although naval Bristol Scouts operated with one or even two wing-mounted machine guns, no effort was made to introduce this arrangement as standard on RFC scouts, although this would not stop some individuals modifying their own machines. Nor did the French Morane N and its deflector system win much official favour. The three ordered for trials arrived in September; according to Baring, Trenchard's aide, pilots who tried it out were impressed and wanted more, but Trenchard did not share their enthusiasm and no order was placed.[15]

Trenchard wanted planes with higher endurance, not single-engine single-seaters. Indeed, Trenchard was increasing his endurance requirement—he now wanted planes with eight hours' endurance. He considered the R.E.7, the largest machine yet ordered by the RFC with six hours' endurance, as just a first step in this direction. The first of these began arriving in France towards the end of 1915 and an impressed Trenchard demanded the War Office double the number on order. The twin-engine Vickers E.F.B.7 and E.F.B.8 fighting biplanes were lined up to follow, although Trenchard was soon making it clear that their three hours' endurance was totally inadequate.

The Factory F.E.4 was more like what Trenchard wanted and 100 had already been ordered, even though the prototype was yet to fly. Even this was not good enough for Trenchard. When he was told it might only have an endurance of seven hours, he sent off another stiff note to the War Office pointing out that anything less than eight hours would be totally unacceptable.[16] De Havilland had hit Trenchard's endurance target with his twin-engine three-seater D.H.3, and fifty of these were ordered.[17] The Factory were already looking ahead to the next generation of fighters with the huge three-engine F.E.5 biplane, the ultimate fighting machine with three gunners—one in the nose and two behind the wing-mounted engines—operating five guns in all. If air fighting was to develop along the lines of naval battleships, this was a true aerial dreadnought, a plane that could bully and blast its way through enemy airspace.

These huge multi-seater combat planes were the very antithesis of the small, nimble, single-seater 'fighting scout' the RNAS and French air force were turning to. Vickers warned Trenchard he could not expect such large planes to be as manoeuvrable as his single-engine machines,[18] but manoeuvrability would not be a factor in the sort of air combat Trenchard was envisaging. Training schools, he informed London, should emphasise the importance of pilots taking up positions so their gunners had a clear field of fire.[19] The opposing planes would engage each other like battleships at sea. If naval warfare was anything to go by, the larger and more heavily armed machine ought to prevail.

However, as autumn turned to winter, it was the single-seat Fokker that was causing problems. Instead of using the Fokker as a passive escort, two German pilots, Immelmann and Boelcke, had begun using it to hunt down enemy planes. They would patrol at altitude and use their height advantage to dive on their opponent out of the sun, wherever possible, to maximise surprise. The energy gained in the dive could then be used to regain altitude and repeat the attack. These hit and run tactics were entirely different to the ponderous manoeuvring of the two-seaters. Planes like the Vickers Gunbus and the larger ones Trenchard wanted were literally 'fighters', planes designed to slug it out toe to toe with the enemy, with the pilot flying as straight and steady as possible to allow his gunner the best chance of hitting his target. The Fokker pilots were 'hunters', using stealth and surprise, and this would be reflected in the designation their squadrons were given: 'Jadgstaffel' or 'hunting squadrons'. The French too were already using the term 'escadrilles de chasse' for squadrons equipped with the Nieuport 10 and

11. On the British side, pilots like Hawker were pioneering the hunting approach with armed scouts. Eventually, the distinction between a 'fighter' and an 'armed scout' or 'fighting scout' would disappear in RFC terminology and both types would both be referred to as 'fighters'. Initially, however, they represented two entirely different approaches to the air combat problem, and as far as Trenchard was concerned, the 'armed scouts' were not proper 'fighters'.

The new Fokker tactics came as a shock to Allied airmen. There was something unnerving about the lightning strikes of the high-flying and often invisible Fokkers. In this scenario, the built-in stability of the F.E.2 and especially the B.E.2 now became a major liability. These planes could not manoeuvre out of the German gun sights and the gunner could only fire backwards with the greatest of difficulty over the pilot's head, and in the case of the F.E.2, the engine as well. The armed German two-seaters had earned the respect of RFC pilots, but the Fokker fighters were causing panic. Encounters with the Fokker were still relatively rare. There were not many Fokkers at the front and there were even fewer German pilots who knew how to get the best out of the machine, but morale among front line RFC squadrons slumped as news of the odd encounter spread. The German fighter acquired almost mystical capabilities.

Trenchard did not appear overly concerned about the Fokker until the loss of some fifty pilots and observers between early November 1915 and early January 1916.[20] In fact, there was nothing particularly unusual or excessive about these losses. Since May, monthly casualties had usually exceeded twenty per month. The first indication of a change in attitude came on 27 December with an urgent note demanding to know what steps had been taken to develop an efficient deflector system. It was a matter of 'great importance' and he hoped private companies were being brought in to solve the problem.[21]

On 5 January, two more aircraft were shot down by Fokkers. In the overall context of the war, especially in the context of what was happening on the ground, it was scarcely a catastrophe, but the loss of two aircraft on the same day was highly unusual. The Fokker was shaking the confidence of the RFC and its commander. Trenchard decided his RFC had to have its own Fokker and the previously rejected Morane-Saulnier N seemed to fit the bill. Like the Fokker, it was a single-seater monoplane tractor with a fixed forward-firing machine gun, albeit with an inefficient deflector system. Despite his earlier reservations and undeterred by its limited endurance, on 7 January, Trenchard instructed Lord Innes-Ker, responsible for co-ordinating RFC and RNAS orders for French aircraft, to order a batch of twenty-four Morane-Saulnier Ns. It was rather a knee-jerk reaction, a decision dictated more by the need to sustain RFC morale than a clear tactical plan to defeat the Fokker. It was not envisaged that the Morane-Saulnier monoplane would engage the Fokker in combat. 'As a defence against the Fokker,' Baring emphasised, 'they would have been useless.'[22] The idea of two single-seaters dogfighting had not yet occurred to anyone at RFC HQ.

The Fokker would be defeated by the Fighting Experimentals that Trenchard set such great store by. The French fighter would be used as an offensive interceptor, giving the RFC the same capability as the Fokker to surprise and shoot down reconnaissance planes. Trenchard needed to be able to say he had something similar to the Fokker and demanded rapid delivery. Fortunately for Trenchard, Morane-Saulnier was equally anxious and able to comply. The French air force had abandoned the Morane-Saulnier N and moved on to the superior Nieuport biplane, and Morane-Saulnier was in need of new customers. Trenchard was ordering a French air force reject, but at least the single-seater tractor scout was now on the RFC agenda.

Five days after Trenchard issued instructions to get hold of the Morane-Saulnier N, the RFC suffered its worst day yet with four aircraft shot down, three of which Trenchard credited to Fokkers. An alarmed Trenchard sent a note to the War Office, demonstrating just how quickly his ideas were changing. He now emphasised the need for a 'handy' machine capable of over 100 mph at 6,000 feet and capable of firing directly ahead.[23] To speed up the delivery of scouts with the required performance, Trenchard turned again to Morane-Saulnier. If a more powerful version of their monoplane could achieve the 100 mph target speed and endurance could be increased to three hours, the French company could expect more orders.

On 17 January, Henderson was reassuring Trenchard that he was doing everything possible to come up with a British system for firing through the propeller. The Royal Aircraft Factory was looking into French-style deflectors and Henderson promised he would see if a private company could improvise something along the lines of the German synchronisation system. He did not seem particularly optimistic but a solution was already at hand. Ten days after this letter was written, Vickers applied for a patent for their Vickers-Challenger synchronisation gear. There was nothing technically particularly difficult about developing a synchronisation system, but British efforts had been held up by the particularly erratic firing patterns of the Lewis gun and the low priority attached to the work. In November, the crucial decision was made to abandon the Lewis and use the heavier Vickers machine gun. By mid-January, the Vickers-Challenger system was up and running, and all future tractor aeroplanes, single and two-seater, would now be required to carry a synchronised gun. In March, a Bristol Scout was equipped with the system and sent to France for trials. There was still time for the Bristol Scout to make a name for itself as a fighter.

Trenchard was moving in the right direction, but it was far from a total conversion to the single-seater tractor scout configuration. As impressed as Trenchard was by the Morane-Saulnier N, he was even more impressed by the two-seater Morane-Saulnier BB biplane, the only plane that 'touches the Fokker', he insisted.[24] Far more of these had been ordered than the Morane-Saulnier N. Nor was it the end of the pusher. Trenchard was still demanding a wide field of forward fire from his single-seater and two-seater fighters, which meant pusher designs were still very much preferred. The single-engine single-seater 'local protection plane' was only intended for the defence of the short-range corps planes and rear lines of communication, essentially a short-range interceptor/escort. The emphasis was still on extending the long-range air combat capability of the air force with planes like the F.E.4 and, eventually, the F.E.5. Eight hours' endurance was still the goal.[25]

In the meantime, Trenchard would do the best he could with what he had. An instruction issued on 14 January, perhaps rather too candidly, blamed RFC problems on the superiority of the Fokker, which can scarcely have done anything for the confidence of those who had to face the German monoplane. Until better equipment started arriving, all long and short-range reconnaissance missions were to be escorted by at least three armed planes, and if any of these become detached from the main formation, the mission was to be abandoned. By sending out stronger formations with a better chance of battling their way through, Trenchard's force would, he hoped, maintain the offensive.

The improved equipment Trenchard was relying on was beginning to arrive. The first of the Fighting Experimentals, the single-engine F.E.2b, finally began to appear in some numbers. No. 20 Squadron, the first to be completely equipped with this plane, arrived in January 1916, followed by a second, No. 25 Squadron, in February, but early versions powered by the 120-hp Beardmore were scarcely better than the Vickers Gunbus.[26] The second new fighter to appear, de Havilland's Airco D.H.2 single-seater scout, proved to be in a very different class. Hawker returned to France in February 1916 with No. 24 Squadron, the RFC's first specialist single-seater fighter squadron. Although a pusher, de Havilland's fighter was superior to the Fokker in terms of speed, ceiling and climb, and Trenchard soon appreciated that the plane he had been so dismissive of was the best fighter available to him.[27]

Around March, the F.E.2b with the more powerful 160-hp Beardmore began to arrive. With this engine the plane virtually matched the performance of the Fokker E, quite an achievement given that it was a two-seater and a pusher. In truth, this was more a reflection of the very average quality of the Fokker basic design than the brilliance of the F.E.2. Even with the more powerful engines, Hubbard, the commander of No. 11 Squadron, was not over-impressed. 'In spite of the handicap of fighting against scouts with a machine that had an enormous blind spot behind and beneath, and was very heavy in manoeuvre and not particularly fast, the squadron accounted for a great number of the enemy, and though suffering considerable casualties never lost for a moment its high spirits and dashing qualities.'[28] It was scarcely a ringing endorsement.

The D.H.2 pilots were much happier with their equipment. In March, No. 24 Squadron started flying patrols and escort missions over the Somme. Although the D.H.2's gun was moveable, in practice pilots preferred to leave the gun fixed and aim the plane at the enemy rather than try to fly the plane and move the gun simultaneously. Therefore, the field of fire the pusher provided was not relevant, but the excellent view was much appreciated. On patrols over the front line, the D.H.2s initially flew singly, but towards the end of April, the squadron started flying in formations of two or more with pairs of fighters considered to be a particularly efficient combination. On escort duties, the D.H.2s would fly to the rear and slightly higher than the main formation, giving pilots the tactical freedom to deal with any threats. No. 24 Squadron prided itself on its record of never losing a plane in its care to enemy action.[29]

Henderson and Brancker assumed Trenchard would form more specialist fighter squadrons with the large numbers of Morane-Saulnier fighters they thought he was acquiring from France; however, the few that were delivered were distributed among the corps squadrons as their scout allocation. Trenchard's new found enthusiasm for using the D.H.2 scouts in specialist fighter squadrons did not extend to the French Morane. Trenchard had only ordered twenty-four and did not plan to order many more, even if Morane-Saulnier achieved the performance targets he had set. The French single-seater was not a major factor in Trenchard's plans.

Trenchard was delighted when he was told the improved Morane-Saulnier I could climb to 9,000 feet in less than nine minutes. He ordered twelve, but was less pleased when he discovered it only carried sufficient fuel for less than two hours. He visited the Morane-Saulnier works late in March to pass on his dissatisfaction in person and made sure that they were aware he had just witnessed an impressive display of synchronised machine-gun fire at the nearby Nieuport factory. They responded by achieving the required three hours' endurance with the much-modified Mark V version of their fighter. Trenchard seemed pleased with his little ruse, although he would have done better simply to carry out his threat and order the far superior Nieuport fighter.[30]

The British press made much of the 'Fokker Scourge'. The quality of the machines RFC pilots were fighting in was criticised and the Royal Aircraft Factory came in for particularly harsh criticism with its B.E.2 ridiculed as mere 'Fokker Fodder'. In parliament, the controversial and outspoken Pemberton-Billing, commander of the naval force involved in the 1914 Friedrichshafen raid, provoked outrage by describing the way airmen were being sent to their deaths in inadequate machines as an act of murder.[31]

The shrill tone of some of the wilder accusations tended to undermine the underlying truth. The machines RFC aircrews were flying were not suitable for the type of aerial warfare that was emerging and the RFC was slow to react. The desire for total stability was understandable given the temperamental characteristics of early planes, and indeed the need to provide a stable firing platform, but the reluctance to upset the delicate balance achieved in the B.E./R.E. designs by putting the observer in the more useful rear position resulted in machines that were both un-manoeuvrable and un-defendable.

With hindsight, the slump in RFC morale the Fokker caused seems disproportionate to the scale of actual losses. Using so many reconnaissance machines as escorts was not ideal as it necessarily reduced the number of missions that could be flown, but the escorts were effective. Although aircraft losses were rising, RFC front line strength was increasing more rapidly and as a proportion of aircraft strength, losses were falling. From October 1915 to May 1916, the RFC lost 134 planes in action, seventy-six of them as a result of air combat. In the same period, sixty-one aircrews had been killed and 133 wounded or captured.[32] These were heavy losses compared to the first year of war, but not unacceptably heavy. Nevertheless, they were enough to slow down expansion. Brancker, now back at the War Office, was struggling to get the RFC in France up to the required strength for the forthcoming Somme offensive. The twenty-seven-squadron scheme to provide air support for three armies was supposed to be achieved by the end of March, and Trenchard was expecting an additional five squadrons by the end of April for the new 4th Army. To make matters more difficult, in March, Trenchard decided to restore squadron strength to the originally intended eighteen machines by the end of July, which was even more necessary now that squadrons had to use some of their planes for escorts. Corps squadrons were to have priority with three more observation planes and three more scout escorts attached to each squadron.[33]

Trenchard also wanted a doubling of the force under the control of GHQ. In total, Trenchard now wanted forty-four squadrons. Looking further ahead, plans to form a 5th Army led Trenchard to expect fifty-six squadrons by the spring of 1917,[34] with an additional ten long-range bombing squadrons once this basic requirement had been met. After Trenchard's initial, rather modest demands, he now wanted more squadrons than Brancker and Henderson had allocated him. The surplus for Henderson's long-range bomber force was drifting further into the future.

Since December 1915, Brancker had been managing to send two squadrons a month to France and had been hoping to do better, but by the spring of 1916, even two a month was problematic. Poor weather had disrupted training programmes and increasing losses at the front had put extra strain on the system. In March, he was warning Trenchard that the five extra squadrons he had been expecting in April were unlikely to arrive. The best he could manage was three squadrons in March, followed by just one in April. Trenchard was running out of time. The Somme offensive was set for July and the RFC desperately needed to find more aircraft and pilots before then. The solution did not seem so far away. Just a few miles north, at the naval airbases around Dunkirk, there seemed to be no shortage of pilots or planes.

CHAPTER 5

Naval Help and Flying Dreadnoughts

For some time both Trenchard and Brancker had been casting envious eyes in the direction of Dunkirk. The RNAS bases were close to the front line and the naval squadrons were making a contribution to the Allied air effort over the northern sector of the British front, but the plan for the summer offensive involved a joint Anglo-French offensive much further south on either side of the River Somme, nearly 100 miles from Dunkirk. Trenchard needed the RNAS aircraft and their pilots to play their part. Since the outbreak of war, the War Office had been suggesting that the Admiralty help the Army by transferring naval planes and pilots to the RFC. The Admiralty were quite happy to transfer entire squadrons, even place them under the temporary operational control of the RFC, but they insisted that they remain naval squadrons. The War Office were equally adamant naval crews and equipment had to be integrated into RFC squadrons.[1]

This was just one of several issues causing friction between the War Office and Admiralty. The War Office were unhappy that many aircraft companies such as Sopwith seemed to be 'in the Admiralty's pocket', although this was hardly surprising given that the Admiralty had been far more willing to do business with them than the War Office. There were also squabbles over the acquisition of French equipment with accusations that the Admiralty were getting more than their fair share. The Admiralty also seemed to have a monopoly on larger engines. Again, the War Office only had itself to blame as it had been convinced Army planes would not need anything more powerful than 160-hp engines. The Navy had always needed larger engines to haul clumsy floatplanes and heavy loads into the air, and it was the Admiralty that was largely responsible for getting Rolls-Royce to develop the 250-hp Eagle. Now the RFC needed engines like this to beef up the performance of the struggling F.E.2, not to mention getting the twin-engine F.E.4 and huge F.E.5 into the air. The fundamental grievance the War Office had with the Admiralty was that it was absorbing resources it did not need. Naval air support was fine, but the Admiralty had taken their non-naval air interests too far. Dealing with the Zeppelin menace rather than supporting the fleet appeared to have become the

RNAS's principal occupation. For purely naval purposes, the RNAS did not need so many aircraft.

Long-range bombing in particular had become a major naval commitment. Following the successful attack on the Düsseldorf Zeppelin shed, Sueter called in Handley Page and his chief designer, Volkert, to see how the naval bombing capability might be developed. Sueter was less than impressed with what they proposed. 'What I want is a bloody paralyser, not a toy,' he snapped, and with this exhortation ringing in their ears, the chastened pair returned to their design office to start work on the huge Handley Page O/100, a true 'paralyser' capable of carrying up to sixteen 112-lb bombs.[2] However, building such a plane was an enormous undertaking, and it would be some time before even a prototype appeared. As a stopgap, Sueter ordered a landplane version of the Short 184 seaplane torpedo-bomber, although even this was a major development project. By the spring of 1916, the only suitable plane available was the much smaller and far less ambitious Sopwith 1½ Strutter, which was being built as a single-seater bomber and two-seater fighter.

The Admiralty planned to create a long-range force with 180 aircraft (fifty heavy bombers, eighty light bombers and fifty escort fighters) to attack any targets which 'the Navy would wish to destroy but cannot be reached by water'.[3] Henderson had no objection to the idea in principle. He had set out his own proposals for a similar capability and there was a growing enthusiasm for long-range bombing within the War Office.[4] Henderson, however, insisted forces for long-range bombing 'against military or national objectives' should be an Army, not a Navy responsibility, and Admiralty efforts to create a parallel force would only result in two weak forces rather than a single strong one.[5] Furthermore, he stated that this force should only be created in addition to those forces required for tactical air operations. The RFC in France was seven squadrons and 275 planes short of what it needed, and many of the available planes, Henderson admitted, were of doubtful quality or suitability. This was not the time to be pouring resources into long-range bomber fleets.[6]

High on the list of unsuitable planes was the B.E.2. The summer 1915 RFC programme had required a tractor with a good rearwards field of fire and rather belatedly the Factory had started work on their R.E.8. This was similar in concept to its R.E.5 and B.E.2 forebears, with the same emphasis on stability, but crucially with a gunner/observer positioned behind the pilot. But the first prototype would not fly until June 1916.[7] The Navy, however, already had just such a machine. Details of the Sopwith 1½ Strutter reached RFC HQ in January 1916 soon after the plane's first flight. It was an exceptional plane. At low level it could manage 107 mph, it was 20 mph faster than the F.E.2b at 10,000 feet and took less than half the time to climb to that altitude. It was not particularly manoeuvrable or rugged, but despite being a two-seater, it had a superior performance to the single-seater Fokker monoplane.[8] The War Office tried ordering the plane from

Sopwith, but the plant was already fully occupied with Admiralty contracts. Licence production was organised with other companies, but deliveries could not be expected until the end of July after the opening of the Somme offensive.

There was little sympathy from the Admiralty. If the War Office had not insisted on relying so heavily on Factory designs, they would not find themselves in such a mess. For the Admiralty, it was a dilemma they really felt they ought not to have been burdened with. The Sea Lords were convinced that long-range bombing was the future and they had the backing of Balfour, Churchill's successor at the Admiralty.[9]

Diverting resources to the Army would inevitably delay the opening of a full-scale strategic air offensive, and this, the Admiralty suggested, was at least as important as the Army's planned Somme offensive. If the War Office did not agree, said the Sea Lords, then perhaps the government would have to decide. For the Admiralty, strategic bombing combined with the economic blockade was much more than just a way of helping the Army—it was part of an alternative strategy for winning the war. The problem for the Admiralty was that even the Sea Lords thought the Navy had more planes than it needed.[10] In February 1916, including aircraft of all types, the Navy possessed over 950 planes compared to the Army's 800, yet had fewer pilots.[11]

The Admiralty had justified its large front line strength by highlighting naval willingness to 'assist the Army whenever and wherever required', and as proof, had pointed to the large-scale naval air operations in support of British and Dominion ground forces in the Mediterranean and Africa. The withdrawal from the Dardanelles, however, had removed one major commitment, and with the Somme offensive approaching, the Admiralty felt under pressure to put its willingness to support the Army into effect on the Western Front.[12] The Admiralty was determined to hang on to the Sopwith bombers required for its bombing offensive, but an understanding was reached whereby naval contracts placed with French firms for light aircraft and 110-hp rotaries would be transferred to the RFC. As far as the RFC was concerned, the engines were the most important element of the deal. It also meant the RFC would take over an order for Nieuport single-seater fighters and acquired subsequent Admiralty allocations of the French plane. At the end of March, the first Nieuports arrived. Oblivious of the significance of the acquisition, these were shared out among observation/reconnaissance squadrons like other single-seater tractor scouts.[13] The Admiralty also offered Trenchard pilots. Trenchard wanted them to fly RFC machines, insisting this would avoid the servicing and spares complications involved in yet more different types being deployed at the front. Initially, the Admiralty agreed to transfer fifteen pilots, but then changed its mind when the pilots protested that RFC aircraft were 'unsuitable for flying in the presence of the enemy'.[14] The naval pilots had a point, although it was extraordinary that the Admiralty apparently seemed so relaxed about this act of defiance.

Henderson was told a group of four naval pilots were particularly anxious to get involved on the Western Front, provided they could take their Nieuport fighters with them. Henderson objected but Lord Derby, the chair of the Joint War/Air Committee co-ordinating naval and Army requirements, was keen on the idea. With naval pilots refusing to fly RFC planes, he was particularly interested to see how RNAS equipment compared to standard RFC equipment. Henderson claimed it was a pointless exercise as the RFC was already very familiar with the capabilities of the Nieuport fighter. Henderson, however, was clearly not familiar with how highly the fighter was rated. After flying the plane, pilots suggested that, in a Nieuport, even average pilots could take on the Fokker with confidence.[15] It was unfortunate that 'average' RFC pilots had not been given a chance to discover this for themselves. Henderson was forced to concede and it was agreed that the four naval pilots would transfer to the RFC, taking their Nieuport fighters with them.[16]

The latest Nieuport 16 the RFC was getting was far superior to the D.H.2. Trials with an example with No. 1 Squadron in April revealed it was 10–12 mph faster than the D.H.2 and climbed to 10,000 feet in half the time, information that was hastily passed on to Brancker in London.[17] By this time, the more refined Nieuport 17, armed with a synchronised machine gun, was already in production. In mid-June, the RFC tested this version and discovered it flew and climbed even quicker.[18] With naval pilots getting fighters like these, their attitude to standard RFC equipment was understandable. Trenchard thought the naval Nieuports would be 'a beastly nuisance' and Henderson dispatched them with a sympathetic 'Gawd help you!'[19] At the end of March 1916, the four RNAS Nieuports were attached to No. 29 Squadron, which was just converting to the inferior D.H.2.[20] Trenchard's main objection, the maintenance problem of operating yet another type at the front, was scarcely valid since the RFC was already getting its first Nieuport fighters, courtesy of the agreement with the Admiralty. Indeed, if Trenchard had wanted, he could have put all the RFC and RNAS Nieuports in one squadron, which, apart from any operational advantage, would have eased the maintenance problem he was so worried about.[21]

Initially, the Admiralty were able to hang on to the Strutters, but more pleas from Trenchard led to these too being passed over to the Army, with production priority switched from the single-seater bomber version to the two-seater fighter version the RFC needed. From May, two Strutters per week—about one third of expected deliveries—would be diverted to the RFC,[22] and No. 70 Squadron was formed in Britain to operate the plane. Its relatively high endurance—close to four hours—made it perfect for the long-range fighter patrols Trenchard's HQ Wing was expected to perform. So anxious was Trenchard to get the plane to the front, each flight of No. 70 Squadron was sent to France as soon as it became operational—the first arriving on 29 May, the second on 29 June, and the third on 30 July.

Naval Help and Flying Dreadnoughts

The only other tractor two-seaters that were readily available were the French Morane-Saulnier BB biplane and the Nieuport two-seater that had spawned the single-seater Nieuport 11, 16 and 17. In March, Trenchard was told the latest version of the two-seater Nieuport had a top speed of 95 mph at 6,500 feet and climbed to that altitude in fourteen minutes. This was not that impressive when compared to the Sopwith Strutter, but Trenchard was desperate—so desperate that he was happy to swap a number of Nieuport single-seaters the Admiralty were redirecting his way for the two-seater version.[23] Trenchard was handing back his best fighter. Ironically, while Trenchard was spurning the Nieuport single-seaters, the enemy were sending captured examples off to manufacturers with instructions to copy them.

There was no interest in making more use of the Bristol Scout, still the best British single-seater in production. A succession of War Office and Admiralty contracts ensured unarmed examples of the scout were still rolling off the Bristol production line. In March, the example armed with the Vickers-Challenger synchronisation system arrived in France for squadrons to try out, and in April, No. 25 Squadron had the plane. Two Bristol Scouts, one with the synchronised gun and the other with a machine gun fixed to the top wing, came across a Fokker. According to the squadron commander, they 'did what they liked with the Fokker', only gun failure preventing the planes from completing the kill. In May, Albert Ball also tried out the synchronised-gun-armed Bristol Scout and shot down a German two-seater.

Under intense pressure from Lord Derby to make as much use as possible of all available equipment, however unsuitable, Henderson and Brancker felt obliged to reconsider the Bristol Scout, but even the gravity of the shortage could not induce a change in attitude. Brancker insisted planes with 80-hp engines like the Scout were totally unsuitable for combat in 1916,[24] although more powerful versions were flying and proving just as capable as the Nieuport of benefitting from the extra power.[25] When the Navy offered Brancker a dozen of Scout Ds powered by a 100-hp engine, he gratefully accepted and immediately whipped the engines out for use in other planes.[26] So little use was being made of the Scout that it was the only plane where deliveries to France exceeded required replacements. Bristol Scouts arriving with synchronised guns were kept, but those without were sent back to England, with RFC HQ claiming they had neither the manpower nor the time to modify them. In July, RFC HQ instructed London not to deliver any more.[27] Nearly 400 Bristol Scouts were built, 236 of which were delivered to the RFC, but only eighty of these ever crossed the Channel.[28] There were only ever half a dozen in front line squadrons at any one time and they made no significant contribution to the struggle. It was a waste of an excellent plane.

While Henderson and Brancker were assuring Derby that even in the current equipment crisis, the Bristol Scouts could not make a useful contribution, they were convinced the Aircraft Factory's single-seater B.E.12 'scout' version of the B.E.2 could. This was supposed to be a scout in the original reconnaissance meaning of the word, and had none of the required attributes of a fighter. Some months before, Henderson had lectured Trenchard on the importance of looking on the armed scout as a fighter. Henderson was now having a problem recognising when an armed scout was not a fighter.

The latest scout from Sopwith was most definitely a fighter. The Pup, so called because it looked like a scaled-down version of the Strutter, was, by First World War standards, a delight to fly. With the same 80-hp Le Rhone rotary as the Bristol Scout, the Pup was 18 mph faster and could climb 3,000 feet higher, a measure of the advances being made in airframe design. When Trenchard heard about the fighter's predicted speed of 110 mph and its ability to climb to 10,000 feet in little more than twelve minutes—half the time it took the D.H.2—he immediately demanded a squadron of the planes for France.[29] Like so many of Trenchard's decisions, it was a spur of the moment affair and did not reflect any fundamental change of heart on the importance of single-seater tractor fighters. As spectacular as the performance of the Pup was, it was no faster and climbed a lot slower than the Nieuport single-seaters Trenchard was quite happily exchanging for the two-seater version. Ironically, there was now a frantic effort to get a plane to the front that was powered by an 80-hp engine—an engine which, when powering a Bristol Scout, had been declared unsuitable for front line use. Brancker reacted promptly to Trenchard's request for Pups, but as with the Strutter, it was too late to make use of the Sopwith plant. In May, Standard Motors was given a contract to build the plane under licence, but deliveries could not begin until the autumn at the earliest. That same month, the first prototype Pup arrived in France for trials and delighted naval and RFC pilots with its speed and manoeuvrability. RFC pilots stepped up the pressure for the immediate delivery of the plane, but Trenchard continued to believe the future was with twin-engine and multi-seater fighters.

These, Trenchard hoped, would also be capable of bombing, which was not unreasonable given that they looked more like bombers than fighters. Indeed, they were soon proving how unsuitable they were for the fighter role. By the time the F.E.4 flew in March 1916, it was a three-seater with an additional gunner behind the main wing. Only 140-hp Factory engines were available and it struggled to achieve 80 mph.[30] Barnwell's conceptually similar Bristol TTA flew soon after, but did not do much better. Both design teams set to work redesigning their prototypes to take much more powerful 250-hp Eagles.

Discouraging reports sent to Trenchard on the slow progress these planes were making were greeted with equally disheartening evaluations from St Omer on the value of the interim R.E.7. Trenchard had grown disenchanted with the large ungainly plane. It looked impressive, 'like a giant magical bird' according to Baring,[31] but flew like 'a heavy lump of a thing' according to the pilots.[32] Not so long ago, Trenchard had been lambasting London over the delays with deliveries of the plane. Large numbers had been ordered and now a concerned Directorate was asking Trenchard if he still wanted the plane. The rather alarming answer was an emphatic no.[33]

Meanwhile, the improved F.E.4 with 250-hp Eagles took to the air in June 1916, but was scarcely any faster. No amount of extra power, it seemed, could induce such large airframes to fly significantly quicker. The design was abandoned and the production contract cancelled. It seemed unlikely that the even larger three-engine F.E.5 was going to be any more successful and this was abandoned before it got off the drawing board.[34] It was also the end of similar projects from Bristol (TTA), Vickers (E.F.B.7 and E.F.B.8) and Airco (D.H.3), as fighters at least. Designers began to consider how these designs might do better as bombers.

The demise of the twin-engine multi-seater fighting planes did not lead to a reassessment of the single-seater tractor. Instead, the two-seater fighter took on the mantle of the flying dreadnought. With a forward-firing synchronised gun, the Directorate in London noted that single-engine two-seaters could effectively be used just like the Fokker. They seemed to offer the best of both worlds with fixed forward and moveable rearward-firing guns; the two-seater fighter was now the definitive preferred option.[35] The twenty Army fighter squadrons required by Trenchard's June 1916 expansion plan were to be equipped entirely with two-seaters.[36]

It was naval interest in single-seater tractor scouts that ensured excellent British designs continued to emerge, and the latest was another from Sopwith. The plane had narrower wings to improve the pilot's view, but three wings ensured it had the same surface area as the Pup. The narrower wings permitted a shorter fuselage, making the plane even more compact and manoeuvrable. With the greater power of the 110-hp Clerget rotary, maximum speed and climb were also improved. The first prototype Sopwith Triplane flew on 28 May 1916. The next day, Lieutenant-Colonel Hugh Dowding, at this time in charge of the Administrative Wing in France, was informed the new fighter had achieved 121 mph and could climb to 10,000 feet in under ten minutes—figures which suggested the plane had 'great possibilities'.[37] It was a view confirmed by RNAS pilots when they got hold of the fighter the following month. Its speed, climb and manoeuvrability made it 'vastly superior to any machine on either side' and the Admiralty were soon ordering a first batch.[38] RFC pilots were just as enthusiastic, but there were no immediate plans to order any for the RFC.

Reports were also coming in of the excellent performance achieved by the latest French scout built around a powerful new water-cooled engine, the Hispano-Suiza HS 8Aa. With the coolant and associated plumbing, planes powered by liquid-cooled engines were inevitably heavier, larger and less manoeuvrable than ones powered by air-cooled rotaries, but they were much faster. The French Spad company used the new 150-hp engine to power their Spad 7 single-seater. A British observer described how the unarmed prototype had achieved 133 mph at ground level and seemed to climb extraordinarily fast.[39] In April, official French performance figures put horizontal speed at 116 mph at 6,600 feet and climb to 10,000 feet at just over thirteen minutes. Initially, the British were more interested in the engine than the Spad airframe.[40] The Royal Aircraft Factory was set the task of seeing what they could achieve with the new power plant, and Dowding was delighted to hear they expected to get 135 mph with their S.E.5 scout.[41] This, however, was merely a design proposal while the Spad 7 was about to be delivered to French air force squadrons. The Royal Aircraft Factory was instructed to push ahead with their design as quickly as possible and three Spad 7s were ordered from the French for trials.

Ever so slowly, the single-seater tractor was edging its way into RFC thinking. Henderson tried to force Trenchard's hand by sending him the newly formed No. 60 Squadron without any planes and telling Trenchard to equip it with the Morane-Saulnier N; this eventually became the first RFC squadron equipped entirely with single-seater tractors. At the end of May, Trenchard reported that Nieuport and Morane single-seaters were doing well.[42] RFC HQ even requested that more attention be paid to 'trick flying' in pilot training, and Trenchard warned the War Office about the failure of the Royal Aircraft Factory to attach sufficient importance to manoeuvrability.[43] This message did not seem to be getting through to Farnborough. Trenchard's warnings coincided with the official trials of the new B.E.12 'scout', the single-seater version of the B.E.2. Whereas the Pup had impressed all with its manoeuvrability, the B.E.12 retained the inherent stability of its B.E.2 predecessor. Indeed, the Central Flying School report claimed the B.E.12 was even less manoeuvrable than the B.E.2.[44] Despite this, production went ahead with the production model armed with a fixed synchronised gun and with air combat as its principal role.

Synchronised guns were still not seen as necessarily the best way forward. Even though D.H.2 pilots preferred to fix their gun, there was still a reluctance to abandon the option of moveable guns the pusher provided, and the view would always be better with the engine in the rear. Production of the single-seater F.E.8 pusher was going ahead and Vickers were busy developing the next generation of their pushers. For a single-seater, the rear-mounted engine did not get in the way and even provided the pilot with some protection. The case for two-seater pushers with the engine blocking rearward fire was far less convincing. Yet production of the F.E.2, now powered by the far more powerful Rolls-Royce Eagle engine, was being stepped up. Meanwhile, the Factory was determined to get round the problem of firing backwards over the engine with their latest F.E.9 pusher where the nose gunner was positioned above a much lower upper wing. Work on this design did not start until the late summer of 1916, long after synchronisation systems had become available.

Naval Help and Flying Dreadnoughts

The disadvantages of the pushers were to some extent concealed by the quality of the opposition they faced. Planes like the D.H.2 and F.E.2 might be inferior to the Nieuport, but RFC pilots did not have to fight the French plane. Their opponent was the Fokker. In April 1916, an example of the German fighter landed at a British airfield by mistake and RFC pilots discovered the plane was far from the wonder machine its reputation had suggested. It was a handful to fly and when it was tested against a Morane-Saulnier N, the French fighter was faster in level flight and climb, and 'had everything its own way'. Even the Morane-Saulnier Parasol and BB biplane two-seaters could hold their own.[45] More significantly, the D.H.2 was superior and even the F.E.2b could compete. Pilots would go into combat with more confidence in their equipment. There was no need to forsake the advantages of the pusher while the Fokker was the opposition, but relying on the enemy to continue using rather ordinary designs was a dangerous game to play as RFC pilots would discover soon enough.

That problem, however, lay in the future. For the opening of the Battle of the Somme, the RFC would have the technical edge.

CHAPTER 6

Ascendancy and the Seeds of Disaster

Trenchard hoped to take full advantage of this technical superiority by introducing new, more aggressive tactics. They were tactics inspired by Commandant du Peuty, the commander of the French air force on the Verdun front, where, since February, the French had been fending off a furious German assault on the forts around the town. Du Peuty and Trenchard had formed a close working relationship and spent many hours discussing air tactics. Du Peuty's approach emphasised the importance of grouping fighters together and employing them offensively in strength deep inside enemy airspace.[1] British observers in the Verdun sector commented on how the air superiority established by these tactics had enabled individual French planes to operate freely over the battlefield unescorted.[2] These were precisely the sort of tactics the offensive-minded Trenchard could relate to.

There was no compelling operational reason for the RFC to change the tactics it was using. The panic that had characterised RFC thinking early in 1916 at the beginning of the Fokker crisis had proven to be somewhat of an overreaction. Corps observation planes regularly flew short-range missions, often without escort, and without suffering excessive losses. As long as the corps planes stayed fairly close to the front line, friendly fighter patrols and anti-aircraft guns were never usually too far away. They were also close to friendly territory if they got into trouble. Only fifteen planes were lost on artillery observation missions in the first six months of 1916.[3] For longer range missions, escorts were proving effective. The 'Fokker Scourge' was as much a myth as the invincibility of the fighter itself.

The future prospects for the RFC seemed even brighter when on 18 June, Immelmann—with fifteen confirmed victories and established as one of the greatest exponents of the Fokker—was shot down and killed in a combat with an F.E.2b. The German nation was stunned by his death. The possibility of losing Boelcke as well, credited with eighteen victories, was too great to contemplate. The German ace was grounded and sent on a morale boosting tour of the Eastern Front. The German air force had effectively lost its two best fighter pilots, who between them had been responsible for a disproportionate number of Allied losses.

There was therefore no urgent necessity to change tactics, but from late June, RFC squadrons were ordered to start flying patrols up to 10 miles behind the front line. The new tactics did not initially bring any great success. Hawker's No. 24 Squadron, operating on the Somme front, flew its first offensive patrol on 20 June, and in the last week of June, the squadron flew offensive patrols every day flying was possible. Only on two occasions were enemy planes encountered and neither combat brought any success. It was by no means an all-out offensive. The squadron also continued to fly patrols along the front line and escort missions. It was perhaps not as offensive as Trenchard wanted, but long-range fighter sweeps were now a regular feature of RFC fighter operations.[4]

For the Somme offensive, Trenchard had twenty-seven squadrons serving four armies, most of which were close to the eighteen-plane target strength. The RFC mustered 421 aircraft along the entire British front, a substantial increase on the 150 that existed the previous October. It was a force dominated by B.E.2s and pushers. The RFC had 186 planes with an air combat role, of which 135 were single or two-seater pushers. There were forty-three single-seater tractor scouts, but twenty of these were Martinsyde G100 'Elephants', considered especially valuable by Trenchard due to their range, but with little manoeuvring capability. The remaining eleven Morane-Saulnier Ns, six Nieuport 16s, and six Bristol Scouts represented the effective tractor single-seater force supported by eight of the new two-seater Strutters. The corps squadrons were for the most part equipped with B.E.2s with a handful of Morane-Saulnier Parasols and BB biplanes.[5] Of these, the B.E.2 was least capable of defending itself, but as long as they limited their operations to short-range observation and were not expected to penetrate too far into enemy airspace, they could still perform a very useful role. Unfortunately for their crews, Trenchard was expecting much more.

The main offensive took place along Rawlinson's 4th Army front with the 3rd Army operating on the fringes to the north. Rawlinson had 109 planes directly attached to his Army with Dowding's 9th HQ Wing adding another fifty-eight. The total immediately available, 167, was not much more than a third of the total RFC force. Rawlinson had just two Army squadrons for fighting purposes, Nos 22 and 24 Squadrons, the former with eighteen F.E.2bs and the latter with nineteen D.H.2s. As reinforcement, three Bristol Scouts and two Morane-Saulnier Ns were extracted from the corps squadrons and attached to No. 24 Squadron. The Strutters, Martinsydes and Moranes of 9th HQ Wing would also be available, but on the front of the offensive there were only eighty fighters. All the available Nieuport single-seaters were deployed further north and would take no part in the fighting. The corps squadrons from the uninvolved armies further north would be used as makeshift bombers against communication targets in the enemy rear. The Germans, still focusing their efforts on Verdun, had just 140 planes with which to oppose the RFC.

The original objective of the offensive had been to achieve a decisive breakthrough of the German lines, allowing the cavalry to romp through the undefended countryside beyond. A more realistic secondary aim was to relieve pressure on the French at Verdun and prevent reinforcements being sent to the Eastern Front where the Russians were advancing. Once again, aeroplane-directed artillery fire was seen as a key to success. The Somme offensive was to be supported by the most intensive artillery barrage yet, 1,500 guns along a 14-mile front. The bombardment began a week before the infantry were to attack, with enemy positions being constantly re-photographed to assess damage and identify new targets. Special processing units had to be established at squadron airfields to deal with the volume of work.

Artillery and air co-operation was becoming ever more sophisticated. The number of planes directing artillery fire along any stretch of the front had been doubled by varying the pitch of the signals to distinguish one transmitter from its neighbours. Pre-planned shoots still involved close co-ordination between airmen and a particular battery, but call procedures had been standardised and the grid reference maps extended to cover the entire battle zone. This enabled more flexibility about which battery a plane could direct towards fleeting targets of opportunity. The corps plane would indicate where the target was, a battery would be assigned the target, and the corps plane would correct the fire, without ever being aware of which battery they were directing.[6]

On the eve of the offensive, bombers joined in the assault, attacking communication targets in the rear. Formations of R.E.7s, benefitting from close escorts, delivered their attacks without loss, but twenty-eight B.E.2s sent off individually on 1 July to bomb railway stations and cut lines in and around Cambrai, St Quentin and Busigny, 20–30 miles behind the front line, were not so fortunate. Carrying bombs instead of a gunner meant the planes were completely defenceless. Protection was supposed to be provided by Trenchard's new offensive patrols. The Moranes of No. 60 Squadron were to fly inner patrols in an arc from Arras–Cambrai–Bapaume up to 20 miles beyond the front line. Meanwhile, the Martinsydes of No. 27 Squadron were to fly on a huge arc from Arras in the north to Péronne in the south, flying as far as Le Cateau some 40 miles from the front line. Only one patrol from the two squadrons encountered any enemy planes, while the lone B.E.2s were less fortunate and five were shot down.

The B.E.2 railway offensive was resumed on 3 July and Moranes and Martinsydes were again responsible for providing an indirect escort. The Martinsydes did not encounter the enemy, and even if they had, it is difficult to see how this would have helped the scattered B.E.2s. A number of Moranes at least engaged the enemy—the squadron losing its commanding officer in a

Ascendancy and the Seeds of Disaster

fight with Fokkers over Cambrai—but their efforts could not prevent another three B.E.2s being shot down and others limping home badly damaged.[7] The indirect escort concept was not working. Dowding, now commanding the GHQ 9th Wing, was particularly critical of these long-range fighter sweeps; views which did not go down well with Trenchard. Nevertheless, on hearing of the losses suffered by the B.E.2 bombers, Trenchard cancelled further solo daylight bombing missions. Raids continued either by night or escorted by day.

On 1 July, the first wave of 60,000 infantry set off for what they hoped was crushed barbed wire and shattered defensive positions; however, the enemy defences remained intact, resistance fierce, progress slow, and casualties unprecedented. Low-flying contact patrols kept Army commanders informed of any progress the infantry managed to make. Forward troops used flares to indicate their position, and for the first time, the contact patrols flew low enough to confirm their identity. Commanders in the rear at least knew how badly the battle was going. 'Trench patrols' flying equally low monitored activity in enemy defensive positions. Despite the perilously low altitudes these planes flew, only two machines were lost in July,[8] demonstrating that flying low over the front line was not as hazardous as some had feared. The RFC was dominant and the omnipresent Allied planes had an oppressive effect on the front line German forces, especially as their own air force was conspicuous by its absence. German prisoners confessed to being reluctant to fire at anything when an enemy plane was in the vicinity, for fear of giving away their position and inviting an artillery barrage.

The opening of the offensive saw an escalation in the number of offensive fighter sweeps, with No. 24 Squadron flying four on 1 July alone. However, not all RFC fighter operations were deep inside enemy territory. Nos 22 and 24 Squadrons also flew pairs of fighters in continuous patrols along the front from dawn until dusk, never more than 3 to 5 miles inside enemy territory.[9] By patrolling in and around the battlefield, fighters were able to give far more protection than fighters patrolling 20 or more miles behind the front. It was not what du Peuty had suggested or Trenchard wanted, but it was working.

Combat losses remained relatively low. Eight planes were lost to enemy action on the first day of the offensive, another five the following day and seven the day after that, but nearly half of these were the vulnerable B.E.2s sent out individually to bomb railway lines. Once these missions were abandoned, daily combat losses were very low, with only fourteen corps planes lost in the entire month on tactical reconnaissance/observation missions. Losses in August were even lower. Whatever the pros and cons of the different tactics and equipment, it seemed to be working and the RFC controlled the skies.

On the ground, any hopes of a decisive breakthrough soon evaporated as the offensive degenerated into a seemingly endless series of actions designed to eliminate a particular German stronghold or capture a vantage point. The corps squadrons performed well. They continued to identify and direct fire towards enemy gun positions, and enabled the artillery to engage troops caught on the move. After the war, General Ludendorff praised the effectiveness of British artillery/air co-operation, especially in the early stages of the offensive when it 'kept down our fire and destroyed our artillery'.[10] It did not, however, help achieve a breakthrough. Artillery on both sides was making movement on the battlefield impossible. Ironically, any success the corps planes achieved was only contributing to the stalemate.

As the battle wore on, the strain increased on RFC squadrons. Total combat losses for July were seventy-two planes, which given the scale of the offensive and the number of aircraft involved, was scarcely disproportionate. Even in the hardest hit squadrons, losses did not equate to the carnage inflicted on the infantry. Nevertheless, losses were no longer infrequent events and they were keenly felt. The relative serenity of the airfields from which the squadrons were operating heightened the sense of loss, ensuring each casualty had a disproportionate effect on morale. Trenchard was aware of this and insisted personnel lost in action should be replaced immediately to ensure there were no empty places at the dining table to remind aircrews of those who had not returned. It was a policy that put an enormous strain on the training system and exposed less than ready pilots to front line action far too soon. The strain on aircrews was increased by the sortie rates expected with two patrols a day the norm. In July and August, with few German aircraft operating over the battlefield, this was manageable for the corps squadrons whose pilots could find the time and energy for makeshift attempts at bombing local targets in between regular observation duties.[11] It was far more demanding for squadrons expected to operate far in the enemy rear, invariably facing a headwind when the time came to get back to their own lines, and flying aircraft that were not easy to fly.

Trenchard made sure his three headquarters squadrons—Nos 60, 27 and 70 Squadrons—followed his offensive fighter policy, even though often they failed to encounter the enemy. Dowding questioned the value of these missions and objected to the high sortie rates expected by Trenchard. After losing half of its Moranes, he asked for No. 60 Squadron to be rested. Trenchard reluctantly agreed, but was unimpressed by Dowding's apparent lack of stomach for the fight and made sure that he was posted back to the United Kingdom.[12] The experience made a deep impression on the future leader of Fighter Command. Many years later, Dowding would bitterly recall the pointlessness of sending out tiny formations deep into enemy airspace merely to be shot at.[13] Army squadrons were also beginning to see the pointlessness of long-range patrols. Responsible only for their particular front, they did not feel the need to patrol so far inside enemy airspace and began to interpret Trenchard's instructions for offensive patrols rather liberally. Terms like 'offensive line patrol' began to appear in reports as squadrons attempted to make sure their fighters were not too distant from the planes they were supposed to be protecting, while paying lip service to Trenchard's offensive vision.

Meanwhile, Brancker was struggling to replace the planes lost. The accident rate was still very high. Combat damage and pilot fatigue were factors—damaged planes that made it back to base and crashed were considered accidents, not combat losses, but the lack of adequate training was also a major factor. By the end of the first month Brancker had to replace over 200 planes, with accidents more than doubling the number of planes lost. This was a heavy price to pay for the air superiority the RFC had established.[14] Brancker was just about able to replace these, but only at the expense of planes intended for the training programme. Combat losses in August were lower than in July, but the number of accidents increased dramatically—a measure of the stress crews were under and the number of ill-trained replacements arriving at the front. Total losses rose to 257, which was beyond Brancker's ability to replace. Even Trenchard was rather ill at ease with the heavy losses his offensive policy involved, but he insisted his strategy was a necessary bluff. He had to maintain the offensive to prevent the Germans seeing the opportunities that existed for their fighters over the front. However, if it was a bluff, it was a bluff that was about to be called. Boelcke was on his way back from his tour of the Eastern Front with instructions to create fighter units that would carry the fight to the British, and he would have the machines and the tactics to succeed.

While the Germans prepared to challenge British air superiority, the RFC was reviewing the lessons learned from the fighting so far. The conclusions Trenchard reached were not going to help prepare for the impending onslaught. It seemed the first two months of the Battle of the Somme had been a triumph for pusher and two-seater fighters, while single-seater tractor squadrons had done little to enhance their reputation. The Martinsyde 'Elephant' squadron was used more for bombing and reconnaissance than fighting, roles for which it was much better suited, and No. 60 Squadron with the single-seater Morane-Saulnier N was the only squadron that had had to be withdrawn to rest and refit. The arrival in August of No. 19 Squadron with its ungainly B.E.12 'scout' conversion of the B.E.2 was scarcely likely to enhance the reputation of the single-seater tractor.

By the end of the Battle of the Somme, the ideal ratio of two-seater F.E.2s to single-seater scouts was considered to be 2:1, with the scout category predominantly consisting of pushers like the D.H.2 and F.E.8. Interest may have faded in the monstrous twin-engine multi-seater Fighting Experimental types, but the smaller two-seater F.E.2 had now assumed the role of the heavy fighter, the new aerial battleship, with the faster scouts taking on the secondary role of swifter and lightweight naval destroyers.[15] The parallels with naval strategy might have had a certain logic when massive multi-engine machines bristling with guns were envisaged, but it was difficult to see how F.E.2s could dominate any degree of airspace in the way battleships might dominate the seas. According to No. 23 Squadron, to maintain formation, F.E.2bs had to fly at a stately 50 mph and such a flotilla could not possibly pose a threat. It would simply be allowed to go on its way, just as the early Vickers Gunbus had been ignored. There were some rather imaginative ideas about how the Fighting Experimentals might get round this problem, with talk of the scouts driving the enemy planes on to the guns of the F.E.s, although why enemy pilots would allow themselves to be corralled in this way was not explained.[16]

There were some dissenting voices. Hubbard, the commander of No. 11 Squadron, was no great fan of the pusher. Having operated Gunbuses and F.E.2s along with a sprinkling of Bristol Scouts and Nieuports, he was aware of the alternatives.[17] He was not the least bit impressed with the tactics the two-seater pushers had forced on his squadron. Flying in formation deep behind enemy lines waiting to be attacked scarcely seemed an approach that encouraged initiative. Indeed, it bred insecurity, but he got no support from Higgins, his brigade commander. In a covering note, he put Hubbard's comments down to a lack of squadron experience at flying in formation with the recently acquired F.E.2bs.[18] Trenchard was also not particularly impressed by his line of thinking, but agreed with his squadron commander that fighting planes needed to have the performance to operate outside passive defensive formations, which was why Trenchard wanted planes like the Sopwith Strutter and two-seater Nieuport, planes he believed had the performance to operate like single-seaters if required. Whether this was a reasonable expectation was another matter.

Trials early in July with the Nieuport 12 scarcely suggested it was. Although the two-seater had a top speed of less than 100 mph and climbed to 10,000 feet in twenty-two minutes,[19] far inferior to the Strutter, the official report claimed it was 'probably one of the best fighting machines there are'. It was conceded the climb performance of the plane was poor, but its other qualities were so impressive that it was felt it could quite easily fly without escort and take on any attacker. Such powerful planes would transform the contribution that the corps squadrons could make. Not only could they observe and reconnoitre, they could participate in the battle for air superiority. The Nieuport 12 was the combat plane of the future and plans were laid to mass produce it under licence in Britain.[20]

The Factory R.E.8 reconnaissance plane, the B.E.2's successor, seemed to be another combat plane in the Nieuport 12 and Strutter mould. It was fast and could fly at 13,500 feet, which was respectable for a two-seater. Like the Strutter and Nieuport, it had a forward-firing synchronised gun as well as a rear-firing weapon, and there seemed no reason why it should not prove to be as capable as the Nieuport 12. When it became apparent early in August that Brancker might have difficulty supplying Trenchard with sufficient fighters, Trenchard told him that he was quite happy to use the new R.E.8 as a fighter if necessary.[21] Like its B.E.2 predecessor, the plane had been designed to be as stable as possible, but as far as Trenchard was concerned, any plane with a synchronised forward-

Ascendancy and the Seeds of Disaster

firing gun and a gunner in the rear was a fighter. At the end of August 1916, Trenchard issued clear instructions on how he envisaged two-seaters being used. Crews were told that in planes with a synchronised gun and a rear gunner, the forward-firing gun should be the principal method of engaging the enemy. The rear gun was only for warding off attacks if a damaged plane was forced to head for home prematurely. Crews were being told to use their two-seaters as single-seater scouts.[22]

The value of the fixed gun was now recognised, but two-seaters were preferred to single-seaters, and pushers were considered better than tractors. Some single-seater tractors were still required, not least to replace the Morane-Saulnier Ns of No. 60 Squadron. Losses had been heavy and French supplies were uncertain; enthusiasm for the plane was on the wane. It had always been considered a difficult and tiring plane to fly, and was credited with 'the gliding angle of a brick'.[23] There were urgent enquiries from RFC HQ about when the first Sopwith Pups could be expected, and as a stopgap, the squadron was re-equipped with Nieuport single-seaters. Supply problems had finally forced the RFC into forming its first squadron equipped entirely with what was at the time the best single-seater fighter in the world. The single-seater pusher, however, had achieved too much to be dispensed with. There was, in RFC eyes, nothing incongruous about a new single-seater pusher fighter, the Royal Aircraft Factory F.E.8 making its operational debut in August 1916, and there were more pusher prototypes in the pipeline. Even the likes of Hawker felt the excellent view the pusher provided its pilot was worth the 10 per cent loss of performance.[24]

To meet the latest British pushers and two-seaters, German designers were preparing something altogether more advanced, and Boelcke was making sure the pilots had the tactics to make best use of their new equipment.

CHAPTER 7

RFC in Crisis

Arguably, the only real quality the Fokker E possessed was its synchronised gun. During the summer, the Germans introduced more advanced fighters, all of which were tractor single-seaters. Initially, there was nothing to concern the Allied pilots too much. The rotary-powered Fokker D.II and D.III biplanes were only a slight improvement on the Fokker E monoplane, but the Halberstadt D.II made more of an impression. It was not superior to the D.H.2, but the Sopwith Strutters and F.E.2 two-seaters would now begin to struggle. More significantly, the arrival of the Halberstadt coincided with the introduction of more aggressive fighter tactics. The best pilots were chosen to join the new Jadgstaffel (Jasta) 'hunting' formations where they were given further training in fighter tactics by Boelcke. The first of these units, Jasta 2, became operational at the beginning of September. In the hands of well-trained pilots that were skilfully led, even the Halberstadt D.II could prove a handful as Boelcke demonstrated on 15 September when he single-handedly savaged a formation of No. 70 Squadron Strutters, shooting down no less than four. It was the beginning of a new phase in the air war.

At the beginning of September, the German fighter force began receiving a new fighter, the Albatros D.I, the first German fighter to make use of 150-hp Benz and 160-hp Daimler liquid-cooled engines. Like the Spad 7, the fighter was relatively heavy, not especially manoeuvrable, but fast. Both sides were beginning to appreciate the initiative altitude gave the pilot in combat, and liquid-cooled engines enabled the Albatros to fly much higher than rotary-powered fighters. The German fighter had a top speed of 109 mph and could get to 10,000 feet in a little over fifteen minutes. By French standards this was respectable without being sensational, but it was still ten minutes faster than the D.H.2. Trenchard's latest tractor single-seater, the B.E.12, had a top speed of 100 mph and took over half an hour to get to 10,000 feet. The high performance of the Albatros was impressive enough, but what made it a truly deadly opponent was its armament. A single light machine gun had never been considered satisfactory by any air force, and efforts had been made to fit fighters with more, but the effect on performance was always too great. The Albatros, however, achieved its remarkable performance and carried two synchronised machine guns. The combination of excellent performance and heavy firepower made the Albatros devastatingly effective.

On 17 September, two days after his success with the Halberstadt, Boelcke led his Jasta into action with the new Albatros fighter for the first time. For the RFC, it was an ominous operational debut. Boelcke and his formation intercepted six F.E.2bs escorting eight bomb-carrying B.E.2s. Four F.E.2bs and two B.E.2s were shot down without loss. Poor weather restricted operations over the next few days, but the return of fine weather brought more heavy losses. The next plane to experience the fighting efficiency of the Albatros-equipped Jastas was the B.E.12. A second squadron, No. 19, had arrived in France and on 22 September, on two offensive patrols, three B.E.12s were lost in clashes with the new German fighter. Not surprisingly, the German pilots thought they were engaging its two-seater B.E.2 predecessor. The possibility that they had taken on Britain's latest fighter never occurred to them. Over the days to come, the B.E.12 squadrons would lose a plane virtually every time they flew. On 23 September, it was the turn of the Martinsydes of No. 27 Squadron. Three were lost in a clash with the Jastas, with a fourth crashing on reaching its base. On 27 September, the squadron suffered again. Of six planes carrying out an offensive patrol, two were shot down, one crash landed in friendly territory, and a fourth made it back to base badly damaged.

After a relatively quiet first half to the month, September became the worst on record with RFC combat losses exceeding 100 machines for the first time. Pilots fresh out of training school were rushed to the front as replacements, but they faced a daunting task. If they managed to get their planes safely into the air, they were now going to be pitted against confident, well-trained and experienced pilots in superior fighters. By the end of the month, B.E.12 losses had risen to thirteen. Trenchard was forced to withdraw both squadrons from operations and told London not to send any more. The F.E.2s were not faring much better; the pusher had always been vulnerable to attacks from the rear, but with its altitude advantage, the Albatros wreaked havoc. Thirty-one F.E.2 fighters were shot down during the course of the month.[1]

The Jastas were not just better equipped, they were noticeably more aggressive and determined to make a difference over the battlefield. No longer could the B.E.2s go about their business undisturbed. The corps squadrons' losses doubled in September and again in October with twenty-eight aircraft lost, even though, with the fighting on the ground petering out and weather deteriorating, the number of sorties being flown was dropping. Trenchard was seriously shaken by the impact the Albatros was having and was forced to reassess the value of the single-seater tractor as a fighter. Trenchard admitted to Haig and Henderson that the only plane he had that was faster than the Albatros were the Spads he had acquired for trials.² Of the rest, the best was the Nieuport single-seater, the fighter that up until this point Trenchard had been happily exchanging for the two-seater version. Trenchard was not giving up on two-seaters or the pushers yet. The new F.E.2d, thanks to its Rolls-Royce 250-hp Eagle engine, was one of the few RFC planes capable of flying as high as the Albatros and Trenchard rated it as valuable as the Nieuport single-seater, although in truth as a fighter it had little going for it. Even the Strutter was rated as 'inferior to the enemy's new machine in some respects, though superior in others',³ although in what respects it was superior was not clear. Nevertheless, in Trenchard's estimation, single-seaters were at least now considered as important as two-seaters.

Indeed, there was a new urgency bordering on panic about acquiring single-seater tractor scouts. Innes-Ker was instructed to speed up deliveries of Nieuport single-seaters.⁴ Any doubts about the relative value of the single-seater and two-seater versions of the Nieuport were removed by the assessment of the first British-built Nieuport 12s to roll off British production lines. The once best fighting machine in the world was now declared to be 'useless for military purposes' with all round performance rated as far worse than the B.E.2c.⁵ Suddenly, Trenchard's policy of converting orders for single-seater Nieuports into two-seaters was thrown into reverse. On 15 October, RFC HQ asked Innes-Ker to acquire the French-built Nieuport single-seater and two-seaters in the ratio of two-to-one. A week later, this instruction was cancelled and Innes-Ker was instructed to see if he could get the entire Nieuport order converted back to single-seaters.⁶ RFC HQ was suddenly urgently enquiring from London what had happened to the Sopwith Pups promised for early September. The answer was not encouraging. 'Misunderstandings' between Sopwith and the licence producers had delayed production. At best, there might be sufficient to keep a flight going by the second week of October.⁷ On 20 September, Trenchard wrote directly to Bares, the head of the French air force, pleading for Spad 7s, but Bares was unable to help. The French were also desperate for something to challenge the Albatros. Deliveries to the French air force were already well behind schedule and Bares thought it unlikely any would become available before the end of the year. He could only suggest the British set up their own production line.⁸ Plans were laid to produce the fighter in Britain while renewed pressure on the French managed to secure a promise of thirty Spad 7s by the end of the year.⁹

Meanwhile, the first Sopwith Pups were beginning to reach the RNAS at Dunkirk. Trenchard was infuriated by the RNAS having 'machines and pilots sitting about all over the world doing nothing', especially if the machines were the ones he wanted. He demanded the RNAS deploy the Pups where they were needed: on the Somme front.¹⁰ On 27 October, the Navy sent a composite squadron, No. 8 RNAS, with one flight each of Pups, Strutters and Nieuports. The only other squadron Trenchard had with modern fighters was No. 60, now converted to Nieuports, no longer an unwanted stopgap but the best fighter available. Lest there be any doubt about what Trenchard wanted—he told Brancker to send as many single-seater fighters as possible powered by either the 110-hp Clerget engine of the Nieuport or the 150-hp Hispano-Suiza of the Spad.

While Brancker set about seeing what could be done, Trenchard turned his mind to how existing equipment could be used better. The solution was simple in Trenchard's eyes at least—superior tactics would have to compensate for technical inferiority. Even before the Albatros appeared, Trenchard had been concerned about the way squadron reports were full of references to 'offensive line-patrols', 'defensive line-patrols' and even 'offensive-defensive-patrols'.[11] Clearly, his orders to fly offensive patrols deep behind the front line were not always being followed. His offensive strategy had been diluted and only the total superiority of RFC equipment had prevented the full consequences becoming apparent. Now the German air force had technical superiority, the offensive doctrine would have to be followed more rigidly—the deeper in the enemy rear the RFC operated the better. It was not necessarily unwelcome among pilots. The irrepressible Lanoe Hawker revelled in the opportunity to get behind the German fighter patrols and cut off their line of retreat.

It was, however, a complete misreading of the situation. Only the performance advantage of RFC fighters had saved Trenchard's offensive policy from catastrophe during the first two months of the Somme offensive. The ability to engage or disengage at will is crucial in any offensive operations deep inside enemy airspace. Without it, the fighter pilot could find himself trapped on the wrong side of the lines, unable to make a break for home without giving the enemy the opportunity to attack from the rear. This ability to disengage had begun to disappear with the appearance of the Halberstadt D.II, and totally evaporated with the arrival of the Albatros D.I. The German pilots now enjoyed the technical edge and initiative—an offensive strategy in these circumstances was suicidal.

Ironically, Hawker was to pay the price for this vain attempt to maintain the offensive. On 23 November, he was piloting one of three D.H.2s on an offensive fighter sweep that was surprised by Albatros fighters. Hawker was separated from the formation and chased by no less than Germany's current highest scoring ace, Manfred von Richthofen. For nearly half an hour, Hawker's brilliant airmanship and desperate manoeuvring kept him out of German gun sights, but with fuel running low, he was forced to make a break for Allied lines. Just weeks before, Hawker had been praising the advantages of the pusher, claiming the 10 per cent loss of performance the pusher layout imposed was worth the better view.[12] Hawker now paid dearly for that 10 per cent loss. Long before Hawker reached the safety of the front line, he was overhauled by the faster Albatros, shot down and killed.

Even Trenchard admitted a more rigid offensive policy would inevitably involve heavy losses. On fine days, Trenchard admitted he could count on losing as many as eight to twelve pilots, but convinced himself that it was a price worth paying. It was an attitude that mirrored the repeated offensives on land and was just as senseless. All that could protect RFC pilots now was the autumnal weather or German disinterest. As the RFC offensive fighter sweeps presented no danger to the Germans, they were often ignored. Only if German pilots found themselves in a particularly favourable position did they choose to engage. The only hope for RFC pilots was that their enemy would let them go on their way. This was happening far too often for Trenchard's liking, and to stop it he ordered bombers to accompany the fighters to provoke a German response. Indeed, if the targets were deep in the enemy rear, the German air force would be forced to withdraw their fighters from the front to defend them and the corps planes would be spared. It was a strategy that could not possibly succeed. The damage the bombers could inflict simply did not warrant desperate defensive measures, especially as the bombs were falling on French and Belgian territories. German fighter pilots were quite happy to take advantage of the RFC tactics when it suited them, but they were not going to be lured into battles they did not want to fight. 'It is better if the customer comes to the shop' was von Richthofen's sardonic appraisal of RFC tactics.

It certainly did not help that the most numerous 'bomber' available to Trenchard as bait was the B.E.2. On 9 November, twelve B.E.2s, with an escort of fourteen F.E.2ds, D.H.2s and Nieuports set off with 20-lb bombs to destroy an ammunition dump north-west of Bapaume. The formation was intercepted as it crossed the front line, and while the escort succeeded in preventing a massacre of the defenceless B.E.2s, two bombers and four fighters were lost—a quarter of the attacking force.[13] It did not appear to be a very efficient way of establishing air superiority.

The desperate plight fighter pilots found themselves in at least encouraged a closer look at the tactics fighter pilots used, and some progressive ideas were emerging. Teamwork and flexibility were seen as the key to greater efficiency. Commanders were becoming aware of the disadvantages of flying in tight formations with pilots paying more attention to their neighbour than looking out for the enemy. A flight of six was the recommended maximum size for a fighter formation and some were promoting the advantages of widely spaced pairs, with one pilot covering the rear of his leader, which would turn out to be the basis of fighter tactics for generations to come.[14] The flight might break up in the heat of battle, but the pair, it was suggested, should try to stick together.[15] There is not much evidence the pair was used extensively. On operations, the entire flight tended to be responsible for covering the tail of the leader,[16] but teamwork of some description was seen as the way forward.

Meanwhile, the way the B.E.2 was being used as a bomber was one of the reasons why the artillery wanted the corps squadrons taken away from the RFC and placed under their direct operational control. This would, artillery officers insisted, ensure closer co-operation and greater efficiency, but it was also a measure of a growing feeling that the RFC was distancing itself from everyday Army needs. Too often, B.E.2s were sent off on unnecessary and dangerous long-range missions when they were needed for artillery observation duties. The artillery felt it needed more control. Trenchard firmly resisted this division of his forces on the not unreasonable grounds that corps machines were expected to perform many roles other than artillery observation. Trenchard cited the various tactical reconnaissance applications, trench patrols, contact patrols and photo-reconnaissance as obvious additional roles. He might also have added bombing and air combat, but no doubt thought better of it. The RFC chief saw the corps planes as combat planes in every sense of the word; with Trenchard still regularly sending off precious B.E.2s on bombing missions and instructing two-seaters to use their synchronised gun offensively, it is easy to see why the artillery wanted tighter control. There was a growing feeling within the Army that the RFC was becoming a law unto itself. Indeed, elements within the RFC were becoming increasingly frustrated at being at the beck and call of the Army they were supposed to be serving. In a rather patronising way, there was a growing feeling that the RFC knew best how to use a force they felt a conservative Army hierarchy did not understand. The more indirect support the RFC was favouring with long-range bombing and fighter patrols was symptomatic of this growing detachment. The air force seemed to want to fight its own private war far from the battlefield. Haig, however, backed Trenchard and the corps squadrons remained under his control. Trenchard was more than happy to hand over observation balloons to the artillery, but since the Army did not have to worry about balloons being sent off on bombing missions, the offer was never taken up.[17]

The Somme series of offensives fizzled out in the late autumn, bringing some relief to the hard-pressed RFC squadrons. Despite the lack of progress on the ground, Haig was convinced that the arrival of winter had robbed him of the chance to take full advantage of the pounding he felt the German Army had taken; he was anxious to get the offensive going again as soon as the worst of the winter weather had passed. However, changes in the French High Command—with the more adventurous Nivelle taking over from Joffre—and a sudden German withdrawal to the more easily defensible Hindenburg Line would delay the resumption of the British offensive until early April. It gave Trenchard precious time to get his battered air units into some sort of shape.

Trenchard's first priority was fighters capable of taking on the Albatros on reasonably equal terms. Throughout the winter of 1916–17, Trenchard kept up a constant stream of increasingly frantic notes, official and unofficial, to Brancker and Henderson about the immense difficulties his RFC faced. He was convinced the scale of the problem was not understood in London and feared he was being seen as a panicky doom-monger.[18] He was wrong about the former, but definitely right about the latter. Brancker did the best he could by ordering just about anything he could lay his hands on that was powered by the Clerget and

Hispano-Suiza engines Trenchard wanted. The phenomenal Sopwith Triplane was a priority, but Brancker found the Admiralty had again been quicker off the mark, taking up all the available Sopwith production capacity. They had so many on order that they were even planning to send some to the Russians. Brancker soon got that changed. The Russians were told they would have to make do with Strutters and a proportion of the Admiralty order was diverted to the RFC, but there were only likely to be enough to equip a couple of RFC squadrons by the spring of 1917.[19]

De Havilland's latest scout was soon attracting Brancker's interest. With his D.H.5, de Havilland had abandoned the pusher layout, but was determined to retain its excellent forward view by having a back staggered upper wing, which greatly improved the forward view but only at the expense of the rearward view, the direction from which German fighters liked to achieve surprise. During official trials in December, the plane proved pleasant enough to fly, but despite its more powerful engine, it was inferior in performance to the Pup, especially at altitude. Even so, it was better than the D.H.2 and production went ahead.

Neither the Airco D.H.5 nor the Sopwith Triplane could carry a second machine gun. The first British fighter powerful enough to do this was the Factory S.E.5, although one would be an unsynchronised moveable wing-mounted Lewis gun, apparently on the recommendation of Albert Ball.[20] The Factory's obsession with stability was still apparent in the S.E.5 and manoeuvrability would never be the fighter's forte, but it was a far smaller and more compact design than the Factory's B.E.12 scout. The prototype flew in November 1916 and although it did not achieve the predicted 135 mph, its top speed of 119 mph was impressive enough.[21] A contract for seventy-five was placed with the Factory and by January 1917, 400 were on order from various contractors.[22] The Scout Experimental series had finally produced a plane that had gone into production, but it was arguably the least remarkable of the series.

Meanwhile, yet another fighter had emerged from the Sopwith stable, one which promised to be even better than the Triplane. Sopwith went back to the biplane format, which meant a lower service ceiling and rate of climb than the Triplane, but it was stronger and lighter, and the savings in weight enabled a second machine gun to be carried. The second gun would only just about fit, and partially obscured the view forward—the hump the machine gun installation required earning the plane its 'camel' name. In January 1917, Brancker was enthusiastically describing to Trenchard how the prototype had achieved a speed of 127 mph at 10,000 feet; he promised to get the fighter into service as quickly as possible. The problem again was that the Sopwith plant was fully occupied with Strutters, Pups and Triplanes, with the Strutters still a very important part of the Navy's long-range bombing plans. Brancker managed to get some of the Strutters cancelled, which enabled first Camel deliveries to be brought forward to May 1917.[23] Other companies were brought into the Camel production programme, but these would take even longer to set up production lines. No Camels from any source could arrive in time for the spring offensive.

Two-seater fighters were still seen as just as crucial as single-seaters. Some excellent two-seaters were emerging, although whether they would make good fighters was another matter. The Airco D.H.4 had started life as a reconnaissance plane, but by the autumn of 1916, was being touted as a bomber/reconnaissance plane capable of carrying 112-lb and 230-lb bombs. With a 160-hp Beardmore engine, it could cruise comfortably at 16,000 feet, and with a top speed of 115 mph, it could cause problems for any fighter trying to intercept it. Even better performance was expected from the production version with the new 230-hp BHP (Beardmore–Halford–Pullinger) engine. When the prototype was sent to France for trials, local commanders were not particularly impressed with the plane as a bomber. It was, however, considered remarkably manoeuvrable for such a large machine and therefore likely to make a first rate reconnaissance-fighter. Trenchard insisted that the plane be developed primarily for this role. Deliveries were not to be delayed by fitting bombing equipment[24] but problems with the BHP engine was holding up production; it was therefore decided to make do with the Rolls-Royce Eagle instead.[25]

Another reconnaissance two-seater that Trenchard had already suggested could operate as a fighter was the Royal Aircraft Factory R.E.8. Too late for the Somme offensive, it was expected to be available in substantial numbers by the spring of 1917, finally allowing the B.E.2 to be phased out. Unfortunately, the plane seemed determined to prove the Factory had been right to resist the complication of having the gunner behind the pilot. Its tendency to nose over and catch fire on landing—and even more alarmingly, its habit of going into a spin at the slightest provocation—were two of its less endearing features. The first squadron to get the plane, No. 52, lost one plane in combat and eleven in accidents, and was so traumatised by the experience Trenchard had to let them have their B.E.2s back. The more experienced No. 34 Squadron had a go, but they too suffered fatal accidents. The plane that Trenchard hoped would be good enough to operate as a two-seater fighter scarcely seemed safe to fly.

The woes of the Factory R.E.8 must have left Frank Barnwell and his Bristol design team feeling particularly pleased with their latest offering. The company had been asked to build the R.E.8 under licence, but insisted they could do far better and offered their R2A reconnaissance plane as an alternative. With the new emphasis on two-seater reconnaissance planes having a fighter capability, the R2A became the F2A, and in case anyone missed the change in designation, it was henceforth referred to as the Bristol Fighter. The prototype flew in September, performance exceeded expectations and the plane was immediately ordered into production, although Brancker could only promise Trenchard two squadrons by the following spring. Armstrong Whitworth chipped in with their F.K.8 as another alternative to the R.E.8, and like the Bristol Fighter, it had none of the problems the Factory R.E.8 was experiencing. One hundred were ordered as an interim B.E.2 replacement, although it already seemed like a better long-term proposition. Far more unconventional was the company's F.K. 9 two-seater fighter, which took the triplane philosophy one stage further by adding a fourth wing. Trials with the Quadruplane suggested four wings was not the right direction to go. The plane took twenty-four minutes to reach 10,000 feet and with a top speed of just 87.5 mph at this altitude, it is difficult to see what it had going for it apart from being powered by the Clerget engine Trenchard was insisting on. It was a measure of how desperate Brancker and Henderson were that fifty were ordered anyway.

Brancker was not neglecting the pusher option, which he believed Trenchard still wanted. The Royal Aircraft Factory F.E.9 was not ready to fly. The Vickers F.B.12 single-seater pusher had flown, but even with a 110-hp engine, the prototype failed to reach 100 mph. Nevertheless, a contract was placed for fifty with the production version to be powered by the 150-hp Hart, an experimental radial engine. An example of the pusher was sent to France for operational trials in December 1916 with a temporary 100-hp rotary substituting for the Hart, but Trenchard was not the least bit impressed. The plane offered no advantages over the existing F.E.8 and Trenchard was not convinced the Hart engine would make much difference. Suddenly, pushers were not wanted.[26] Trenchard made it very clear to Brancker exactly what he did want. The Directorate was to concentrate all its efforts on the S.E.5, D.H.5 and Sopwith Pup single-seaters, and for the two-seater fighter role, the D.H.4 and Bristol Fighter and Armstrong Whitworth Quadruplane, all of which were equally important.[27] No pushers, not even the F.E.9 and certainly not the previously favoured F.E.2d, were on the list. Brancker cancelled the contracts for the Vickers F.B.12 and the Factory F.B.9 pushers.[28] The contract for the Armstrong Whitworth Quadruplane was also cancelled before Trenchard had a chance to find out what that plane was capable of.

It was not just better fighters Trenchard wanted, he also needed more. At the opening of the Somme offensive, Trenchard had fifteen corps, twelve Army and GHQ squadrons, eleven of which had a fighter or fighter/reconnaissance role. The June expansion programme required fifty-six squadrons by the end of the year, of which twenty-four would be fighter (twenty attached to the armies and four at GHQ). As soon as the Albatros burst on the scene, Trenchard was demanding a doubling of the number of Army fighter squadrons. The new programme, approved in November, required seventy-six squadrons by the end of 1917, of which forty-four would be fighters. In December 1916, Trenchard only had fifteen fighter squadrons and there was no chance of reaching even the original twenty-four-squadron target by April 1917. Only one squadron had what Trenchard considered to be modern machines (No. 60 Squadron with Nieuports) and Brancker's promise of thirteen fighter squadrons with modern planes by the beginning of March had already been cut back to just nine by the end of March.[29]

To help make up the difference between what Brancker could offer and what he felt he needed, Trenchard again turned to the Navy. Trenchard asked the Admiralty to provide another four naval fighter squadrons by the end of March together with fifty Eagle, fifty Falcon and fifty Hispano-Suiza engines, which would enable him to build sufficient planes for two D.H.4, two Bristol Fighter and two Spad squadrons. This, with Brancker's promised nine squadrons and the two squadrons (No. 60 and the RNAS composite squadron) he already had, would give Trenchard twenty-one squadrons equipped with single and two-seater fighters better than or at least equal to the Albatros by the middle of March. With this, Trenchard felt the RFC could 'hold its own'.[30] The Admiralty was being asked to provide the bulk of the material for nearly half the RFC fighter force.

Initially at least, the Admiralty was in no mood to bail out their sister service. They were keen to get their strategic bombing offensive going and had promised the French a 200-strong force to support their long-range bombers. The opening of the offensive had already been held up by the diversion of naval planes and engines to the RFC for the Somme offensive. There was also the growing U-boat threat to deal with. The Admiralty insisted the onslaught against the U-boat bases in Belgium was just as important as any renewal of the Somme offensive and begrudged any reinforcements from its Dunkirk force. In some pretty acrimonious exchanges, the Admiralty suggested the RFC losses would not be so high if their pilots were trained properly, to which Henderson's stinging response was that it was easy for the Navy to maintain high levels of training since their pilots were hardly ever engaged in combat.[31]

However, Vaughan-Lee, Sueter's successor, needed Trenchard's help. With the War Office demanding control of any bombers the Navy had in France, he needed Trenchard's support for the continued presence of the independent naval bomber force being set up in eastern France. In exchange for this, Trenchard got his reinforcements.[32] Although they could not meet Trenchard's engine demands in full, the Admiralty offered twenty-five Eagles and thirty Falcons, and instead of the fifty Hispano-Suiza engines, they handed over half of their French Spad 7 contract, amounting to some sixty fighters. They also promised to get four extra fighter squadrons to the front by March 1917. With some of their Triplane production also redirected towards the RFC, Trenchard had no reason to complain.

Until these modern fighters arrived, the winter of 1916–17 promised to be a grim time for the squadrons on the Western Front. Fortunately for the RFC, poor weather often prevented flying, but when the weather did clear, the exchanges between the two air forces were often sharp and one sided. Squadrons tried to implement Trenchard's instructions to patrol deep inside enemy airspace, but were often intercepted long before they got to their intended patrol line. Army corps planes were flying in pairs to try and give each other some sort of protection, and despite Trenchard's orders, line patrols and direct escorts were a common feature of fighter operations. Common sense and sheer necessity were prevailing in the face of Trenchard's dogma. For all their efforts, the fighters were unable to offer much protection. Reduced aerial activity helped keep overall losses down, but loss rates were still steadily increasing. In August 1916, before the introduction of the Albatros, the RFC was suffering one casualty for every 295 combat hours flown. By December, this had increased to one casualty for every 133 hours.[33]

Trenchard was close to despair. His fears that he was being seen as scaremonger did not stop him maintaining a barrage of increasingly critical correspondence with Henderson and Brancker, which first Henderson and then Brancker began to find tiresome and insulting. Twice German fighter technology had surged forward, Trenchard maintained, first with the Fokker biplanes in the summer of 1916 and then the Albatros in the autumn, while his squadrons were still using the same planes they had started the Battle of the Somme with. He predicted 'enormous' losses if better equipment did not reach the front before the British spring offensive. Even in January and February with the weather limiting operations, losses were heavy. Once serious fighting began, he predicted every F.E.2, F.E.8 and D.H.2 in France would be 'wiped out'. Only a postponement of the offensive could save the RFC from disaster.[34] As spring approached, an increasingly desperate Trenchard urged the latest planes be rushed to the front even if they had not yet been properly tested.[35] Trenchard, apparently oblivious to the irritation his constant complaints were causing, was puzzled by the lack of response.[36]

Trenchard got Haig to weigh in with his support. The Army commander insisted that nothing should be allowed to stand in the way of increasing aircraft production and backed this by suggesting an order for 700 tanks be cancelled if that helped.[37] 'The seriousness of the situation cannot be overrated,' he warned. The reply was less than sympathetic.[38] Delays were blamed on Trenchard's insistence that planes be flown across the Channel rather than shipped. There was a hint of quiet satisfaction that poor weather had intervened to upset Trenchard's apparently sensible way of speeding up deliveries. Trenchard was accused of reducing his own strength by ordering certain squadrons to stay in Britain, even though they were ready to move to France. It turned out to be a Strutter squadron that Trenchard saw no point in having until it was equipped with something better.[39] Relations between France and London were collapsing. Trenchard's shrill demands were becoming increasingly counterproductive. Nevertheless, he was right about the disaster that was coming.

The lengthening casualty lists intensified Trenchard's growing sense of doom. RFC units escaped lightly in January 1917, but loss rates increased in February and by March, one casualty was being suffered for every 100 combat hours flown, the worst loss rate of the war so far. The Sopwith Strutter's fragility and lack of manoeuvrability was now being exposed with twenty lost in March.

The D.H.2 was also struggling. For a while, D.H.2 pilots could hope to achieve something against less experienced German pilots by exploiting the excellent manoeuvrability of their machine, but as the winter wore on, inexperienced German fighter pilots were becoming a rarity. Not even experienced D.H.2 pilots had much chance against the prowling Albatros.

With the tractor now firmly established as the most effective configuration, the arrival of the Royal Aircraft Factory F.E.8 pusher was almost an embarrassment. The first F.E.8 squadron, No. 40, arrived in August and a second, No. 41, in October. Initially, they seemed to be coping well. The two squadrons only lost three planes in combat in 1916, and on 22 October, No. 40 claimed no less than five enemy aircraft in one day. It seemed too good to last, and so it proved. Losses began rising in 1917, culminating in a disastrous mission on 9 March when nine F.E.8s of No. 40 Squadron were attacked by von Richthofen's Jasta. Four were shot down, four severely damaged and the ninth caught fire on landing.[40] The F.E.2s were now useless as fighters and used mostly for photo-reconnaissance, but even in this less demanding role, losses were rising.[41]

The need to replace the B.E.2 was becoming more urgent with each passing month, but the technical problems plaguing the new R.E.8 reconnaissance planes refused to go away. Production lines had been set up to mass produce the R.E.8 and large numbers of RAF 4a engines had been ordered to power it, long before the plane had been properly tested. Now, with large numbers rolling off the production lines, stories of the plane dropping out of the sky for no apparent reason were spreading like wildfire. Pilots were refusing to fly the plane even when threatened with court martial.[42] The press latched on to the story and the problems became very public with the cabinet demanding to know what was going on. It was not surprising the R.E.8 should cause problems for those used to the more forgiving B.E.2. Higher performance and greater capability inevitably meant aeroplanes that were more difficult to fly. If Trenchard wanted a plane that was capable of long-range reconnaissance, bombing and air combat, it could not possibly be as easy to fly as the B.E.2. Even so, the R.E.8 seemed a particularly difficult plane for the B.E.2 crews to graduate to, and even experienced crews were struggling. Trenchard insisted the problems were all in the mind and claimed that an unspecified squadron considered the plane 'faster and better' than the Nieuport 17, a claim surely born of frustration and desperation. Brancker was no more sympathetic. Trials, he insisted, had demonstrated that claims that the plane was unstable were 'rot'; it just needed 'good piloting', which might have been a reasonable expectation if the training programme had not been sending such inadequately trained pilots to the front to fly it.[43]

The alternative Armstrong Whitworth F.K.8, which had only been ordered in small numbers, had demonstrated that a more capable corps plane need not be such a handful to fly.[44] Even Trenchard was forced to admit the Armstrong Whitworth plane was the better machine, but with so much production capacity allocated to R.E.8 production, Weir, in charge of production, was reluctant to switch horses midstream. Apart from the airframes that had been built, there was the problem of what to do with the large numbers of RAF 4a engines pouring off the production lines. There were no other planes that used the engine. The F.K.8 airframe was tried with the Factory engine, but the result was even more unsatisfactory than the R.E.8.[45]

Weir predicted it would take five months to restore production levels if the R.E.8 was abandoned in favour of the Armstrong Whitworth. He desperately suggested the higher accident rate might be compensated for by the lower losses in combat, an argument that could not be expected to go down well with aircrews, who might reasonably expect the plane they were flying to be on their side. Production was halted while the plane's problems were investigated. Modifications, including a larger tailplane, were introduced and production was restarted, but very few would be available for the spring 1917 offensive[46] and there was no realistic alternative.[47] One interesting innovation that anticipated future developments was the use of the Nieuport fighters of No. 60 squadron in the low-level tactical[48] and photo-reconnaissance role.[49] The 'scout' concept had turned full circle with the fighters now carrying out their original high-speed reconnaissance role, but with the shortage of fighters this was hardly a solution. The only immediate practical remedy was simply not to expect so much of the B.E.2. Used for low-level and short-range observation, the plane was reasonably adequate.

While the R.E.8 struggled, the Bristol F2A exceeded expectations at every stage of its development. It would need to if it was to live up to its fighter tag. Trenchard fumed at the delays in getting the promised two squadrons to France. He wanted it as a fighter and told Brancker not to allow the fitting of cameras or bomb racks to delay deliveries.[50] The Bristol Fighter was the jewel in the crown as far as Trenchard was concerned. Still favouring the two-seater fighter, he was convinced the arrival of this powerful plane would come as a huge shock to the enemy. No. 48 Squadron finally reached France at the beginning of March, but it would be the only squadron to reach him before the Arras spring offensive. Trenchard jealously guarded his latest arrival. The squadron was to be held back until the eve of the offensive, before being let loose on an unsuspecting German air force.[51]

Exactly how two-seaters like the Bristol Fighter were supposed to be used as an air superiority fighter was the subject of much debate. Trials at Martlesham Heath seemed to support Trenchard's contention that the fixed forward-firing gun should be the principal weapon. The trials involved single-seaters engaging various two-seaters, including the Strutter, Armstrong Whitworth F.K.8, D.H.4 and the R.E.8. It was concluded that if the rear gun could be fixed to fire forward when required, to supplement the synchronised gun, then these 'light two-seaters' could be used 'almost as scouts', although this seemed a rather liberal interpretation of the actual results as two-seaters engaging single-seaters scarcely got a shot on target with their forward-firing guns. Nevertheless, training units in Britain were encouraging two-seater crews to fly their equipment aggressively. RFC HQ in France was having second thoughts and was sending out mixed messages on the role of the two-seater. It was argued there was little practical difference between a two-seater fighter-reconnaissance plane and a two-seater fighter. The latter could be used as aggressively as a single-seater, but both were also capable of 'sustaining a prolonged combat' by flying in formation.[52]

Meanwhile, the single-seaters Trenchard was relying on to regain technical parity with the Albatros were encountering unexpected problems. The first Sopwith Pups finally reached the RFC in December. It was immediately recognised by RFC pilots and German opponents as substantially superior to any previous British design. Considering the Sopwith Pup was only powered by an 80-hp engine, the fighter's performance was remarkable, but to achieve it, Sopwith had kept weight down to an absolute minimum, and there was soon good reason to believe they had gone too far. In December, a Pup suffered structural failure pulling out of a dive, killing the pilot. Brancker advised Trenchard that the problem could be solved with some strengthening, but this would inevitably affect performance. Trenchard insisted on no strengthening, and would take the Pup as it was. Pilots would have to work within the limitations of the plane—a desperate step to take.[53] Even in its somewhat fragile state, the Pup scarcely possessed the performance to be a long-term solution. With only an 80-hp engine, acceleration was inevitably sluggish, and the fighter would need every ounce of its excellent manoeuvrability to stay out of the Albatros' gun sights. At the beginning of March, there was a spate of heavy losses, including the loss of three No. 3 (Naval) Squadron pilots in a single day, raising fears that just three months after entering service, the Pup was already outclassed. Suddenly, the talk was of cutting back Pup production.[54]

The D.H.5 did not even make it to the front. The first batch of D.H.5 fighters suffered such excessive engine vibrations that plans to deploy the fighter operationally had to be suspended until the problem could be ironed out. Trenchard was able to acquire sixty Nieuports to compensate for the loss of the de Havilland fighter, but structural problems were also emerging with the French fighter. Early in 1917, there had been a series of incidents in which the wings of Nieuport fighters had buckled in flight. Pilots had managed to land their stricken planes successfully, but it was disconcerting to say the least, and certainly discouraged pilots from taking the fighter to its limits in combat.[55] On 28 March, the inevitable occurred and a pilot was killed as a result of structural failure. Just days before the launching of the spring offensive, confidence in the plane plummeted.[56]

The solid Spad, rated by Trenchard as his best fighter, had no such problems. When the Admiralty complained that their promise to divert Triplanes to the RFC was delaying their commitment to send four fighter squadrons to the front,

Trenchard jumped at the opportunity to allow the Admiralty to take delivery of all Triplanes in exchange for any Spads they had.[57] By the spring of 1917, however, the French were already conceding that the Spad 7 could not cope with the latest versions of the Albatros, and were rushing the Spad 13, powered by the latest 200-hp Hispano-Suiza engine, into production. While the French were preparing to move on to the next generation of fighter, Trenchard was grateful for any Spad 7s he could lay his hands on, and he had not even got his first S.E.5, the British equivalent of the Spad 7. The first of these were reaching RFC squadrons, just as the French were deciding their Spad 7 was no longer good enough. To make matters worse, British pilots soon came to the conclusion that the S.E.5 was inferior to the lighter Spad 7, especially in manoeuvrability and climb.[58] The British fighter was in even more need of the 200-hp Hispano-Suiza engine. Trials were already taking place and the more powerful engine considerably improved performance, but it would be some time before the British could expect to get hold of the French engine in numbers. The first S.E.5 squadron, No. 56, did not reach France until 8 April, the day before Haig was due to launch his offensive. The production version had the first semi-enclosed cockpit, which might have looked like an advanced feature, but added weight and restricted the pilots' view. Trenchard exploded when he saw what he described as a 'conservatory' covering the cockpit.[59] The squadron commander declared his squadron was non-operational until the cockpit canopies had been removed; production was suspended while these and other required modifications were introduced.[60]

For the Arras offensive, Trenchard had nothing like the twenty-one modern fighter squadrons he had been hoping for back in December. The RFC mustered one and a half Spad 7, three Nieuport 17, and two Sopwith Pup squadrons. The Navy had four of the promised five squadrons at the front, two on Triplanes and one each on Nieuport 17s and Pups. With the RNAS contribution, the British had just ten and a half effective single-seater fighters. The three squadrons of Strutters were still the best two-seater fighters flying operationally, although the first Bristol Fighter squadron was ready for its first mission. The rest of the single-seater fighter force was equipped with pushers—two D.H.2 squadrons, one with the F.E.8, and eight and a half squadrons with the F.E.2. There may have been doubts about the ability of the latest fighters to take on the Albatros, but they had far more chance than the F.E.2, F.E.8 and D.H.2.

Despite the heavy losses suffered by the RFC in March, Trenchard still believed that offensive patrols flown behind enemy lines would create the circumstances in which other planes could operate unescorted. Even long-range reconnaissance and bombing missions would only receive an indirect escort provided by fighters patrolling the general area of attack. The one exception was the B.E.2 when flown as a bomber. Even Trenchard would concede a close escort was justified for this plane, although this rather begged the question why the RFC should want to use the B.E.2 as a bomber in 1917.

With fifty squadrons and a front line strength of 891 machines, it was a much-expanded RFC that prepared to support Haig's resumption of the offensive in the spring of 1917. It was an air force that Trenchard knew was desperately short of up-to-date equipment, but he hoped that the handful of modern planes that had arrived would have an impact out of all proportion to their numbers.[61] Opposing this force, the Germans on the British front mustered just six fighter squadrons, increased to eight from 12 April, each with twelve machines and far fewer available at any given time. This tiny number of fighters was about to inflict carnage on the massive force that confronted them.

The Arras offensive was essentially no more than a large-scale diversion to draw German forces away from the front further south where Nivelle was hoping his French armies would achieve the decisive breakthrough. The British offensive was to be launched on 9 April and 3,000 guns were massed for a five-day pre-offensive barrage—nearly twice as many as had been used at the Somme. The preparatory air offensive began on 5 April and the time had come to unleash Trenchard's secret weapon, the Bristol Fighter. On its first mission, six set off in formation on an offensive patrol, which as squadron commander Hubbard had put it the previous summer, essentially involved 'waiting to be attacked'. The formation did not have to wait long. Albatros fighters accepted the challenge and four Bristol Fighters were shot down, while two survivors limped back to base badly damaged. It was a catastrophic operational debut. No. 59 Squadron also found flying in formation provided little security. On 6 April, the squadron sent a formation of R.E.8s on a photo-reconnaissance mission and lost three. On the same day, the 9th GHQ Wing, still trying to use its F.E.2s for offensive fighter patrols, sent out six F.E.2s to the Cambrai region. One returned with engine trouble and the remainder were shot out of the skies by Albatros fighters. A flight of F.E.2s from No. 11 Squadron carried out a reconnaissance mission with a protection flight of F.E.2s from No. 25 Squadron—one of the former and three of the latter were shot down. Again, the fighters were relying on formation flying and their combined firepower to slug it out with the enemy. In truth, the F.E.2 lacked the performance to be used any other way, but flying in formation could not provide the solution to the plane's vulnerability. Persisting with the two-seater pusher as a front line day fighter was simply wasting brave aircrews.

The Nieuport pilots were also suffering. On 7 April, a flight of six from No. 60 Squadron encountered Richthofen's Jasta and lost two with three more damaged. The squadron had five of its Nieuports shot down in three days. Ironically, the one aircraft that was making an impression on German pilots was the Sopwith Triplane, the plane Trenchard had handed over to the Navy. The fighter made such an impression that German aircraft manufacturers were ordered to copy the triplane configuration, which would eventually lead to the Fokker Dr.1. On 5 April, the RFC lost fifteen planes, and the next day, this rose to twenty-four. Poor weather brought some relief to the crews, but in the four days preceding the offensive, sixty-one planes did not return.[62] Nevertheless, on the eve of the ground assault, Trenchard remained confident that his tactics were correct. In a memorandum on 8 April, he reasserted that the aeroplane was essentially an offensive weapon and 'owing to the unlimited space in the free manoeuvring in three dimensions ... and the difficulty of one plane seeing another, no number of planes acting on the defensive will prevent a hostile pilot of initiative and determination from reaching his objective'.[63] However, apart from Trenchard's unshakeable belief that aggressive offence was always the best strategy, regardless of circumstances, there was no reason why patrols flying along a 75-mile perimeter 20 miles from the front line would be any more likely to see the enemy and stop him reaching his objective. Trenchard braced himself for heavy losses and Henderson warned the government to expect the worst.[64]

Once the offensive was underway, Trenchard seemed determined to put the most positive spin on events. He took comfort from the fact that fighters were suffering losses five times those of the corps planes. It was, for him, proof that the offensive tactics were working, and the number of victories his fighters were claiming was also encouraging. In the first eight days of April, the RFC claimed the destruction of thirty-one enemy aircraft with another fifty-three seen going down 'out of control'. Apparently buoyed by these successes, Trenchard seemed to have forgotten his previous predictions of impending disaster. Only the poor weather was saving the German air force, he insisted; he even found himself hoping for a long stretch of fine weather to ensure the German air force had no opportunity to recover from the mauling he was suddenly confident his RFC was inflicting.[65] Not even Trenchard appeared to realise that what he had so confidently predicted was coming to pass. The successes his squadrons were reporting were an illusion—the enemy aircraft going down 'out of control' were merely German pilots using their higher diving speed to escape. In these eight days, the German air force had lost only sixteen aircraft along the entire Western Front. It was the RFC that needed the respite poor weather might provide.

On 9 April, in poor weather with frequent snow showers, the infantry launched their assault on the German lines. Despite the heavy losses suffered by the corps squadrons in the build up to the offensive, the position of most batteries was known on the opening day of the assault and enemy fire was successfully suppressed. Despite the weather, planes were out in force, observing and directing artillery, and reporting on progress. This air support, along with more effective creeping barrages and artillery shell fuses sensitive enough to react to barbed wire, not to mention some poor visibility, helped the infantry make some good progress with advances of up to 4 miles on the northern sector by the end of the first day. The poor weather also kept the German air force away and only three RFC planes were lost. Indeed, throughout the rest of the month, low clouds and frequent snow and rainstorms would often limit aerial activity, but there was still sufficient fine weather for the Germans to inflict on the RFC its heaviest casualties of the war so far. Reasonable weather on 11 April saw losses jump to fifteen planes. For a force of over 800, this could not be considered excessive, and if the breakthrough on the ground had been achieved, such losses would have been insignificant; however, a breakthrough was not achieved. The northern thrust would not attempt to make more progress until the artillery moved up to support it, and the southern thrust, launched on 11 April, was immediately repulsed. In the air, as on the ground, a war of attrition was emerging in which acceptable losses in the short term became unsustainable as days stretched into weeks.

RFC losses on 11 April included five B.E.2s operating over the front as German fighter pilots showed a new determination to disrupt the corps plane and artillery combination. As the offensive wore on and the B.E.2s found it more difficult to operate, British artillery would become progressively less effective. Losses also included another two B.E.2s, carrying bombs instead of a gunner, attempting a raid on Cambrai, 20 miles behind the front line. Spads of No. 23 Squadron were supposed to provide indirect escort, but took-off forty minutes after the B.E.2s and arrived at Cambrai after the bombers had left the target area. After the experiences over the Somme the year before, using the B.E.2 as a day bomber seemed inexplicable.

Poor weather limited air operations on 12 April, but on the following day both sides were out in force. No. 59 Squadron flew a photo-reconnaissance mission with no less than six of its R.E.8s, only to have the entire formation wiped out by Albatros fighters. Trenchard felt obliged to pay the squadron a visit to restore morale, but how long Trenchard could sustain his struggling squadrons by sheer strength of personality was open to question.[66] Formation flying was not dominating airspace as theory demanded, and attempting to use two-seaters like single-seater fighters was even less likely to succeed. Newly arrived pilots had to be specifically ordered to ignore the emphasis home training units were putting on using two-seaters so aggressively.[67] When the conclusions from the two-seater versus single-seater fighter trials at Martlesham Heath reached RFC HQ in France late in April 1917, they were considered little short of heresy and far too dangerous to pass on to brigade commanders. Encouraging reconnaissance pilots to use the manoeuvring capability of their two-seaters to bring the synchronised gun into play seemed little short of lunacy to front line commanders attempting to deal with the Albatros fighter that none of their single-seaters could master.[68]

The day after the R.E.8 massacre, a formation of No. 60 Squadron Nieuports on an offensive patrol in the Douai region ran into Richthofen's Jasta and lost four fighters in eight minutes. The squadron would go on to lose thirteen pilots in ten days, forcing the commander to request the squadron be taken off offensive patrols to allow it time to recover. The Sopwith 1½ Strutters were also suffering. This once 'bloody fine fighter' was now 'more bloody than fine', as one patrol leader from No. 45 Squadron described it after four bullet-riddled survivors of a formation of seven limped home. For his troubles, he was sent home with reduced rank. The Strutter-equipped No. 43 Squadron, commanded by Major Douglas, a future commander of Fighter Command, suffered 100 per cent losses in a month.[69]

When offensive patrols encountered the enemy, losses were heavy, but very often patrols were returning home having encountered nothing. Either way, they seemed to be achieving little. Even Trenchard had to concede that they were being ignored. It was too easy for German fighter pilots to fly under them and go straight for the vulnerable corps planes, but if the RFC patrols flew lower, they would expose themselves to hit and run tactics by German fighters. On 15 April, Trenchard modified his all-out offensive approach by ordering a proportion of fighters to operate at lower altitudes closer to the corps planes. In fact, many squadrons were doing this already. Close escorts were also being used more, but the losses continued to mount. Plans to use the D.H.4 as a fighter had been quietly dropped, but even as a bomber, its excellent performance was not always enough. Three D.H.4 bombers were lost on 23 April along with two Nieuport escorts. The next day, three out of six F.E.2s of No. 20 Squadron were shot down while escorting a single Strutter on a photo-reconnaissance mission. The F.E.2 was as much in need of an escort as the Strutters they were supposed to be escorting. A flight of three B.E.2s—sent out on a bombing mission with no gunners or escort—was shot down by a single German fighter. Fortunately, the weather intervened to bring some relief to the British squadrons.

The continued use of the B.E.2 in the single-seater day-bomber role was not going unnoticed back home. An anonymous letter, apparently from a disgruntled aircrew, was circulating that laid bare the inadequacies of this plane in the bomber role. The letter described how the plane, weighed down by a couple of 112-lb bombs, struggled along at 50-60 mph and with no gunner was defenceless. Using such a plane as a day bomber was nothing short of 'pure murder'. Speaking in the House of Commons, Baird, the RFC Air Board's political representative, sought to quash these stories by emphatically denying the plane was used for bombing. Trenchard had to correct him. He apologetically claimed he had no choice but to use all the resources available to him to maintain the offensive which he still believed was pinning the German air force back.[70]

On the ground, the infantry on the southern wing of the offensive continued to inch their way forward, still trying to catch up with the initial rapid progress of the now stalled northern wing. RFC squadrons continued to provide support as best they could, but they were paying a heavy price. It was not the dramatic massacre Trenchard had warned of, but the cumulative effect was the same. The tragedy unfolding in the skies was brought home to Trenchard by the loss on 29 April of Harvey-Kelly, the squadron commander of the Spad-equipped No. 19 Squadron and a personal friend, who he had been planning to have dinner with that day. After waiting at the airfield for his return, he was eventually forced to accept the inevitable—the entire flight had disappeared. In all, twenty planes were lost that day. 'Another bad day,' Trenchard recorded.[71] F.E.2s were still being used for patrols over the front line, three from one formation being shot down early on the morning of 30 April. Five Nieuports and three Sopwith Triplanes would also be lost this day. By this time, the S.E.5s of No. 56 Squadron had become operational, but its pilots found the new fighter was no match for the Albatros, especially at altitude.[72] On the last two days of the month, thirty-five planes had been lost.

So ended what would become known as 'Bloody April'. In just one month over 270 RFC and RNAS aircraft failed to return. Many more crashed on return or were so badly damaged they had to be written off. In terms of loss rate, it was the worst month of the war so far, with one casualty for every ninety-two hours flown.[73] The B.E.2 (sixty-nine lost) and F.E.2 (seventy lost) suffered the most heavily.[74] Depressing as these figures were, the true scale of the defeat was not appreciated at the time. With pilots constantly reporting that they were being engaged by twenty to thirty enemy fighters, RFC HQ was convinced they were witnessing a titanic struggle with a numerically superior enemy. In such circumstances, heavy losses were perhaps inevitable. In fact, the losses had been inflicted by a fighter force that rarely possessed more than fifty serviceable machines. If the opposing forces had been more equally matched numerically and the weather had stayed fine, it would have been far worse.

Some consolation appeared to be provided by the heavy losses the RFC had inflicted on the Germans. Some 126 German machines were claimed as destroyed with another 206 seen to be diving away 'out of control', making 332 claimed for the month. With seventy French claims, German losses appeared to have risen to over 400. However, even discounting planes diving away 'out of control', the number claimed destroyed was grossly exaggerated. Total German losses on both British and French fronts for the entire month were less than 100 planes.[75] Trenchard took some comfort from the fact that the German air force had not been able to operate over the front line to the extent the RFC had, but even this contained an element of delusion. With high ground to observe British positions, the German Army did not have to rely on low-level tactical reconnaissance.

The heavy losses the RFC suffered might have been a price worth paying if a decisive victory had been won, but it had not. The horror in the air had been matched by the casualties on the ground, with another 150,000 men lost. The huge sacrifice in airmen and infantry had achieved nothing, nor had the sacrifice paved the way for a French victory further south. Nivelle's offensive on the Aisne proved to be a catastrophic disaster. On sectors of the French front, soldiers began refusing to obey any more senseless orders to advance. The French Army was mutinying.

Back in Britain, Haig's own costly and apparently pointless offensives were the subject of increasing criticism. The nation had been hardened by three years of war, but the sheer scale of the brutality still managed to shock. Lloyd George was reluctant to send Haig the reinforcements he was demanding for fear that they would be swallowed up in more futile attempts to advance. In nearly three years of war, the British Army had suffered enormous losses and had got nowhere. There had to be a better way of winning the war.

CHAPTER 8

The Brave New World of Strategic Bombing

The Admiralty believed they knew what that better way was. The plight of the British Army demonstrated how right they had been all along to oppose a full-scale military intervention on mainland Europe. The British Army was hopelessly bogged down in an apparently never ending war of attrition and suffering losses on a scale that not even the most pessimistic critics had foreseen. Not that the Admiralty alternative strategy had proven any more decisive. After three years of war, the naval blockade was no nearer to defeating Germany than the British Army in France, although it had at least been less costly in human lives. There was also the hope that the long-range bomber might speed up the process.

Developing the equipment for a strategic bombing offensive was not proving easy. It was December 1915 before the prototype Handley Page O/100 'Paralyser' flew, more than a year after work started on the design. Development of the Short Bomber, ordered as an interim, was no quicker.[1] Early in 1916, the only effective bomber available to the Admiralty was the Sopwith Strutter. In its single-seater bomber configuration, it could only carry four 65-lb bombs, and to give it a reasonable range, it normally only flew with two. A rudimentary bombing-aiming device was installed in the floor of the machine, but it was extremely difficult for the pilot to line up the target.[2] It did not look like a war winner, but at the beginning of 1916 it was the best bomber available.

Meanwhile, the Germans were taking the initiative with their own long-range bombing campaign. On the night of 19–20 January 1915, Zeppelins dropped their first bombs on British soil. The raid and reaction of the defence were to be typical of many subsequent airship attacks. The two planes that took off to intercept the giant airships made no contact with the enemy. At least one Zeppelin became hopelessly lost, claiming that King's Lynn and various villages in the region were military targets. Four people were killed and sixteen injured, the first casualties in a campaign that was to last the best part of four years. The Kaiser was initially reluctant to attack London,[3] but on the night of 31 May–1 June the first bombs fell on the capital, killing seven and injuring thirty-five. An alarmed government banned any newspaper comment beyond official government statements.[4] These raids may not have been on the scale, nor had the cataclysmic consequences some pre-war experts had predicted, but the marauding airships had a depressing effect on the civilian population. The mere report of an airship brought factories to a halt across entire swathes of the country, seriously reducing production. While many airship missions failed to inflict any damage or casualties, a sufficient number found a target to ensure the death toll steadily mounted.

There was also the occasional bloody reminder of how serious the threat could be. On the night of 13–14 October 1915, seventy-one were killed and 128 injured in London. On the night of 31 January–1 February 1916, another seventy were killed and 113 injured.[5] The inability of the home defence forces to shoot down these raiders caused much resentment. The civil population vented their rage not just on the government, but any local inhabitants who seemed even vaguely German, and there were inevitable demands for retaliation against German cities. If the government had any doubts about the strength of public concern, the victory of Pemberton-Billing in a March 1916 by-election, standing as an independent and campaigning solely on the air defence issue, made public feelings very clear.[6] There were no angry mobs marching on Buckingham Palace or parliament, but the government could not be so sure the public would continue to air their grievances solely through the ballot box. Stopping the Zeppelins was a very high government priority.

The effort and ingenuity thrown into the task were impressive. The wireless transmissions from incoming Zeppelins were tracked by naval direction finding stations and the intersection of bearings from different stations revealed the airship's position. This was, on occasion, good enough to allow warships to be sent on an intercept course to engage the Zeppelins with seaplanes or anti-aircraft guns before they reached the coast and were still flying in daylight. Zeppelins only approached the coast after sunset and from this point onwards they observed radio silence. Sightings from anti-aircraft batteries and police stations were passed on by direct telephone lines to the Admiralty, which in turn had direct lines with the airfields. This information enabled air raid warnings to be more selective, reducing disruption to industry, but interception proved impossible. Seaplanes launched from ships in the North Sea could not climb fast enough to intercept by day, and by night, pilots were reluctant to patrol anywhere other than over their own airfield. Fighters did not usually take off until the Zeppelin could be heard approaching, which was usually too late. Even those fighters that did reach the altitude of the intruder found the Zeppelin captain always had the option of dropping ballast and climbing far faster than the struggling fighters could manage. To make matters worse, all the favoured means of attack such as bombs, grapnels and explosive darts required the attacking fighter to fly higher than the Zeppelin. The only success was when a RNAS plane operating from Dunkirk on a bombing mission encountered a returning Zeppelin by chance and used its bombs to destroy it. It was, however, a success the home defence squadrons were unable to replicate.

With the departure of Churchill in May 1915, the Admiralty became less enthusiastic about its air defence role and keen to pass the responsibility back to the War Office. As anxious as the War Office was to recover a responsibility it believed had always been rightfully theirs, with its commitments on the Western Front, the Army was in no great rush to take on what appeared to be a hopeless task. Efforts to intercept nine Zeppelins in the 31 January–1 February raid seemed to illustrate the futility of even trying. Fourteen RFC and eight RNAS aircraft took off in appalling weather; no success was achieved while six of the intercepting planes were lost and seven damaged in accidents with two pilots killed. It was the last effort under Admiralty control. In February 1916, the War Office formally took over primary responsibility for air defence, but with the Somme offensive approaching, it was not the top Army priority.

The reluctance of either service to tackle the air defence issue underlined the need for some sort of overarching organisation to take responsibility for air matters. The retaliation some were calling for was also not necessarily an Admiralty or War Office responsibility. With the constant squabbling between the two departments over resources and their own complaints about unnecessary duplication, it was not surprising many were suggesting the solution was an air force independent of both the Army and Navy. Lord Sydenham, an ex-secretary of the CID and advocate of long-range bombing, wanted an independent air arm 'under the direct orders of the government'.[7] So too did Lord Montagu, one of the notable pre-war prophets of doom. Even Sueter was calling for an independent air force, making himself so unpopular with the Admiralty that he was replaced by Vaughan-Lee as the commander of the Naval Air Service.[8] At cabinet level, Lord Curzon agreed with the logic, but was on balance against a merger of the two air services in the middle of a war, but he believed a ministry, with fully fledged executive powers, or at least a board with strong recommendatory powers, should be created to co-ordinate air matters.[9] There was little enthusiasm for even this among his cabinet colleagues, but Hankey suggested the pre-war Air Committee should be revived; the result was the Joint War Air Committee. It was the first of a series of committees and boards, each of which would be bitterly opposed by the Admiralty and eventually defeated by Admiralty intransigence, only to be replaced by a body with the greater powers the Admiralty did not want to surrender. These successive committees progressively introduced a stronger political element into the debate. Politicians were not just worried about public opinion; air power also offered an alternative way of ending a war that had already lasted far longer than anyone had anticipated. The growing number of members from the pro-bombing lobby appointed to these air committees was a strong indication of the way the government was leaning, and the enthusiasm with which the Admiralty was presenting the case for long-range bombing could only encourage this inclination.

The Joint War Air Committee was set up under the Earl of Derby to establish the roles of the two services, the relative importance of these roles, and the resources that each should get. Sueter and Vaughan-Lee represented the Admiralty and Henderson the War Office. Lord Montagu also joined the committee as an additional adviser. Most of the committee's brief existence was spent attempting to maximise air resources for the forthcoming Somme offensive, but Derby did float the idea of a long-range bomber force independent of the Army and Navy—an idea that was roundly rejected by all except the maverick Sueter.[10] After six weeks of inter-service bickering, Derby resigned, claiming that without any executive power it was impossible to achieve anything. Curzon had a go with a more high-powered Air Board and was joined by Lord Sydenham, Brancker and the Third Sea Lord, Rear Admiral Tudor, who replaced the out of line and out of favour Sueter. The House of Commons also had its own representative, the MP Major Baird. Curzon emphasised the importance of a long-range bomber force and repeated Derby's suggestion that it be independent of both services. The Admiralty and War Office agreed that it was important, but Henderson insisted such a force had to be under Army command. Furthermore, it could only be created after the Army's tactical air requirements had been met. The Admiralty did not begrudge the War Office having its own bomber force; indeed, Vaughan-Lee felt the more RFC participation the better. Balfour believed it was the duty of the War Office to play its part in a bombing campaign, taking on targets that affected the land battle while the Admiralty took on targets that affected the war at sea.[11] If the Admiralty appeared to be monopolising long-range bombing, he claimed it was only because the War Office was failing to develop its own bombing strategy.

The issue that divided the services was essentially one of priority. The War Office was not willing to neglect the needs of the Army to construct a long-range bomber force whereas the Admiralty was convinced there was an overwhelming case for getting the bomber offensive under way as soon as possible. As far as the Admiralty was concerned, the Zeppelin raids were ample proof of the success of long-range bombing. Vaughan-Lee raged at the 'absurd' War Office position that airship raids were of no military value. They were clearly damaging the British war effort by slowing down munitions output and in a 'thousand other ways'. Tapping into the potential political need and popular desire for revenge, Vaughan-Lee insisted there were only two ways of dealing with the Zeppelin threat: anti-aircraft guns and 'a definite policy of Retaliation', with a capital 'R' adding ominous emphasis. It was the latter that Vaughan-Lee considered to be the most likely to succeed. 'An organised and systematic attack on the German at home' would restrict Zeppelin activities and 'have an immense moral effect on Germany itself'. Curzon agreed: 'An aggressive retaliatory policy is of the first importance and the air fleet should be created which will carry it out.' The political need for retaliation dovetailed neatly with the naval economic argument for bombing.

Interception was not mentioned as a way of stopping the Zeppelin, but given the lack of success so far achieved this was hardly surprising. It seemed that airships, and by extension any long-range bombers, were and would continue to be immune to defences. Destroying airships on the ground or the factories which built them seemed the only alternative, and the sooner Britain launched an offensive against these targets the better. Vaughan-Lee was so anxious to get a 'sustained offensive' going, he recommended naval air resources be switched from anti-submarine coastal reconnaissance squadrons, nor should bombs be wasted on U-boat bases in Belgium. All effort should be focused on targets in Germany.[12]

For the Admiralty, the Somme offensive was a frustrating distraction from the main task. 'Further delays are dangerous to the whole course of the war and action should be taken forthwith,' Vaughan-Lee warned.[13] So sure was the Admiralty of the correctness of the long-range bombing strategy, there was a general feeling the War Office was only objecting to Admiralty plans because the Army was not ready to launch a strategic offensive of its own and did not want the Navy 'to have the honour' of doing it first.[14] It was a complete misreading of War Office motives. They wanted to control the long-range bomber force so that it did not get a priority they felt it did not deserve.

On the eve of the Somme offensive, Trenchard came over from France to make an impassioned personal appeal to Curzon's Board for more support from the Admiralty. He read a statement from Haig emphasising that 'Admiralty plans for a RNAS long-distance bombing are regarded as having secondary military importance and inferior military effect.'[15] The Admiralty was forced to concede and Trenchard got his Strutters, but the naval representatives vented their frustration. They insisted that War Office priorities were at the heart of the problems facing Britain and the entire British war policy was flawed. The whole idea of a British Army involved in a continental war was a major mistake. Tudor was already thinking ahead to a post-war situation where there would be no massive conscript Army and no need to build a tactical air force to support it. The air resources freed would enable the Admiralty to develop a long-range strategic bomber capability the country needed. The power of the offence was important, he insisted, and someone had to develop an offensive air capability. If the War Office wanted to, that was fine, but if no one else was going to do it, the Admiralty would.[16] Talks were held with the French on their long-range bombing plans in secret, so as not to arouse the wrath of the War Office. In a further subterfuge, it was suggested the French might be persuaded to make a formal request for RNAS air support on their sector of the front, which would provide a perfect pretext for sending bomber squadrons to eastern France.[17]

Captain Elder, who was to command the proposed naval bomber force, represented the Admiralty in these talks. He ascertained that under the direction of Bares, the French air force commander and a passionate advocate of long-range bombing, the French did indeed have a well thought out strategic plan and were happy to have the RNAS join them.[18] These discussions did not stay secret for very long, provoking another acrimonious exchange of memos between the War Office and Admiralty.[19] However, with the War Office showing no interest in an immediate bombing offensive, Curzon felt he had little choice but to abandon plans for an independent bomber force and let the Admiralty get on with it. The first naval planes arrived in eastern France in July 1916, but it would be October before a sufficient number had been assembled to open the offensive.[20] In the meantime, to pep up support for a bombing campaign, the Admiralty invited Bares to come to London and speak to the Air Board. The French air force commander conjured up a frightening picture of future wars being decided by the systematic bombing of towns and cities. The bomber could also act as a very effective deterrent, the general suggested. The bombing of German cities on the same day as a Zeppelin attack or submarine outrage would soon bring home to the German people the futility of waging war in this way.[21]

There was a contradiction in this line of thinking, which would become a familiar flaw in long-range bombing strategies. Using a weapon as a deterrent relied on the enemy taking the initiative with some heinous act. Using it to win a war relied on using it regardless of enemy actions, which necessarily meant abandoning its deterrent value, indeed inviting the sort of counterattack it might have deterred. It could not be used for both attack and deterrent.

Haig was furious that the Admiralty and Air Board were consulting the French commander on 'the future aerial policy to be pursued in France'. 'I am not aware aerial policy in France is an Admiralty responsibility,' Haig snarled. He put Bares' views down to 'enthusiasm for his own particular service rather than sound military judgement', and doubted the British Government would ever resort to terrorising civilian populations as a means of waging war. Haig insisted that only 'decisive victory over the enemy's forces in the field' could bring the war to a victorious conclusion.[22] The War Office passed on Haig's memo to the Admiralty with a sharp note expecting them to make it clear to their air service that any RNAS units in eastern France would be under Haig's command.[23] The Admiralty simply ignored the note. However, the tide was turning against the pro-bombing naval lobby. For a start, the political need for a retaliatory capability was suddenly no longer so strong. The Zeppelins had been defeated.

Success had come rather suddenly. Initially, the air defences under Army command had no more success shooting down the German airships than the Navy. The short summer nights brought a welcome pause in the raids and gave the War Office time to take stock of the situation. The B.E.2c was selected as the standard night fighter. It was slow but the extreme stability of the plane, which had been its undoing in the fighting in France, made it ideal for night flying, and no great manoeuvrability or speed was required to engage an airship.

Gradually, pilots became more confident of their night flying skills and no longer felt the need to restrict patrols to the immediate vicinity of the airfield they were operating from. Squadrons began patrolling a belt parallel to the coast, 30 miles behind the coastal observer cordon. With the airships travelling at around 45 mph, this gave the defending fighters sufficient time to climb to a reasonable operating altitude. Explosive bullets were developed, their illegality now of little concern to anyone. Rifle-calibre bullets could only contain a tiny quantity of explosive, but it was just about enough to ignite hydrogen gases, even if they were protected by a layer of inert gas. With incendiary-tracer bullets, pilots could see where their fire was going and increase the chance of igniting the escaping hydrogen.[24] With an upward-firing machine gun as the main weapon, interceptors would no longer have to climb above the airship to drop the assortment of weapons they had previously carried, and airships were much easier to spot from below against a clear sky than they were from above.

Even these advances did not bring immediate success, and doubts continued to grow about whether the defending fighters would ever bring an airship down. However, on the night of 2-3 September 1916, a B.E.2, flown as a single-seater by Lieutenant Robinson, was able to climb into a position to attack the airship SL11 with the new explosive and incendiary-tracer ammunition. Two attempts at spraying the length of the airship with machine-gun fire had no effect, but on his third attempt, Robinson concentrated his fire on one spot. The gas inside ignited and within seconds the airship had become a blazing inferno, visible for miles around. Londoners rejoiced as they watched the doomed airship crash to the ground and the crews of six other Zeppelins in the area could only look on in horror as they witnessed their comrades' fate. In the next four raids, no less than five of the twenty-nine Zeppelins that crossed the coast were destroyed. The Zeppelin attacks were suspended and the first 'Battle of Britain' had been won.[25]

The long-range bomber's retaliatory capability was no longer required and the Admiralty began to pay the price for their uncooperative attitude. Curzon came down firmly on the side of the War Office in recommending that any long-range bomber force based in France should be under the control of the Army commander in the theatre and only created when that commander considered the Army's primary tactical requirements had been met.[26] Vaughan-Lee found himself conducting a desperate rear-guard action. He insisted the naval bombers were already making a significant contribution to the Army cause by forcing the Germans to divert fighter squadrons from the front to the rear. In any case, the Admiralty could not possibly let the French down by withdrawing so soon after committing to support their air offensive. He even managed to get Trenchard to agree to the naval bombers staying in eastern France, albeit at the price of a promise to provide the reinforcements the RFC so urgently needed for the Arras offensive.[27]

In a bold counterattack and a brazen distortion of the truth; Tudor even claimed the bombers had to stay in eastern France as the War Office wanted them to bomb German blast furnaces. It transpired that this referred merely to a letter from a Belgian agent who had identified blast furnaces which he felt could be bombed. He had sent the letter to an uninterested War Office and they had casually passed it on to the Admiralty.[28] It was hardly surprising Curzon was losing patience with the Sea Lords. His frustration poured out in a final report accompanying his resignation, in which he castigated the Admiralty for their total lack of co-operation. Tudor, the leading Admiralty representative on the board, had not even bothered to turn up to half the meetings, and when he did appear, he insisted he did not have the authority to express definitive opinions. One of Curzon's final recommendations was that this problem be solved by creating an Admiralty Fifth Sea Lord responsible for aviation, paralleling the War Office Directorate of Military Aeronautics, ensuring any future Air Board would have a single empowered authority to deal with.[29]

Meanwhile, the RNAS 3rd Wing in eastern France was launching its strategic air offensive. Bares' gruesome vision of future war seemed somewhat at odds with the capabilities of the aircraft available. Both the Admiralty and the French were placing great faith in high-speed bombers carrying relatively small bomb loads. The early success of 20-lb bombs in the Zeppelin attacks tended to give a misleading idea of the damage tiny bombs could achieve. Large targets full of highly combustible hydrogen gas would prove to be a rare combination. Elder believed the ideal day bomber was a small two-seater, capable of defending itself. Two 65-lb bombs were perfectly adequate and in no circumstances should the bomb load be increased to the detriment of performance.[30] Future advocates of long-range bombing, with far more advanced planes at their disposal, would be equally guilty of overestimating the destructive capabilities of the bomber.

The first missions by the joint Franco/RNAS bombing force were flown in October 1916. The French had identified the Saar-Lorraine-Luxembourg regions as the only industrial zone within range of existing bombers. Lorraine was a region the French considered rightfully their territory and Luxembourg was an occupied country, so most of the bombs would be falling on supposedly friendly populations.[31] Even if attacks on targets in this limited region were successful, it was scarcely a plan that was likely to have a decisive effect on overall German output. In the first operation on 12 October, fifteen RNAS bombers, mostly Strutters and a few Breguet pushers borrowed from the French, together with sixteen French bombers, all escorted by around twenty fighters, set off in daylight to bomb the Mauser factory in Oberndorf. It was a triumph for the German defences and a disaster for the Anglo-French force, with six French and three British bombers failing to return. The French immediately switched to bombing at night, although the failure of some of the bombers to bomb the right town in daylight did not auger well for the continuation of the offensive by night.

The RNAS squadrons persevered by day, but late autumn was not the best time to begin such an offensive. By the end of the year, some eighty sorties in nine raids had been flown.[32] The aircrews were convinced they were succeeding. With only basic air defences in place, bombing could take place from low altitudes and the pilots brought back enthusiastic reports of direct hits.[33] By the New Year, however, the writing was on the wall for the force. In the end, it was not pressure from the War Office that brought about its downfall, it was a change of policy within the Admiralty. In December 1916, Lloyd George took over from Asquith as Prime Minister, and in his new government, Carson took Balfour's place. Curzon's recommendation of a Fifth Sea Lord was reluctantly accepted by the Admiralty, but the post went to Godfrey Paine, not Balfour's close ally Vaughan-Lee. Jellicoe took over from Jackson as the First Sea Lord and Beatty replaced Jellicoe as commander of the Grand Fleet.[34] The new team believed naval aircraft had better things to do than scatter 65-lb bombs on the German munitions industry.

It was the beginning of a long overdue reappraisal of naval air policy. In the enthusiasm for the development of a long-range bomber force, the tactical use of aviation to support the fleet had been almost entirely forgotten. As Asquith's private secretary once noted when commenting on Sueter's proposals to create an independent air force:

> The military wing is a success largely because it has been developed and trained as a branch of the Army and with military objects strictly in view. The naval wing is a failure because it has not been designed for naval objectives ... What is wanted is to make the naval wing more naval, not more 'aerial'.[35]

In the Battle of Jutland (31 May–1 June 1916), the only major naval encounter in the war, the RNAS played virtually no part. There was a seaplane carrier attached to both Jellicoe's Battle Fleet and Beatty's Battle Cruiser Fleet, but Jellicoe contrived to leave port without his and Beatty ordered his seaplane carrier to fly just one sortie during the entire engagement. The plane successfully sighted and radioed back the movement of German naval units, but the information never reached Beatty.[36] It was all in very stark contrast to the extensive use of aviation in the Battle of the Somme a month later.

Naval ideas about how air power should be used were now changing rapidly. On 21 January, Beatty reported the air resources available to the fleet were 'insufficient to enable the full use to be made of this new Arm, which has such great possibilities'. It seemed remarkably late in the war to come to this conclusion. Beatty wanted not just better seaplane carriers, but also aircraft carriers that could carry reconnaissance planes to spot for the fleet, fighters to deal with the German Navy's reconnaissance Zeppelins, and torpedo bombers to strike the German fleet in port. He also wanted more shore-based long-range seaplanes to patrol the North Sea. He noted disapprovingly 'only a small proportion of RNAS is employed upon naval air service' and wanted all naval personnel not supporting the fleet redeployed.[37] That meant not just the RNAS squadrons attached to the RFC at the front, but the 3rd Bomber Wing in eastern France. Not so long ago, Vaughan-Lee had been suggesting coastal naval squadrons be redeployed as long-range bombers. Now the process was in reverse.

On 1 February 1917, the urgency increased when the German Government declared that any merchant shipping in the seas around the British Isles, no matter what its country of origin, could expect to be sunk without warning. The U-boats were soon taking their toll, with shipping losses doubling in February. Surveillance of British coastal waters would be a crucial part of the anti-submarine campaign, and bombing their bases in Belgium was now the priority, not targets in Germany. Haig assured Paine the naval bombers had not caused any redeployment of German fighters nor weakened the German Army in any way,[38] and in March, the Naval 3rd Wing was recalled to Dunkirk to reinforce the naval attacks on U-boat bases in Belgium.

The withdrawal of the RNAS force was briefly delayed by the British Government for one further operation. German U-boats had torpedoed two British hospital ships and naval bombers were instructed to bomb the centre of Freiburg as a reprisal. On 14 April, fifteen British and six French bombers dropped two and a half tons of bombs on the most heavily populated area of the city. Given the cold blooded purpose of the operation, casualties were surprisingly light, with twelve dead and eighteen injured, but for the first time British aircraft had deliberately aimed their bombs at civilians.[39] Lloyd George's government seemed to be embracing this new brutal aspect of war.

Just as the naval bomber force was being withdrawn from France, the first generation of heavy bombers were becoming operational. The first mission by the interim single-engine Short Bomber was against Zeebrugge on the night of 15 November, with each bomber carrying eight 65-lb bombs. The Handley Page O/100 flew its first mission from eastern France on 16–17 March dropping twelve 100-lb bombs on a railway station. Neither would now have much opportunity to operate against the targets in Germany they had been designed to attack.

It was all very disappointing for the advocates of strategic bombing. They could blame the poor results on the weather and argue that the naval force had been denied the opportunity to demonstrate what it could do with the more capable bombers that were beginning to arrive. However, there was a realisation that the damage being inflicted was relatively light and the argument for maintaining an air offensive was moving from the damage it would inflict on the enemy to the resources it would divert. It was a reasonable argument, provided the resources poured into the offence did not exceed those the enemy was forced to switch to defence. With huge and expensive Handley Page bombers joining the offensive, it was an argument that would become increasingly difficult to sustain.

When Cowdray's Second Air Board took over from Curzon's board in January 1917, one of its tasks was to consider an independent air strategy and whether an independent Air Service and Air Ministry would be required to deliver it. However, under the Admiralty's new leadership, long-range bombing was not a priority, and with the Navy focusing on the U-boat threat, the Army preparing for its Arras offensive, and no Zeppelins to concern the government, the question of an independent air force was shelved. The new board would be responsible for releasing specifications for the planes required by both services and for placing orders. Organising production was to be left in the hands of the Munitions Ministry. William Weir, an experienced industrialist whose own companies had been involved in the licence production of aircraft for the Royal Aircraft Factory, was included on the new board as the Ministry of Munitions representative. The task facing him was enormous. Aircraft production depended on engine production. Raising the strength of the RFC to the required 106 squadrons (eighty-six in France, ten home defence and ten overseas), making good losses and meeting naval and other requirements would require 2,000 engines a month. Existing monthly output was around 600.[40] Just meeting the tactical needs of the Army and Navy was going to be challenging enough, without the complication of creating a long-range bomber fleet. Weir set himself the target of achieving the required 2,000 engines a month by the end of the year.

More resources were poured into the aircraft industry, and to get better value for money, the number of types of aircraft and engines on order were reduced and the size of contracts increased. Teams of inspectors toured factories advising on ways in which efficiency might be improved, but whether these steps would be enough to treble engine production in twelve months was another matter.

The best engines available were the Rolls-Royce Falcon and Eagle. They were both beautifully engineered, wonderfully reliable, and the soundness of the basic designs ensured considerable development potential. Rolls-Royce had adopted the simple expedient of running their engines at higher power levels until a component failed and then strengthening or redesigning that component. The results were spectacular with the 225-hp Eagle I eventually producing 375 hp as the Eagle VIII, and the 190-hp Falcon I emerging as the 275-hp Falcon III.[41] The problem was that these engines were handmade, the products of skilled craftsmen. The whole ethos of Rolls-Royce was the maintenance of the company's reputation for high-quality products at the expense of quantity. There was no 'mass production' culture, parts were not standardised, and no two engines were necessarily the same. As a result, repairs could not always be carried out in the field and engines had to be returned to the Derby factory. The plant was soon overwhelmed with repair work. The company was also reluctant to allow their engines to be built under licence. Only their own craftsmen could achieve the required level of precision, Rolls-Royce insisted. The company was not going to have their reputations tainted by workers they had no control over. Even subcontracting the production of engine parts was problematic. Rolls-Royce developed atrocious relations with subcontractors as they insisted on a standard of quality the subcontractors, and indeed Weir, did not always consider necessary. It also made their engines very expensive. Frustration with Rolls-Royce was so intense that when the company suggested the acquisition of a new factory would allow them to build an additional 250 Eagle engines a month, the proposal was turned down.[42]

Weir did not feel he needed Rolls-Royce. Excellent alternative British designs seemed to be emerging, engines which were not only powerful, but also easy to mass produce and far cheaper than Rolls-Royce power plants. In January 1917, the Beardmore–Halford–Pullinger BHP and the Sunbeam Arab liquid-cooled engines seemed extremely promising. Both were expected to produce at least 200 hp and were considered superior to Rolls-Royce engines. Thousands were ordered and it was these engines that Weir hoped would enable him to hit his targets.

Meanwhile on the home front, there was the odd reminder that the danger of air attack still existed. On 28 November, a German naval plane flew up the Thames Estuary in broad daylight and dropped six light bombs on central London, injuring ten people. Twenty-two planes took off to intercept, but none made contact. It was a timely warning that London was still vulnerable. Over the next six months, German aircraft restricted themselves to occasional attacks on coastal towns and shipping targets. On the night of 6–7 May 1917, an intrepid German Army officer set off in a reconnaissance plane for London where he dropped four 22-lb bombs, killing one person. If the pilot expected to be praised for his daring exploit, he was to be disappointed. His superiors were furious at this unauthorised demonstration of initiative. They were planning a far more ambitious assault, not under the cover of darkness, but in broad daylight. The last thing the German air force wanted was for the air defences of London to be alerted.

On 25 May 1917, twenty-three Gotha G IV medium bombers, each carrying 660-lbs of bombs, set course for London. The new German bomber was an impressive machine, capable of cruising at an altitude of 15,000 feet, a very challenging altitude for the interceptors that opposed it. Poor weather prevented the bombers from reaching their primary target, so the German formation turned south and bombed Folkestone instead. Ninety-five people were killed and 195 injured—a higher number of casualties than in any airship raid. There was fury in the town at the failure to provide any warning. Public meetings were called and enquiries called for, but there were no demands for the overthrow of the British Government and certainly no suggestion of surrendering to the perpetrator of these atrocities. Instead, there were just demands that German towns be bombed in retaliation.

For the defenders, the first Gotha raid had been a catalogue of errors. It was only twenty minutes after the *Tongue* lightship transmitted information on the approaching formation that RFC planes were scrambled to intercept and the

1 Dunne's remarkable tailless 'flying wing' biplane. The sweptback wings helped achieve exceptional stability, but severely limited the plane's ability to manoeuvre. Dunne was later involved in the Westland 'Pterodactyl' flying wing designs of the Twenties and Thirties, which relied on the same principles.

2 The French Henri Farman pusher was one of the first planes to be armed with a machine gun. The planes were delivered to the RFC with the passenger behind the pilot, but the positions were switched to give the gunner the nose position and a wide field of fire.

3 A Bleriot XII monoplane and similar to the plane used to make the first cross-Channel flight. Examples acquired by the War Office tended to be accident prone. (*P. R. Hare*)

4 A Bleriot monoplane 'repaired' by the Royal Aircraft Factory. The tractor monoplane had been transformed into a pusher biplane. The 'repair' became the S.E.1 and the Factory's first design. With its Wright Flyer-style forward elevator, it was technically a step backwards and the plane was a failure. (*P. R. Hare*)

5 The Cody II. Cody used the same basic configuration with Wright Flyer-style forward elevators for most of his designs. By the time his design won the 1912 military aircraft competition, this configuration was looking decidedly dated. (*P. R. Hare*)

6 An early Royal Aircraft Factory B.E.2. The Factory biplane represented a much more advanced approach to aeroplane design. (*P. R. Hare*)

Left: 7 The nose of the pusher was the ideal position for a gunner firing forwards, but defending the plane from attack from the rear required agility and nerve as demonstrated by the gunner of this F.E.2d. (*Imperial War Museum*)

Below: 8 Two engines provided more power and made it easier to have gunners firing forwards and backwards, which led to fighters like the three-seater Royal Aircraft Factory F.E.4. (*P. R. Hare*)

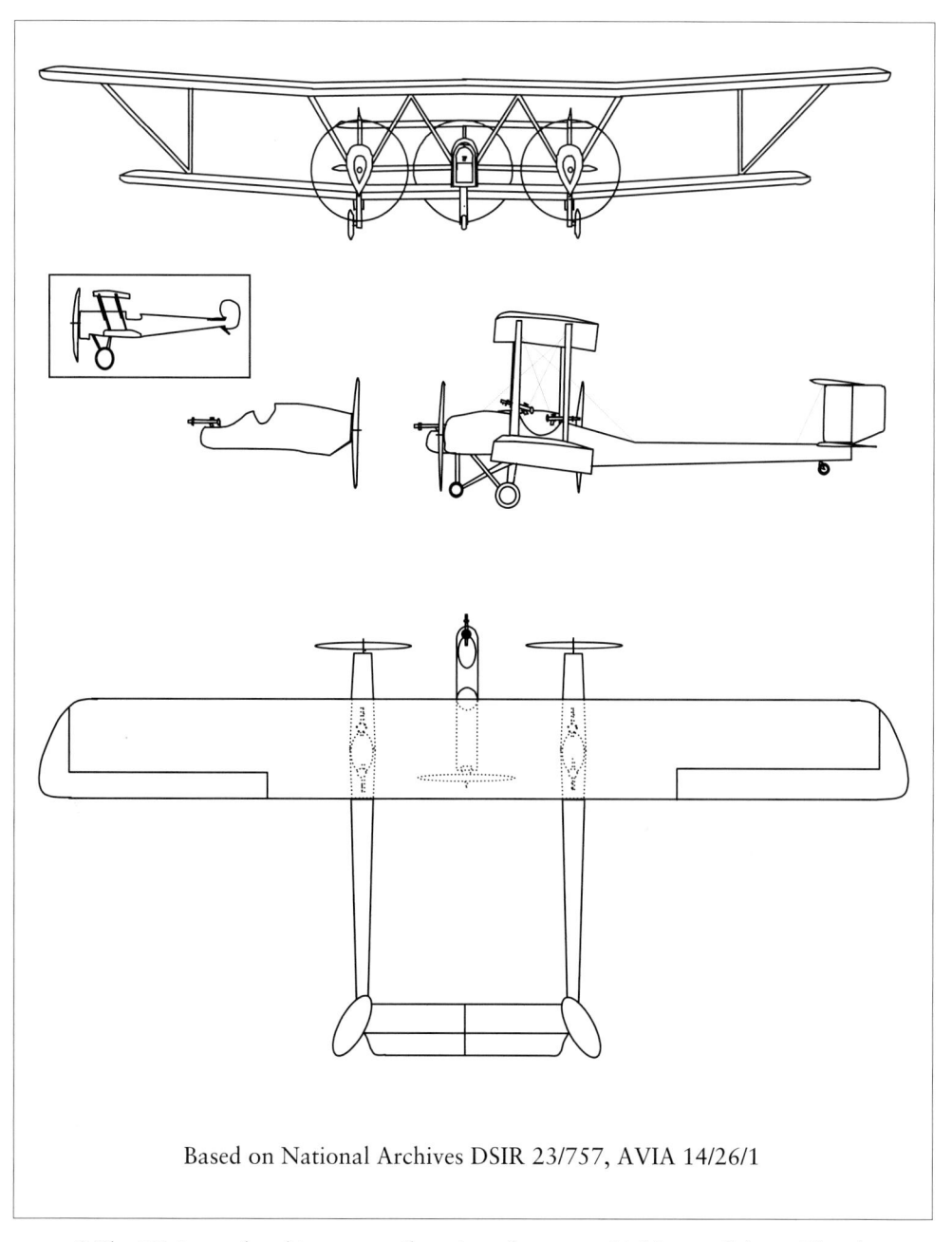

Based on National Archives DSIR 23/757, AVIA 14/26/1

9 The F.E.5 was the ultimate manifestation of pre-war thinking on fighters. The plane was to have a gunner in the nose and two more behind the wing-mounted engines. The outline of a Bristol Scout gives some idea of the size of the plane—it would have been as large as the Handley Page O/100 heavy bomber.

10 Having the gunner of the B.E.2 in the front cockpit put the pilot in a rather precarious position when pursuing Fokkers had to be beaten off. The trace of a smile visible on the pilot's face was probably not present when his gunner was firing for real. (*Canada Aviation and Space Museum/Image Bank Collection*)

11 The single-seater Morane Saulnier N was acquired off the French to give the RFC an equivalent to the Fokker E. Metal grooves on the propeller deflected bullets from the fixed forward-firing machine gun. (*P. Carradice*)

12 There was no shortage of British designs that could have been used as single-seater fighters. The S.E.2, built for high-speed reconnaissance, had all the qualities required by a fighter. (*P. R. Hare*)

13 The S.E.4, built to break the world air speed record, was another potential fighter. To reduce drag, the original design had a streamlined and enclosed cockpit. Such was the shortage of planes at the outbreak of war that the prototype was earmarked for frontline service, but crashed before it could leave for France. (*P. R. Hare*)

14 The privately developed Sopwith Tabloid was built as a racer, ordered as a high-speed reconnaissance plane and used, albeit on a very small scale, as a fighter. Its first kill was achieved by an unarmed pilot who frightened a German pilot into landing. (*P. R. Hare*)

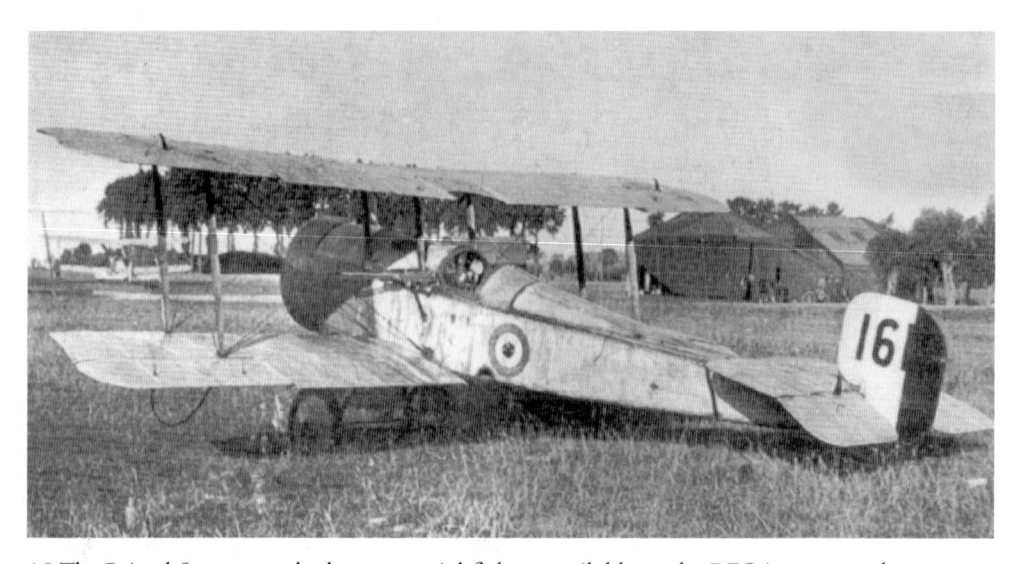

15 The Bristol Scout was the best potential fighter available to the RFC in any numbers, but like all scouts, it was initially delivered unarmed. Pilots had to improvise their own armament like the Lewis machine gun in this picture, fixed to fire at an angle from the cockpit. This particular machine was flown by Lanoe Hawker. (*P. R. Hare*)

16 The S.E.4a high-speed scout was tried with a fixed forward-firing machine gun on the upper wing, but only five were built and was only used as a fighter by home defence squadrons. (*P. R. Hare*).

17 The preferred single-seater option for fighting duties was the Airco D.H.2, a pusher whose pilot was supposed to aim his weapon and fly the plane at the same time. The un-aerodynamic framing around the propeller reduced performance, but the pusher arrangement gave the pilot an excellent view forward. (*P. R. Hare*)

18 When the twin-engine fighters failed, the RFC turned to single-engine two-seaters such as the Sopwith 1½ Strutter. (*P. Carradice*)

19 The D.H.4 was designed as a reconnaissance-bomber but despite its size, Trenchard saw it as a fighter. (*P. R. Hare*)

20 Smaller single-seaters such as the Sopwith Pup were far more agile than two-seaters. Concentrating weight as close to the centre of gravity as possible improved manoeuvrability, but inevitably put the pilot in a position where his view was limited. Forward-staggered upper wings and an un-aerodynamic hole cut in the upper wing helped, but the view forwards was very poor. (*P. Carradice*)

21 The ground crew surrounding this Sopwith Camel underline how compact this particular design was. (*P. Carradice*)

22 The Airco D.H.5 offered the pilot an excellent forward view by using an unusual back-staggered upper wing. It was not as aerodynamically efficient as the more conventional forward-stagger and merely replaced a poor forward view with poor rearward view.

23 Trenchard was furious when he saw the 'conservatory' semi-enclosed cockpit of the S.E.5. Pilots complained it restricted their view and it was removed. Being able to see the enemy was more important than being protected from the slipstream. (*P. R. Hare*)

24 Heavier water-cooled engines meant higher speed but less manoeuvrability. The Martinsyde F.4 was one of the fastest, but also one of the largest single-seater fighters developed in the First World War. (*P. R. Hare*)

25 The lighter rotary-powered Sopwith Snipe was more manoeuvrable but much slower than the Martinsyde F.3/4. (*P. Carradice*)

Above: 26 The Handley Page O/400 'Paralyser' was a huge plane for its time. Bombers like this were difficult to develop and expensive to build. (*P. R. Hare*)

Left: 27 German personnel inspecting captured Allied planes. The Nieuport 17 in the foreground gives some idea of the size of the Handley Page bomber. Five single-seater fighters could be built for the price of a Handley Page bomber. (*P. Carradice*)

28 The Vickers Vimy bomber was developed from the unsuccessful Vickers E.F.B.7 twin-engine fighter. (*P. R. Hare*)

29 The Airco D.H.10 was developed from the Airco D.H.3 twin-engine fighter, which in turn was a scaled-down version of the Factory F.E.4. The D.H.10 bomber had a shorter wingspan than the F.E.4 fighter. (*Crown via Phil Butler*)

30 The enormous four-engine Handley Page V/1500, which was designed to bomb Berlin, was twice as heavy and expensive to build as the Handley Page O/400. (*Library of Congress*)

31 The huge six-engined Tarrant Tabor was the ultimate folly in long-range bombers. The photo shows the prototype being prepared for its maiden flight in 1919. The gantry was required to start the upper engines. The plane crashed on take-off, killing its two pilots. (*RAF Museum*)

thirty-three B.E.2s; B.E.12s were not even capable of climbing to 15,000 feet. The RNAS squadrons responded faster and with fighters such as the Sopwith Pup, Triplane and Camel, they had the performance to reach the altitude the German bombers were flying. However, once in the air, hazy conditions prevented the pilots gleaning any information from ground signals on the location of the enemy bombers. With the Gothas initially heading for London and then diverting to Folkestone, the German formation had spent nearly an hour and a half in British airspace, yet only one fighter pilot got close enough to open fire. Only one Gotha was shot down, and that was a victim of Nieuports scrambled from Dunkirk against the returning bombers. With the death toll inflicted and the apparent ineffectiveness of the defences, it seemed like a triumph for the attacking force and a humiliation for the defence. The defences were undoubtedly ill-prepared and the Bleriot Experimentals were clearly inadequate for intercepting aeroplanes. Training units were ordered to put any modern fighters they possessed on standby to deal with any follow-up attack. These, however, were to play very little part in arguably the most significant air raid flown by either side in the entire war.

On 13 June, fourteen Gothas reached central London and scattered nearly four tons of bombs over the city. The inhabitants of the capital were given no warning and, until the bombs fell, many assumed the planes were friendly. 162 people died and 432 were injured—an unprecedented number of casualties. The casualties included sixteen children killed by a single bomb that hit a primary school in Poplar. As in Folkestone, feelings ran high, but again the desire for revenge was the predominant emotion, not capitulation. The defending fighters flew 94 sorties, but the more capable Bristol Fighters, Pups and Camels on standby at the training schools were only ordered into the air some ten to fifteen minutes after the front line squadrons. Only five pilots got within effective firing range and no enemy planes were shot down. It was another dismal performance by the defence.

The question of air defence was immediately put on the agenda of the next War Cabinet meeting. Curzon was one of its members as was a recent addition, Jan Smuts, a South African who had achieved some notable victories against German colonial forces in Africa and who had impressed Lloyd George with his original and progressive thinking at the recent Imperial Conference. The meeting was held the day after the raid. The mood was sombre and the outlook seemed grim. Robertson, the Chief of the Imperial General Staff, claimed it was impossible to intercept bombers before they reached London when they could fly from the coast to the capital in just forty-five minutes. There was, he claimed, simply not enough time for fighters to reach 15,000 feet. This was true of many of the planes assigned to home defence for anti-Zeppelin duties, but modern fighters like the Pup and Camel could climb to this altitude in less than thirty minutes. Interception was by no means as impossible as Robertson was claiming.[43]

The government were certainly not willing to accept his analysis. The cabinet ordered that 'the best fighters and pilots' should be concentrated in the south-east of England to ensure any further attempt to bomb London was met with an 'exceptionally hot reception'.[44] A batch of twenty-four Camels intended for the conversion of two squadrons in France was reallocated to home defence and the cabinet ordered Trenchard to move two fighter squadrons from the Western Front to Britain. Trenchard and Haig were furious. They insisted the bombing of targets in Britain, however tragic and unfortunate, could not in any circumstances be militarily significant. Any move to weaken the British armed forces in France in order to strengthen home defences would be playing into enemy hands. Haig, who was preparing for his Ypres offensive in northern Belgium, and Trenchard suggested the Germans had probably bombed London simply to get squadrons transferred away from the front. Haig was forced to accept the transfer, but he imposed the condition that the squadrons return by 6 July, in time to take part in the preparatory air operations for his planned offensive. No. 56 Squadron with S.E.5s moved to England, but No. 66 with Pups only got as far as Calais where, it was argued, it would be well placed to intercept future raids as the Gothas returned to their continental bases.

The retaliation the public and press were demanding was very much on the agenda. It had been considered after the Folkestone raid, but the cabinet were well aware that Folkestone was no less a military target than the ports the Navy had been bombing in Belgium.[45] Retaliation for the raid on London seemed more justified and various targets were considered, including Strasbourg, Mannheim and Frankfurt ('...a centre of finance and socialism'). To be successful, such raids had to be concentrated and powerful, but with the disbandment of the RNAS 3rd Wing, there was no way of delivering effective retaliation.[46]

In any case, there was not much confidence within cabinet that such acts of 'frightfulness' would achieve anything. It was noted that the bombing of British cities had merely sharpened the public's appetite for retaliation. A decision was postponed,[47] but the question of creating a long-range bomber force capable of delivering retaliation was now very much back on the Air Board agenda. In the wake of the Folkestone raid, Weir was expecting the government to order retaliation and Cowdray felt it was the right time to revive the idea of an independent bomber force that might deliver it. The bomber force, however, would still have to be created in addition to the air forces required by the other two services for tactical operations. Weir believed this was possible. He predicted engine output would reach 2,600 by the end of the year, comfortably exceeding the 2,000 target required for the existing expansion programme. By this time, there would be a total of 3,000 surplus engines and this excess would continue to grow in 1918. A bomber force of ten squadrons with ten aircraft each would require 1,000 engines to establish and 200 per month to maintain. This seemed well within the capabilities of the industry.[48]

At the 14 June cabinet meeting, the government decided much more was required. They wanted the greatest possible expansion of the air force and the

The Brave New World of Strategic Bombing

Air Board was set the task of determining exactly what was possible, and how this might affect arms production in other areas.[49] Weir was expecting engine production to rise to over 4,000 a month by the summer of 1918, double the number required to maintain the existing 100 squadron target, which suggested sufficient aircraft could be built to equip 200 squadrons. Henderson, Brancker and Paine all questioned whether it would be possible to train the aircrews to man these squadrons, but Weir saw no problem in building the 2,500 D.H.6 trainers that this enormous undertaking would require.[50] Henderson, Brancker and Paine were persuaded 200 front line squadrons could be achieved by the end of 1918.[51] There was a brief discussion about what these squadrons might be used for. Henderson suggested the new formations should be more fighter and bomber squadrons, but Cowdray was only interested in bombers, which, he believed, could ultimately be deployed in 'tens of thousands'.[52]

On 2 July, Derby, now the Secretary of State for War, reported back to the cabinet confirming that the doubling of RFC and RNAS strength was well within the future production capabilities of the aircraft industry and 200 front line squadrons became the RFC target strength.[53] The cabinet were not told, nor did they appear to ask, exactly what this new found strength would consist of, but an extra forty fighter and sixty bomber squadrons was banded around at subsequent Air Board meetings. At no point in the process were Haig or Trenchard consulted.

Meanwhile, the more immediate task was to defend London. Despite the cabinet's wish that any repeat attack would get 'an exceptionally hot reception', the immediate improvements to the defences were makeshift and temporary. In addition to the squadrons transferred from France, a fighter training unit was moved to the south-east to bolster the defences, which scarcely constituted the movement of the 'best pilots and planes' the cabinet had wanted. In letters to Henderson and the CIGS Robertson, French, who as Commander-in-Chief of Home Forces was also responsible for the air defence of Great Britain, warned that if the two squadrons transferred from France were allowed to return to the Western Front as planned, the forces at his disposal would constitute an unsatisfactory collection of second-line units and obsolete aircraft. As it might jeopardise the return of the loaned fighter squadrons, Henderson chose not to pass this warning on. On 6 July, the two borrowed fighter squadrons duly returned to the Western Front. Twenty-four hours later, the Gothas struck again.

For this second raid, over 100 planes rose to defend the capital, but only around twenty were modern single-seater fighters. A number of fighters managed to engage the bombers before they reached their target and more harried the Gothas as they retreated to the coast, but only one was shot down. This time, civilians took cover more quickly and casualties were lower, but the fifty-seven death toll was still a huge shock for the nation. Within hours of the raid, the war cabinet sat in an emergency session to discuss how to respond. Ministers were furious to discover that the two fighter squadrons transferred from the Western Front had been sent back on the eve of the raid and that French's warnings had not reached them. They demanded the squadrons return immediately. Henderson stood by the decision to return the squadrons, again insisting that the Germans were probably only attacking London to draw crucial British air resources away from the battlefront. However, a furious French repeated the warning in his undelivered note that without these two front line fighter squadrons, London's air defences were a 'patchwork affair' relying far too heavily on training aircraft.[54] The cabinet sided with French. The outcome of the war 'depends almost as much on the endurance of the people as that of the armies' and defences would have to be improved. Haig was allowed to hang on to one of the two squadrons that he was supposed to return, but three new home defence fighter squadrons would be formed, squadrons that Haig might have otherwise expected would go to him.[55]

There was now a real urgency about expanding the air force and Weir was called in for the 9 July cabinet meeting to explain how this might be achieved. He assured the cabinet that the planes could be built to equip 200 squadrons and the crews could be trained to fly them.[56] Haig was informed of the decision and told to prepare airfields in France for forty bombing squadrons by August 1918. He was none too impressed at this sudden influx of bombers, about which he had not been consulted. His first priority was not long-range bombers, but the seventy-six squadrons that were promised to him to meet his fighter/reconnaissance requirement. Nor was he impressed with the inability of the War Office to explain exactly what targets these bombers were supposed to attack.[57]

Meanwhile, a week after the second Gotha raid, the Prime Minister created a two-man committee, comprising himself and General Smuts to consider what further action should be taken to strengthen the air defences and improve the organisation of the air force as a whole. Lloyd George did not participate directly in the enquiry, but his influence was clear with many of Smuts' conclusions reflecting the Prime Minister's fears about the pointlessness of Haig's offensives. His nominal participation was a clear signal that whatever conclusions Smuts came to would be accepted. Smuts was not ideally qualified for the job. He did not have an aeronautical background and only limited use had been made of aviation in his African campaigns. He had no first-hand experience of the large-scale air operations that were taking place on the Western Front, but he had experienced the attacks on London and was aware of the effects they had on a city, its population and its political leaders, and this was bound to influence his thinking. It was a rather select band Smuts chose to consult. It included Derby, Curzon, Cowdray, Paine, Brancker, Henderson, who drafted much of the subsequent reports, Churchill and Rear Admiral Mark Kerr, most of whom had at some time shown an interest in long-range bombing. The most fervent was Kerr, who had worked closely with the now banished Sueter and held very similar views on the potential of air power. Haig and Trenchard were not consulted, never mind asked to attend. All those

Smuts spoke to agreed that the aeroplane surplus should be used to create a long-range bomber force and the only debate was about whether an Air Ministry should be created to organise it and an independent air force created to deliver the assault. The basic premise that there would be an aeroplane surplus was not questioned.

In his first report, Smuts concentrated on the immediate need to improve the defences of London. The main recommendation was that all aspects of the air defence of the capital should be in the hands of a single person and that this force should be independent of French and his GHQ Home forces, the command responsible for dealing with invasion. It was not the first time this had been suggested and the reorganisation was entirely sensible and uncontroversial. By 2 August, all three of the new squadrons required by the cabinet had started forming, one on Camels and two on Pups. On 8 August, Major-General Ashmore became the commander of all fighter, anti-aircraft and searchlight units in the London Air Defence Area (LADA), a zone that included all targets within range of the Gotha and which therefore possessed all the day-fighter squadrons. As it turned out, Ashmore would never get an opportunity to see how his reinforced and reorganised day defences would fare. The Gothas would make a further three daylight raids on Britain, all on coastal towns. These were met with growing confidence by the RNAS coastal squadrons, supported by squadrons based on the French coast. A Gotha was shot down on 22 July, another on 12 August with four more crash landing, and three were lost in action on 22 August. These high losses forced the German High Command to suspend daylight raids. On the last two occasions, Ashmore had believed that London was the target and behind the RNAS coastal patrols, substantial numbers of fighters were patrolling the airspace between the coast and the capital. In the end, the efforts of the naval fighters alone proved sufficient. The Gotha daylight offensive had been defeated quite easily and far more speedily than the Zeppelin menace.

Meanwhile, Smuts, now warming to the task, prepared a second report. In this, Smuts pointed out, like many before him, the vulnerability of London. His view that the steps taken to defend London had to be 'without prejudice to operations in the field and on the high seas, as the fighting forces must, as a matter of general principle, have the first call upon our output of aircraft and anti-aircraft guns' mirrored Army and Henderson's thinking. However, there was little else in his report that would comfort the commanders of Britain's land and sea forces. Smuts spoke dismissively of the 'snail's pace' progress being made in France by ineffective armies and he could not imagine how armies would ever again be capable of acting decisively. For the air arm, on the other hand, there was no limit to the scale of future operations. 'The day may not be far off when aerial operations with their devastation of enemy lands and destruction of industrial and populous centres on a vast scale may become the principal operations of war, to which the older forms of military and naval operations may become secondary and subordinate.' Future wars would be waged well behind traditional front lines. Germany had shown the way by its attacks on London and unless Britain reacted quickly, took to the offensive and ensured the struggle for air supremacy was fought far beyond the Rhine, Britain would remain in peril. There was not much evidence for these predictions. It was pure speculation, but it was a belief that would remain the cornerstone of British air strategy for decades to come.

To achieve the kind of air force capable of winning wars, Smuts believed a unified air service had to be created and administered by its own Air Ministry. Smuts emphasised that the possibility of decisive long-range air operations was not some distant prospect; 1918 would see the dawn of this new era in warfare. With the Air Board planning on a force of 400 bombers by the beginning of 1918, this did not seem like wild speculation. None of these ideas were new. They had been around since the Zeppelin paranoia of the pre-war days. A single united air force had been the original idea behind the creation of the Royal Flying Corps. An independent Air Ministry had been seen as inevitable by each successive committee or board set up to co-ordinate aviation and Cowdray's Air Board was an embryonic Air Ministry in waiting. All that had stopped proposals like Smuts' being introduced before was the belief that it would be impossible in the middle of a war and the opposition of the Admiralty and War Office. This time the commanders of the Army and Navy would not be consulted. Before the services had a chance to comment on Smuts' report, it was approved 'in principle' by the cabinet. There was plenty in it for both services to be unhappy about and the criticisms the service chiefs would come up with would anticipate the problems that would plague British defence policy for decades to come.

Haig saw no evidence at all for the conclusions Smuts had come to and questioned whether the surplus Smuts was relying on would ever materialise. He still did not have the fifty-six squadrons he had been promised for the end of 1916 and his requirements had increased considerably since then. Even if the proposed bomber fleet could be built, he did not believe there was any evidence to suggest it could cause the level of destruction Smuts claimed. Even if it did, it did not seem to be in Britain's best interests to try and win a war by the wholesale destruction of enemy cities. He recognised the value of a deterrent that could be used to 'punish' and possibly deter such attacks by an enemy, but Britain was far too vulnerable to air attack to use such a force to win a war. Haig feared an Air Ministry bent on developing such a long-range bomber force would not be prepared to devote the necessary resources to Army and Navy co-operation. With independence for the air force, a rift would inevitably develop between the services and future generations of air force officers would lack the Army background to understand the needs and requirements of land forces. Each of these predictions would come to pass in the decades ahead. Haig appealed to Robertson to get officers with 'practical knowledge' to re-examine the claims that had been made for long-range bombing.[58]

On the naval side, Geddes, who had taken over from Carson, and the Admiralty were also opposed. Air units attached to a fleet needed specialist aircraft flown by crews with specialist training. The Admiralty also feared a separate Air Ministry preoccupied with long-range bombing would inevitably neglect naval requirements.[59] This was particularly ironic given that the Admiralty's previous infatuation with long-range bombing had done just that. Beatty, however, surprised his colleagues by suggesting it was 'a move in the right direction' and perhaps provoked some embarrassment by suggesting that an Air Ministry might provide the naval air force with a much more coherent air policy than the Admiralty had so far managed. Naval aviation might finally be able to catch up with its Army counterpart, he rather provocatively suggested.[60] Beatty saw all the same potential problems that worried the War Office and his naval colleagues, but believed they were not insurmountable. The Admiralty attitude was too parochial, he insisted.[61] Indeed, Geddes feared Admiralty objections amounted to little more than a failure to trust an independent ministry to do its job properly.[62] Whether the trusting Beatty or the suspicious Geddes was right would be revealed soon enough.

Meanwhile, Weir was driving ahead as fast as he could with his increased aircraft production programme. Large orders for engines were placed in Italy and the United States to supplement the efforts of British manufacturers. Early in September, Weir was assuring the Air Board that surplus engine production would enable a front line force of 165 squadrons to be created as early as June 1918.[63] By this time, he was expecting the delivery of at least 300 Handley Page O/400 bombers,[64] which would allow the creation of no less than seventeen new heavy bomber squadrons between March and July 1918.[65] The personnel brought in to help the Air Board prepare for a fully-fledged Air Ministry were not exactly what Haig had in mind when he suggested the need for people with 'practical knowledge'. Rear Admiral Kerr was seconded to the Air Board in August 1917. Lord Tiverton was another who perhaps did not have the sort of practical knowledge Haig was talking about. Tiverton had worked as the armaments officer with the naval No. 3 Wing in France and had shown a keen interest in the problems long-range bombing involved. In late 1917, he was working with the British Aviation Commission in Paris, but was set the task of preparing a plan for the Air Board for the systematic destruction of the German munitions industry. He was told to assume a force of 2,000 bombers would be available.[66]

Tiverton attacked the task with gusto. Operating from eastern France would bring the Düsseldorf, Cologne, Mannheim and Saar Valley industrial zones well within range. Bombing by day would be best. Apart from finding their targets more easily, day bombers were smaller, required fewer aircrews and were cheaper to build. The effect on morale would also be greater if civilians felt attacks might come while they were going about their everyday business.

Concentration was crucial, he insisted, with one target being attacked at a time until obliterated. With 100 squadrons available, a city like Mannheim could be subjected to a five-hour bombardment, with one squadron arriving every three minutes. Frankfurt might be dealt with next, by which time it was 'quite possible that Cologne would create such trouble that the German Government might be forced to suggest terms before that town [sic] was also attacked'.[67] The Air Board set about ordering the bombers that might cause such mayhem. The naval members of the Board preferred night bombers, which could carry more bombs, could drop them from lower altitudes and suffered fewer losses. Paine insisted the naval squadrons at Dunkirk had no difficulty finding their targets even on moonless nights and one Handley Page squadron could drop more bombs than six D.H.4 squadrons.[68]

Henderson wanted to keep the option of bombing by day open and pointed out that the Dunkirk squadrons were only attacking coastal targets, which were always easier to find in darkness. Targets deep inside Germany would be quite a different proposition. To cover the day-bomber option, the range of the D.H.4 would be stretched to 450 miles. Henderson wanted the extra range to be at the expense of bomb load rather than speed but was overruled. The plane would carry the same bomb load, which would reduce speed of the interim Eagle-powered version to just 95 mph, but the supposedly superior BHP engine would, Weir insisted, fully restore the plane's performance. The long-range BHP version would be so different it was effectively a new plane and became the D.H.9. Switching from the D.H.4 to the D.H.9 would involve the loss of four to ten weeks' worth of output, but Weir was sure the superior performance of the D.H.9 would more than make up for this—an enormous misjudgement as it would turn out. An order for 300 D.H.4s was converted into an equal number of D.H.9s and orders for the new de Havilland bomber soon ran into thousands.[69]

However, Weir needed the greater lifting capacity night bombers could provide. The best available night bomber was the Handley Page O/100, but Vickers was promising more with a bomber adaptation of their failed E.F.B.7 two-seater fighter. Despite Henderson's objections, prototypes of the Vickers plane, the future Vimy, were ordered and large contracts placed for the Handley Page O/400, an improved version of the Handley Page O/100.[70] Meanwhile, the political urgency to create a long-range bomber force seemed to subside almost as quickly as it had erupted. The home front was quiet and the Gothas had not returned to London. The cabinet began to wonder if the turmoil of creating a new service in the middle of a war was really so necessary after all. While Smuts had been writing his reports and the Air Board preparing for a decisive air offensive in 1918, Jellicoe was expressing doubts that Britain could survive that long.[71] In June, nearly 600,000 tons of shipping was sunk by German submarines and the Navy was in danger of losing control of the seas around Britain. The Belgian ports that the U-boats were operating from had to be eliminated and bombers did not seem to be capable of doing this.

Haig seemed to have the solution. He suggested his proposed offensive in northern Belgium in the Ypres region might result in the capture of these ports and, for good measure, the airfields the Gothas were operating from. Lloyd George was extremely reluctant to embark on yet another costly land offensive, but in June, a small preparatory tactical operation at Messines brought rapid success with light losses. Perhaps the prospects for the proposed offensive were not quite so bleak. Haig promised the offensive would not continue if the casualties were excessive. A not entirely convinced Lloyd George gave the Army one last chance. Once again the focus was back on the Western Front.

CHAPTER 9

A Modern Tactical Air Force

Trenchard could not have been any more enthusiastic about the proposed offensive than Lloyd George. The RFC chief's main concern was not how to save British merchant shipping, but how to prevent his own air force from being wiped out. April 1917 would, however, prove to be the lowest point of RFC fortunes. The second half of 1917 would see a gradual improvement. Better equipment arrived creating a transition from a force equipped for the static trench warfare that typified so much of the First World War, to a more versatile force better suited to the more mobile operations that would characterise the closing stages of the conflict. The success of the Albatros D fighter had left no one in any doubt that the single-seater tractor was the key to establishing air superiority. The RFC had paid a heavy price for the ineffectiveness of its fighter force in the Arras offensive and Trenchard's first priority was to complete the conversion of his fighter squadrons to more modern planes. The problem was that the planes Trenchard considered modern before the Arras offensive had hardly distinguished themselves, and some of the new fighters that arrived after the offensive were even less effective.

One such fighter was the D.H.5. Large numbers were delivered before it was realised that unless ground crews prepared the plane for flight with meticulous attention, excessive vibrations made it almost impossible to fly.[1] Some strengthening solved the problem and 300 would eventually find their way to front line squadrons, but the increased weight further reduced the performance of a fighter that had always been mediocre at best. Pilots converting from the D.H.2 pusher were far from convinced they were getting a better plane. The Nieuport 17 was reaching the end of its useful life; in May, Nieuport contracts were cancelled and Camels ordered instead.[2] The Sopwith fighter was a huge improvement, although very much a mixed blessing. Manoeuvrable to the point of being dangerously unstable, this quirky fighter was a handful for any but the most experienced pilot to fly, but if the pilot could master its idiosyncrasies, it was a difficult plane for the enemy to keep in their sights. The first Camels reached RFC squadrons in June.[3] The Factory S.E.5 had proven to be another disappointment, but the 200-hp S.E.5a version climbed faster, flew higher and was 23 mph faster at 15,000 feet. It was a much more effective fighter.

While trials with the S.E.5a were taking place, an even better fighter was taking to the air. The Sopwith Dolphin, powered by the same 200-hp Hispano-Suiza engine, not only flew even faster and higher than the S.E.5a, it was also far more manoeuvrable and armed with three machine guns.[4] Even before trials were completed, the fighter was rushed to France to see what RFC pilots made of it. A young Cecil Lewis with No. 56 Squadron came across the prototype Dolphin while testing out the newly arrived S.E.5a. Determined to show off his own piloting skills and the capabilities of his new fighter, Lewis set about engaging the Dolphin in mock combat, only to discover the Dolphin outclassed his S.E.5a in every respect.[5] Pilots from No. 60 Squadron reported the Dolphin was extraordinarily quick in turns and praised the excellent view;[6] Trenchard was keen to get the fighter in production as quickly as possible.[7]

Initially, Weir was also anxious to get production going.[8] He suggested one third of the next batch of 1,000 Hispano-Suiza-powered fighters to be ordered should be Dolphins and the rest S.E.5as. Some board members thought this was not going far enough. There was a strong feeling that the Dolphin represented the next stage in fighter development and merited a higher priority. The Admiralty agreed. Naval pilots had developed an almost unshakeable aversion to liquid-cooled engine fighters, but the Dolphin was a fighter even they wanted.[9] Sopwith claimed deliveries could begin in September if the plane was ordered straight away. Three hundred Dolphins were ordered to get production going, but Sopwith was also just beginning to turn out desperately needed Camels, which rather complicated the situation. For the time being, a decision about more substantial contracts was put on hold.

Like the S.E.5, the disappointing F2a Bristol Fighter was rescued by the application of more power. It was only when the plane was fitted with the 220-hp Falcon II and later the 275-hp Falcon III, becoming the F2b, that the plane started living up to its 'fighter' designation. Deliveries of the Falcon II began in May 1917 and the Falcon III in September. With the latter, it was 13 mph faster, could climb to 15,000 feet seven minutes quicker, and although a two-seater, its Rolls-Royce engine gave it a power/weight ratio comparable to any single-seater. Its size inevitably limited its manoeuvrability, but at medium and low altitudes, it was a formidable opponent for even the best German fighters. It was superior to the Albatros in terms of speed and climb—quite an achievement for a two-seater—and the improved performance enabled crews to begin using the synchronised gun as the main weapon as had originally been intended. Ironically, by this time Trenchard had decided the single-seater was the way forwards in the air superiority role,[10] but for a while the Bristol Fighter proved to be a surprisingly useful low to medium altitude fighter.

In the months following Arras, RFC equipment underwent a transformation. The last D.H.2 pushers were withdrawn from service in June and the F.E.8 went the following month. By the end of July, the B.E.2 equipped two squadrons and the F.E.2 just one, a major achievement given that three months before, these two types had constituted such a high proportion of front line strength. The Nieuports and Pups were also slowly phased out. Production of the Camel and S.E.5a gradually accelerated. S.E.5a deliveries were initially held up by a shortage of Hispano-Suiza engines—at one point there were 400 engineless fuselages in storage—and following the Gotha raids, Camels and S.E.5as were also being diverted to home defence. By the end of July, there were four squadrons equipped with the Camel with just one S.E.5a squadron, but by the end of November, this had risen to six Camels and five S.E.5a squadrons. By the end of the year, over 700 Camels and S.E.5as had crossed the Channel.

During the summer of 1917, German pilots were all too aware of the increasing quality of the aircraft that opposed them. The more aerodynamically refined and lighter Albatros V appeared in May 1917, but only offered a slight improvement in performance. Even such a notable ace as von Richthofen was alarmed and despondent by the way the Camel, Triplane and Spad 13 'play with our D Vs' and was forced to admit that the Albatros did not even have the speed to catch the two-seater Bristol Fighter.[11] The German fighter force would have to wait until the late summer of 1917 before a significantly better fighter reached their squadrons, the Fokker Dr.1, but this suffered from structural problems and never won the complete confidence of the pilots who flew it.

The Germans may have been impressed by the latest British fighter designs, but on the British side there was disappointment. Brooke-Popham found it perplexing that the S.E.5a was clearly inferior to the similarly powered Spad 13, especially in terms of climb, a weakness that would become very apparent when the Fokker Triplane arrived.[12] Another cause for concern was the performance of the Camel. Production models reaching the squadrons simply did not achieve the performance of the early prototypes, particularly at altitude. The plane was supposed to have a service ceiling of nearly 20,000 feet, but pilots claimed it was impossible to maintain formation at 16,000 feet.[13] Test pilots insisted there was no problem with the machines they tried.[14] The problem was never entirely resolved, although it seems the inferior quality of the British produced version of the Clerget engine was partly to blame.[15] Confidence in the Camel slumped and it was accepted that it could not remain a front line plane for long.

The obvious solution as far as Brancker was concerned was to accelerate the introduction of the Dolphin on Sopwith production lines.[16] This, however, would mean more engine problems for Weir. A key element of Weir's expansion programme was the placement of large orders to reduce costs. Large numbers of Clerget engines had been ordered for the Camel, and with the failure of the D.H.5, no other major RFC plane used the French rotary. To use up the Clerget engines, huge orders for Camels continued to be placed, even though it had effectively been decided to phase out the fighter.[17] This clogged up the Sopwith production lines with a machine that was no longer wanted when it could have been building Dolphins.

All sorts of reasons were conjured up for not increasing orders for the Dolphin. There was a genuine shortage of the Hispano-Suiza engine that powered the Dolphin, although the superior performance of the Dolphin seemed to justify priority for the Sopwith fighter over the similarly powered Factory S.E.5a. Trenchard did not help by insisting the Dolphin be thoroughly tested before more were ordered. Also, dubious data was supplied to the Air Board claiming that although the Dolphin had demonstrated its superior climb at low and medium altitudes, at 20,000 feet the S.E.5a, rather mysteriously, could climb twice as fast.[18] Where this information came from is not quite clear, for the trials unit at Martlesham had not even speculated about the climb performance of either fighter at 20,000 feet. Their measurements stopped at 18,000 feet and up to that altitude the Dolphin out-climbed the S.E.5a and there was no reason why it would not continue to do so above this altitude.[19] There were also concerns about the safety of the pilot. The pilot had an excellent view because his head protruded above the upper wing, but this put him in a vulnerable position if the plane overturned on landing. This had not stopped planes like the Morane-Saulnier N being used by the RFC and Martlesham Heath insisted a simple protective head bar solved the problem. Nevertheless, there seemed to be a determination not to let the introduction of the Dolphin slow down overall production. Weir had his targets to meet and a lot of Clerget engines to use up.

Weir's production priorities were also affecting the next generation of fighter planes. It seemed the useful life of any particular fighter design was remarkably brief and Trenchard had no doubts the German aircraft industry would soon produce another fighter as advanced as the Fokker E and the Albatros D had been in their time. He scolded himself for not putting his requirements forward forcefully enough to anticipate planes like the Albatros, although in reality it was only after the Albatros appeared that he fully recognised the importance of the single-seater tractor.[20] To ensure his RFC was not taken by surprise again, in March 1917, Trenchard laid down the performance required by the next generation of fighter. The emphasis was very much on performance at altitude with a top speed of 135 mph at 15,000 feet and a ceiling of 25,000 feet,[21] which was well in advance of anything current fighters were capable of. He also wanted this new fighter entering service by the early winter of 1917–18 so that his pilots would have plenty of time to become familiar with the plane before the following spring.[22]

The Air Board specification that emerged in April 1917 was broadly similar in expectations, but was different in one key respect. While Trenchard wanted a liquid-cooled engine, the Board preferred an air-cooled rotary. Trenchard pointed to the success of the Albatros and Spad as proof of the advantages of the liquid-cooled engine, but Brancker assured Trenchard that any 200-hp rotary-powered fighter would be superior.[23] The Air Board were pinning their hopes on the Bentley BR2, a more powerful, reliable and cheaper version of the French Clerget. A whole series of fighters powered by the Bentley engine were being designed to meet the Air Board requirement, including an updated version of the Camel, which would become the Snipe. In tests in October 1917, prototypes of the Bentley engine were managing over 230 hp, but it was already too late for such an engine to be in production in time to power large numbers of front line fighters by the spring of 1918. There was, however, an alternative, a high-performance fighter that was already flying in 1917 and did not rely on an experimental engine.

The engine it used was the Rolls-Royce Falcon. It should not have been surprising that an engine capable of hauling the two-seater Bristol Fighter through the air in a way that embarrassed the pilots of German single-seater fighters would be capable of even more when only required to power a single-seater. Martinsyde were working on Falcon-powered single-seaters,[24] the latest of which was the F.3. In July 1917 Henderson enthusiastically described to the Air Board how this fighter had achieved 128 mph at 15,000 feet and could climb to that altitude in under thirteen minutes.[25] Weir, however, insisted that there were no spare Falcon engines in his programme for any such fighter, and the firm had to consider an alternative engine.[26] However, he could not stop interest in the fighter growing. In November, Lieutenant-Colonel Pitcher (Controller of the Technical Department) reported the prototype had achieved between 130–140 mph at 10,000 feet and could climb to that altitude in six minutes. Pitcher reminded the Air Board that this was a plane that was actually flying, not some paper project, and the performance was extremely close to what they were expecting from the next generation of single-seaters.[27] It was a large and heavy fighter by the standards of 1917, but Martlesham Heath considered it had excellent manoeuvrability 'for a machine of this size and power' and generally considered it 'a great advance on all existing fighting scouts'.[28] All this was being achieved with a tried and tested engine that was already in production.

The case for ordering the Martinsyde fighter seemed overwhelming. It was estimated it would take Martinsyde ten weeks to get production going and output would be up to forty fighters a month within three months. The new fighter would start reaching the front line in the spring of 1918, which Paine was quick to point out was sooner than the Bentley-powered fighters could arrive.[29] Weir insisted there were simply no plans to build the Falcon on the scale planned for the Bentley, and there were not even enough being built to satisfy Bristol Fighter production. Indeed, Weir was hoping to phase the Falcon out completely so that Rolls-Royce could concentrate on the larger Eagle engines the proposed bomber fleet would require. It might be possible to free sufficient Falcons to allow two or three squadrons to be equipped with the Martinsyde fighter, but large-scale production would, Weir repeated, be quite impossible.[30]

Weir argued the fighter was not needed and that the new development programme with the Bentley rotary would produce something far better.[31] Unfortunately, there was little sign of this happening. A prototype Bentley BR2 was tried in a Sopwith Camel late in November, but Martlesham Heath did not think it was an improvement. There was no doubt that the Martinsyde F.3 was the best available British fighter and not to introduce it into service was very difficult to justify. Baird, the Board's political representative, was particularly aware of the potential for embarrassment. Ever since the 'Fokker Scourge' of 1916, the quality of RFC equipment had come under more public scrutiny than any other item of military equipment. Baird was very concerned that if it should become public knowledge that a superior fighter had been available but had not been ordered, the Air Board would be severely criticised.

Weir suggested production should wait until the latest Hispano-Suiza 8Fb (300 hp) engines became available, which would give the Martinsyde an even higher performance, but when this engine would be sufficiently developed for operational use was far from clear. It was scarcely a satisfactory alternative to a fighter that was already flying with an engine that was already in production. As a compromise, it was decided to order 150 Martinsydes powered by the Falcon, enough to equip and maintain two squadrons.[32] The first squadron with the type was scheduled to move to France in April and the second in May; however, the whole process was thrown into confusion when Trenchard got to see the prototype in November 1917. RFC pilots who tried the plane were impressed by its performance, particularly above 12,000 feet where its speed, climb and ability to maintain height in a turn were highly praised. Nonetheless, below 12,000 feet the plane was not considered sufficiently responsive, and the view from the cockpit was also criticised. Trenchard curtly informed the Air Board the fighter they had been agonising over was too heavy, had insufficient endurance, a poor view, was not 'handy' and 'does not appear will ever become satisfactory'. It was a very harsh interpretation of the pilots' reports and rather a surprising one, given that Trenchard's preference was a fighter powered by a liquid-cooled engine and his priority was the best possible performance at altitude.[33] A frustrated Directorate suggested that if the RFC in France did not want them, then the home defence squadrons would be more than delighted to acquire such a high-performance fighter.[34] Ironically, a few weeks later, unbeknown to Trenchard, the next great leap forward in German fighter performance he so feared materialised with the first flight of the Fokker D.VII.

For the time being, the RFC fighter squadrons could continue to count on a degree of technical superiority the S.E.5a and the Camel provided. Frustratingly, RFC fighter losses remained high, partly because RFC formations usually only consisted of a single flight of six planes while the German air force was hunting in larger fighter wings (Jagdgeschwader) with up to fifty to seventy fighters. Flying offensive patrols deep inside enemy airspace did not help, but at least these were becoming a less prominent feature of RFC fighter operations. The aggressive spirit inherent in Trenchard's offensive tactics was sound. The problem was Trenchard's belief that 'aggressive' was equated to 'distance behind the front line'. Fighters did not have to be 20 miles inside enemy territory to be aggressive. There seemed to be a constant struggle between Trenchard's desire to pursue these long-range tactics and his commanders' preference for the more focused approach common sense dictated. Common sense was, however, slowly prevailing.

As the Arras offensive had worn on, the RFC had been compelled to adapt and fly lower and nearer the front line, and this trend continued in the months that followed. For the June Messines assault, fighter patrols were flying over the front at altitudes as low as 5,000 feet with protection provided by a second layer of fighters flying above 15,000 feet, with all fighters instructed to operate within six miles of the front line.[35] For the first day of the Ypres offensive, fighters were to maintain a permanent low-level patrol over the advancing infantry. High-altitude offensive sweeps behind the front were still to be flown, but before setting off for their patrol lines, they were to pass over the front line and 'clear' the air above the troops. It was not ideal. The permanent low-level patrols consisted of just four fighters and the offensive patrols were far from certain to encounter anything on their brief passage over the front line. The Army might quite justifiably have asked why these offensive patrols could not stay over the front and continue to 'clear' the air. They were certainly needed. At the end of the first day, after struggling forward a mile in atrocious weather, the infantry were encountering fierce counterattacks supported by strafing German planes, with frustrated front line troops complaining that the RFC was nowhere to be seen. So infuriated were Army commanders, Trenchard had to issue a lengthy explanation of RFC tactics, in the words of the official history, to clear up 'the haziness about the work and limitations of the arm' that existed within the Army. The instruction emphasised the need to 'educate troops to the need for the RFC to operate offensively out of sight of the troops on the ground'.[36] Both sides had a point. Fighters need space for tactical flexibility. They cannot operate immediately above the heads of the troops, and even when providing close protection they might be out of sight. The problem was all too often the fighters were so far 'out of sight' they became an irrelevance.

Although in his explanation Trenchard insisted that it was impossible for the air force to respond to every enemy plane that was sighted over the front, this was precisely what the RFC had started doing with its compass stations. These had been set up along the front to gather intelligence on German activity by listening into enemy wireless transmissions and using direction-finding techniques to locate their source, which often identified the position of specific German observation planes. This information was passed on to the RFC, initially to provide information on trends in enemy air operations and to indicate areas where fighters might more profitably operate. However, following the Arras debacle, the RFC started using this information to direct fighters to enemy planes. For the Messines assault, 11th Army Wing set aside one squadron each day to act on information received from the compass station. In the first week of June, on forty-seven occasions, the station passed on the location of German observation aircraft, and on twenty-two occasions, the RFC claimed to have shot down or chased off the enemy plane.[37]

More use of escorts was another way of putting the fighters where they were needed. Even during the Arras offensive, far more use was made of close escorts than Trenchard had wanted. Even if a direct escort was not provided, offensive patrols were often so tightly co-ordinated with long-range bombing or reconnaissance missions they became, to all intents and purposes, escorts. On the issue of the size of RFC fighter formations, Trenchard was trying to move in the right direction. He ideally wanted all fighter squadrons to operate at three-flight strength with 2,000 feet separating the flights vertically, and hoped to increase fighter squadron strength to twenty-four machines to make this possible. Ultimately, he wanted two or three squadron strength formations working together at different altitudes, giving his pilots the chance to take on the German 'circuses' on far more equal terms.[38] The higher quality and more focused use of available fighters was slowly enabling the RFC to gain control of the skies. It helped that the planes they were protecting were also more capable of looking after themselves. For all its faults, the R.E.8 was faster, tougher and better armed than the B.E.2, and for this the aircrews had to be grateful, especially if they were expected to carry out longer range reconnaissance and bombing missions.

Bombing was an aspect of RFC operations Trenchard had always been very anxious to expand, mainly because he wanted to carry the fight well into the enemy rear. The D.H.4 was the first effective day bomber to reach the front. It flew faster and higher than any previous plane used for bombing, although its ability to bomb from 15,000 feet was not matched by the ability to hit anything from that altitude. A far more useful development was tactical bombing under the cover of darkness. By night, bombers could fly as low as they liked in reasonable safety. The destruction of an ammunition dump at Audruicq by German bombers in July 1916 with the loss of 8,000 tons of ammunition was a spectacular illustration of how successful nocturnal bombing could be.[39] Impressed by this German success, Trenchard ordered an intensification of RFC efforts, which meant more work for the corps squadrons.[40] Slowly, aircrews gained the confidence to fly their B.E.2s by night and crews set off on roving missions attacking any target that gave its presence away with lights. It rarely achieved anything more than a nuisance value, but it was another way of wearing down the enemy. So successful were these nocturnal bombing efforts, Trenchard decided it was worth creating specialist bomber squadrons equipped with the F.E.2.s that were being phased out. As with the B.E.2, the stability which had made the aeroplane so vulnerable by day became a priceless asset when flying by night. In February 1917, Nos 100 and 101 Squadrons started forming, using experienced night-flying pilots from a now underemployed home defence force. No. 100 Squadron moved to France in March and picked up the F.E.2s No. 23 Squadron was relinquishing as it converted to Spads.[41] No. 100 Squadron flew its first mission on the night of 5–6 April when eighteen F.E.2s—flying at 500 feet or under and using phosphorus bombs dropped by the leading F.E.2 to illuminate the target—maintained an all-night attack on von Richthofen's base at Douai. It was the beginning of a continuous night offensive against aerodromes, railway stations, convoys and any other targets of opportunity that presented themselves.[42]

The only way day bombing could match the accuracy achieved by night was to fly as low. Since the beginning of the war, pilots had been dropping bombs and strafing targets of opportunity, but often from too great a height to be effective and on too small a scale to be useful. During the Somme, the number of low-level contact and trench patrols increased substantially. As they were operating so low, on completing a mission the pilot would often take the opportunity to use any remaining ammunition against the nearest enemy target. They did not know it at the time, but they were inventing close air support. Ground strafing was only a secondary aim, but these impromptu close air support missions provoked considerable alarm among the defenders. Indeed, German soldiers became convinced these 'battle planes' had ground attack as their primary purpose. It might seem quite an achievement that the offensive efforts of these aircraft were even noticed on the shell drenched and machine gun raked battlefield, but there was something very different about attack from the air. To the soldier, it always looked as if he had been picked out personally by the attacking plane. So impressed were the Germans by the improvised British air support, in the autumn of 1916, the German air force stepped up its own ground-attack efforts and the British infantry were equally alarmed, giving their own commanders some inkling of the potential of this type of support.

A March 1917 RFC memorandum recognised the huge psychological advantage on troops if they were able to witness 'numbers of our machines continually at work over the enemy' and observed how 'the mere presence of a hostile machine above them inspired those on the ground with an exaggerated forebodings of what it is capable of doing'.[43] During the Arras offensive, fighters ordered to fly low defensive patrols over the battlefield often joined the corps planes in these improvised attacks on targets of opportunity. As much as these ground-attack efforts made an impression on German troops, their random nature meant that they rarely brought any immediate advantage to British infantry. However, in May 1917 during the closing stages of the Arras offensive, the RFC began co-ordinating close support more closely with action on the ground. Two-seater F.E.2b and single-seater Nieuports, the former carrying light bombs, were specifically assigned the task of supporting assaulting infantry, although to prevent friendly forces being attacked by mistake, targets were mostly beyond the creeping barrage. These were therefore mostly out of sight of the attacking infantry, but on occasions when an artillery barrage lifted, the infantry were able to witness these efforts.[44]

At Messines in June 1917, fighters were specifically tasked with attacking targets of opportunity, although again the focus was on targets well to the rear of the battlefield, extending as far as enemy airfields.[45] For the opening day of the Ypres offensive, three fighters from each of the four Army squadrons were assigned the task of strafing enemy airfields and other targets of opportunity in the rear. On the eve of the offensive, a last minute decision was made to fit these fighters with improvised bomb racks for four 25-lb bombs. The next day, the Pups, Camels, Spads and S.E.5a fighters made their operational debut as fighter-bombers.[46] The fighters bombed airfields and on their return strafed any target that presented itself, some of which were close enough to the front line to be observed and appreciated by troops on the ground. The demoralising effect they had on German troops was noted by commanders; however, as the pilots were choosing the targets and these were often well beyond the front line, there was little opportunity for the infantry to take advantage of any confusion they might temporarily cause.

Army commanders needed this air support to be much more closely co-ordinated with planned infantry assaults. Complaints from the front that German counterattacks were being regularly supported by low-flying planes striking targets immediately in front of the advancing infantry were supported by captured German documents indicating these were the instructions German pilots were getting; Trenchard was persuaded to order his brigade commanders to do likewise.[47] This was first tried in a minor operation involving the 12th Division on 9 August 1917 when three D.H.5s strafed enemy positions as the troops left their trenches, and four more flew over the advancing infantry at a height of 500 feet, attacking targets immediately in front of them. The psychological lift for the advancing infantry was enormous.

On 15 August, a Sopwith Strutter squadron was specifically assigned the task of dealing with enemy infantry counterattacks. The squadron, operating from a temporary forward base, observed the build-up of enemy reinforcements and reported these to the artillery or engaged them directly. The Strutters were also responsible for helping to keep the front line clear of low-level enemy tactical reconnaissance planes. The concept of the multi-role tactical fighter was emerging. For an assault on 16 August, two D.H.5s were allocated to each division with instructions to attack targets that had survived the creeping barrage and were holding up the advance. Co-ordinating such support so close to advancing friendly forces was far from easy and only a few enemy strongpoints were attacked, but a start had been made to providing an intimate close air support capability. All fighters were soon being encouraged to attack ground targets, whatever their primary mission. Fighters flying offensive patrols for an attack in late September were ordered to dive to ground level at the end of their patrol to attack targets of opportunity with any unused ammunition.[48] In practice, most pilots needed no such instruction to have a go at any target that presented itself. Fighter pilots were beginning to treat ground attack as a normal mission.

It would be idle to suggest it was not dangerous work. After the war, much would be made of these dangers by an air force trying to distance itself from the need to support an Army on the battlefield. Ground attack was portrayed as a pointless waste of expensive machines and highly trained aircrew. It was risky and not particularly popular. Many fighter pilots liked the idea of being in control of their destiny; if they were killed, it was because they were careless or made a mistake, unlike the luckless infantryman who could do nothing about an artillery shell that had his name on it.[49] Ground strafing put the pilot in the same predicament as the infantryman. Yet, there was a realisation among airmen that they were fortunate in avoiding the squalor of the trenches and there was a desire to do something to make the lot of the soldier a little less precarious. There was an affinity between airman and soldier that air force dogma would never be able to break. Fighter pilots threw themselves into ground strafing just as they would unhesitatingly dive into a large formation of enemy planes to help out a fellow pilot in trouble. It was dangerous but arguably less dangerous than advancing across no man's land towards machine guns, or indeed following Trenchard's instructions to patrol 20 miles inside enemy airspace in an obsolete fighter.

Ground attack became the principal role for fighters that did not possess the performance for air-to-air combat. The D.H.5 may have lacked performance at altitude, but at ground level, it was fast, manoeuvrable, rugged, and had an air-cooled engine that was less vulnerable to ground fire. It was almost designed for the ground-attack role. Less capable fighters like the D.H.5 were used for low-level work while the more sophisticated and refined fighters such as the S.E.5a dealt with the enemy at altitude. In RFC parlance of the time, these two types of fighter were referred to as 'ground work' and 'high flying' fighters respectively, or later 'low' and 'high' fighters. They were the future multi-purpose tactical and the specialist air superiority fighter. Initially, Camels were needed for the air superiority role, but as more S.E.5as became available, this fighter, with its superior performance at altitude, assumed responsibility for air superiority, leaving the less capable Camel free for fighter-bomber operations.

Low-level air defence and close support became a regular feature of RFC operations throughout the ill-fated 'Third Battle of Ypres'. It was, nevertheless, the air and artillery combination that was dominating the battlefield. Corps planes were becoming less necessary for identifying the location of enemy batteries, as ground-based sound ranging and flash location methods became more efficient, but they were still hugely valuable for directing fire and identifying targets of opportunity. The latter was particularly valuable with an increasing proportion of the artillery being used just to engage fleeting targets spotted by aircraft.[50] During the Ypres offensive, time and time again, corps planes reported the development of German counterattacks to artillery batteries, which were able to bring prompt and accurate fire to bear on German concentrations.

Low-level fighter-bomber missions, tactical nocturnal bombing, and the need to operate fighters in larger formations at high, medium and low altitudes, all pointed to the need for a larger tactical air force. In November 1917, Trenchard and Haig outlined the force they wanted for 1919. In total, 113 squadrons would be required, a substantial increase on the eighty-six of the current plan. The number of 'high' fighter squadrons for the air superiority role would remain fixed at forty, but with squadron strength increased from eighteen to twenty-four aircraft.[51] There would also have to be an additional fifteen 'ground-attacking' fighter squadrons to provide low-level support. Tactical bombing would be covered by the ten short-range day bombers, but the increasingly effective tactical night-bomber force would require another ten squadrons. In total, the tactical force being proposed would be some 2,400 aircraft strong. In addition to this, Haig was expecting to control the long-range bomber force that was being proposed following the Gotha raids, which, Trenchard and Haig anticipated, would consist of twenty-five day and twenty night-bomber squadrons, twenty escort fighter squadrons and one long-range reconnaissance squadron. First priority, however, was the 113 squadrons for the basic tactical force.[52]

Haig's demands for more aircraft, men and guns was coming on the back of what had turned out to be one of the most fruitless offensives of the entire war. The Ypres region was mostly reclaimed marshland. The shells that poured into the Flanders mud smashed what was left of the drainage channels and even light rain turned the battlefield into a quagmire. The offensive was a disaster. By the end of October, even the ever-optimistic Haig had given up hope. In one last push, Haig insisted the village of Passchendaele and surrounding ridge must be taken, and on 6 November, the village fell; with this minor tactical victory the battle ended. Allied forces were no nearer the submarine bases or Gotha airfields. Strategically, nothing had been gained, but despite Haig's promised caution, another 310,000 men had been lost. Lloyd George was aghast at the horrendous loss of life and the sheer pointlessness of it all. The bloodletting had to stop. Smuts' alternative vision of a war fought solely in the air was beginning to look increasingly attractive once more.

CHAPTER 10

The Government Opts for the Bomber

At the end of August 1917, as the battle around Ypres ground on, the prospects for the creation of a long-range bomber force run by an independent Air Ministry were fading fast. The failure of the Germans to follow up their initial attacks on London and the need to do something about the enemy submarine menace contributed to the independent air force and its long-range bomber fleet slipping down the government's list of priorities. Even Smuts was having second thoughts about the programme he had set in motion. Trenchard had been explaining to him the realities of wartime expansion programmes. All talk of a 200-squadron air force was irrelevant when existing expansion plans were so far behind schedule. On 31 July 1917, the RFC had forty-seven squadrons in France—nine short of the target that was supposed to have been achieved the previous December. The plan had been to increase the RFC to seventy-six squadrons by the end of 1917, but there was little prospect of these arriving even by the following spring.

Smuts was genuinely shocked. He had assumed the production estimates Weir had passed on to him were realistic. All Smuts' talk of a decision on the battlefield being impossible was suddenly forgotten as he contemplated the possibility that, with air superiority, the Germans might punch through the British lines. He remained convinced Britain could not win the war on the battlefields of France, but somewhat paradoxically, he feared she might lose it there. Smuts told the cabinet that it was vital that the basic needs of the RFC in France be met. Once the RFC and British Army had established a sufficient degree of ascendancy on the Western Front to defeat a German offensive, the way would then be clear for the long-range bomber to deliver victory.[1]

The Gothas, however, had returned, attacking under cover of darkness. On the night of 3–4 September, four Gothas bombed Chatham, a single bomb hitting a naval dormitory and killing 130 recruits. More worryingly from the government's point of view, the following night the first bombs fell on London since the second Gotha raid, killing nineteen civilians. Nearly three weeks passed without any further attacks but then six Gotha raids in eight nights resulted in the deaths of ninety-five civilians.

Once more, public and political attention was focused on the horrors of this new indiscriminate form of warfare. Kerr warned the War Cabinet that, according to his Italian sources, Germany was planning to build a 4,000-strong bomber force. He left the cabinet in no doubt about what the consequences would be of 'several hundred machines every night, each one carrying several tons of explosives'. He predicted 'Woolwich, Chatham and all the factories in the London district will be laid flat, parts of London will be wiped out, and workshops in the south-east of England will be destroyed'. The country, he claimed, was now in a race to build an effective long-range bomber force first, and immediate action was required if this race, and with it the war, was not to be lost.[2]

The tragic loss of life at Chatham made such a nightmare scenario highly plausible, and there seemed no way of stopping it. The Gothas by day had been dealt with, but Smuts held out no possibility of the defences coming to terms with bomb-carrying aeroplanes operating under the cover of darkness. Planes were smaller and faster than Zeppelins, and even if the interceptors caught up with them, pilots would have to get within 200 yards before they could even see an intruder. Interception would be impossible. In Smuts' view, balloon barrages to force the bombers to fly higher and searchlights to dazzle the pilots were about the best that could be achieved.[3]

To make matters worse, intelligence reports were coming in of a new six-engine German bomber that was twice the size of the Gotha. The plane was the Zeppelin-Staaken R bomber, capable of carrying three times the Gotha's bomb load, which unbeknown to the defences, had already flown its first mission over London on the night of 28–29 September.[4] Nor was the Zeppelin threat over. Reports of Zeppelins operating beyond the effective ceiling of searchlights were confirmed on the night of 16–17 June, when a new streamlined and lightweight Zeppelin was forced to a lower altitude by engine trouble and shot down. In the wreckage, documents were found revealing the airship had achieved nearly 20,000 feet in trials. There were also reports of a version of the Gotha that was capable of flying at 25,000 feet. If no effective defence was possible against such machines, future wars might become a question of which side could build the most long-range bombers and which country could endure the greatest civilian casualties.

Weir was doing his best to ensure Britain won this race. Trenchard's new interest in night bombing, following the success of his F.E.2 squadrons, undermined Henderson's objections to heavy night bombers; large orders were placed for the Handley Page O/400. Trenchard was warming to the idea of a long-range bomber fleet that he saw as 'part and parcel' of his tactical offensive air policy. He now believed that bombing the sources of iron ore in the Lorraine/Luxembourg area—the targets he had criticised the Navy for bombing—was a good idea, and wanted to go further by attacking German cities and striking a blow at German morale.[5] Trenchard's offensive philosophy was taking the future aerial battle deep inside Germany; the future father of the RAF was taking his first steps towards a strategically orientated vision of aerial warfare. Work began on creating the airfields in France the promised bombers would require.[6]

With the government under increasing pressure to respond to the latest German raids, Trenchard was summoned to London and told by the War Cabinet to arrange an offensive against German targets with whatever was available. Trenchard set up the 41st Wing in the Nancy region in eastern France and put Lieutenant-Colonel Newall in charge. This time the British would be on their own—Bares had departed and with him had gone most French interest in strategic bombing. Newall, a future Chief of Air Staff, was given just three squadrons: one with D.H.4s, one with tactical short-range F.E.2 night bombers, and a squadron provided by the RNAS with a mixture of Handley Page O/400s and F.E.2s. The first mission was flown against the Burbach ironworks on 17 October with eight D.H.4s. A bomb fell on a railway line and two others damaged buildings nearby.[7] It was another inauspicious start to a strategic bombing campaign.

Trenchard was assured seventeen new night-bomber squadrons would be created by July 1918, with the first becoming operational in March. These night bombers, along with the twenty-five long-range day bomber squadrons and twenty long-range escort squadrons, would provide Trenchard with an opportunity to fulfil his vision of dominating airspace deep in the enemy rear. He was soon proposing medium and long-range 'gun machine' squadrons equipped with planes that were essentially similar to the 'flying dreadnoughts' abandoned in 1916. These long-range fighters would not be so different from the long-range reconnaissance planes and bombers Trenchard wanted.

The aircraft that would fill these roles was the twin-engine Airco D.H.10, which was a distant relative of the 1916 Fighting Experimental F.E.4. The first prototype would not fly until March 1918, by which time the plane was being pencilled in to meet over a third of all RFC requirements. Meanwhile, the Vickers F.B.27, the future Vimy, which was another design that owed its origins to the 'flying dreadnought' concept (the E.F.B 7), was emerging as the best solution to the night-bomber requirement.[8] Both the D.H.10 and F.B.27 had ample range for Trenchard's purposes, but Weir needed bombers that could fly much further. For an aerial assault to seriously threaten Germany, bombers had to be able to strike at any target in Germany, not just targets close to her western frontier. There could be no hiding place or safe haven for German civilians and industry that the bombers could not reach. Even the capital had to be within range. Berlin was 450 miles from French-held territory, which meant a bomber would have to be capable of flying at least 1,100 miles.

Weir, however, did not just want bombers capable of reaching Berlin from France—he wanted them to reach the German capital from airfields in Britain. There were too many potential complications to basing a long-range bomber force in France. Haig had made it clear that any continental-based bomber force would be under his command, which raised doubts about how these squadrons might be used. The French might also object to bombing German targets from their bases if it provoked reprisals on French towns and cities. All these problems would be removed if the bomber force operated from Britain, but this added another 200 miles to the round trip to Berlin. Carrying a useful bomb load that distance would require an enormous increase in lifting capability. In November, Weir called Handley Page in to his office to discuss what might be involved in building such a bomber.[9] The response was the Handley Page V/1500 bomber, an enormous plane with nearly twice the wing area of the Handley Page O/400 and powered by two huge 35-litre 600-hp Rolls-Royce Condor engines.[10] The project was a colossal undertaking and Volkert and his Handley Page design team would need all the experience they had acquired in the development of their O/100 and O/400 bombers.

Another designer with ambitions to build large planes, but with far less experience than the Handley Page team, was W. G. Tarrant. He ran a carpentry business in Byfleet, Surrey, and after the outbreak of war, had become involved in manufacturing components for various aircraft. His company's first venture into aircraft design was an audacious four-engine triplane bomber that would have a range of 650 miles and carry a staggering bomb load of 12,000 lbs. Tarrant sent his idea to the Air Board in October 1917 and got a polite reply explaining that his proposal had been carefully considered and rejected.[11] Undeterred, he sent a revised proposal in December, this time sending copies to Trenchard[12] and Weir. Trenchard showed no interest but Weir was very keen, and at the end of January, he summoned Tarrant to his office.[13] Weir suggested a version with the new American Liberty engine ought to be able to reach Berlin. Tarrant doubted four Liberty engines would be enough, but promised to do the best he could. Weir was not discouraged by this tentative response and demanded twenty bombers be built by the following August.[14] It was an extraordinary proposition that underlined the growing air of unreality about the entire strategic bombing venture.

While the process of designing a new generation of heavy bombers was underway, the entire strategic bombing project was being undermined by the collapse of Weir's engine production programme. Neither of the key engines, the Sunbeam Arab and BHP, was proving satisfactory. In the haste to increase output, both had been cleared for production before they were running satisfactorily, despite warnings from the Air Board's own technical department that the experimental features both engines relied on scarcely justified such faith.[15] Even if they could be made to work properly, they were not going to be as good as the Rolls-Royce Falcon or Eagle. Thousands of both were supposed to be delivered by the end of 1917 but deliveries were less than 400.[16] Even before the new version reached France, de Havilland was warning Trenchard that the performance of the BHP-powered D.H.9 would be considerably inferior to the Rolls-Royce-powered D.H.4, which was only supposed to be a temporary and inferior stopgap. Despite all these problems, D.H.4 orders were still being converted into D.H.9 contracts.[17]

When Trenchard discovered the truth about the D.H.9, he was furious and insisted that the bombers on order revert to the Rolls-Royce Eagles, but Weir had to admit there were simply not enough Eagles being produced. It was the BHP-powered D.H.9 or nothing. 'Morale is bound to suffer if they (the aircrews) are called upon to carry out persistently and repeatedly a task for which they know by experience their machines are not thoroughly suited to,' Trenchard fumed.[18] To order so many of an aircraft that was so poor was, in the eyes of Trenchard, sheer incompetence. There were also problems with the other engines Weir was relying on. The American Liberty engine looked like a promising alternative to the Arab and BHP, but deliveries were also running behind schedule.[19] Even production of the Hispano-Suiza was encountering problems. The quality of engines from a subcontractor in France were so poor they had to be rebuilt on arrival, and engines being built in Britain by Wolseley also needed numerous modifications before they could be considered suitable for front line use. So desperate was the shortage, some were sent to the front without the necessary modifications and with warnings for the pilots to treat them with care. It was an appalling demand to make of men risking their lives in combat.

Even including these substandard engines, Weir was not meeting his production targets. Two thousand engines a month were required just to attain the November 1916 seventy-six squadron programme, which Weir had been expecting home production alone would meet, but in December, British output was still hovering around the 1,000 mark. Imports helped make up some of the shortfall, but total engine output was well below 2,000 units. There were insufficient engines to meet the tactical needs of the RFC, never mind create the promised huge engine surplus that was supposed to power the long-range bomber fleet. The Air Board was forced to turn to Rolls-Royce, and the company started getting the investment to expand production of its excellent, albeit expensive engines. Weir was not short of explanations for his failure to meet the targets he had set. He complained that the importance of air power had emerged too late for it to get its fair share of industrial resources and that it was impossible to compete with the huge Navy and Army arms production programmes. As far as Weir was concerned, the only solution was a radical realignment of the country's resources with a higher proportion going to aircraft production.[20]

It was true that the British aircraft industry had been underdeveloped at the outbreak of war, but it was not the allocation of resources to aeronautical and non-aeronautical armaments that was the problem. The Admiralty and War Office might not have devoted sufficient resources to aircraft production, but it was within their power to allocate whatever proportion of the budget they felt it deserved. Weir's problem was the balance between tactical and strategic aircraft production. He was beginning to realise a strategic bomber force could only be built at the expense of, not in addition to, Army and Navy requirements. Testing the waters, Weir tentatively suggested two Army reconnaissance squadrons might be transferred to the bomber force to speed things up. Trenchard and Henderson soon scotched that idea and reinforced their objections by demanding the fighter force be expanded by the formation of eight new Dolphin squadrons, which they pointedly emphasised, were far more important than bombers.[21] The battle for resources was on, but with the Air Board having no executive power, it was a battle the War Office was going to win. Weir needed the backing of the independent Air Ministry Smuts had proposed, and he was about to get it.

The combined pressure of German air raids on London, growing calls for a more centrally organised air programme, criticism in the press of a dithering government, and Rear Admiral Kerr's dire warning that 'the country who strikes first with its big bombing machines at the enemy's vital spots, will win the war',[22] forced Lloyd George to act. In November, the government announced an Air Ministry was to be formed with full executive control of all military and naval aviation. A decision-making Air Council equivalent to the Army Council and Admiralty Board, headed by a Chief of Air Staff, would come into being on 3 January 1918. This would be followed by the creation of an entirely independent air force, bringing together the RNAS and RFC, and the new service would have the formation of an independent long-range bomber force as its top priority. Cowdray, president of the existing Second Air Board, was the logical choice to run the new ministry and Weir was another fancied candidate, but Lloyd George hoped to curry favour with an increasingly hostile press by offering the post to Lord Northcliffe, the pre-war champion of air power and owner of the *Daily Mail* and *The Times*. It would, Lloyd George reasoned, be an opportunity for the newspaper tycoon to do something about the problems his newspapers had spent so many column inches highlighting over the years. It was also an opportunity to silence one of his biggest critics by bringing him into the decision-making process.

Northcliffe, however, rejected the offer publicly in an open letter published in his own newspaper, while Cowdray immediately resigned in protest at being so obviously overlooked. Weir seemed the most likely to fill the vacuum, but Lloyd George, still anxious to get some press opinion on his side, turned to Northcliffe's younger brother Lord Rothermere, the owner of the *Daily Mirror*. From an organisational point of view, an independent air force and Air Ministry was not such a dramatic step to take. The Air Board was a sound foundation for the new ministry and the Directorate of Military Aeronautics was already a semi-autonomous body within the War Office, which could easily be transferred to the new ministry. This was not so much the case with the Navy, where the centralisation of aeronautics forced on the Admiralty by the creation of a Fifth Sea Lord had not yet had time to take effect.

In the new organisation, the disempowered War Office Directorate of Military Aeronautics would become the Army department that would liaise with the new Air Ministry. It would be a key position with a seat on the Army Council, and for the War Office it was important to get someone into this position who could be relied on to toe their line. The current director, Henderson, was not considered to be that person. Henderson's involvement with Smuts was already taking him away from his work at the War Office. Indeed, his close association with Smuts provided both a good reason and excuse to get rid of him. Brancker saw no reason why he should not move into the top job. For most of the previous three years, he had effectively been running the air department, but was told his youth (he was just forty years old) counted against him. In fact, Brancker was no more trusted by the War Office than Henderson. Both had shown an enthusiasm for long-range bombing and had incurred the wrath of Trenchard for failing to provide the RFC with all it needed in France. Indeed, far from getting the top job, Brancker found himself banished to command RFC squadrons in the Middle East.[23]

John Salmond became the new Director General of Military Aeronautics. He had been one of Trenchard's first brigade commanders, and since 1916 had been impressing all with the way he had transformed the pilot training programme. He was one of a new generation of RFC officers. He was just thirty-six years old when he was appointed, becoming the youngest member of the War Council, which did not impress the overlooked and supposedly too youthful forty-year-old Brancker. Brancker's position was taken by the equally youthful Ellington. Before the outbreak of war, Ellington had been briefly involved in the organisation of the RFC and was also attached to Derby's Joint War Air Committee, but had spent most of the war serving with the Royal Artillery. Salmond and Ellington were rising stars destined to reach the very top. Both could be relied on to hold reasonably conventional views on the importance of tactical air power.

While the War Office had to decide who might best protect the interests of their tactical air force, the government had to choose someone to head the new independent air force. If the fledging independent air force was to have any chance of succeeding, it would have to be led by someone with the strength of personality to stand up to the War Office and Admiralty, and overcome any reluctance within the RFC and RNAS to unite. Henderson was the logical candidate, but it was not just the War Office that did not trust him. Advocates of long-range bombing had not been impressed by his insistence that the RFC's tactical requirements should be met before a long-range bomber force was created. There was a dearth of suitable candidates for the new Chief of Air Staff position; the single outstanding dominant figure in British military aviation was Trenchard. He was scarcely the most diplomatic of candidates. He did not want the job and the fact that he did not believe in the need for an independent Air Ministry or air force was scarcely a recommendation, but there seemed to be no one else with the strength of personality to hold the new organisation together. At least there was a good chance his appointment would win over a reluctant RFC and placate a nervous War Office. Haig was loath to lose his air force commander, but there was the undoubted compensation that he would have his man in the key position. Nor was it such an entirely illogical move for Trenchard. For some time he and his RFC commanders had been pulling in different directions, with Trenchard emphasising the need to operate deep in the enemy rear and his more pragmatic commanders reining in these offensive tendencies. Although it would not have occurred to Trenchard, the Air Ministry was a conducive environment for the policies he was tending towards. John Salmond would take over from Trenchard in France and Ellington would replace Salmond in the War Office.

However, as the government marshalled the resources to fight this new revolutionary form of warfare, yet again the bomber threat was being dealt with. Nocturnal air defence was not proving as impossible as Smuts had predicted, and one by one the problems were overcome. The first problem for night interceptors was to reach the altitude the bombers flew. Single-seater tractors had the best rate of climb but were difficult to fly by night, and it seemed to be expecting too much of the lone pilot to look out for the enemy as well. As an alternative, the Royal Aircraft Factory was working on the specialist two-seater N.E.1 night fighter, a pleasant and stable but pedestrian adaptation of the F.E.9 pusher. However, while the Factory persevered with the two-seater pusher, pilots of the Sopwith Camel-equipped No. 44 Squadron were regularly taking off to intercept night raiders without suffering any accidents. Unfortunately, encounters with the enemy were just as infrequent, until the night of 18–19 December 1917 when a Camel pilot from No. 44 Squadron spotted the exhaust flames of a Gotha. Searchlights illuminated the bomber and the Camel attacked from below; after the fourth pass, the Gotha began to lose altitude and ditched in the sea just off Folkestone.[24] It was ironic that one of the more difficult single-seaters to fly should achieve the first nocturnal success against a bomber. However, the fighter had advantages. Its air-cooled engine, unlike liquid-cooled engines, did not need to warm up, a significant factor when every minute counted if the fighters were to have a chance of reaching the bombers. With the lighter Lewis gun replacing the Vickers and less fuel, the plane climbed quicker, and the Camel, perhaps the most capricious of all the available single-seater fighters, became the LADA night fighter of choice. The fighters were backed by an increasingly efficient early warning and tracking system. Experimental sound mirrors operating on the path the bombers took to London could provide up to seven minutes of additional warning, enough time for a Camel to climb 8,000 feet.[25] On the approach to London, observers using stereophonic headphones were able to provide the approximate location of the approaching bombers which gave the searchlight crews an idea of where to start looking.

The occasional loss to fighters or anti-aircraft fire might have been acceptable, but the defences were just one of the problems facing the German bombers. The freezing temperatures and lack of oxygen at the altitudes the Zeppelins were now operating made for extremely harsh conditions for the crews. Furthermore, with the airships operating on the fringes of the jetstream, crews were encountering unexpectedly strong winds which made navigation extremely difficult and flying airships a dangerous occupation, as demonstrated in a raid on the night of 19–20 October. A Zeppelin crew bombed Birmingham, thinking it was Manchester, and the thirty-three civilians killed in London that night were the unlucky victims of bombs dropped by a Zeppelin that was blown of course by high winds and by chance found itself over London. The Zeppelin eventually crashed on the continent, along with three others swept to similar fates that night.[26] Following this, no more Zeppelin raids would be flown until the following March.

Aeroplanes at lower altitudes were not finding it much easier. On the night of 31 October–1 November, an all-out effort against London—using new incendiary bombs, which were supposed to set off huge conflagrations—ended in failure. Twenty-two Gothas set off for London but only ten reached the target; the remainder lost their way and bombed towns on the coast. Ten civilians were killed but the incendiaries were too inefficient and the concentration too low to cause any major fires. To complete a miserable night for the attackers, five Gothas crashed as they approached their airfields in Belgium. The defences had been totally ineffective, but the Germans had still managed to lose nearly a quarter of the attacking force. The offensive was in danger of inflicting more casualties on the participating German aircrews than the defenceless civilians they were trying to bomb. On the night of the Camel fighter's first success, the Germans lost another two bombers destroyed and five damaged in landing accidents. No further Gotha attacks took place until 28–29 January, when another German bomber was caught in searchlights and destroyed by two Camels from No. 44 Squadron.[27] The Gotha units were stood down for rest and re-equipment, leaving the Zeppelin–Staaken bombers to persevere alone. Five raids were carried out by these enormous bombers in the first three months of 1918, the last and largest with just six machines took place on 7–8 March.

The small numbers involved in these raids was perhaps the most damning statistic of all. As well as underestimating the operational difficulties, the advocates of long-range bombing continually underestimated the enormous effort required to create a sizeable long-range bomber force. Zeppelins and heavy bombers were very expensive to build and required highly trained crews. Kerr's exaggerated estimate that the Germans would have 4,000 bombers by the summer was hopelessly wide of the mark. 'Nonsense! Forty,' was Trenchard's curt response when Lloyd George confronted him with Kerr's figure.[28] Even predictions of raids of up to 500 bombers turned out to be wild exaggerations. The Air Council soon downgraded the estimates to a more modest threat of eighty bombers by the summer of 1918. Even Trenchard's figure of forty proved to be an overestimate. Only on one occasion during the winter of 1917–18 did the German air force manage to put more than twenty bombers over a British target on a single night. In the spring of 1918, there was no indication that parts of London would be 'wiped out' and its factories 'laid flat' as Kerr had predicted. By the time the Gotha and Zeppelin units were ready to return to operations in March, Germany had realised the futility of their air offensive and the Gothas and Zeppelin–Staakens were switched to tactical targets in the rear of Allied lines in France. This was where the German High Command now expected the war to be decided.

Newall's 41st Wing was not finding long-range bombing any easier. The French could no longer see any point in attacking targets in Germany and risking retaliation for no gain and wanted the British bombers to concentrate on rail communications running eastwards from the Lorraine basin. Haig, however, insisted Newall's bombers concentrate on targets in Germany proper where bombs would kill Germans. As German aircrews were finding, the weather was a far more dangerous enemy than the opposing defences. On the first nocturnal raid against Saarbrucken on 24–25 October, twenty-five F.E.2s and Handley Page bombers were dispatched, but two of the former and two of the latter failed to return, probably victims of the poor weather, but still an uncomfortably high 16 per cent loss rate.

On 4–5 December, the base the British bombers were operating from was bombed. Although little damage was done, Newall feared that a sustained offensive against his airfield would decimate his already meagre resources so he diverted part of his effort to attacking local German aerodromes. In the New Year, Newall also began focusing more on railway targets in Alsace-Loraine the French wanted bombed, all of which meant much less effort was being devoted to targets in Germany proper. Newall gained permission to extend these raids to occupied Luxembourg, although he was instructed to make sure targets were military and the risk to innocent civilians was minimal. There was still very little idea of how inaccurate aerial bombing was and how unrealistic this request was. Whatever their targets were, with only three squadrons and a small chance of reinforcements, Newall's force was unlikely to achieve much. Trenchard still believed 'an offensive policy from the air on German territory is of paramount importance' but only when the 'primary and indispensable' seventy-six squadrons required by the Army had arrived.[29] Like the Germans, the British were giving priority to building up their tactical air force. The decisive battle in 1918 would be fought on the battlefields of France, not in the skies above London or the Ruhr.

CHAPTER 11

New Options on the Battlefield

Before returning to London to take up the post of Chief of Air Staff, Trenchard was involved in one last offensive, a relatively small-scale attack on the Cambrai sector of the front. Although the full significance of the encounter was not so obvious at the time—and like most previous offensives, ended with both sides holding virtually the same ground as they had started with—the engagement was in many ways a watershed in the development of military tactics. The action saw both sides move away from a reliance on lengthy pre-offensive artillery barrages and towards an effective and substantial use of low-level air support.

Two innovations would influence the way this and future battles were fought. Instead of mass frontal assaults, the German Army introduced flexible infantry tactics based on initiative, movement and surprise with small groups of troops seeking weak points in the defensive lines, bypassing strongpoints and pushing into the enemy rear. The British Army was moving in the same direction with smaller and more flexible infantry platoons. Both sides were moving away from lengthy pre-assault artillery barrages. The new emphasis was on achieving surprise and using firepower to cover an advance rather than expecting it to destroy the defences.

The second innovation was the large-scale deployment of the tank. The tank had first been tried out in September 1916 when forty-nine were assembled to support an infantry attack. Although they caused considerable panic among the German defenders, one of the first acts of air-tank co-operation was the reporting by contact patrols of the position of machines that had broken down. However, there were glimpses of what was to come. In what the official history would later describe as 'an example of perfect co-operation between the air, tanks, artillery and infantry', a German trench defending the village of Gueudecourt was occupied at two points separated by about a mile. The two groups of infantry then converged, with the group approaching from the north supported by a single tank. A spotter plane followed their progress and when the German infantry became sufficiently compressed to present an attractive target, the plane called for an artillery barrage. As the pincers closed, the plane called off the artillery support to avoid friendly casualties and provided its own support by strafing the enemy forces caught in the trench. Soon afterwards, the remaining German forces surrendered. The entire action had cost the lives of just five British soldiers.[1] The role of the tank or the sole 'ground-attack' aircraft was scarcely central or decisive, but the action did show infantry, tanks, artillery and aircraft working together in a way that would not always prove easy to replicate in the decades to come.

Rushed into action before they were fully developed, tanks did not particularly impress British commanders, nor did they inspire the Germans to copy the idea. During the Ypres offensive, tanks found it more difficult to move in the quagmire than infantry; however, following the Ypres disaster, the Tank Corps was given the opportunity to try out their new weapon in large numbers and in conditions that suited it. The dry, chalky countryside around Cambrai was perfect tank country.

Both sides might have developed very different methods for breaking through strong defences, but both could agree that close support by low-flying aircraft should play an important part in supporting the attacking forces. So far the aeroplane had contributed to a vicious circle in which reconnaissance and directed artillery fire had helped squeeze all mobility out of military operations, but the circle now started moving in the opposite direction. Close air support was an excellent way of providing covering fire, which would help enable mobility to return to the battlefield. The more mobility there was, the more scope there would be for aviation to demonstrate how influential it could be.

For the Cambrai attack, nearly 400 tanks were to support six divisions along a 6-mile front. The 3rd Brigade supporting the attack possessed six corps squadrons, seven fighter squadrons and one squadron of fighter-reconnaissance planes. With the addition of a handful of D.H.4 bombers, there were 289 planes in all.[2] The three S.E.5a squadrons would be responsible for maintaining air superiority while the D.H.5 and Camel squadrons would fly low-level fighter-bomber missions with four machines on standby to intercept German observation machines over the battlefield. They were opposed by seventy-eight German aircraft, twelve of which were fighters.[3] The lack of a pre-offensive artillery barrage would help ensure surprise. Meanwhile, aircraft droned up and down overhead to conceal the noise of the tanks moving into position. To help compensate for the lack of artillery, four fighter-bomber squadrons were assigned the task of attacking German artillery positions in the Flesquieres, Lateau Wood and Vaucelles Wood areas with machine guns and 25-lb bombs. Other fighters would attack targets of opportunity, initially over a broad front to disguise the direction of the main effort, but from two hours into the attack, they would concentrate on targets in front of the advancing tanks. Poor, misty weather on the day of the attack did not lead to postponement. The tanks and infantry would be attacking with some protection from the weather. Aircraft would have to do the best they could.

The resources available were far too limited to maintain the attack once German reinforcements began to arrive, which Haig believed gave him around forty-eight hours to achieve something significant. The air attacks on the artillery batteries were not particularly effective. The mist did not help, but even if the aircraft found their targets, small bombs and machine-gun fire were not enough to knock out gun emplacements. The batteries in the Flesquieres and Lateau Wood areas were soon slowing the advance; the German defences in the centre held, and with mist and low cloud covering the battlefield, the corps planes were unable call the artillery in. However, the advantages of the mist far outweighed the disadvantages. The Germans were caught by surprise and on either side of Flesquieres, their defences were rapidly over-run. By midday, Lateau Wood had also fallen. The slow relentless advance of the tanks was causing panic among the defenders and as the mists lifted, the low-flying fighters added to the confusion. The artillery batteries may have remained too tough a target for the fighter-bombers, but troops caught in the open were very vulnerable.

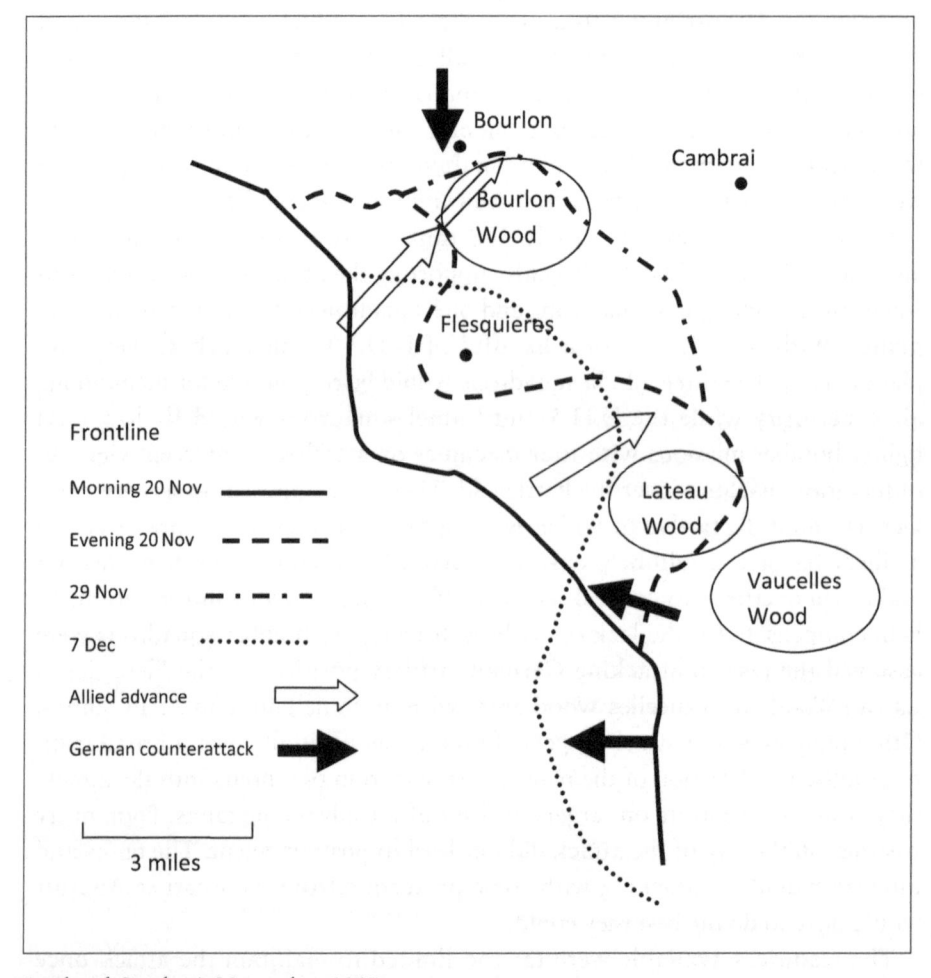

Battle of Cambrai: November 1917.

RFC losses were heavy. On the first day, of the seventy-five planes that flew repeated low-level ground-attack missions, nine failed to return, four were write-offs and thirteen were severely damaged. Most of these were lost against airfields and artillery positions in the rear during low-level attacks carried out in early morning mists, with some of the losses the result of aircraft hitting the ground or trees. Attacks later in the day against disorganised retreating German forces were less costly.[4]

Although the advance was held in the centre at Flesquieres, by the end of the day, the tanks had advanced up to four miles on either side. A partial breakthrough had been achieved, and with no lengthy artillery assault giving advance notice of the attack, the Germans did not have adequate reserves immediately available. During the night, the Germans evacuated the Flesquieres Salient, and the Bourlon Ridge, with its dominant position over the surrounding countryside, became the crucial battleground. It was now the German Army that benefited from effective close air support as low-flying two-seater Halberstadts and Hannovers disorganised British efforts to capture Bourlon Wood. The 62nd Division took the brunt of these attacks and requested fighter support for the following day, and four S.E.5as were given the task of providing low-level cover.[5] The numbers may seem tiny, but the shift in mentality was significant. The Army was no longer being protected by theories about dominating the airspace above the battlefield by flying distant offensive patrols well beyond the front line. The fighters were in the battle zone. At the end of the day, Bourlon Ridge remained in enemy hands—Haig's original forty-eight-hour deadline was up and enemy reserves were arriving. Haig, however, felt he had to take the ridge at least. The German reinforcements included Richthofen's fighter wing, JG1, and the S.E.5a squadrons suddenly had their work cut out protecting the low-flying Camels and D.H.5s, but the escorts did enough to ensure the fighter-bombers were able to provide very effective support, bombing and strafing enemy strongpoints often in full view of the British troops.[6] Losses were heavy,[7] but there would be no need to 'educate' the British soldier about the value of this sort of air support.

Poor weather kept RFC air activity to a minimum on subsequent days. As the German defences recovered from the shock, resistance stiffened with artillery firing over open sights inflicting heavy losses on the tanks. The fighting was fierce, positions changed hands several times, Bourlon Wood was occupied, but the Germans hung on in the village.

On 30 November, the Germans hit back, attacking the flanks of the salient the British advance had created from north and south. Again, there was no preliminary artillery bombardment and the new German infantry infiltration tactics, being used on the Western Front for the first time, proved as difficult to combat as the British tanks had been. Air support also played its part. The low-flying German 'battle-flights' might have inflicted relatively few casualties, but they caused enormous alarm and confusion. Even if they only succeeded in making defending British infantry keep their heads down, it was often enough for the attacking Germans to gain the upper hand. Once the retreat started, the low-level air attacks turned it into a near rout with panic-stricken troops abandoning guns and equipment in their haste to escape. RFC fighter-bombers were thrown against the advancing German forces, and fighters were ordered to provide low-level cover. The advance was halted, but in a remarkably short space of time, the Germans had regained much of the lost ground.[8]

The net result may have been the same as all the previous indecisive battles on the Western Front, but the pace at which events had unfolded had been dramatically quicker. Both sides had advanced distances in days that had previously often taken weeks or months, and close air support had been an important factor. Air attack was provoking far stronger feelings among the infantry than the deadlier weight of fire artillery could bring to bear; artillery never induced panic, but it seemed aircraft could. Nor was it just a question of morale. Aircraft had provided very real assistance with British tank crews and infantry reporting that on occasion it was only the intervention of aircraft that had enabled friendly forces pinned down by enemy fire to continue their advance.

There was much to ponder on during the winter months of 1917–18. The overall strategic balance of power was shifting dramatically. The German unrestricted submarine campaign resulted in American ships being sunk, and in response the United States declared war on Germany. It would take time for the United States to mobilise, but inevitably the long-term numerical and material advantage on the Western Front would tip decisively in favour of the Franco-British-American alliance. On the other hand, Russia was in turmoil. In November 1917, the Bolsheviks took control of the country and began negotiating peace terms with Germany. German forces on the Eastern Front could now be switched to France, giving Germany a short-term numerical advantage and the opportunity to go on to the offensive before the Americans arrived. Both sides appreciated that Germany would have one last chance of victory. The British and French were confident that if they could avoid defeat in 1918, ultimate victory was assured. Haig and Trenchard were instructed to conserve their forces and prepare for a defensive battle. It was a welcome breathing space for the RFC and one which would be well exploited. The new defensive attitude coincided with a determined effort to resolve the long-standing deficiencies in the training programme, which had churned out underprepared replacement aircrews. RFC front line strength was also being boosted by growing numbers of airmen from Canada, Australia, South Africa and other parts of the Empire.

As Trenchard prepared to return to London to take up his new responsibilities, he was leaving behind an air force that was growing in confidence and capable of much more than reconnoitring and observing. Although he tended to favour indirect rather than direct support for the Army and continued to argue that the air battle should be fought at the enemy's rear, Trenchard still believed air power was primarily a tactical weapon; he expected it to play a crucial role in the forthcoming defensive battle. Supporting the artillery was still the most important air force role, but any unemployed corps planes should be used to attack targets in the battle zone 1–2 miles beyond the enemy front line. Even this, he conceded, was unlikely to satisfy the Army—an indication that the infantry was coming to expect ever closer support. Even Trenchard conceded that there would have to be some very close support, simply because of the huge effect it had on the morale of the troops, not to mention the need to pre-empt criticisms that the RFC was not fully engaged in the battle.[9]

For the counterattacks the Allies would inevitably mount, Trenchard did anticipate very close air support along the lines developed at Cambrai with fighter-bombers flying low over the advancing infantry, but supporting the artillery and bombing targets in the rear were still the primary air force roles.[10] Trenchard's first task as Chief of Air Staff was to make sure that the RFC was ready to provide the Army with all the support it might require.

CHAPTER 12

Tactical Air Support Comes of Age

On 3 January 1918, Trenchard took up his new position as Chief of Air Staff in Rothermere's newly created Air Ministry. With the autocratic press baron and the single-minded air commander both used to doing things their own way, it was a combination that was doomed from the start. Trenchard was soon complaining that he had no real power; his Secretary of State could overrule him and his new ministry was simply not doing his biding. 'It is impossible for me to impress myself on them as a dictator,' he complained.[1] Rothermere was harbouring similar sentiments.

The organisation of the new ministry mirrored the War Office Directorate with three departments controlling strategy, personnel and equipment. Kerr was appointed Deputy Chief of Air Staff (DCAS), and with Trenchard would be responsible for strategy and operational matters. Personnel was run by Paine, the ex-Fifth Sea Lord, and equipment was taken over by Brancker who had been hastily recalled from the Middle East.[2] These four formed the Air Staff.

At the first meeting of the Air Council, Trenchard found himself confronted by some formidable advocates of an independent bombing strategy. His deputy, Admiral Kerr, had made his views on strategic bombing very clear, and Weir was there to support him. Rothermere and Baird, now Rothermere's Under Secretary of State, ensured that the popular political requirement for a retaliatory bomber force was met. Brancker and Henderson, back as vice-president, could scarcely be counted as automatic allies after the fractious relationship that had developed between them while Trenchard was in command in France.

If the ranks of the Air Council were supposed to steer Trenchard in the right direction, it failed to do so. As many had predicted, the administrative complications of creating such a significant new organisation were bound to take up a fair proportion of the available time. The name of the new force, the Royal Air Force, was decided, and the date for its creation, 1 April, agreed. The administrative infrastructure of the new service was discussed and the colour of the uniforms chosen—at this stage a 'nasty pale blue'[3] dictated by the large quantities of material available from a cancelled pre-revolution Russian contract—but long-range bombing hardly got a mention in Air Council deliberations. There was an inertia on the issue that Trenchard had little desire to do anything about.[4]

It was not just administrative detail that was putting a brake on the development of strategic bombing. When the talking did get round to air policy, it was difficult to justify an immediate effort to build up the long-range bombing arm when a German offensive was expected in the spring and the U-boat battle was still far from won. Brancker's experience in the Middle East had reinforced his belief in the importance of tactical air power, and Henderson had always insisted the needs of the Army came before the long-range bombing force. Even Kerr, in his prediction of cataclysmic destruction, had insisted the new Air Ministry he was advocating would have to supply the Army and Navy with sufficient machines to ensure mastery over the enemy at sea and on the battlefield.[5]

Both tactical air forces were still a long way short of what the Army and Navy required. Haig only had forty-eight of the seventy-six squadrons he had demanded in November 1916, and since then his requirements had increased to 113 squadrons. Admiralty demands were accelerating even faster. To deal with the U-boat menace, the Admiralty wanted 1,200 places just to patrol British coastal waters,[6] and Beatty was demanding more fighters, torpedo bombers and reconnaissance planes for operations from warships and aircraft carriers. On 1 January 1918, the Navy had 2,851 planes of all types, nearly three times as many as it had in January 1916. Two years before, Trenchard had mockingly asked the Admiralty what they had planned to do with all the aircraft they were acquiring and the Admiralty had had no convincing answer. In 1918, they knew exactly what they wanted to do with them, and they wanted a lot more. By early 1918, front line requirements had risen to a staggering 3,742 planes.[7] With Weir promising a massive increase in aircraft production, Rothermere casually promised the Admiralty 4,000 planes, which was merely leading the Admiralty 'up the garden path', according to Trenchard.[8]

The latest Admiralty and War Office demands pushed the creation of the promised aircraft surplus further into the future. To complicate matters further, casualties on the battlefield meant Britain was suffering a major manpower crisis. The Army was short of men and the War Office insisted that its infantry requirements had to have priority over the manpower requirements of any air programme. It was difficult to see where the resources and manpower for a long-range bomber fleet could possibly come from.

The prospect of imminent defeat, either on the battlefields of France or the coastal waters of Britain, was something that even the most ardent military or naval advocate of long-range bombing could not ignore. Submarines were sinking British ships and German divisions were moving from Russia to the Western Front while the skies above London were quiet. Whatever grandiose ambitions Lloyd George, Weir and Rothermere might have, until the War Office and the Admiralty got their basic tactical requirements, the long-range strategic bomber force would have to wait. In the new era of an independent Air Ministry, things carried on pretty much as before, and Salmond's tactical air force in France continued to get priority. Not that Salmond would necessarily have approved of all the decisions Trenchard's Air Ministry was making on his behalf.

By the end of 1917, it was clear the Camel was struggling in the fighter-versus-fighter role, but the Camel continued to pour off the production lines. Over 4,000 Camels were built in 1918, simply to keep production lines occupied until the similar Snipe and its Bentley BR2 engine were ready for production. Over 4,000 of the Hispano-Suiza-powered S.E.5a were also built, while in the same time period, production of Britain's best fighter, the Sopwith Dolphin, numbered fewer than 1,500.[9]

The Martinsyde F.3 was even better, but Trenchard had taken an instant dislike to the plane. Only a small number had been ordered and one of his first decisions of the new Air Ministry was to shelve their production; in addition, Martinsyde were told another engine had to be used instead of the Falcon. The 300-hp Hispano-Suiza was the leading contender, but it was not expected to become available until the summer. The order for 150 Falcon-powered F.3s was converted into an order for the Hispano-Suiza-powered F.4 version, and if the airframes were completed before the French engines became available, they would be put into storage. Weir and Trenchard had torpedoed any chance the RFC had of getting a significantly better fighter into service for the spring or summer of 1918.[10] A March 1918 review of the state of British fighter development highlighted how serious the situation was. The BR2-powered Snipe prototype, the only other new fighter on the horizon, was only offering a marginal improvement in performance over the existing Camel, and was rated as substantially inferior to the existing S.E.5a and Dolphin.[11]

The report was encouraged by two new engines, which seemed capable of rescuing the Snipe and saving the day. The engines had been developed by ABC— the All British (Engine) Company—and had first been proposed in the summer of 1917. With fixed rather than the rotating cylinders of the conventional rotary, they were very experimental. The seven-cylinder ABC Wasp was expected to produce 170 hp and the nine-cylinder Dragonfly was predicted to achieve 340 hp. Both engines would be simple and easy to produce, and for their power, were extraordinarily light.[12] Rival manufacturers were particularly sceptical, claiming such performances were impossible and that ABC had cut far too many corners to get the weight so low, but this was viewed as sour grapes. If ABC's forecasts were right, it was predicted that the Dragonfly would enable a fighter to achieve 156 mph at 15,000 feet and climb to that height in under nine minutes.[13] In the autumn of 1917, the Air Board was just about able to resist the temptation to order them immediately, but as soon as the first test runs began in the spring of 1918, the Air Ministry could contain its excitement no longer.

Higher performance was required and the ABC engines conveniently justified the decision to keep the Camel–Snipe line of fighters going.

The March report concluded that with the Bentley BR2 already in production, there was little alternative but to persevere with the Snipe, but a minimum number were to be built with production switching to the ABC-powered version as soon as the Dragonfly was running reliably. Although the Dragonfly was still being tested, the first 300 were ordered on 12 March.[14] A Snipe was fitted with the engine and took to the air in April 1918; when the engine worked properly, the fighter managed a sensational 150 mph. This, however, was a rare event. In truth, the Dragonfly and the Wasp were far from ready for production. To try and speed things up, the Wasp was dropped and all effort was focused on the Dragonfly, with the Royal Aircraft Factory brought in to help sort out the problems. Even though there was little evidence these were close to being resolved, orders for the Dragonfly had soon risen to a staggering 12,000.

One fighter not even mentioned in the March report was the Martinsyde F.3/4. Martinsyde had completed the prototype of the Hispano-Suiza-powered F.4, and in April the first example of the French engine arrived. It would not appear there was any great urgency about testing the plane as it did not go to Martlesham Heath until June. It was better than the Falcon-powered F.3, but the RFC would now have to wait for deliveries of the 300-hp Hispano-Suiza engine before the fighter could go into service.[15] The Bentley BR2-powered Snipe prototype was rushed to France in March 1918 and pilots were pleasantly surprised by its performance.[16] In its final form, it flew faster, higher, and climbed quicker than its predecessor. It was also less capricious, which was a mixed blessing. For the novice pilot, it was good news, but for the old hands who knew how to get the best out of the quirky Camel, it was the fighter's instability that often proved their salvation. An improvement it might be, but the Snipe came nowhere near matching the S.E.5a and Sopwith Dolphin or the requirements of Trenchard and the Air Board. It was just an improvement on the Camel.

As well as an air superiority fighter, Salmond would also need a low-level fighter-bomber. This role was currently being carried out by standard fighters, but losses to ground fire had been heavy and there was a case for giving the pilots more protection. How much was a matter of debate as more armour meant less manoeuvrability and air combat capability. In January 1918, a specification was released for an armoured ground-attack fighter. Sopwith put forward two proposals: a modified Camel with 130 lbs of armour, the TF1 (Trench Fighter 1); and a more heavily armoured plane, the Sopwith Salamander TF2, based on the Snipe, with no less than 600 lbs of defensive armour. As the Snipe was not yet in production, the Camel-based TF1 would be available long before the TF2. Weir, for production reasons, and Trenchard, for tactical reasons, favoured the lighter and more manoeuvrable Camel TF1, while the Air Ministry Technical Department preferred the more heavily armoured Salamander.[17] Within a month, Sopwith had a prototype of the lightly armoured Camel TF1 in the air. In March, two prototypes were flown to France for service trials and the pilots felt the light armour would be perfectly adequate.[18] A couple of squadrons were to be equipped with the plane as quickly as possible for trials, although work on the more heavily armoured Salamander still continued.[19] Neither these nor many other new designs would arrive in time to meet the German spring offensive. A couple of squadrons converted to the Dolphin. The first D.H.9 became operational in March, but this was inferior to the D.H.4. With the disappointing Snipe, the next fighter to enter service, British aircraft development seemed to have stalled. The RFC would fight the crucial battles of 1918 largely with the same aircraft it had used in the summer of 1917.

Meticulous preparations were made for the coming offensive. To counter the infiltration tactics used by the Germans at Cambrai, Haig prepared a flexible defence with lightly held forward positions covered by strongpoints that dominated the battlefield and fall back positions behind that. This 'battle-zone' stretched for up to five miles. Haig was confident these defences would hold, but Salmond was not so sure and prepared for the worst. Possible new sites for airfields in the rear were reconnoitred and more motorised transport was allocated to enable the squadrons to retreat to them.

Wherever and whenever the attack came, everyone would know what to do. The day and night bombers stood ready to strike at communication targets in the rear while the corps squadrons prepared to bring down artillery fire on the advancing German forces. The fighters were under instructions to concentrate their efforts in the battle zone. Flights of fighters were to be kept on standby to intercept any enemy planes reported over the front. Close escorts were to be provided for corps planes as well as 'inner protective patrols' and 'close offensive patrols'. These would be supplemented by 'distant offensive patrols', but 'distant' now meant just a few miles beyond the front line.[20] As the March days lengthened, the build-up of enemy units on the 3rd and 5th Army fronts suggested this was where the attack was coming. The RFC, just days away from officially becoming the Royal Air Force, stood ready.

The German plan was to attack the British 3rd and 5th Armies along a 45-mile stretch of the front with the main weight of the attack falling on the southern wing of the 3rd Army. The German forces would advance as far as Albert-Bapaume and then swing north to take Arras from the south. The southern flank of this drive would be covered by an advance on the British 5th Army front as far as the Somme-Crozat Canal line. It was anticipated that the capture of Arras would compel the British Army to retreat northwards towards the English Channel, separating them from the French and pinning them against the Channel where they would be destroyed. The British also saw the crucial importance of holding Arras, and their defences were strongest there. Further south along the 5th Army's front, the line was more thinly held.

The sixty-three German divisions would be supported by 6,000 guns and 730 aircraft, including twenty-seven specialist close-support squadrons. RFC strength in France, excluding the three squadrons with the 41st Wing, stood at fifty-eight squadrons with a further two squadrons provided by the Navy. This was still well below the seventy-six squadrons the RFC was supposed to have the previous December. The bulk of the fighter force was made up of an equal number of S.E.5a and Camel squadrons, with just a couple of Dolphin squadrons. The S.E.5a was good enough and the Dolphin more than adequate as long as the Albatros and Fokker Triplane remained the opposition. Total front line RFC strength was over 1,200 aircraft, with 500 planes supporting the twenty-eight British divisions in the path of the German assault and another 150 planes of the HQ 9th Brigade available to reinforce the forces attached to the 3rd and 5th Armies.

The offensive was launched on 21 March. A fierce and accurate artillery barrage hit front line trenches, artillery positions, communication lines, headquarters and ammunition dumps. After four hours of bombardment, the lightly equipped stormtroopers, taking full advantage of early morning fog, picked their way through the outer defences. The fog would be the most significant factor in the fighting that followed. Along some sectors of the front it would persist for much of the day, blinding the artillery in the rear and the strongpoints in the heart of the battle zone and easing the path of the German infantry. German progress was greatest where the fog was thickest.

Where the fog and mists lifted, RFC corps planes were busy directing artillery fire against the advancing German infantry. German accounts describe how the appearance of an RFC plane above the battlefield was invariably followed by heavy and accurate artillery fire. These efforts were supported by at least four single-seater squadrons flying fighter-bomber sorties and others were involved in ground strafing. An unassigned R.E.8 squadron and a Bristol Fighter squadron were also used exclusively for low-level bombing. Even this relatively low scale of attack made an impression on the enemy with numerous German accounts describing how these daring low-level bombing and strafing attacks had disrupted their advance.[21] In the early stages of the battle, however, it was the more numerous attacks by the German ground-attack formations on the retreating British forces that were having the greater impact on the course of the battle.

As soon as the fog cleared, fighters from both sides were out in strength. Most combats took place over the battle zone, usually at low altitudes, but neither side achieved decisive results. Many RFC planes were attacked, but just five planes were shot down or forced to crash land. D.H.4s began bombing railway stations and bridges to the rear of the battle zone, but from altitudes of 15,000 feet, they were never likely to inflict much damage.[22]

For the British Army, it was a day of retreat. Along a ten-mile stretch of the 3rd Army front and a twenty-mile stretch of the 5th Army front either side of the Flesquieres salient, the Germans had bitten deep into the British defensive positions, pushing British forces to the very rear of their fortified battle zone. Indeed, at the extreme southern end of the assault, Gough's 5th Army had abandoned the

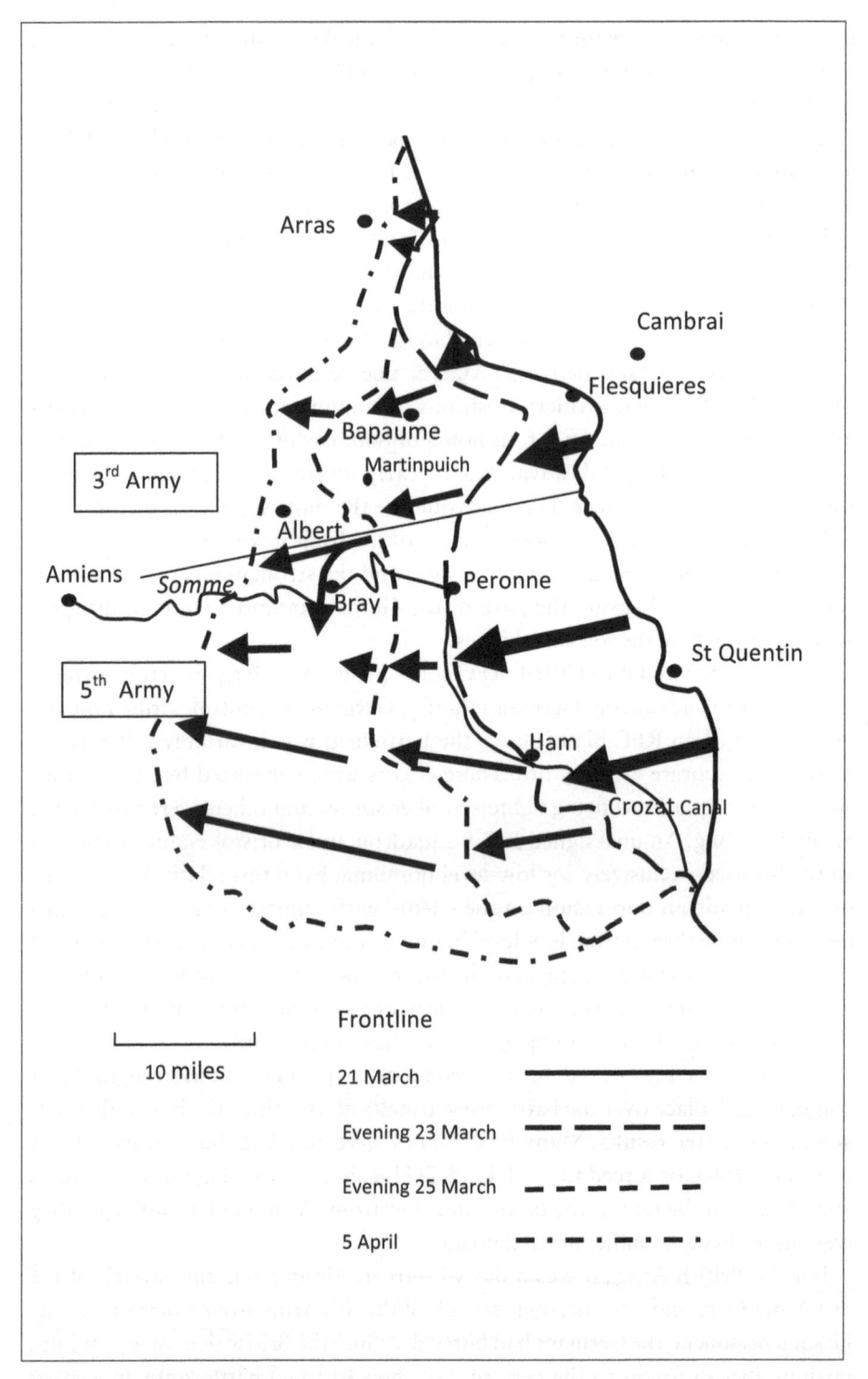

German spring offensive: March 1918.

prepared defensive positions and pulled back to the Crozat Canal. Haig remained confident that the worst was over and assured a worried Gough that German efforts would now slacken.[23] Instead, German efforts intensified and while defences on the 3rd Army front held, Gough's 5th Army crumbled with the German forces pushing on to the Somme, their original objective, and further south bursting past the Crozat Canal. Up to this point, fighter-bombers had been supplementing the artillery and supporting the defences, but along some sectors of the front there were now no defences to support. The fighter-bombers were being called in to slow down German troops advancing unopposed through the gaps opening up in front of them. Even where the retreating forces retained some sort of cohesion, in the confusion of retreat there was little time to erect the tall aerials required to receive wireless transmissions from aircraft. Many artillery units simply abandoned their radio equipment in their haste to escape the German advance.[24] Army planes hovered above the battlefield indicating the location of suitable targets for the artillery, but all too often no one was listening. On the southern front, air support was no longer an additional means of supporting the forces on the ground. Along some sectors it was now the only opposition.

As the German advance gathered pace, the RFC had to abandon airfields. Salmond's foresight in preparing airfields in the rear was paying off and the squadrons were able to operate from their new bases with remarkably little loss of efficiency. The focus was now providing the most direct support possible for the struggling ground forces. During the night of 22–23 March, the two F.E.2 night-bomber squadrons were switched from more distant communication targets to suspected enemy artillery positions and ammunition dumps in and around the battle zone. The F.E.2s were sent off on low-level patrols[25] with crews flying repeated missions throughout the hours of darkness. Using flares to identify targets, the pushers did sterling work bombing and strafing troops and transport, ensuring German forces had no respite.

Ironically, although the 5th Army was crumbling, it was the 3rd Army that was bearing the brunt of the attack. Although its southern wing had been forced out of its battle zone, it maintained a coherent front line and the corps planes were still able to call in the artillery. However, throughout 23 March, the reconnaissance planes continued to bring back discouraging news of the serious inroads the German forces were making, especially on the road to Bapaume. Fighter squadrons were asked to step up their low-level attacks in this area and squadrons from the 1st and 2nd Armies further north were switched south to help. On the second and third days of the offensive, the scale of RFC ground strafing doubled.

The battle for air superiority grew in intensity as the weather improved. For the first few days, it was an even affair, but from 23 March, the RFC squadrons began to gain the ascendancy. RFC pilots continued to make grossly exaggerated claims, but their own losses were low, even though many fighter squadrons were heavily involved in low-level strafing attacks.[26] It was the low offensive patrols that were scoring most successes. Losses among the German ground-attack squadrons rose and the scale of the Allied low-level attacks began to discourage the German infantry from putting out the cloth panels they were using to mark the extent of their advance and direction of the targets they wanted attacked. To the German infantry, there seemed to be more RFC planes in the air to take advantage of these indicators. Fighter squadrons were not reluctant to combine ground attack with their offensive patrols. In the early afternoon of 23 March, during what was described as an offensive patrol, S.E.5as of No. 84 Squadron strafed columns of German troops north-east of Ham. Apparently encouraged by their success, the same squadron set off that evening on another 'offensive patrol' with eleven S.E.5as, although the fact they were carrying 25-lb bombs suggests it was targets on the ground they were after rather than enemy planes in the air.[27]

To the south, the French took some of the pressure off Gough's 5th Army by covering the southern flank of Gough's front; from 24 March, the French air force was engaged in low-level strikes on the German advance, enabling Haig to focus on the threat to Arras. On the same day, corps planes reported that a gap was opening up between Bapaume and Peronne. Scratch formations were rushed to try and contain the threat while a reserve division moved up to plug the gap. The RFC was instructed to buy as much time as possible for these reinforcements by concentrating all its efforts in this area. Continuous low-level attacks were carried out throughout the day, which according to German accounts 'imposed a very cautious advance'. By the end of the day, a tenuous defensive line had been re-established, but a huge chunk of territory south of Arras had been lost. Bapaume had fallen and German forces were less than 10 miles from Albert, the other end of the start line for the planned second phase of the offensive, the drive north to Arras.

There was a real danger of the 3rd and 5th Armies becoming separated, and again the air force was called in to buy time. On eight occasions on 25 March, 3rd Army planes identified threatening enemy troop concentrations and called in the artillery to deal with them. As effective as these artillery assaults were, it was not enough. Haig demanded maximum air support, and in response Salmond ordered the 9th Wing to send every fighter and bomber to attack anything moving east of an arc from Bapaume through Martinpuich to the Somme. The attacking squadrons would include the two D.H.4 squadrons, previously used to bomb targets in the rear from high altitude, but now ordered to fly low-level strikes in and around the battlefield. Ten squadrons, including five corps squadrons from the 1st Army, were also switched south to support these attacks. Even two squadrons from the hard-pressed 5th Army were switched north. This was where the ground-attack capability of the R.E.8 came in useful. These were missions the B.E.2 could not have performed. 'Very low flying essential. All risks to be taken. Urgent,' Salmond ordered.

24–25 March saw another significant increase in low-level ground-attack sorties with nearly twice the weight of attack of the previous day. With the fighting becoming more mobile and both sides struggling to get their artillery into position, air support was crucial; however, while the RFC was able to intensify its efforts, the German ground-attack planes had been largely driven from the skies. On 26 March, all 3rd Army squadrons (apart from one corps squadron), along with squadrons from the 1st, 2nd and 5th Armies, covered by the 3rd Army's six fighter squadrons, were thrown into a furious assault on German ground forces. On this day, thirty-seven of the sixty squadrons based in France were active on the 3rd Army front. The assault was continuous, with the scale of low-level attack ten times greater than had been delivered on the first day of the offensive. The continuous air attack and the timely arrival of reinforcements on the ground ensured the front held. By the end of 26 March, the crisis on the southern flank of the 3rd Army had passed.

Nevertheless, the situation remained critical. During the night of 26–27 March, Albert fell and further south the German forces were now well beyond their initial objective of the Somme and Crozat Canal. The British retreat south of the River Somme was complicated by an ill-timed withdrawal on the right flank of the 3rd Army that enabled enemy forces to cross the Somme at Bray and threaten the 5th Army from the rear. The 5th Army threw all its available squadrons against the German threat and received the full support of the 1st, 2nd and 3rd Brigades as these switched their efforts south of the river. Once again, the RFC was able to focus its effort precisely where it was most needed.

27 March was to be the day of greatest activity for the RFC with a 50 per cent increase on the previous day's ground-attack efforts. Despite losses and the confusion of retreating to new airfields, since the opening of the offensive, daily ground strafing had grown fifteen-fold and the tonnage of bombs dropped had doubled. The same day also saw the greatest losses with some forty planes missing, bringing combat losses to over 160 since the beginning of the offensive, with many more abandoned in the retreat.[28] The British and French east of Amiens had to concede more ground, but their air forces were slowly sucking the momentum out of the enemy offensive. After an advance of 30 miles in a week, the German supply lines were stretched and the horse-drawn supply columns were proving especially vulnerable to strafing RFC fighters. The artillery could not move forwards quickly enough and the German air force failed to provide any alternative support.

On 28 March, Ludendorff launched a full-scale attack on the untouched defences immediately east of Arras, an attack that had been planned as the *coup de grâce* but was now more an act of desperation. There was no fog to protect the attacking infantry and British artillery was brought to bear on the approaching German infantry by the circling planes with devastating effect, with low-level attacks by six squadrons of Camels, S.E.5s and D.H.4s adding to the mayhem. The attack on Arras was comfortably held. Further south, German forces continued to push towards Amiens, the last major town before Abbeville and the coast. For the 5th Army corps squadrons, there was virtually no artillery left to direct. Just one plane from each squadron was retained for tactical reconnaissance while the remainder were ordered to fly low-level ground-attack missions with 9th Wing bombers and fighters in support. By 30 March, the German advance had been held on this front too, with German units less than ten miles of Amiens.

It had been a dramatic ten days for the RFC. For the first time, aircraft were able to demonstrate the direct influence they could have on a battle that involved ground forces on the move in open country, unprotected by trenches or bunkers. In the rapidly changing situation on the ground, aerial reconnaissance had played a crucial role in assessing where the main danger lay, just as it had in 1914. This time, by disrupting the advancing columns and hindering the flow of supplies, aircraft had also played an important and decisive role in slowing down an advance. The effects were not just material—the continuous air assault had a huge effect on the morale of both sides. British Army commanders enthusiastically reported that RFC aircraft were 'so thick in the air ... there was every danger of collision', while German troops cursed their own airmen who, as the battle progressed, became more and more conspicuous by their absence.

It was a very tactical air battle. Fighters on high-altitude air superiority missions soon found themselves sucked into the crucial battle below, as both sides sought to provide the maximum support for their ground forces. The rigid organisation of the RFC, with most squadrons attached to particular armies, had delayed but not prevented air power being concentrated at whatever sector of the front needed support. It was an impressive display of air power operating in 'fire brigade' mode, reacting promptly to crises wherever they arose. The first reinforcement to reach a threatened sector was always the air force. During the battle, forty-five new airfields were set up to accommodate the retreating squadrons and from these improvised airstrips, squadrons were able to maintain a remarkably high sortie rate. It was a brilliant performance.

For years to come, the exploits of the RFC during the German March 1918 offensive would become the most often quoted example of an air force exerting a decisive influence on a land battle. Indeed, so often would this particular example of tactical air support be referred to, it came to be considered an extraordinary exception—an unusual application of air power provoked by a desperate emergency. It was a desperate emergency, but the air force had not switched to a role it was not familiar with and the only planes operating in an unfamiliar role were the D.H.4 bombers used for low-level strikes. By the spring of 1918, there was nothing exceptional about tactical or close air support, and by this stage of the war all corps and fighter squadrons were familiar with the low-level attack role. It had always been planned to use fighter-bombers and other aircraft if available for air support to supplement the efforts of the artillery. What no one had expected was that on certain sectors of the front, the vital artillery-aircraft combination would collapse, and that ground attack would become the primary role for so many squadrons, effectively acting as a substitute for the missing artillery.

It was not a victory for air power acting alone. Defeating the German Army single-handedly was quite beyond the capabilities of the air force; in the end, it was the troops on the ground that had stopped the German advance. The RFC contribution was to support the efforts of the retreating forces and give the reinforcements precious time to get into position. It was, however, a crucial contribution—during the retreat, the Army came to rely on air support in a way it had never needed to before. The victory came at a price. Around 200 planes were lost in combat, over half of these crash landing in friendly territory. In normal circumstances, some of these might have been recovered and repaired, but these and a large number of other unserviceable planes had to be destroyed as air units retreated, bringing total losses for the period 21–31 March to 478 aircraft. It was a high price, but given the seriousness of the situation and the scale of the disaster that was narrowly averted, it was a price worth paying.

It was a coming of age for the air force and the RFC's finest hour. Ironically, as the battle came to an end, so were the RFC and its sister RNAS; both were about to be incorporated into the new Royal Air Force. For the RFC it was a fine note to end on. With the initial crisis passed, squadrons were ordered to resume normal activities, which meant D.H.4s bombing targets from 15,000 feet and fighters flying offensive patrols at altitude. But with the fighters encountering empty skies there did not seem any point in these 'normal' operations. On 1 April, Foch, who had taken over as Supreme Commander of all Allied Armies on the Western Front, summed up the new thinking on how fighters should be used:

> At the present time, the first duty of fighting aeroplanes is to assist the troops on the ground, by incessant attacks, with bombs and machine-guns on columns, concentrations or bivouacs. Air fighting is not to be sought except so far as necessary for the fulfilment of this duty.[29]

It was perhaps an over-reaction to the ill-conceived all-out offensive fighter strategies favoured by du Peuty and copied by Trenchard, which tended to take the fighters away from the forces they were supposed to be supporting. The primary role of fighters would always be to engage enemy aircraft, whether they were fighter, bomber or reconnaissance; however, fighters had to get involved in the main battle. They could not seek to fight their own private war for supremacy over the opposing fighter forces, regardless of what was happening on the battlefield below. If fighters were the only way of holding up the enemy advance, then that was how they had to be used. There would always be situations where even pure air superiority fighters could contribute more by attacking enemy troops on the ground than engaging the enemy in the air. Over-specialisation and compartmentalisation of roles was a danger that had to be avoided.

There would soon be more opportunities for fighter and bomber forces to get involved in the land battle. With American troops already being encountered, the German High Command knew they were running out of time. The March offensive had come frustratingly close to achieving a decisive victory. The Anglo-

French forces had taken a hammering and had at the very least been knocked off balance. Ludendorff had no choice but to try again. On 9 April, the German Army struck further north on the Belgian frontier—the target was Hazebrouck, a key rail centre fifteen miles behind the front line, the capture of which would cut communications between British and Belgian units and the Allied forces to the south. Again, German infantry made use of the thick early morning fog to cover their advance and were soon making rapid progress. Poor weather throughout the first two days restricted air operations, but on the afternoon of 11 April, with German forces advancing on a 30-mile front, the weather finally cleared and intensive low-level ground-attack missions began in earnest. The next day, German units were just five miles from Hazebrouck and the situation became critical. Haig ordered his troops to fight where they stood, to the last man if necessary.

After a brief flurry of activity on 9 April, the German air force had faded rapidly, which allowed what had now become the Royal Air Force to devote all its attention to ground attack. The weather remained fine throughout 12 April and more hours were flown on this day than on any previous day of the war. Once again, the air assault played its part in slowing down the Germans sufficiently for reinforcements to stiffen the line and another crisis had passed. In May, June and July, there were further German offensives against French-held lines further south. On the Aisne (27 May), Noyon–Montdidier (9 June) and Champagne (15 July), enemy forces made progress, but were held and thrown back by an increasingly confident French Army, well supported by the French air force. The German Army had shot its bolt.

In all these defensive battles, these low-level close air support operations had been, in the words of Salmond, 'exceedingly necessary and effective'. However, as Salmond emphasised, it was the air superiority fighter that was the crucial weapon; it was only when the enemy air force had been driven from the skies that the full weight of British air power could be turned on the enemy ground forces. Salmond ideally wanted specialist planes for both roles, but if that was not possible, he insisted that the air superiority fighter should have priority. It was easier to use specialist fighters for ground attack than specialist ground-attack planes for fighting.[30]

With the Camel struggling in the pure fighter role, Salmond was already aware of the need for better fighters. The need became even greater in May 1918 when Allied pilots began to encounter an entirely new fighter with remarkable characteristics: the Fokker D.VII. The early versions were not particularly fast, but the plane's other qualities more than made up for this. Its thick high-lift upper wing and excellent engine gave the fighter outstanding flying characteristics, especially at high altitudes. From July, more powerful and faster versions began to appear which totally outclassed the Allied opposition. The RFC had nothing in the pipeline that might challenge the German fighter; in the battles to come, the RFC would be finding itself at an increasing disadvantage.

CHAPTER 13

A Glimpse into the Future

Having blunted Germany's last drives for victory, Foch was anxious to get the Allied armies moving forwards. Haig was anxious to give his forces defending Amiens a little more room for manoeuvre and his plan to push German forces back became the first instalment of Foch's grand counteroffensive. The attack was set for 8 August. Tanks were to play a key role in helping the infantry smash the German forward defences, but to get maximum benefit from them, a way had to be found of dealing with the improvised anti-tank artillery the Germans had used with increasing success during the Cambrai operation.

Anti-tank guns were difficult to spot, and to see if the air force could help in any way, No. 8 Army Corps Squadron, commanded by Major Trafford Leigh-Mallory, who commanded Allied air units in the 1944 Normandy landings, was attached to the Tank Corps. Aircrews demonstrated they could spot anti-tank guns, but passing the information on to the tanks by wireless proved impractical, while calling in artillery proved impossible as the guns only engaged the tanks at short range. Trials in March, however, demonstrated that there was no reason why Leigh-Mallory's machines should not eliminate as well as locate the guns.[1] During a small-scale action at Hamel, his squadron accompanied the tanks and successfully identified and eliminated at least one enemy battery and helped beat off several infantry counterattacks.[2] Leigh-Mallory's squadron became a permanent attachment to the Tank Corps.[3]

The Amiens attack was spearheaded by over 500 tanks, supporting seven British, Australian and Canadian divisions of the 4th Army, with French forces covering their right flank and 800 RAF and 1,100 French planes providing air support. In the air, the German air force had less than 400 planes, but they included the new Fokker D.VII. Initially, the light bombers were to strike at enemy airfields and fighter-bombers would support the infantry and tanks. In line with Foch's preference for fighters to be employed for ground attack wherever possible, all eight fighter squadrons attached to the 4th Army were to be used in this role while the five day fighter squadrons of the HQ 9th Brigade provided cover. Four fighter squadrons of the 3rd Brigade to the north were ready to assist if required. The assault would begin with the now standard short, sharp artillery barrage. It was anticipated that the movement of German reserves would be in full swing towards the end of the first day; to disrupt these efforts, bomber and fighter-bomber squadrons would switch their attention from the battlefield to the key railway stations at Péronne and Chaulnes.

The attack began at 4.20 a.m. on 8 August. The artillery barrage did not begin until the infantry and tanks had started moving forwards, and complete surprise was achieved. Early morning mists prevented any of the planned close air support taking place and severely disrupted attacks on German airfields, but for the infantry it was once again priceless protection. The defenders immediately started reeling back and when the mists lifted at 9.00 a.m., Allied troops had already advanced up to three miles and the German defences were in considerable disarray. Setting off in pairs at regular intervals, fighter-bomber pilots found a host of targets among the retreating German forces. Losses were heavy: No. 201 Squadron alone lost no less than seven Camels in the morning's fighting, but the tactics appeared to have worked. As at Cambrai, the sudden appearance of so many tanks and the continuous low-level strafing and bombing proved too much for the front line German units. By early afternoon, marauding armoured cars were shooting up a German headquarters at Framerville, seven miles behind the front line. The German forces were in retreat, but this was no orderly withdrawal. German commanders were hearing stories of troops laying down their weapons and fleeing, openly expressing the pointlessness of continuing the war. By the end of the day, the advance stretched up to eight miles and an unprecedented 16,000 prisoners of war had been taken. The German Army appeared to be on the point of disintegrating—for Ludendorff, it was a 'black day' in the history of the German Army. The Allies seemed to be on the verge of achieving a breakthrough as dramatic as the Germans had achieved in their spring offensive. Instead, the attack stalled and the opportunity disappeared, which some would later argue was the result of a crucial change of plan on the opening day.

At midday on 8 August, with the Germans in full retreat, instead of targeting Péronne and Chaulnes stations to prevent the arrival of reinforcements, it was decided to destroy the bridges over the Somme, some fifteen to twenty miles behind the front. This would cut off the line of retreat, trapping German forces on the west bank of the river where they would be destroyed. It was a bold plan. From early afternoon, all fighter-bombers supporting the advance and the bomber squadrons that were going to attack the railway stations were thrown against the bridges.

For the next two days, the RFC flew repeated missions against the dozen or so bridges from Péronne to Ham. Attacking fixed and well-defined targets in the enemy rear would prove to be a very different proposition to harrying retreating and disorganised forces on the battlefield. Once the bridges became the target, German fighter squadrons knew exactly where to find the enemy. To have any chance of hitting such small targets, the bombers had to fly low; Fokker D.VIIs

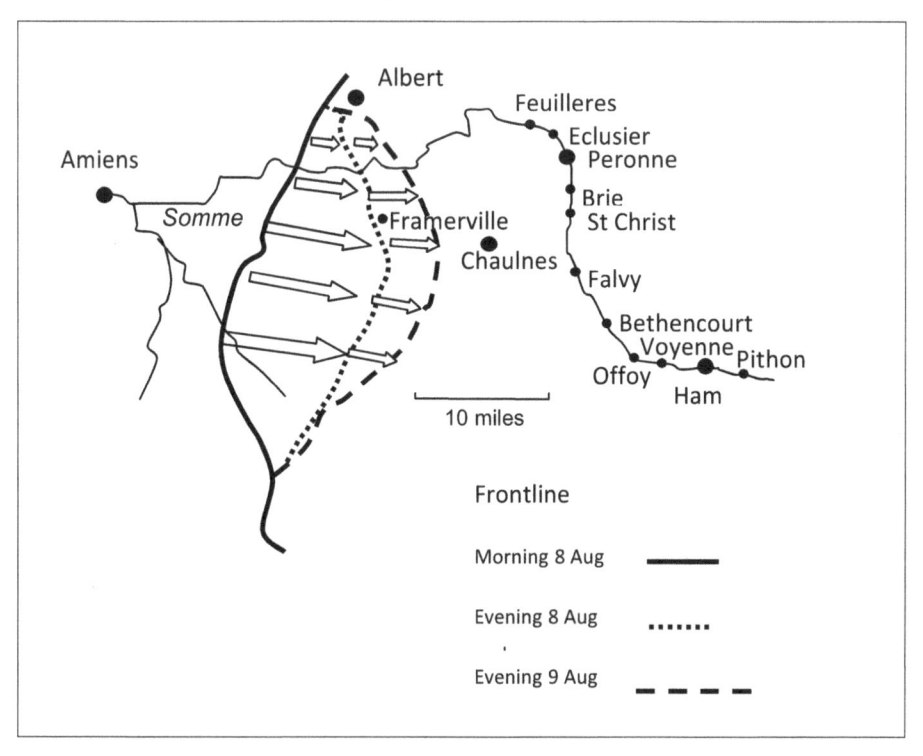

Amiens August 1918: army advance and bridges bombed.

tore into the hapless D.H.4 and D.H.9 formations.[4] Those that managed to get their bombs on target found that the bridges made particularly unrewarding targets. To cause any damage, direct hits were required, which even from low-altitude were rare, and the largest bomb available (the 112-lb bomb) was not powerful enough to have much of an impact. As bomber losses rose, fighter-bombers were switched from attacking the bridges to escort duties. Eventually, nearly 500 fighters, about 70 per cent of RAF fighter strength, were operating in the area, but the British fighters were completely outclassed by the Fokker D.VII and bomber losses continued to mount. No bridges were destroyed; instead, they were used by reinforcements arriving to stabilise the front rather than by a fleeing German Army. Meanwhile at the front, the advance was slowing. Less progress was made on 9 August and by 10 August the advance had ground to a halt. While the RAF was focusing on the bridges, the German air force was controlling the skies over the battlefield and Allied troops were now the victims of low-flying aircraft.[5] On the ground, German reinforcements were arriving in strength, Allied casualties were rising, and Haig felt he had to suspend the advance until more artillery could be brought up.[6]

In the years to come, critics would claim that if the railway stations had remained the target, these reinforcements would not have arrived and a glorious breakthrough would have been achieved. Cleary, the destruction of either the stations or the bridges would have been very useful, even decisive. Railway stations are easier targets to hit than bridges, but previous experience provided little evidence that attacks on these would be any more successful.[7] The truth was that the RAF did not have the means to destroy bridges or stations. Arguably, it was not the switching of the bombers to the bridges that was most significant; it was the parallel decision to remove close support from the advancing tanks and infantry. The support the RAF was providing on the battlefield was one of the reasons for the initial collapse of German morale; it was withdrawn just as the tanks and infantry were beginning to move beyond effective artillery range and needed it even more. The advance was slowing even before the first German reinforcements arrived.

There were many reasons apart from the lack of air support for the slowing of the advance. Tank losses were very heavy. On the morning of 9 August, only 145 tanks remained serviceable. The German anti-tank guns were taking their toll and Leigh-Mallory's No. 8 Squadron was clearly not sufficient to deal with the threat. Charlton, the commander of the RAF 5th Brigade, believed it was the inability to eliminate the German guns that prevented an 'irresistible' advance,[8] which was perhaps rather overstating the case. In reality, the mechanical unreliability of the tanks was at least as significant a factor as their vulnerability to enemy fire. However, if the advancing troops and tanks had continued to get more substantial close support on the battlefield, the advance might have maintained enough momentum to ensure the arriving reinforcements did not have time to establish a defensive foothold.

In truth, the offensive was probably doomed to achieve little more than an initial success. The Army had no clear strategic objective beyond the limited tactical aim of pushing the enemy back. By attacking the bridges, the RAF was trying to do what the Army should have done—to sweep round the enemy rear and block the line of retreat. In its search for a grander and more significant role, the air force was making the mistake of drifting beyond the immediate battlefield and attempting tasks that were beyond its capabilities. In the end, all it proved was that air power tends to be less effective when trying to achieve results on its own. It was on the battlefield, in concert with other arms, that the Allied air forces had their best chance of making a difference. Airpower could have supported an Army drive to cut off the enemy retreat, but it could not substitute for one. It was the Army that needed to be more imaginative.

Following the Amiens assault, Haig seemed prepared to be more imaginative. He urged his commanders to be bolder in future offensives and strike deeper into the enemy rear—no longer was it necessary to advance on a continuous front. Commanders should reinforce success rather than units that were being held up, and advances should not be slowed for fear of counterattacks on exposed flanks.[9] It was a bold vision, one in which air power was capable of providing the mobile firepower such adventure would require, but after four years of heavy losses, it was a brave general who would risk throwing caution to the wind. It had backfired far too often in the past and it is perhaps not surprising that Foch settled for a more cautious approach. Instead of bold strikes in the enemy rear, offensives with limited objectives would follow each other at different points on the front. Once one had stated to lose momentum, another would be launched. The aim was to continue pushing the enemy back rather than destroy him.

If close air support was to continue to play an important role in these offensives, a way had to be found of reducing losses to ground fire. Armour was one solution and in the wake of the Amiens offensive, the more heavily armoured Salamander, rather than the lightly armed Camel TF1, found itself back in favour.[10] The prototype Salamander had flown in April and in May was sent to France for trials. Pilots were generally favourable, and considering its weight, they felt the plane handled fairly well. It was as manoeuvrable as the Bristol Fighter and below 10,000 feet 'could almost be used for fighting an Albatros Scout',[11] which was perhaps a little optimistic. The first Salamander squadron was due to arrive in France by mid-September.[12]

Armour, however, was not the only way of reducing losses. The commander of the 22nd Wing saw a tactical rather than a technical solution. He noted that in the early stages of an attack, when the enemy might be expected to be confused, losses tended to be light; in these circumstances, widespread and indiscriminate air support seemed justified. Losses only rose as the defences became more organised, and in these circumstances it was better to use air support in a more focused way, meeting specific requests to eliminate particular strongpoints holding up an advance, or help beat off counterattacks, rather than roaming the battlefield looking for targets.[13] During the Amiens attack, there had been many examples of planes spotting targets for fighter-bombers, but no procedure equivalent to the artillery call system existed to direct aircraft to these targets. Information could only be passed on after the corps plane had finished its mission and landed, by which time it was usually too late. There was a clear case for bringing air support in line with artillery support, and to do this a Central Information Bureau (CIB) was set up to collate requests for support and pass on suitable targets to the artillery or fighter-bomber squadrons, whichever was more appropriate. New instructions stated that in future '…wireless calls will largely control the action of low-flying scouts subsequent to zero hour. This system marks a large stride in the direction of close co-operation in battle.'[14] Indeed it did. To produce an even faster response, it was suggested the reporting corps plane could fire a flare of predetermined colour in the direction of the target on the off chance there were fighter-bombers in the vicinity. It was in essence the cab-rank system developed in the Second World War, lacking only the lightweight wireless equipment that forward troops and fighters might be able to carry into action to provide a more efficient way of passing on target information.

It was the air/tank combination that was generating most excitement. The tank was the only means of carrying wireless equipment on to the battlefield, but communicating with aircraft overhead was proving difficult. However, once these problems were overcome, Leigh-Mallory envisaged huge possibilities for air supported armoured warfare.[15] To increase the strike capability available to the tanks, the Camel fighter-bombers of No. 71 Squadron joined No. 8 Squadron on attachment to the Tank Corps.

There would be plenty of opportunities to develop these ideas in the coming months. With increasing numbers of American troops arriving, the Allies had the resources to maintain the offensive and stretch the German Army. The advance would be remorseless and steady rather than dramatic and decisive. It was still very much a war of attrition, but at least one where Allied soldiers were constantly moving forwards, and it was a war that the Franco-British-American alliance knew they would inevitably win.

The different approaches to providing close air support for the various British contributions to Foch's offensive would demonstrate how thinking was still very much in a state of flux. Significantly, the level of support tended to be on a lower scale than had been possible during the Amiens attack, mainly because an increasingly higher proportion of the available fighter strength had to be used

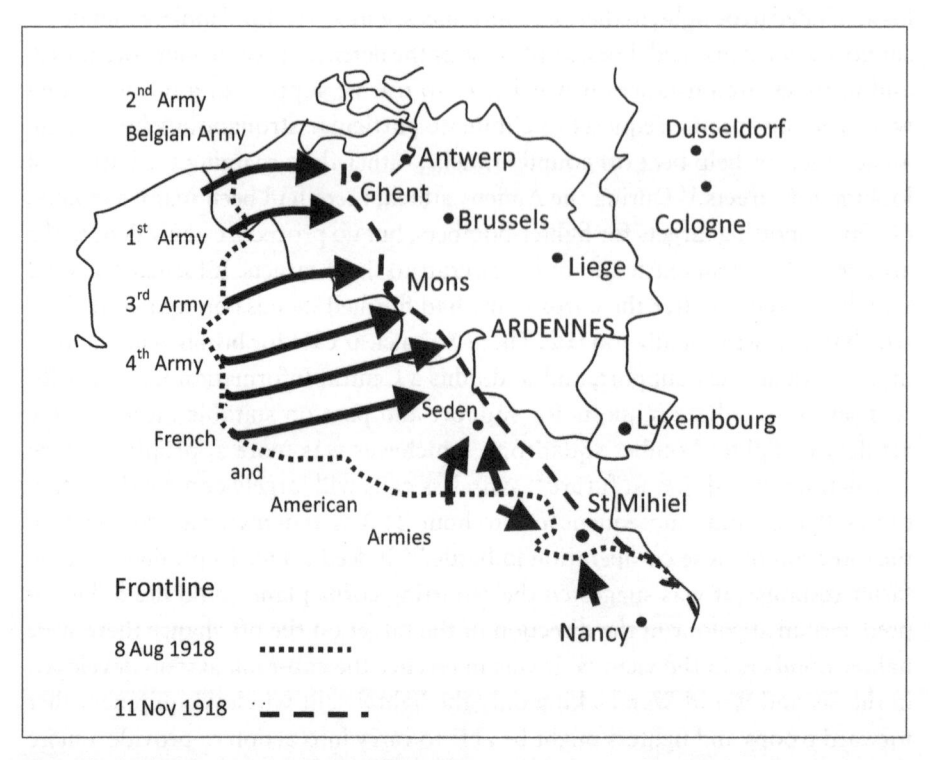

The Allied advance: August–November 1918.

to counter the growing threat of the Fokker D.VII. For the 3rd Army's assault on 21 August, each of the three attacking corps would be supported by just one fighter-bomber squadron with a fourth attached to the Tanks Corps; the rest of the fighter force would provide air cover. The support for the infantry was indirect with each squadron sending off pairs of fighters at half-hourly intervals throughout the day to patrol the roads that local reinforcements were likely to take. The Camels supporting the Tank Corps provided much closer battlefield support, engaging enemy anti-tank guns holding up the advance.[16]

On 23 August, the 4th Army joined the assault. For the first time, the fighters assigned the fighter-bomber role were directed to specific targets reported by the squadrons via the CIB. The aircrews were instructed to look out in particular for anti-tank guns. A study of local terrain and captured German documents describing where anti-tank guns should be sited gave the aerial observers an idea of where to look, and active batteries were often spotted as soon as they opened fire. Six fighter squadrons, including the Camel squadron attached to the Tank Corps, responded to requests to attack these and other targets.[17]

On 26 August, the 1st Army extended the offensive and No. 73 Squadron and No. 8 Squadron were switched north with the Tank Corps. In this operation, four fighter squadrons were assigned the ground-attack role, and in an effort to centralise fighter-bomber support, all four were based at the same airfield under a single commander, Major Smythies. During the day, and despite the poor weather, the four squadrons, operating in flight strength, flew at least 150 fighter-bomber sorties, mostly in response to requests from aircraft over the front. Losses were light with just one plane failing to return and another three written off in crash landings.[18] The first day of the offensive ended with a powerful demonstration of the flexibility and value of air support when a strong German counterattack hit the 3rd Canadian Division. All available aircraft of Nos 208 and 209 Squadrons, some twenty-seven aircraft, were immediately ordered to the area to help the Canadians beat off the attack.

For an assault on the Hindenburg Line by the 1st and 3rd Armies on 2 September, a more systematic approach was adopted with predetermined targets integrated into the planned artillery support programme. Enemy strongpoints were bombed throughout the previous night by F.E.2 bombers, and from dawn, Smythies' squadrons supported the infantry assault with another 200 fighter-bomber sorties. Losses to ground fire were relatively light with six planes missing or crashed landed and three shot down by fighters.[19] The overall conclusion of these operations was that the closer fighter-bomber missions were to the front line, the more impact they had, and the more specific the target, the lower the losses. With Fokker fighters on the prowl, pilots did not want to spend too long looking for a target.[20] This battlefield intervention was far more useful than the efforts of the day bombers, which were still attempting to cut lines of communication from altitudes as high as 13,000 feet.[21]

Aircraft could never match the weight and ferocity of artillery, but air support was offering different options. Apart from extending the range of support, there were targets within artillery range that could be more effectively and precisely engaged by aeroplanes, such as enemy forces marching along roads, or targets very close to friendly forces. There was also the enormous psychological impact air strikes had on the morale of both sides. Air support was proving to be supplementary and complementary to artillery support. Even when substantial artillery support was available, there was a place for close air support.

The offensives since 8 August had recovered the ground lost in the spring and even captured a sector of the formidable Hindenburg Line, but the advance had taken its toll. The RAF and Army were instructed to pause and conserve their resources for future battles. RAF squadrons needed the break. August was the worst month of the war so far for British squadrons on the Western Front with 436 aircraft failing to return and many more damaged machines being written off. Losses to ground fire were still causing concern but a high proportion of these had been suffered during the Amiens offensive, especially during the low-level attacks on the Somme bridges. Once these were called off and close air support was used more selectively, losses to ground fire were not so excessive. As the contact and trench patrols had discovered, the immediate front line was not such a dangerous place to be. It was against targets in the rear of the tactical zone, where air defences were more organised, that losses tended to be higher.

The biggest problem for the RAF was the German fighter force, which was responsible for 70 per cent of losses in August. The 258 aircraft known to have been shot down by enemy fighters represented a 60 per cent increase on the previous month. The latest German fighters, and in particular the Fokker D.VII, were making their mark. Escorts did their best but Camels were totally outclassed by the Fokkers, especially at the altitudes the day bombers usually operated. On 29 August, in a particularly disastrous mission, three out twelve D.H.9s and five out of fifteen escorting Camels from No. 43 Squadron were shot down.[22] At low level in the fighter-bomber role, the Camel's extraordinary manoeuvrability gave its pilot some chance when engaged by enemy fighters, but conceding the altitude advantage to the enemy and lacking the necessary speed to disengage, the Camel pilot often found himself trapped. In August, the RAF lost 121 Camels and seventy-two D.H.9s; both types urgently needed replacing. Even the S.E.5a was beginning to struggle with losses doubling in August. Bristol Fighter losses were also heavy and the continued use of the two-seater as an offensive fighter was becoming increasingly dubious. Only the Dolphin was holding its own.[23] Salmond's fighter force was facing a crisis and the need for a better fighter was suddenly very urgent.

With the new Bentley-powered Sopwith Snipe, judged to be inferior to the S.E.5a and Dolphin, the only immediate hope was the improved ABC-powered version of the fighter. In tests, speeds of nearly 150 mph had been achieved with the prototype, and it was expected to climb to 10,000 feet in less than eight minutes and have a service ceiling of 25,000 feet. These were potentially sensational capabilities, giving the fighter a comfortable margin of performance over the Fokker D.VII. The Air Ministry's determination to persevere with its temperamental engine is understandable, but the problems defied a solution. Suddenly, the Martinsyde F.3/4 was back in contention. The fighter was in production, although the plan was to store the airframes until the 300-hp Hispano-Suiza engine became available. By the end of July, it was clear the RAF could not afford to wait for the French engine. On 30 July, it was decided that some squadrons would have to be re-equipped with the Martinsyde fighter, even if it meant taking Falcon engines from Bristol Fighter production. In September, the fighter was named the Buzzard and the existing order for 150 was increased by 1,300. It was hoped that the first squadrons would be in France by November, seven months later than need have been the case. In the meantime, the RAF would have to make do with the Snipe. After its mauling on 29 August, No. 43 Squadron was withdrawn to become the first squadron to convert to the fighter.[24]

There was some good news for the D.H.9 squadrons. The American industry was turning out large numbers of the excellent 400-hp Liberty; with this engine, the D.H.9a could fly faster and higher than the BHP-powered D.H.9. The first of these would reach the front in September. The arrival of the Snipe and D.H.9a could not come soon enough for the battered Camel and D.H.9 squadrons. For the Camels, September started as badly as August had finished, with eight out of twelve Camels from No. 70 Squadron shot down in a clash with two squadrons of Fokkers on 4 September.

To add to the problems of technical inferiority, RAF fighters were still operating at single flight strength and were continually finding themselves outnumbered, even though overall Allied air strength far exceeded the opposition. Trenchard wanted squadrons to patrol in strength but there was opposition from many commanders who felt larger formations would discourage German pilots from engaging,[25] a bizarre reason for putting oneself at a disadvantage, but one very much in tune with the 'gung ho' attitude the RAF was so proud of. Efforts to get squadrons to work together were often poorly co-ordinated and since a squadron might only put out one flight as its contribution, no concentration of fighter strength was achieved. On 5 September, a patrol of five Camels of No. 4 (Australian) Squadron was supposed to be protected by a flight of Bristol Fighters from No. 88 Squadron at medium altitude and another of S.E.5as from No. 2 (Australian) Squadron at high altitude, but the Camels lost touch with their cover and lost four of their number in a clash with three squadrons of Fokkers.

Towards the end of September, squadrons were ordered to operate at squadron strength and in pairs with typically two S.E.5a squadrons flying top cover for a couple of lower flying Camel squadrons. The disadvantage was that deploying fighters in larger formations made it more difficult to provide continuous cover, especially as most of the available squadrons were spread evenly among the various armies. The Germans out of necessity and the French out of choice were concentrating their fighters in much larger independent formations that could achieve air superiority where it was required. At least fighter effort was focused where it was needed. Pilots were under strict instructions not to fly too far east; long gone were the days when pilots were instructed to patrol 20 or even 40 miles behind the front.[26]

In the first five days of September, the RAF lost ninety planes and squadrons had to be told to limit their activities to the barest minimum in order to conserve resources. A long spell of poor weather helped reduce losses, but the return of fine weather in the middle of the month saw fighter losses soar to twenty a day. This was unsustainable. Despite the unseasonably poor weather, losses in September were even heavier than they had been in August.

The British and Belgian armies resumed their offensive towards the end of September. The air operations that accompanied these offensives underlined how fluid ideas on air support were as each Army brigade struggled to come up with the best approach in skies dominated by the Fokker. The 1st Army's 1st Brigade committed most of its fighter squadrons to the ground-attack role with five fighter squadrons under Smythies' control flying around 175 fighter-bomber sorties during the course of the first day of the attack. The majority were flown along predetermined and well-defined routes local reserves were expected to take—or retreating forces might be fleeing along—but two requests to attack strongpoints holding up the advance were also met. This only left two fighter squadrons for air defence, and these, operating as a pair, were to fly morning, midday and evening patrols, which meant for much of the day there would be no air cover at all. However, when No 4 Squadron, on a fighter-bomber mission, was caught by Fokker D.VIIs and lost four planes, Smythies was forced to divert two more S.E.5a squadrons to the pure fighter role.[27]

To support 3rd Army operations, the 3rd Brigade felt obliged to reserve nearly all of its fighters for the air superiority role, leaving just one squadron, No. 201, for fighter-bomber duties, with one flight allocated to each of the attacking corps. These were to support the initial assault by breaking up any counterattacks and eliminating strongpoints holding up the advance. After this initial phase, the flights were put on standby and responded only to direct requests for air support via the CIB. This freed sufficient squadrons to maintain fighter patrols at low and high altitude at two squadron strength, although in an attempt to squeeze a little more ground-attack capability out of the fighter force, the Camel squadrons flying the lower patrols carried bombs to attack targets of opportunity. The disadvantage of CIB-directed missions was that if suitable targets did not emerge, a useful striking force was left idle on airfields while the battle raged. The air support the 5th Brigade provided the 4th Army on 29 September was a case in point. Three squadrons and a flight were on standby throughout the day, but the first day of this particular offensive was one of very confused fighting; no request for air support was made until midday, and by 4.00 p.m. only four missions had been flown. Far more sorties were flown on the 2nd Army front, where fighter squadrons were given maximum licence to seek out and strike targets of opportunity. The targets, however, were inevitably less relevant and losses were heavy. The de Havilland bomber squadrons suffered especially high losses when used for low-level attack, underlining the advantages of smaller and more manoeuvrable fighters in this role.

However it was applied, close air support was proving its worth. It was not a decisive factor in the relentless Allied advance—it was just one element of the merciless pressure the Allied armies were able to apply. All along the front, tanks, artillery, air strikes and the infantry were helping to lever the Germans out of their defensive positions. It was in co-operation with other arms that air power was proving most effective.

By the beginning of October, the mighty Hindenburg Line had been broken. Yet, as the German Army fell back on less well-prepared defensive positions, and despite the terrible losses it had suffered, it remained a cohesive and effective fighting force. Crucially, the German air force had not lost control of the skies. The outnumbered German fighter squadrons fought fiercely and, with the best fighter available to either side, very effectively. Throughout the summer and early autumn of 1918, RAF losses as a percentage of front line strength were increasing and approaching the levels suffered during the catastrophic April 1917 offensive. September 1918 saw the RAF in France endure its heaviest losses of the war with over 500 aircraft destroyed. Two hundred fighters were lost during the course of the month as they attempted to grapple with a better equipped enemy, compared to just forty-three on the supposedly more dangerous ground-attack missions, and many of these were the victims of prowling German fighters.

The German fighter force was not preventing the RAF from supporting the Army, but without a fighter to negate the Fokker D.VII, it could only do so at a very high cost. The German Army bemoaned the increasing numbers of Allied planes and the apparent failure of its own air force to make an impression, but the Allies did not have air supremacy and for this the German Army had to be grateful. The very presence of an effective German fighter force meant that fighter squadrons which would otherwise have been used for ground attack had to be used for air combat. Events elsewhere would demonstrate what could happen if retreating armies completely lost control of the skies above them.

In the summer of 1918, the RAF enjoyed total air supremacy in Palestine and General Allenby planned to exploit it in an offensive with the straightforward aim of eliminating all Turkish forces in the region. A short artillery bombardment ensured maximum surprise; the breakthrough was rapidly achieved and cavalry swept round to the enemy rear. With routes to the north blocked, the Turkish Army sought to escape eastwards through the Jordan hills, the main route of escape being the narrow Wadi El Far'a road. On the morning of 21 September, Bristol Fighters spotted the withdrawing Turkish forces and all available aircraft were ordered to attack. Throughout the day, RAF aircraft strafed and bombed the roads with 20-lb and 112-lb bombs in what turned into a massacre. The narrow roads were easily blocked, the steep hills and ravines prevented much lateral movement, and the dispirited Turkish forces offered no effective anti-aircraft fire. The road was soon blocked with the wreckage of a defeated enemy.

Aircraft had turned a retreat into a rout and the victory would rival the March 1918 defensive efforts in post-war RAF folklore as an example of tactical air power at its most effective.[28] Elsewhere, total loss of control of the skies resulted in similar scenes. In Macedonia, an Allied offensive struck north on 18 September 1918. Outflanked by the advance of the French and Serbs to the west, the Bulgarian Army facing the British was forced to retreat and a handful of RFC squadrons wrought havoc among the retreating Bulgarian columns.[29]

On the Western Front, however, the German fighter force ensured that the degree of air superiority the Allies possessed in Palestine and Macedonia was never achieved. At the beginning of October, and with winter approaching, it seemed that the German Army would be able to hold on and take the war into 1919. For the next campaigning season, it was planned to assemble huge numbers of tanks. The British Army alone would have three massive formations, each with 300 to 400 tanks, each supported by its own squadron of corps planes and fighter-bombers.[30] Fuller was envisaging an Allied force of 5,000 tanks, many of which would have the speed to strike deep in the enemy rear, where they would destroy communication centres and eliminate the means to control an Army, tactics which embodied the shock effect of the future 'Blitzkrieg', without perhaps the strategic focus of the German doctrine. However, it was good enough to impress Foch and Fuller's ideas became the basis for Allied offensives planned for 1919. The RAF Trenchard and Haig were planning for 1919 would be able to provide all the mobile firepower Fuller's plans required.

The advocates of strategic bombing also had plans for 1919. A war stretching into another year might have been an appalling prospect for the war weary nations of Europe, but for the apostles of this brave new world of strategic bombing, at least it meant there was still time for long-range bombing to make an important, even possibly decisive, contribution to victory.

CHAPTER 14

Strategic Bombing in Retreat

At the beginning of 1918, the development of a war-winning long-range bomber force seemed a very distant dream. The surplus aircraft production the Air Board had been relying on was not materialising and with everyone accepting that a decisive battle was going to be fought on the Western Front in the spring of 1918, the Army had first call on manpower and resources. Military realities, production realities, manpower realities, indeed reality itself, seemed to be against the advocates of long-range bombing. All they were left with was a gut instinct that strategic air power had to be a better way of winning wars than the carnage taking place on the Western Front, and a conviction that their time would come. With Trenchard in charge, it seemed that their time might not come in this particular conflict.

Trenchard had left no one in any doubt that long-range bombing was not his priority, which must have left Lloyd George wondering why Trenchard had seemed like such a good appointment in the first place. One of Trenchard's first acts as Chief of Air Staff was to inform the Prime Minister that all the talk of having a powerful bomber fleet of forty squadrons by June was nonsense. Nine was a more likely figure and possibly thirty by October.[1] Rothermere also found Trenchard's attitude extremely unhelpful, if not downright obstructive. He was hearing far more upbeat assessments of the potential of independent air power from sources outside the Air Ministry. Tiverton, still kicking his heels with the British Aviation Commission in Paris, kept in regular touch with Kerr and sent reports outlining the industrial targets that could be attacked to maximise the return. In November 1917, still using the figures on bomber strength he had been given and assuming 1,000 of the expected 2,000 bombers would be available for operations at any given time, Kerr assured the Air Board that concentrated attacks starting at the beginning of April would cripple the German chemical industry by the middle of May.[2]

At the time, Newall's 41st Wing was only managing around 100 sorties a month, but Air Ministry analysts were drawing encouragement from the results even this tiny effort was achieving. All reports from any source that mentioned the effects of bombing were carefully documented. Captured soldiers' letters from home contained information such as 'three wagons of food, two of hay and one of tobacco were burnt or destroyed and railway workshops were much damaged' and were dutifully recorded by Air Ministry staff as evidence of the efficacy of long-range bombing.[3] In terms of physical damage, the sum of these comments did not add up to much, although perhaps the letters did at least reveal the bombing was playing on the minds of German civilians. A resident of Mannheim complained in January 1918 that every day 100 or so bombers were operating in the vicinity of the city.[4] This was clearly a gross exaggeration. The most recent raid had been two weeks before this letter was written and was carried out by ten D.H.4s, killing two and injuring twelve, not a death toll that seemed likely to bring a nation to its knees. Nevertheless, the way the effects were being exaggerated could be interpreted to mean German morale was being disproportionately affected by the bombing.[5]

Newall, however, was increasingly turning away from targets inside Germany to railways in occupied friendly territory; by April, attacks on industrial targets inside Germany proper had virtually ceased. On 1 April, the very day the RAF came into being to pursue an independent strategy against targets inside Germany, Newall agreed to move two of his three bomber squadrons to the Reims region to support French bombers attacking communications in anticipation of a German offensive.[6] The RAF would start its existence with a strategic bombing force consisting of one short-range single-engine D.H.4 squadron.

Meanwhile, Rothermere, frustrated by Trenchard and his staff's apparent lack of interest in developing a long-range bombing capability, was looking elsewhere for a more positive attitude. He found it in abundance in Henry Norman, an MP, journalist and member of the Aircraft Development Committee, who Rothermere had co-opted on to the Air Council. In a wide-ranging report that was extremely critical of the Air Ministry, Norman insisted the long-range bomber was the only way of breaking the four-year-long deadlock. With a bomber like the Gotha, capable of carrying one ton 250 miles, Essen, Cologne, Frankfurt, Düsseldorf, Stuttgart and Mannheim would be within range from bases in France. These 'provincial towns' did not have the sophisticated fire-fighting equipment available to a city like London and rescue services would soon be overwhelmed by any concentrated attack. He suggested that with a force of 500 bombers, two cities could be bombed simultaneously. With twenty-five bombers setting off every hour, after ten hours the towns would be wiped out. 'Imagination fails to picture the effect upon the doomed town,' he melodramatically concluded.[7]

This apocalyptic vision of what existing bombers might be capable of achieving was followed by a crude assessment of how the German people would cope with such catastrophic events. Speaking from his personal experience of living in Germany as a schoolboy, he assured Rothermere that 'German morale would almost certainly prove to be very poor'. With Stuttgart and Mannheim 'wiped off the face' one week, Frankfurt and Cologne 'reduced to virtual ruin' the next and Essen and Düsseldorf similarly dealt with a week later, 'the rest of Germany would approach a state of panic'. Within a month, 'victory would be in sight'. With better planning, the British bomber force would already be meting out such devastation; it was not too late, but there was not a day to waste in establishing such a force. 'The future of our race and Empire may depend on whether or not we rise now,'[8] he concluded. This was more the sort of talk Rothermere wanted to hear.

None of this impressed Trenchard. He was furious Rothermere was getting advice from whomever he pleased, effectively bypassing his Chief of Staff. Not only was he consulting them, he was bringing them into the Air Ministry and on to the Air Council without any reference to him. As Chief of Staff, Trenchard believed he should be Rothermere's sole source of advice on aeronautical matters, but Rothermere saw no reason why he should not get advice from any quarter he chose. On 19 March, Trenchard resigned, citing the lack of faith Rothermere had shown in his professional judgement as the reason.[9] It was a remarkable step for Trenchard to take. Just a few months before, during the political intrigue that surrounded the formation of the Air Ministry and Trenchard's own appointment, Salmond had been considering resignation and an appalled Trenchard told him he could not possibly consider such a move at a time of war.[10] Such restrictions, it would appear, did not apply to Trenchard. It was scarcely out of character—in 1914, he had wanted to resign command of the First Wing as soon as he discovered Sykes would be his commander. For the government, Trenchard's decision could not have come at a worse time. The sudden resignation of the Chief of Staff just two weeks before the new Royal Air Force was due to come into being was potentially a huge political embarrassment. It scarcely suggested unanimity of purpose and an already controversial unification might become a political disaster. Rothermere attempted to placate Trenchard by suggesting that if the problem was just a personality clash, Trenchard should reconsider for he too was planning to resign in a few weeks. Rothermere's health was poor and he had been devastated by the recent death of a second son from wounds suffered in action.

Two days later, the Germans launched their spring offensive and Trenchard was persuaded to delay the announcement until 20 April, by which time Rothermere had assured Trenchard he would be gone.[11] Doubtless, Trenchard thought he was going to get his way as he had in 1914, but on 13 April, Rothermere decided he would accept Trenchard's resignation. He did not mince his words in his letter of acceptance. Trenchard's act, on the eve of the creation of the Royal Air Force, he considered 'an unparalleled incident in the public life of this nation' which he put down to 'instability of purpose, which I have observed in you on several occasions recently'.[12] The decision split the nation with Trenchard's allies in parliament making life very uncomfortable for Rothermere and the government, while others considered Trenchard's action to be nothing short of treasonable. Desperate to minimise the political fallout, the government promised that suitable employment would be found for the ex-Chief of Air Staff.

Finding someone to fill the vacant position was no easier than it had been when Trenchard was appointed, and the solution took everyone by surprise, not least Trenchard.[13] The vacuum was filled by none other than Trenchard's despised foe of old, Frederick Sykes. It was a remarkable return from the wilderness for the RFC's first commander. Following his work in the Dardanelles in 1915, Sykes had not been involved in any aspect of military aviation. Since 1917, he had been on the staff of the new Supreme War Council Lloyd George had helped instigate to provide better overall control of Allied policy and, more specifically, to blunt Haig's desire for ever more costly and futile ground offensives. With Britain and France running out of men to man the factories and fill the divisions, one of the council's tasks was to consider alternative ways of winning the war. Sykes' solution was to turn to machines: tanks and aircraft would replace the massed ranks of the unprotected infantry.[14] These ideas had got Sykes noticed, especially as a strategic bombing offensive fitted neatly within this philosophy.

The appointment came as much as a surprise to Sykes as anyone else, but he did seem to tick all the boxes. His previous involvement in both Army and Navy aviation meant he had the experience, albeit rather dated, of dealing with both air services, and his recent lack of direct involvement in aviation matters meant he could be seen by both Army and Navy factions as reasonably neutral. Crucially, he was sympathetic to the idea of the long-range bomber. Sykes did not believe bombing could win the war, but nor did he believe the armies on the battlefield could bring victory. Only a combination of pressure at the front, naval blockade and the bombing of German sources of production could bring success.[15] Sykes' appointment caused more ruptures. Henderson, who had never forgiven Sykes for his attempts to unseat him in 1915, declared he could not work with his archenemy and made his final exit. On 25 April, Rothermere followed, as he had promised Trenchard, although the fallout from the Trenchard resignation made his departure more of a sacking than a resignation. He left convinced that his greatest contribution to the future of the RAF had been getting rid of Trenchard.[16] Henry Norman followed his patron and Kerr returned to the Admiralty. A restless Brancker accepted the opportunity to go to the United States to help co-ordinate American aircraft production. Weir took over from Rothermere and Ellington moved from the War Office to replace Brancker.

With Sykes in control, the build-up of the bomber force gained momentum. The appointment of Brigadier-General P. R. C. Groves as Director of Flying Operations gave a very clear indication of the way Sykes and Weir wanted the air force to develop. Groves, a close friend of Sykes, had become fascinated by the power and potential of the bomber ever since a small force he led in Africa had caused panic among local rebellious tribesman with a few B.E.2s.[17] By 1917,

Groves was speculating about what more formidable bombers might achieve against better organised enemies. He sent the War Office a note in November 1917 that reached John Salmond via Ellington in which he predicted a 'new and tremendous phase' in the air war was about to begin with giant planes, which would make the Gotha and Handley Page O/400 look like toys. He predicted by the following spring, the Germans would be capable of launching a low-level attack on London, strafing and dropping delayed-action explosive and poison gas bombs on 'Parliament, the headquarters of the fighting services and innocent shoppers in the West End. The loss of life, the material damage, the disorganisation would be enormous and the moral effect would be greater.' It would cost too much to defend every target the Germans might bomb, so the only choice was to attack, either by bombing enemy aircraft factories and aerodromes, or if that failed, bombing German cities in retaliation.[18] This was the sort of talk Weir wanted to hear.

Tiverton was brought back from France to pep up Air Ministry efforts. On arrival, he discovered the 2,000-strong bomber force he had been assured would exist was sheer fantasy. In anticipation of future expansion, Newall's force had been raised to the status of a brigade, but by the beginning of May, he had only received one additional squadron, and predicted strength was down to twelve squadrons by the end of July and twenty-three by the end of October.[19] In the face of such evidence, Tiverton conceded that no decisive offensive was possible in 1918, but at least a start could be made. He suggested a small force of three D.H.9 squadrons, one D.H.4, one Handley Page, and one F.E.2 squadron might be scraped together by the summer, which, along with two or three French bomber groups, might constitute a reasonable striking force. Tiverton emphasised the importance of focusing on economic targets. The temptation to bomb Berlin with its limited war-related output simply because it was the capital should be resisted at all costs. With such limited resources available, Tiverton warned that targets would have to be chosen extremely carefully. Partial damage to any target would give the Germans plenty of warning about the need to relocate vulnerable industries to a safer region. If a particular target could not be eliminated, it should not be bombed. The best that could be hoped for in 1918 was a degree of disruption with perhaps an all-out finale at the end of the summer as a warning to the German nation of what lay in store for its people in 1919.[20]

On taking over, Weir reaffirmed the creation of an effective long-range bomber force as the reason for the existence of the Air Ministry and the first priority for its Air Staff. Ominously for the other services, he emphasised the Air Ministry alone would be responsible for allocating aircraft to their commands.[21] The Admiralty rushed to defend their air assets, insisting that they retain complete control over the number and operational use of naval air units and the Air Ministry should have no say in how or where they deploy them. They reminded Weir that only air resources in addition to the minimum required by the Admiralty and War Office were supposed to be used for the long-range bombing offensive.[22] Weir insisted there was no problem as long-range bombing was the only sphere in which the Air Ministry would be an authority. For naval and Army support, the Air Ministry had to act 'with the advice of and in the closest liaison with representatives of the Army and Navy' and the air forces supporting the Army and Navy would stay under the operational control of those services. Only the long-range bomber force would be under the operational control of the Air Ministry.

Weir accepted 1918 could only be a year of experimentation, but by 1919, he was confident a powerful British, French and American force would be engaged in an aerial offensive against the German homeland.[23] Tiverton enthusiastically set out his plans to 'demunitionise' the German Army with an assault on steel and chemical plants by 4,000 twin-engine D.H.10 or 800 four-engine Handley Page V/1500 bombers. The centrepiece of this offensive would be the dropping in a single blow of 40,000 112-lb bombs on the enormous Krupp works in Essen. 'If Krupp works are not obliterated by such an attack, there is something very peculiar about them,' he suggested.[24] Just how 'peculiar' the Krupp works were, Bomber Command would discover in the Second World War. To carry out this mission, the 8th Brigade would provide the nucleus for a new Long Distance Independent Bombing Force, soon shortened to the Independent Force, which would have as its sole purpose the bombing of Germany on a large scale.[25] It would be based in France but controlled by the Air Ministry, not Haig.[26] Controlling from London a force on French soil was not only going to upset Haig—the French were not going to be happy about it either. The timing for Weir was particularly unfortunate. Foch had only just been appointed Commander-in-Chief of all Allied Forces in France and was hardly likely to take too kindly to having his newly acquired authority undermined so soon.

The commander of the bomber force would be in an enormously difficult situation. He would be relying on French co-operation, which might not be forthcoming if the French disputed the independent status of the force. Nor could he expect much enthusiasm from Haig and Salmond; the new RAF commander in France was as staunchly against the whole idea of an Independent Force as Haig. Commanding the new force would require a strong personality, dogged determination and a fair amount of obstinacy. As far as Weir was concerned, there was only one candidate.[27] Trenchard was unemployed and a nation was waiting to find out how the government planned to make use of his immense talents and experience. He certainly had the qualities to see off any threat to the fledging force and his personal relationship with Haig and French Army commanders ought to stand him in good stead. Perhaps most significantly of all, appointing a former commander of the RFC and Chief of Air Staff would demonstrate to friend and foe alike just how important this new command was. The only snag was that

Trenchard did not believe the new command was necessary and he certainly did not want the job of commanding it. Anxious to make good their promise to make full use of his experience, the government offered Trenchard various posts, including command of the Independent Force, but he was not interested in any of them. A week passed and Weir made it clear that choosing none of these posts was not an option, and he hoped Trenchard would command the new bomber force. Trenchard decided this was the least unattractive and accepted, although even in his letter of acceptance he made it clear he did not believe the command was a good idea.[28] So it was that the former head of one of the world's mightiest air forces came to be the reluctant commander of three squadrons in the east of France whose mission their own commander did not believe in.

Trenchard was promised a rapid expansion of his force and as soon as Handley Page V/1500 squadrons were operating from Britain, he would command these too. In May 1918, the prototype Handley Page bomber took to the air, powered by two pairs of back-to-back Rolls-Royce Eagles in place of the still unproven Condors. On 3 June, the Air Council approved the setting up of a long-range bomber group in Norfolk,[29] and on 13 June, the formation of the first V/1500 squadron, No. 166, was authorised.[30] The V/1500 would have twice the lifting power of a Handley Page O/400 but was also twice as expensive to build.[31] They were so expensive, each squadron would have just four front line planes with a reserve of two. The order for the bomber was increased to fifty with a third company brought into the production programme, but only a handful of these huge machines could be turned out each month.[32] It was difficult to see how a substantial force, let alone the 800 Tiverton was talking about, could ever be assembled. Meanwhile, Tarrant was busy on his huge Triplane Tabor bomber, which, he insisted, would be a much cheaper alternative to the Handley Page giant. The plane would be built mostly by unskilled labour and make minimal use of metal and maximum use of locally produced wood.[33] Tarrant was given every encouragement and the resources of the nearby Royal Aircraft Factory were put at his disposal. With four huge 600-hp Rolls-Royce Condor engines, it was calculated the Tabor could carry 4,400 lbs to Berlin or 8,800 lbs to Hamburg from airfields in Norfolk.[34] Groves could scarcely contain his excitement at the prospect of deploying these mammoth machines. They were 'a thing of joy' he confided to Geoffrey Salmond, his former commander in the Middle East. 'I go to Hendon and "stroke" this whenever I get the chance,' he told Salmond, referring to the V/1500 prototype. Following the V/1500, he assured Salmond that there was the tantalising prospect of the Tarrant Triplane.[35]

In the meantime, Tiverton was fretting at the delays in getting the air offensive underway. On 22 May, he was warning reasonable summer weather could only be expected to last twenty weeks and four of these had already been wasted. Nor was he impressed by Newall's preference for bombing rolling stock and aerodromes, neither of which was part of his master plan to 'demunitionise' the German Army.[36]

The Independent Force formally came into being on 6 June 1918. It was a far more significant landmark than the formation of the Royal Air Force. The new force marked the beginning of a new era, or at least what the advocates of independent air power hoped would be a new era. Trenchard's instructions were to pursue vigorously an intensification of bombing against German industrial targets for which he would be answerable solely to the Air Ministry.[37] How co-operative the French would be remained to be seen. The best way of securing their support was to secure their participation, but this was unlikely with Bares no longer in charge. The latest French air force commander, Colonel Duval, was a more practically minded officer, or less imaginative, depending on one's views on long-range bombing, whose priority was to support the French Army. Sykes and Weir made a determined effort to get the French and other Allies involved and took their ideas to the Supreme War Council in Versailles. They hoped that the Council would control the International Independent Force when it came into being, much as the Air Ministry planned to control the British Independent Force; however, it was difficult to see how the Council would do anything other than put such a force, including its British element, under Foch's command to use as he saw fit.

Initially, to the relief of Weir and Sykes, things seemed to be going unexpectedly smoothly. The Supreme War Council set up a subcommittee to discuss aerial matters and at the first meeting on 9 May, the question of long-range bombing was discussed in general non-controversial terms. The British War Cabinet approved Weir's request that the French Prime Minister, Clemenceau, who conveniently also happened to be the French War Minister, be formally requested to provide Trenchard's 'Independent Long-range Bombing Command' with all the support he needed. A telegram was dispatched to Clemenceau who raised no objections and passed the telegram on to Duval.[38]

Trenchard arrived in France in mid-May and began setting up his new command. When he officially took over early in June, his command had expanded to five squadrons. Initially, he received the full co-operation of the French authorities, but then it suddenly ceased and French authorities began quizzing Trenchard about what organisation he represented. The British Government's telegram had reached Foch, and the Independent Force had suddenly become an organisation non grata.[39] The second meeting of the Supreme War Council's subcommittee on air policy would be a far livelier affair than the first. This meeting took place on 31 May with Sykes and Trenchard both present. Duval arrived, armed with the offending telegram, and made it clear that the British Independent Force was a problem. He could not believe that so soon after the principle of a unified military command in the French theatre had been accepted, the British were proposing a separate Independent Force based on French soil. 'Independent from what exactly?' he asked the committee. The whole point of appointing Foch as Supreme Commander had been the need for co-ordination and concentration of the available resources. Sykes insisted the Independent Force was quite a different issue—the primary role of the new force was unconnected with the war on the Western Front. Its task was to attack economic targets inside Germany. Its location in France was an incidental geographical accident, although a fortuitous coincidence, as it would always be available to support ground forces if circumstances demanded. Foch need only ask. Such tactical deployment, however, was not its purpose.[40]

Duval insisted that the British were getting their priorities mixed up—the land battle was the priority. The idea of the Commander-in-Chief of all military forces in France having to rely on the whim of the British Independent Force commander at the height of a crucial battle did not appeal. 'From the military point of view, orders are usually better than requests,' Duval suggested. The British delegation reminded Duval that the resources of the Independent Force were only those above and beyond the declared needs of the British Army, a convenient argument that was scarcely true anymore and did not impress Duval. 'I would be grateful to any authority who could establish the limits of what is necessary to a battle,' the French air force commander replied.[41] The Supreme War Council reached no definite decision but Foch made his feelings very clear. If no ground operations were underway the French Commander-in-Chief would be perfectly happy to allow the force to perform whatever strategic operations the British had in mind, but if 'serious operations' were underway on the ground, the Independent Force would have to be under his command.[42] Weir told Trenchard to ignore this, assume he was answerable only to the Air Ministry, and push on as best he could. Trenchard was able to do this largely due to the excellent relations he had built up with local French commanders. Indeed, Trenchard claimed, apart from Foch, Duval and his 'aviation people', he found the French keen to help.[43] For the time being, this was as much as the Air Ministry could hope for.

When Trenchard would have a bomber force worth arguing over was far from clear. A year had passed since the Gotha raids and the decision to establish a large bomber fleet, but Weir had little to show for his efforts. Nevertheless, Sykes assured the War Cabinet that the bomber fleet would soon be producing decisive results. With the huge industrial resources of the United States, the Allies now had the equipment and industrial capacity to take the offensive. Although he had given up on the French, the Italians might contribute, and the Americans, he believed, might eventually provide 50 per cent of the bomber fleet; indeed, it might possibly end up as a purely Anglo-American force.[44]

Sykes believed even the existing Handley Page O/400 operating from bases in France could 'dislocate' 40 per cent of iron ore production and 50 per cent of the chemical industry.[45] With such extensive dislocation, the paralysis of the German war machine was just a question of time, and 'far reaching morale and political effects' would follow. Airpower would provide the best and most rapid return on the expenditure the country was investing in its war effort.[46] Sykes was not claiming the bomber could win the war on its own, but he was drifting in that direction. Strategic bombing was, he believed, the way forward, not just as a means of attack, but as the only way of defending the country. Sykes too believed it was impossible to protect every target in Britain; only by bombing enemy aerodromes and aircraft factories could an enemy offensive be defeated. With the Army making slow progress in France, the long-range bomber had become the only truly effective means of pursuing the offensive. Anticipating events a couple of decades on, Sykes suggested that, 'In the event of our retirement from France, the strategic striking force in Norfolk would be our sole offensive arm.'[47] It was a measure of the potential of the long-range bomber, Sykes insisted, that despite the limited resources currently available, 'far reaching' results had already been achieved.[48] 'Airpower if developed, organised and co-ordinated could be accepted even now as the most prominent determining factor for peace.'[49]

Sykes wanted to strike hard in the autumn while Germany was still reeling from recent defeats on the battlefield.[50] It was crucial that the air requirements of the Army and Navy 'be cut to the minimum consistent with maintaining air supremacy over the battlefield'—'kept to' replacing 'cut to' in a later draft.[51] It was a revealing slip of the pen. Weir got cabinet approval for a policy whereby as long as the current level of air superiority on the Western Front was maintained, everything else could go into developing the long-range bomber force.[52] This was significantly different to the Army and Navy getting what they felt they needed and assumed a satisfactory level of superiority existed. Sykes helpfully suggested working out their own air requirements was 'too complicated' for the War Office and Admiralty. The Air Ministry had now taken on this responsibility 'with the aim of devoting as much as possible to the air fleet'.[53] Haig and Salmond immediately felt the winds of change. Much to Salmond's disgust, he was informed that squadrons which had been previously promised to him would now be going to the Independent Force. Indeed, for each new D.H.9 squadron Salmond would receive, two would be going to Trenchard. Also, a number of the naval heavy bomber squadrons at Dunkirk that Salmond had acquired when the RAF was formed would also be transferred. Trenchard was promised that he would have thirteen squadrons by the end of July and twenty-seven by October.[54]

Even before he formally took over control, Trenchard's very presence in France seemed to focus minds. In mid-May, those squadrons loaned to the French Army were returned. The monthly number of sorties flown jumped from an average of around 100 in the first four months of 1918 to 400 in May, and most of these were in the second half of the month. Trenchard's first official month in charge saw the number rise above 500. Most missions were being flown against railways although towards the end of June, a greater proportion of effort was directed towards the industrial targets Tiverton and the Air Ministry wanted eliminated.[55]

In late June, Trenchard, now warming to the task, and despite his traditional and well-justified scepticism of official production forecasts, seemed convinced that sufficient air strength existed to support the Army and bomb Germany simultaneously. Far from being a dilution of air strength, as Duval had suggested, Trenchard maintained the strategic air offensive was a fine example of concentration of effort. 'It seems to me unanswerable that if it is possible to hit the German armies in France and at the same time hit the Germans in Germany, this is a better concentration of effort than if we hit only one part of Germany'—a curious line of reasoning that was scarcely likely to impress Duval and Foch.[56] For Trenchard, the transition from tactical air power practitioner to strategic bombing apostle was proving to be seamless. Trenchard had always wanted bomber squadrons to force the Germans onto the defensive and now he had the opportunity to implement this policy on a much grander scale. Trenchard assured Weir that if he could keep him supplied with sufficient aircraft to maintain ten full strength squadrons this year and forty in 1919, he would 'knock Germany harder than you ever expected'.[57] Even more reassuring for Weir was Trenchard's description of a meeting he had with representatives from Foch in which he had explained that his squadrons were designed for bombing Germany and they could no more be switched from this role to tactical air support than the naval blockade of Germany could be temporarily suspended so that the Fleet could support a land offensive. Weir was no doubt impressed by Trenchard's loyalty and newly found fervour for the cause.[58]

French opposition could still scupper the entire plan. Just days before Haig went on the offensive at Amiens, the Supreme War Council re-emphasised the importance of all resources, land and air, including a strategic 'International Force', working together to achieve victory. Clemenceau instructed Foch to draw up a plan of operation in anticipation of this new international strategic bombing force, which would absorb the British Independent Force.[59] The stakes were rising and tempers were fraying. Foch made it clear that if the Independent Force was not going to be under his control, then it should not be based in France, to which Weir responded by telling the cabinet, if Foch took over the Independent Force, he would not hesitate to move the entire fleet 'lock, stock and barrel' back to England and only use French airfields as forward bases for refuelling.[60] In his correspondence to Foch, Weir took a more diplomatic line, making the modest claim that 'While not for a moment suggesting that such an offensive can of itself be decisive,' he nevertheless felt that as an independent force it offered the Allies 'considerable advantages'.[61] Foch would not disagree. The French Supreme Commander was by no means against strategic bombing, he just wanted to make sure it was under his command. While the row over ownership simmered, Sykes set about supplying Trenchard with the bombers he needed. He was already doing this at the expense of Salmond's tactical air force, but Sykes had a far more ambitious readjustment in mind.

The original response to Smuts' report had been to double Army and Navy air strength, and have a total of some 200 squadrons. The Army had already asked for over 100 squadrons for France and worldwide it would require around 150 squadrons. Just doubling the existing naval fleet of twenty-six squadrons would use up the rest of the planned 200 squadrons. The Admiralty, however, were planning a much more radical expansion, expecting front line strength to rise to 3,742 planes,[62] the equivalent of over 200 squadrons. The figures simply did not add up. In terms of existing production capacity, the Air Ministry's 200-squadron target seemed to belong to a world of fantasy, but even this was nowhere near sufficient to meet the tactical requirements of the Army and Navy, never mind a long-range bomber force.

In March 1918, the non-naval requirement was increased to 240 squadrons, comprising the 113 tactical squadrons Haig wanted for France, the sixty-six long-range squadrons that Haig was assuming he would control, forty squadrons for other theatres, and twenty-one for 'unforeseen eventualities'. A doubling of existing naval squadrons, fifty-two, was added to this to make 292 squadrons. This was scarcely likely to satisfy the Admiralty. In June, the Admiralty had trimmed back their requirements to a more modest 2,992 planes by the summer of 1919, and reduced this again to 2,682 on the understanding that now the United States was in the war the balance would be provided by the US Navy. This was considered an 'irreducible minimum'[63] but it was still vastly in excess of what fifty-two squadrons might provide. Sykes pushed the global figure up to 341 squadrons to provide a little more leeway. This was broken down into 127 Navy squadrons with 2,073 planes (a huge increase but well short of what the Admiralty wanted), 134 squadrons for the Army with 111 in France, twenty home defence squadrons, and a slightly reduced force of sixty squadrons for long-range bombing. Although reduced in number, the strike capability of the long-range bomber force would be doubled by replacing the twenty proposed escort squadrons with an equal number of Handley Page V/1500 heavy bombers.[64]

The 341 squadron scheme was put before the cabinet but not formally approved with very good reason: there were doubts about whether the manpower and resources could be found to build and maintain such a huge force.[65] Sykes, however, wanted more bombers and was working on a radical review of the 341-squadron scheme to provide them. Despite these intended changes and the doubts about the practicality of creating so many squadrons, the 341-squadron scheme in its existing form was sent to the War Office and Admiralty for their comments. It carried with it a warning that in the view of the Air Staff, the scheme did not take sufficient account of the importance of long-range bombing and changes could therefore be expected.[66] Unsurprisingly, the Admiralty was outraged and sent stark warnings to the War Cabinet that the proposed naval provision would seriously compromise the struggle against the U-boat. The War Office was also none too pleased as they now believed they needed more than the 113 squadrons they had requested in November 1917.

While the War Office and the Admiralty prepared their responses, Sykes set about his review. The cabinet had decided 328 squadrons was a more reasonable target, although Smuts and Milner, the new Secretary of State for War, thought this was still far too ambitious.[67] To achieve the 328 target, Sykes shaved six Handley Page V/1500 squadrons off the Independent Force and seven from the naval allocation. He then set to work on the remaining 328 squadrons. By removing another thirty-three squadrons from the naval and seventeen from the Army allocation, he was able to increase the Independent Force by fifty squadrons, taking it up to 104 squadrons. The fourteen remaining Handley Page V/1500 squadrons would be based in Britain, but the French-based force would undergo a massive expansion with a further thirty bomber squadrons, making seventy in all and the twenty escort squadrons reinstated. All in all, accommodation for ninety Independent Force squadrons would eventually have to be found in France.[68]

Expecting a huge backlash from the Admiralty and War Office, Sykes carefully set out for the War Cabinet his justification for this radical shift in the tactical-strategic balance. In a draft note, Sykes emphasised that he was not reducing the size of the tactical air forces, just reducing the proposed increase. Existing forces had achieved the existing level of superiority, so reducing the rate of further expansion did not necessarily mean any loss of superiority. In any case, the Army and Navy would gain far more than they lost by having a strong long-range bomber force. This he justified for naval operations by claiming that since the bombers would destroy the factories that built the submarines, there would be fewer submarines to hunt, so the Navy would not need so many squadrons for anti-submarine patrols, an argument which assumed naval requirements depended on the number of submarines the enemy had rather than the area which needed to be patrolled.[69] Similarly, the Army would benefit from the reduction in munitions output the bombing would cause, which would more than make up for any reduction in tactical air strength over the front. Furthermore, any numerical disadvantage caused by transfers to the Independent Force would be made good by the technical superiority of the equipment RAF tactical forces would soon be getting. Sykes claimed the Germans were relying on an engine that had reached the end of its development potential while the RAF was about to benefit from the new ABC wonder engines. If more tactical air support were ever required for Army or Navy operations, the Independent Force would always be available to assist.[70]

Sykes also argued a strategic air offensive would nip in the bud German plans to build a long-range bomber force, British civilians and industry would be spared and the Army would not come under any pressure to move fighter squadrons to Britain. The squadrons the Army was losing in his scheme, Sykes argued, would be fewer than the squadrons the Army would be expected to transfer to home defence if the British bombers did not stop the German air force bombing Britain.[71]

It was the sort of tortuous and convoluted reasoning that advocates of long-range bombing would often find themselves resorting to in the decades to come. There were a lot of assumptions and just as many flaws in the arguments. The assumptions about British technical superiority were especially ironic given the shambolic state of British engine development with an overreliance on underdeveloped power plants, with the ABC engines Sykes specifically mentioned a prime example. The claim would become even more ironic in the months to come as the Fokker D.VII and its BMW engine dominated the skies over the battlefield. Ironically, while Sykes was composing his justification, a depressed Brooke-Popham, facing the reality of German fighters that were running 'rings round our S.E.5s', was observing that, 'People in England are living in a fool's paradise thinking we are so far ahead of the Hun in all technical matters.'[72]

The most fundamental false assumption of all was that strategic bombing would work, that factories could be found, they could be accurately bombed and destroyed, and German production would be dramatically reduced. None of this was considered guesswork—it was assumed to be true. The only supporting evidence was the theoretical studies made by the likes of Tiverton and the even less scientific musings of 'experts' such as Norman. Set against these theories were the facts that patrolling areas where German submarines operated worked. Similarly, Britain's air defences had succeeded in defeating German air offensives and there seemed no reason why defences could not be as successful in the future. Stopping a German bomber offensive at source was by no means the only and certainly not the easiest option. Sykes and Weir were offering an unproven strategy as an alternative to the tried and tested. Indeed, the very success British defences had achieved against day and night bombing raids should have placed a serious question mark over the theory that the British independent air offensive would achieve a degree of success that had been beyond the capabilities of the German bomber force.

Before these arguments could be presented to the cabinet, the War Office and Admiralty—still unaware of Sykes' reworked 328-squadron scheme—were replying to the original 341 proposal. To emphasis their displeasure, the Admiralty compared the 2,073 Sykes was offering with their original 3,742 requirement. Nevertheless, they were willing to accept Sykes' allocation, provided the Independent Force would, if required, be used to attack naval objectives 'under the general direction of the Navy', which as far as Weir was concerned, would be as bad as handing the force over to Foch. Noting the reference to the possible need for an even greater independent bombing element and further reductions in projected naval tactical air strength, the Admiralty reply warned the Air Ministry that this could not be achieved at the expense of the anti-submarine force, precisely the force Sykes claimed could be reduced.[73]

Salmond had also sent in the Army response to the original 341 scheme. Salmond had been offered broadly what Trenchard had requested in November

1917, but circumstances on the Western Front had changed, Salmond insisted, and the Army's needs were now much greater—he needed more bombers, another nine day squadrons with four squadrons to protect them, and three Handley Page night-bomber squadrons. He also wanted another corps squadron for each Army specifically to direct the growing number of long-range artillery batteries, and the growing Tank Corps would also need its own squadrons.[74] Each Army also needed its own night-fighter squadron to oppose the increasingly successful German bombing raids. Most of all, he needed an additional ten high-altitude fighter squadrons to challenge the increasingly dominant German fighter force.[75] Salmond was prepared to be reasonable; for the time being, he was quite happy to make use of unengaged squadrons to cover the tank and air support requirement. He was also willing to make do with fewer two-seater Bristol Fighter fighter-reconnaissance planes, but even with these concessions, his final requirement was for an additional twenty-five squadrons. Effectively, the gap between what Salmond wanted and what Sykes was prepared to give him in his revised 328-squadron scheme had grown to forty-two squadrons.[76]

Even Sykes' own staff were turning on him. Ellington, recently arrived from the War Office to replace Brancker, was quick to stand up for the Army. He did not believe the Independent Force could be used tactically as Sykes had claimed. He was not impressed that the Admiralty and War Office had been kept in the dark about the proposed reductions, and Ellington thought Sykes was being rather free and easy with the term 'Air Staff'. In his communications with the War Office and Admiralty, Sykes had given the impression that it was the 'Air Staff' who believed long-range bombing represented the best way of winning the war in 1919; however, Ellington pointed out it was something Sykes and Weir had come up with. It had not been discussed by the Air Staff and was certainly not his view.[77] Ellington insisted the proposed expansion of the Independent Force was unnecessarily large and the reduction in fighter-bomber and day bomber strength would seriously weaken the offensive powers of the British Army in France. The requests for more squadrons to support the Army had been drawn up by officers with far more experience than officials in the Air Ministry. It was only the offensive capability of the Army, Ellington insisted, that could ultimately bring victory. Probably well aware of the answer, he wanted to know if Trenchard had asked for the twenty escort squadrons and doubted sufficient airfields could be found in eastern France for the proposed ninety Independent Force squadrons.[78]

Weir felt obliged to find out what Trenchard thought. Given Trenchard's apparent growing enthusiasm for the long-range bombing programme, Weir might have expected a more eager response to the proposed expansion of his force. However, Trenchard was horrified by the plan and agreed with Ellington that there was no way sufficient airfields could be built in time for such a massive increase. Trenchard did not want twenty fighter squadrons, was not even sure what sort of escort fighter he wanted, and was quite happy to let these twenty squadrons go to Salmond.[79] Trenchard was not going to miss an opportunity to throw another spanner in Sykes' Air Ministry works.

It was all going horribly wrong for Weir and Sykes. Sykes reworked his proposal so that the thirty additional bomber squadrons Trenchard had refused would be based in Britain. Sixteen squadrons would have the D.H.10 and fourteen the Vimy,[80] but what they could do from British bases was not clear. Vickers were working on an improved version of the Vimy which the company claimed would be able to reach Berlin from bases in Britain,[81] but in their existing forms, the Vimy and D.H.10 would only be able to reach targets in Germany if permission could be gained to fly across Dutch airspace. Based in Britain, they would only be capable of the anti-submarine patrols the Admiralty wanted.

Weir had little choice but to make concessions. Some of the Independent Force squadrons would be transferred to the Navy for anti-submarine work. Five of the proposed escort squadrons were returned to Salmond for fighter-bomber duties and the remaining fifteen, plus some of the Independent Force bomber squadrons, were put into a reserve available to both the Army and Navy.[82] The Air Ministry solved the Army's night-fighter requirement by declaring that the twenty proposed home defence squadrons would be available to defend the British Isles and British forces in France. It was left to the War Office to decide what proportion they needed to defend the Army, which neatly placed the responsibility for any inadequacies in the air defence of Britain at the door of the War Office.[83]

The Air Ministry plans now stood at 123 Army squadrons (ninety-nine in France) and ninety-five Navy squadrons with twenty-two in reserve with the long-range bomber force cut back to sixty-eight. With five night-fighter squadrons switched from the home defence force and the promise of more squadrons from the reserve,[84] the War Office had clawed back all it had lost. The Admiralty had not done quite so well. This plan was sent off to the War Cabinet with the same letter of justification Sykes had penned for the initial 328 scheme.[85]

Once again, however, the German threat was fast fading. On the night of 19–20 May 1918, twenty-three Gothas and three Zeppelin–Staakens reached the capital. Forty-nine civilians were killed but the Germans encountered a much-modernised defensive force with seventy-four Camels, S.E.5s and Bristol Fighters scrambling to meet the raiders. The bombers were fairly easy to spot in the moonlight and with flames spitting from their exhausts. The fighters shot down three raiders and anti-aircraft fire claimed another two—an unsustainable sixteen per cent loss rate. The raid would be the last effort by aeroplanes during the First World War against targets in Britain.[86]

On 5–6 August, five Zeppelins made the last airship raid on Britain. The brand new Zeppelin L 70, with a hugely improved performance and capable of carrying 8,000 lbs of bombs, was brought down on its first bombing mission. Another Zeppelin limped home badly damaged. The Germans claimed to have bombed targets of opportunity, but nearly all the bombs had fallen in the sea and there were no casualties or damage reported.[87] A couple of days later, the German Army suffered its 'black day' at Amiens. The German Army began its long retreat and was in need of all the support it could get. After 8 August, there was no justification for wasting air resources against civilian targets in Britain.[88] For the remainder of the war, the German bomber fleet concentrated on tactical missions in the Allied rear. The German long-range bomber force had started the war supporting the German Army and it would finish it the same way.

It was a triumph for the British air defences, but there was no complacency. It was assumed that once the short summer nights started to lengthen, the German bombers would return and every effort was made to improve the efficiency of the defences. Guiding the fighters towards the bombers after they had taken off required wireless communication; the first operational use of radio-equipped fighters was probably on the night of 19–20 May during the last Gotha raid. By the end of August 1918, all London Air Defence Area (LADA) squadrons had some fighters equipped with radios.[89] The entire tracking and reporting network was streamlined with the introduction of a system of control that would serve the RAF for decades to come. Information from sound location devices, gun sites, observation posts and searchlights was sent by direct wireless link to twenty-six sub-control centres. Here, the information was sifted and relevant information was passed on to the central operations room at Spring Gardens in London where plotters received it through headphones and moved counters representing the position of raiders on a horizontal map. The time from initial sighting to the counter appearing on the map was on average just thirty seconds. The approach of the bombers was then closely monitored from a raised platform by Brigadier-General E. B. Ashmore and the commander of the fighter wing, Lieutenant-Colonel T. C. R. Higgins. Higgins would order his fighter squadrons to scramble using direct telephone lines to their bases, and the progress of the intercepting fighters was marked on the map. Ashmore estimated the new system improved efficiency by a factor of four.[90]

There was within the defence community no sign of the sense of hopelessness the advocates of long-range bombing often seemed to associate with the air defence problem. Indeed, there was growing confidence that adequate early warning and information on the course of the intruders could be gathered to enable fighters and anti-aircraft defences to be effective. At the speeds aircraft were flying at the time, this confidence in the available technology was by no means misplaced. The defences seemed well prepared for anything the Germans might throw at them, but the new arrangements were never put to the test. No more bombers ever came.

It might have occurred to Weir and Sykes that the problems they were having in finding the resources to create a long-range bomber force were precisely the reasons why the devastating German bomber force that had been predicted had not materialised. The preferred alternative theory was that Britain was highly fortunate that the Germans were taking so long. Weir insisted Germany still saw the bomber as a war-winning weapon. He claimed that even though German industry was severely stretched and the inferiority of the German Army was becoming more marked with each passing day, the Germans were still pouring resources into their long-range bomber fleet with intelligence estimates putting the future bomber force at between 190 and 350 planes. Britain had to force the Germans to redirect their resources to defence, and only in this way could British cities be saved. The Independent Force provided 'home defence by anticipation', and this role was too vital to allow the bomber force to be frittered away in Army and naval support. Weir maintained that using expensive long-range bombers on or near the battlefield in normal circumstances was an unnecessary and unjustified extravagance.[91] The War Office and Admiralty might equally well claim that building expensive long-range bombers in the first place was the unnecessary and unjustified extravagance.

As the summer wore on, with no sustained air threat emerging and the German retreat on land continuing, Weir could feel Government interest slipping away. The War Office sensed it had the initiative and increasingly questioned the need for any independent long-range bombing force. Salmond made his feelings public in an interview with the military correspondent of the *Morning Post* in which he complained the Independent Force was draining away the resources he needed for his squadrons. If Trenchard's bombers had been under his command during the Battle of Amiens, he claimed, he would have turned the German retreat into a rout.[92]

The War Office suggested that unless the Independent Force was placed under Haig's command, it would inevitably pass under the control of Foch, who would use it as he saw fit and a lot of British effort would have been wasted on a force that would end up supporting the French Army. The War Office was sternly warned to forget any ideas they might have about taking over the Independent Force. The Air Ministry would rather pull the entire force back to Britain than have it fall under Army control, British or French.[93] The Independent Force faced the very real prospect of being hounded out of France not by the German air force but by hostile British and French Army commanders.

At the beginning of September, with the Fokker D.VII inflicting heavy casualties on his squadrons, Salmond renewed his plea for the full fifty high-altitude fighter squadrons he had originally demanded,[94] while the Admiralty stepped up their demands by insisting ninety-five squadrons were not enough to deal with the U-boat menace. The Admiralty demand provoked a particularly unsympathetic response. The Air Ministry was never happy with the notion that aircraft could achieve useful results not by engaging the enemy but by simply patrolling, which was what anti-submarine patrols did most of the time. Their role was to keep submarines submerged so they could not close on the convoys. The anti-submarine patrols did not have to sink submarines to win the battle.[95] Weir asked for information on how successful these patrols were, and by 'success' he meant U-boats sunk, not ships saved. Weir knew very well what the answer would be: a huge number of hours spent patrolling for very few sightings of submarines and even fewer U-boat kills.[96] Weir insisted it was a waste of effort and ridiculed the number of planes involved, claiming he would be perfectly within his rights to intervene and slash the number by two-thirds.[97] The Admiralty took exception to this criticism of the way they were running their anti-U-boat campaign. They needed more than ninety-five squadrons and either Weir would have to assure the Admiralty it was physically impossible to build the planes or, if he decided long-range bombing was more important, he would have to get the backing of the War Cabinet.[98]

With the support of the government no longer so certain, the Air Ministry felt compelled to make more concessions. Early in September, Weir agreed to yet another reduction in the proposed long-range bomber force, this time to fifty-six squadrons with forty-two in France. He also reduced the overall reserve by twelve, thereby creating a total of twenty-four squadrons which the Army and Navy could share in any manner they could agree on. The Army ended up with 140 squadrons (113 in France, five in Italy and twenty-two elsewhere) and the Navy with 102 squadrons with twenty Home Defence, fifty-six Independent Force and ten reserve squadrons.[99]

The Air Ministry had been hauled back beyond its starting point. It seemed like a victory for the War Office and Admiralty, but the Army and Navy were by no means getting everything they wanted and the long-range bomber fleet was absorbing a much larger proportion of the available resources than the number of squadrons alone would suggest. Long-range bombers were expensive in terms of manpower and materials, and even with this reduced force, the Air Ministry had established its right to a large chunk of the industry's production capacity and RAF training programme. Despite the fierce and successful resistance of the War Office and Admiralty, Weir was getting the redistribution of industrial resources he wanted. With the battle on the Western Front and the waters around the British Isles raging fiercely, the more senior services were slowing their rate of expansion in order to facilitate the expansion of the independent striking force.

CHAPTER 15

Last Gasp for the Long-Range Bomber

The setbacks in the allocation of air resources to the bomber fleet did not dampen the enthusiasm of Groves and his Directorate of Flying Operations (DFO). The Handley Page V/1500 would soon be available to transform the prospects for strategic bombing and although a front line strength of just fifty-six V/1500 bombers was now envisaged, even this small force was expected to be capable of making a huge impression on the German nation and the course of the war. Indeed, Groves believed even a dozen or so ought to be sufficient to achieve some worthwhile results, although with such a small number, operations might have to be limited to 'moral/political' objectives. The DFO suggested that Hamburg would make a good first target. Not only was it on the coast and therefore easy to find, it was also a key political and economic centre, an attack on which might 'bring the capitalists into conflict with the military'. After this, the aircrews would be ready for an attack on Berlin, an operation that would make it clear to the German people that there was no hiding place from Allied bombs. Cologne might be next and then Hannover, by which time all German cities would be clamouring for anti-aircraft defences, which the German Army would not be able to provide.[1]

This would just be the preliminary stage of the air offensive. From December 1918, when forty V/1500 bombers would be available, the second more decisive phase would begin with the 'obliteration or cessation of certain industrial targets'. A particular war item, submarine accumulators, for example, would be chosen and all industries involved in its production would be bombed until production ceased. This would be impossible from high altitude, it was conceded. Crews would have to be persuaded that low-level bombing was safe, that anti-aircraft guns had great difficulty aiming at low targets, and barrage balloon cables could be sliced away by special cutting devices attached to the bombers. Crews might not be particularly enthusiastic about these tactics, it was admitted, but it was simply a case of educating and training them.[2]

This was all very impressive but Weir and Sykes could not afford to wait for the Handley Page V/1500 to arrive. They desperately needed some positive results from Trenchard's existing bomber force to prove to the growing number of sceptics that such plans were not mere flights of fancy. An increase in the five squadrons Trenchard had started with would help, but Air Ministry plans to strengthen the Independent Force were constantly being disrupted by the needs of the Western Front. In fierce air battles, the Fokker D.VII was taking its toll and the D.H.9 was proving especially vulnerable. Over 100 were lost in June and July, and in these circumstances it was impossible to send Trenchard the reinforcements he had been promised. Every plane and crew was needed to keep RAF tactical bomber squadrons up to strength. Newly formed squadrons promised to Trenchard went to Salmond instead and he was even able to hang on to the ex-naval bomber squadrons he was supposed to be transferring to Trenchard.[3]

To add to Trenchard's woes, his bombers were also having to deal with stronger German air defences. In July, losses began to rise alarmingly, especially when missions were flown against targets inside Germany proper. The month ended with a particularly disastrous raid when nine D.H.9s heading for Mainz were set upon near Saarbrucken. The planes hurriedly scattered their bombs over the city and headed for home, but seven of the nine bombers did not make it back.[4] These heavy losses raised serious doubts about the practicality of maintaining a bombing offensive and Trenchard feared things were about to get a lot worse. On 4 August, Trenchard warned Sykes and Groves there was evidence that a large number of aerodromes were being built on his sector of the front, which he believed would be used to accommodate bombers and fighter squadrons to take on his small force. He was convinced the recent losses were evidence that the fighter build-up had already begun.[5]

Trenchard wanted to know what had happened to his 'Gun Machine' concept—bomber escorts that bristled with machine guns—which, he noted disapprovingly, seemed to have disappeared from air force plans.[6] Alternatively, a day bomber that could operate at 19,000 feet, higher than any German fighter could climb, would solve all his problems.[7] In the meantime, Trenchard believed that he only had one option—he would bomb the enemy fighter airfields. It might have occurred to Trenchard that the fact that the Germans had so far failed to deliver any heavy raids on his airfields suggested that his tiny force was not perceived as the threat he believed it to be. Trenchard had no intention of drawing any such conclusion. He was simply grateful he had the chance to strike first and take the initiative. For Trenchard, the very act of attacking established a degree of moral ascendancy and with it the battle was half won. Enemy airfields would become Trenchard's number one target.

Even before Trenchard raised the issue, Groves' department was very aware that the bomber loss rate was a serious problem that could very easily jeopardise all their plans; Groves' staff were working on solutions, including a long-range escort fighter. While Trenchard favoured large multi-seater twin-engine escorts, the Air Ministry had not given up on using the single-engine single-seater. Of the twenty escort squadrons the Air Ministry were proposing, four were to be the two-seaters and sixteen would be single-seater fighters. The single-seater would prove to be the correct solution, but getting a single-seater to fly as far as the bombers was a daunting task, especially at the speeds the fighters of the time flew. With extra internal and external tanks it was felt it ought to be possible to extend the endurance to the six hours of the D.H.9 bomber, and long-range versions of the Snipe and Martinsyde F.4 were considered. With the extra weight, the Snipe would only be just about safe to fly, but it was hoped the larger Martinsyde fighter would cope better, and still possess a very respectable top speed of 120 mph.[8] Three long-range versions of the Martinsyde fighter were ordered for trials, but since the standard version had yet to come off the production lines, it was scarcely an immediate solution.[9]

A more immediate remedy was to rely on the defensive firepower of larger bomber formations, and there seemed to be some evidence that this would work. A study of Independent Force losses noted that in five raids where the bomber formation consisted of fifteen to twenty-four planes, fifteen enemy fighters had been shot down compared to the loss of just seven bombers. If the intercepting fighters did not outnumber the bomber formation by large numbers, then the advantage seemed to lie with the bombers.[10] Interestingly, the success of this tactic was measured in terms of enemy fighters shot down, not bombers lost—a 7 per cent loss rate was hardly healthy. The conclusions also relied on the claims made by the gunners being accurate. An alternative explanation for the greater success of large bomber formations was that with more gunners firing at the same enemy interceptor, multiple claims for the same aircraft were more likely. Indeed, German losses were nowhere near as high as British claims. Nevertheless, this combination of wishful thinking and suspect analysis led to the conclusion that thirty bombers in formation ought to provide a reasonable degree of security.[11]

The long-range single-seater escort was not abandoned. Trials with the modified Martinsydes were to go ahead, and as an interim, fifty modified Snipes—with a more manageable four-and-a-half hours' endurance—were ordered, which would at least allow the fighters to escort the bombers through the front line zone where there was always likely to be a higher concentration of enemy fighters.[12] However, large self-defending bomber formations was the preferred option, especially as it involved no range limitations.

To try out this tactic, the Air Ministry would first have to ensure Trenchard had thirty day bombers he could put into the air at the same time. In August, Trenchard received his first reinforcements since May. No. 97 Squadron with Handley Page O/400s flew its first mission on 19–20 August, followed by No. 215 Squadron, also with Handley Page bombers, three days later. Also, No. 100 Squadron converted from F.E.2bs to the Handley Page O/400 in August. September would see another Handley Page squadron arrive and the first Liberty-powered D.H.9a squadron.[13] It was an increase, but not on the scale

Trenchard had been promised. Nevertheless, Weir was confident it was sufficient to achieve the decisive results that would impress the growing number of critics at home. The results Weir was looking for need not be of the economic variety. He suggested the aims of the strategic air forces were in some respects 'outside normal military aims' and were not just economic but 'political, being an attack on the morale of the industrial population with the object of reducing output and of producing a tendency towards peace'.[14]

To achieve such far-reaching objectives, something considerably more destructive than the weapons so far used was required and Weir was encouraged by the development of the new BIB ('Baby Incendiary Bomb'). The existing 40-lb phosphorous incendiary relied too much on chance to fall on something inflammable. This new 6½-ounce device could be dropped in far larger numbers, some 860 from a D.H.9 and over 4,000 from a Handley Page O/400, which would greatly improve the chances of making contact with material that would catch fire. The inventor, Professor Dickenson, had no doubts about the significance of the new device. 'That a successful attack with incendiary bombs is likely to be more generally destructive of material and will cause greater dislocation of production or activities than an attack by explosive bombs may now be regarded as an established doctrine,' he stated authoritatively. Solid structures like blast furnaces would not make suitable targets, but chemical plants, munitions factories, crops and 'older German or other towns' would prove vulnerable to the new device. A single Handley Page O/400 could lay a swathe of fire 40 yards wide by 1,200 yards long; a single V/1500 would incinerate an area 60 yards by 2,500 yards.[15] Ideally, the attack would be preceded by conventional high explosives to blow in doors and windows to enable currents of air to flow freely to feed the fires. For the 'average sized Rhine valley town or city' four Handley Page O/400s with conventional bombs followed by four bombers with the new incendiary 'would undoubtedly obviate the necessity of such a city or town to be visited again'. Just eight bombers would be required to destroy a city. When the Handley Page V/1500 became available, the same devastating results would be expected from just four machines.[16]

Successful trials in June were followed by the first operational use in August, and Air Ministry intelligence was gratified to discover the new weapon appeared to have made an immediate impact. On 18 August, a German newspaper article, the first of several on the subject, reported that the Allies were using a new incendiary device and warned people to remain alert, clear any combustible materials out of lofts, and make sure harvests were protected. The advice that the fires started by the incendiary could be put out rapidly 'with a little water' was perhaps not quite so encouraging.[17] Nearly a million of these incendiaries were dropped but no German cities were set ablaze.

With Dickenson's apocalyptic vision in mind it is not surprising Weir felt that Trenchard now had 'quite a strong night force' and was hoping for 'rather decisive' results. Weir's high hopes for the new BIB incendiary were not shared by Trenchard who believed the blast effect of high explosives had a much greater result on morale than just starting fires. Weir disagreed—he believed Trenchard was picking the wrong targets. He encouraged him to choose areas that were likely to burn—cities that contained older wooden structures rather than more solid modern buildings. Weir suggested the historic town of Heidelberg or the older parts of Mannheim, Frankfurt or Cologne. 'I would very much like it if you could start up a really big fire in one of the German towns. I can conceive of nothing so terrifying to a civilian population as bombing from low altitude.' There was no doubt now about the target. 'If I were you I would not be too exacting as regards accuracy in bombing railway stations in the middle of towns. The German is susceptible to bloodiness and I would not mind a few accidents due to inaccuracy.' Trenchard assured Weir he had nothing to worry about on that score. His pilots were already pretty much reduced to aiming their bombs in the general direction of town centres.[18]

By this time, Trenchard was not dropping many bombs on any German towns; his priority was the enemy airfields that threatened his bomber force. In June, around 13 per cent of sorties were flown against aerodromes, but by August, it was up to nearly 50 per cent. Elsewhere, German night bombers were doing enough damage to remind Trenchard of what could happen. On 24–25 August, eleven RAF planes were destroyed and three damaged at Bertangles. On the night of 23–24 September, twenty-six planes were destroyed and seventy-three damaged at the Marquise depot.[19] Trenchard's force lost no bombers but there is no evidence that it was his Independent Force that was preventing German bombers from operating against his airfields or reducing the level of German fighter activity. Indeed, Trenchard's losses on operations continued to rise, and as he was painfully aware, this was not just down to increased German fighter activity. The D.H.9 bombers that were now arriving were simply not as good as the D.H.4. On 11 August, an irate Trenchard reminded the Air Ministry that he had repeatedly told them that the D.H.9s would only remain effective until June or July and made it clear that he wanted the type to be removed from service by October. If there were any of the new Liberty-powered D.H.9a available, he would prefer them to be used to re-equip his existing squadrons rather than form new squadrons.[20]

On 13 August, three D.H.9s were lost attempting to bomb Mannheim and further raids by the bomber over Germany were temporarily suspended. On 22 August, Trenchard tried again—twelve set off to bomb Mannheim and seven were shot down. When he saw an expansion programme envisaging new D.H.9 squadrons arriving in France in the last three months of 1918, Trenchard was furious and made it very clear that he did not want any of them.[21] With large numbers of D.H.9 bombers rolling off the production lines, it was another major setback for the Air Ministry. To make matters worse, faults had been found in the Liberty engines arriving from the United States and correcting them was putting deliveries of the superior D.H.9a behind schedule. Trenchard's rejection of the D.H.9 scuppered any hope of any meaningful increase in his day bomber force in the near future.

By night, the offensive was gaining momentum and the overall bomb tonnage dropped was increasing. After managing just 3 tons in April, 49 tons was dropped in May, 66 in June, and 88 in July. The new Handley Page squadron helped to push this to over 100 tons in August, but fewer of these missions were being flown against economic targets inside Germany.[22] In June, the number of such sorties rose above 500, but it fell to 416 in July and under 300 in August[23] and even these 'economic' targets included railway stations. Trenchard liked Newall's argument that replacing destroyed rolling stock put extra pressure on German industry. Like Newall, he also appreciated railway targets were a lot easier to attack and many were closer to home for his bomber crews, although many were in areas that were sympathetic to the Allied cause and attacking them put the local population in the firing line. On 8 July 1918, twelve D.H.4s of No. 55 Squadron failed to find the Duren explosives factory and bombed the Luxembourg city railway station instead, killing twenty-four civilians and provoking bitter protests from the city's authorities who insisted no damage whatsoever had been inflicted on the target.[24]

The growing proportion of Independent Force effort being directed towards targets that were outside Germany and not industrial was causing frustration and dismay within the Air Ministry. Groves conceded that the increased effort against aerodromes had to be a tactical decision made by the commander on the spot. The increasing use of bombers against rail targets, on the other hand, was unacceptable, especially when the rail targets were inside Germany. Having got that far, the bombers might as well attack a more useful target, Groves suggested. It appeared that Trenchard's bombers were often bombing stations that were very close to excellent industrial targets, and on occasion even flying over perfectly valid industrial targets to get to the railway stations.[25] Groves calculated that the percentage of raids flown against chemical factories and steel works had dropped from 27 per cent in June to just 15 per cent in August. It seemed Trenchard was choosing not to bomb the industrial targets the Independent Force had been set up to attack. It was, in the words of Groves, 'a violation of the policy of the Independent Force'. The Air Ministry was discovering Trenchard's Independent Force was far more independent than they had bargained for. Groves feared that if Trenchard's bombers continued to follow this policy, it would be difficult to justify 'the Army/Navy/Independent Force' division of resources to the War Cabinet. It was an interesting distinction, emphasising that it was the long-range bomber force, not the air force as a whole, which was the new third element in defence thinking.[26]

Weir tackled Trenchard directly on the targeting issue. He explained that he was under pressure for results and, repeating his appeal of the week before, wondered if Trenchard could manage 'one really big concentration' over Stuttgart, Mannheim, Frankfurt or Cologne to impress the doubters back home.[27] Weir had no doubts that Trenchard's force was capable of something 'big'. As he was composing his appeal, Trenchard's latest summary of operations arrived. 'Glad to see you got Stuttgart,' he added encouragingly to the end of his note,[28] but 'getting Stuttgart' involved nine planes struggling to the target with a couple of 112-lb bombs each. Twelve people were killed, eleven injured and much personal distress caused, but it was not going to win the war, nor were such results likely to satisfy Weir's critics in London. Trenchard's explanation for the focus on railway stations was straightforward and frank. Stations tended to be in the middle of cities while munitions and chemical factories tended to be on the outskirts. If his bombers aimed for the stations and missed, their bombs would hit something and he could claim a successful mission. If they aimed for factories, the bombs that failed to hit their target would only fall in fields. Weir, in his quest for a little bloodiness, was scarcely likely to object to this line of reasoning.[29]

Despite all the problems, the Air Ministry still insisted that strategic bombing was not only the most likely way the deadlock might be broken, but was a force that was already achieving 'far reaching' results. An August summary of long-range bombing operations was upbeat, claiming significant damage to the Badische chemical works and destruction of the Thionville goods station. Photographs taken during and immediately after the raids 'and the accumulation of evidence from all quarters of Germany provide indisputable proof of the efficacy of air raids during the period under review'. Captured letters also demonstrated morale had been badly affected,[30] but the evidence for all these 'far reaching' effects was hardly compelling. By day, Trenchard knew high-level bombing was inaccurate. The cover of darkness had at least enabled the bomber crews to fly as low as they liked and bomb more accurately. German eyewitnesses were in awe of the nonchalant way in which two Handley Page bombers of No. 215 Squadron bombed the Badische chemical works near Mannheim on 25–26 August, flying just above the chimneys and low enough to strafe and bomb at leisure. It seemed reasonable to assume such raids were inflicting a lot of damage and evidence to the contrary was ignored. When a German raid on a French blast furnace caused surprisingly little damage, Weir assured Trenchard that German blast furnaces were far more complex affairs and therefore much more vulnerable.[31]

Losses continued to rise. The arrival the Fokker D.VII and other fighters such as the Siemens-Schuckert D.III and D.IV with their superb climbing and altitude performance meant even the high-flying D.H.4 was now very vulnerable. Three D.H.4s were shot down on 16 August and another five were lost on 30 August,[32] taking the overall loss rate for the month to six per cent. Trenchard was beginning to accept that such high losses were inevitable. He warned Weir that one bomber could be expected not to return from each formation of twelve sent into Germany, but whether a 100 per cent squadron turnover every twelve missions was sustainable had to be questioned. It got worse in September: four

D.H.9s were lost on 7 September, three were shot down on 12 September, and a further seven failed to return three days later. The D.H.4 squadrons were not doing much better. Of fifty-four sorties flown in the month, nine D.H.4s failed to return—a loss rate of 17 per cent. Unfortunately, the improved Liberty-powered D.H.9a had no more luck. In No. 110 Squadron's first raid on a target inside Germany on 16 September, two bombers were shot down and the squadron's next incursion into German airspace was a catastrophe with five failing to return from a raid on Frankfurt. With losses rising and bombing accuracy poor, daylight bombing scarcely seemed worth it.[33]

An effective escort was becoming a priority and the Camel-equipped No. 45 Squadron was brought back from Italy to provide it, although it would not start operations until it had re-equipped with the long-range Snipe. Whether the fighter would be up to the task was another matter. The performance of the standard version was fairly ordinary and trials with the prototype long-range version revealed that when the plane was fully loaded, it was a handful to fly and only capable of basic combat manoeuvring once it had burned off some fuel.[34]

Even the cover of darkness was no longer providing complete immunity. The Handley Page bomber crews attacking the Badische chemical works in August might have looked nonchalant but they did not feel it. Flying so low in the vicinity of barrage balloons and anti-aircraft defences was a hair-raising occupation and required a little luck. On 16 September, the squadron was not so lucky, losing four bombers, and three other squadrons operating that night also lost a plane.[35] Bomber crews decided the increased strength of anti-aircraft and searchlight defences meant they could no longer bomb targets from low-level at their leisure. Forced to fly higher, bomb aiming and even finding the target became far more problematic.

With losses increasing and no immediate solutions, the Air Ministry began to look for scapegoats and Trenchard was top of the list. Groves was struck by the large number of Independent Force bombers that were crashing close to their base, a problem Salmond's bomber squadrons did not seem to have. There was a suggestion Trenchard was expecting too much of his aircrews. He was perhaps using too many bombers from the same airfield, overloading bombers in an attempt to carry worthwhile bomb loads to distant targets or sending bombers off when the weather was unsuitable.[36] Any explanation was better than admitting that long-range bombing was an extremely difficult, risky and costly business and getting more so by the month.

The Air Ministry also wanted to know why British bombers that were ordered to attack Cologne had been reported in the Düsseldorf area. The only explanation that the Air Ministry could come up with was that Trenchard had secretly ordered raids on Düsseldorf, a target known to be beyond the effective range of his bombers.[37] There was also a report of two squadrons attacking the same target at roughly the same time, yet one reported attacking in mist, the other in clear weather.[38] The Air Ministry suspected some very strange goings on in Trenchard's command. It never occurred to anyone in the Air Ministry that the bomber crews simply had no idea where they were when they dropped their bombs.

Trenchard's total losses in September amounted to 81 per cent of his front line strength. The heavy losses were all the more discouraging as most of the targets were relatively close aerodromes and railway stations, with many of the latter requested by the French Army. While the Air Ministry steadfastly refused to give Foch control of the Independent Force for fear he would waste it by using it tactically, Trenchard was giving the French Army all the support it asked for. Trenchard's true beliefs often seem hard to fathom. His position on the relative value of tactical air support and strategic bombing appeared somewhat inconsistent to say the least. In August, he was vigorously defending the existence of his Independent Force to Foch's representatives. Early in September, he was warning Weir that Foch would take the first opportunity to bring the Independent Force under his control and then deploy it tactically. Yet, when asked by Foch to support the American offensive against the St Mihiel salient in mid-September and later the Franco-American push against the southern wing of the Hindenburg Line, he seemed more than happy to use his bombers tactically.[39] In truth, the independence of his force from all interference was more important to Trenchard than the actual role it played.[40] Trenchard did not mind what his bombers were attacking, as long as he was giving the orders.

Attacks on airfields, railway communications and air support for the American Army meant less offensive effort against industrial targets. In September, 85 per cent of all Independent Force missions were against airfields and stations, and only ten raids were carried out against industrial targets. The War Office warning that the resources invested in the Independent Force would simply end up supporting other Allied armies was coming to pass, and Trenchard was organising it. With each new Allied success at the front, the argument that no decision was possible in the land battle and only long-range bombing could break the deadlock was losing some of its force. French pressure to put the Independent Force formally under the control of Foch was increasing. Clemenceau repeated that the French were quite happy to let the Independent Force operate independently when Army operations were not in progress, but insisted that it support them when they were.[41] Even Sykes was beginning to appreciate the logic of this argument. The problem for the long-range bombing advocates was that Foch's strategy involved continuous offensives on one part of the front or another. There was now never a time when major Army operations were not in progress somewhere. With Trenchard supporting the American and French forces, the British were effectively already doing what Foch wanted.

By the beginning of October, and with the Hindenburg Line collapsing, the argument for concentrating everything in support of the advancing Allied armies was becoming overwhelming. With Foch delivering repeated blows at different points along the front, the only way the German Army had of dealing with the Allied offensives was to switch its dwindling resources from one sector of the front to another to counter each successive blow. An Allied air offensive against German lines of communication might disrupt these efforts and it seemed Trenchard's bombers would be far more usefully employed striking at these rather than economic targets. The war was being won on the battlefield, not over German cities, and it was in the tactical zone where the maximum effort needed to be applied. 'The spirit of the German people will be shattered more surely by the sight of their beaten armies retiring on the Rhine, than by the knowledge that the inhabitants of Trier and Kaiserslautern have to sleep in their cellars,' a War Office intelligence assessment suggested.[42]

Trenchard firmly rejected the allegations that German civilians had ever been the target, stressing there was no instruction or justification for randomly dropping bombs on civilians, although in practice this was precisely what his bomber aircrews were doing and he knew it.[43] The Air Ministry knew it too and had accepted that the bombing of industrial targets had effectively been abandoned. Trenchard's view that little material damage had been inflicted was 'accepted as official'. The summary of Independent Force effort for the period August to October recognised that 'the material damage was as yet slight' but 'evidence has accumulated as to the immense moral effect of our air raids into Germany'.[44]

The British Government accepted that the situation at the front had changed significantly since the Independent Force policy was laid down. In the new circumstances, the British were willing to concede to Clemenceau's demand. Sykes accepted the logic of the argument but Weir was far less enthusiastic about the new policy the government was hoisting on him. In a letter to the French outlining the new British position, Weir explained that the Independent Force had been created and its role defined at a time when it seemed the front line would remain stable throughout 1918–19. However, there was now the possibility of a rapid and victorious advance, and 'in such an emergency', it was better to place the force under the command of Foch.[45] It was a strange sort of 'emergency'. Weir emphasised the transfer was only on the condition that the French accepted that long-range bombing was still the Independent Force's primary role, not just a role that would be performed when there was no ground offensive underway. Furthermore, Trenchard was to be responsible for targeting.[46] The Air Ministry was reduced to trying to establish the pedantic point that they owned the bomber force and it was they who were loaning it out to Foch, not the other way round.[47]

The government's U-turn left Weir, Groves and Tiverton infuriated and frustrated. Under Foch's control, the force would inevitably be wasted on tactical air operations; however, all was not yet lost. Weir was still looking for that dramatic demonstration of the decisive power of the Independent Force that would prove his point and turn the tide of opinion in his favour. With the French-based Independent Force being increasingly used tactically, the only way

Weir had of ensuring the bombers attacked targets in Germany was to have them based in Britain. With a belief that even 'an attack by twelve planes in one night would be a very serious matter in terms of morale and damage',[48] the sooner the operations got going with the Handley Page V/1500 the better. Early in September, No. 27 Group began forming in Norfolk, but following the crash of the first V/1500 prototype, first deliveries were delayed until August.[49] Then problems with the second prototype put back deliveries to October and even these early production models would only be suitable for training.[50] Weir was running out of time. Germany seemed to be close to defeat. The blockade was hitting the country hard and her allies seemed to be slipping away. Following their crushing defeats on the battlefield, Bulgaria agreed to an armistice on 29 September and Turkey and Austro-Hungary were showing signs of following suit. Even in Germany, there was civil unrest in the air.

At the front, there was no sign of the German Army buckling; victory seemed to be as far away as ever, and Sir Henry Wilson, Chief of the Imperial General Staff, feared Haig's armies were close to exhaustion.[51] In the middle of October, the British forces resumed their advance, capturing the submarine ports on the Belgian coast and forcing the Gothas, now an almost forgotten irrelevance, to abandon their bases. Further south, French and American forces were driving the German Army back, but fierce resistance kept open the German line of retreat through Belgium. Poor weather prevented Allied air forces from taking advantage of German difficulties, and on the ground, as Wilson feared, troops were too exhausted to maintain the advance.[52] It would be early November before the British Army would be ready to tackle the next German defensive line, the Sambre-Oise Canal line. To the troops on the ground it did not seem like the end of the war was near.

For those who believed air power striking at the heart of a nation would be the decisive factor in future wars, Germany looked ripe for an aerial *coup de grâce*. The morale of a civilian population, already depressed by shortages, the flu pandemic and defeat on the battlefield, would surely find bombardment from the air the final straw. With Austro-Hungarian forces also now in retreat, new airfields were becoming available from which bombers could operate against Germany. Groves suggested that as many Mediterranean air units as possible be transferred to southern Europe to take part in a final all-out aerial offensive against Germany.[53] It was not just the Air Ministry who believed it was time to put German civilian morale to the test. British diplomats in Holland were monitoring the situation in Germany closely and encouraged the Foreign Secretary Balfour to believe bombing could have decisive effects on crumbling German morale.[54] Balfour, who as First Lord of the Admiralty had always supported a long-range bombing strategy, needed little encouragement and the tactics of retreating Germans troops seemed to create the ideal justification. Allied governments had been outraged by the wanton destruction of French and Belgian towns and cities as the retreating Germans implemented a scorched earth policy. It seemed to provide the perfect excuse to destroy German towns and cities.

Balfour suggested that in retaliation a number of German towns should be designated as targets for destruction. The targeted towns would be made known to the Germans and several days before the attack, a warning would be given to allow civilians the opportunity to flee—superficially a humanitarian approach, but one that was intended to maximise panic. These, Balfour suggested, should be towns with no particular industrial significance. Balfour believed the Germans would be unlikely to deploy defences to defend towns of secondary importance, even if they received a warning. The objective was to destroy residential areas, not factories.[55]

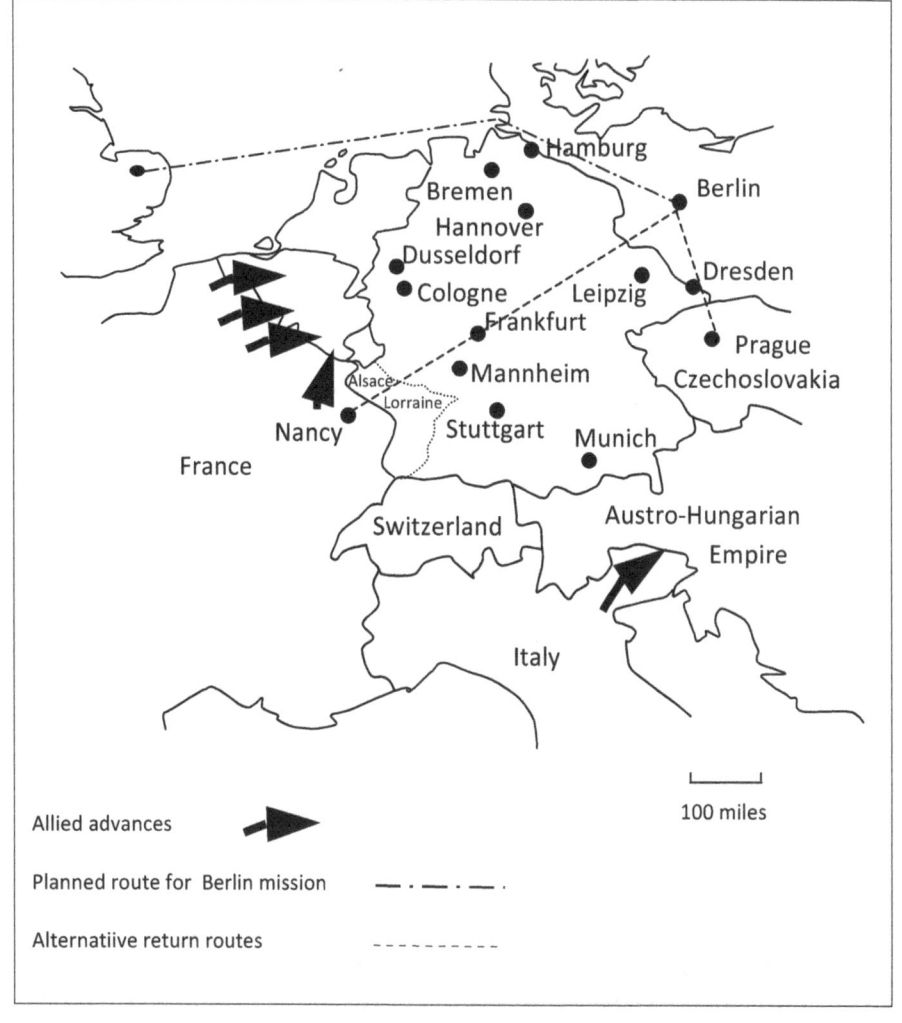

Collapse of Austro-Hungarian Empire exposes Germany to all-round attack.

It was ironic that Trenchard's bombers were being called in to respond to acts of German destruction that were essentially what his bombers had been trying to achieve, but with far less success. Significantly, Balfour apparently believed Trenchard's bomber force was capable of inflicting devastation on a scale that warranted the evacuation of the entire population of a city. The claimed enormous destructive power of the bomber was becoming firmly established as fact in the political mind.

Groves and his DFO section were already considering how such terror raids would be delivered. Dickenson's tactics, with high explosives followed by incendiaries, might provide the terrifying demonstration of air power Balfour wanted. It would not be without risks for any RAF aircrews shot down, the DFO warned, as they might accused of war crimes and face execution if they admitted their targets had not been military.[56] Nor did the DFO share Balfour's optimism that the Germans would choose not to waste defensive resources on towns of little industrial value. Bomber losses were heavy enough already without giving German defences warning of exactly where the next raid was coming, nor were there any particularly convenient targets. Mannheim was the closest city that could be counted as unquestionably German, but this was by no means particularly easy to reach.[57] Balfour got very little support for his scheme in cabinet and even Weir was against it. As the Air Minister candidly admitted, this was precisely what Trenchard's bombers were already doing or at least trying to do, although his main reason for opposing it was political. If the Independent Force was specifically used to retaliate for the damage to French towns, it would justify Foch having permanent control of the bomber force. In the face of Weir's opposition, Balfour did not push the proposal further,[58] but there was a growing political willingness to use the bomber to terrorise.

It was not just the politicians and diplomats who were beginning to see the bomber as a way of accelerating the end of the war. Even the War Office was looking to the air force to provoke a degree of panic on the German home front. Despite the almost continuous advance on the Western Front, Wilson was not optimistic that a clear victory could be achieved on the battlefield before the onset of winter.[59] He suggested an all-out bomber offensive might finish off an enemy tottering on the brink of defeat. He encouraged Sykes to get every possible plane, even trainers, over to the Independent Force to maximise its striking power, and if possible, bomb Berlin.[60] For maximum political effect, the target had to be Berlin, and Weir fully shared Wilson's enthusiasm for bombing the German capital. It was not just that Germany was ripe for attack and such a raid might hasten defeat. A blow against the capital might seal victory and enable the long-range bombing force to claim a decisive contribution.

Groves' DFO enthused over the opportunity to bomb German cities, especially ones that had not been bombed before, which would subject the German people to enormous pressure and might 'frighten them out of the war'. Significant targets that came into this category were Hamburg, Hannover, the more eastern regions of the Ruhr (Westphalia) and Berlin. It was important that these attacks should be sustainable and repeatable. There should be no 'gestures' with planes on one-way missions or with only sufficient fuel to fly as far as neutral Holland on the way back. The problem was that only Westphalia was within range of the best long-range bomber in service, the Handley Page O/400.[61]

Somehow, the bombers had to go further and if possible reach Berlin. No. 27 Group was being set up precisely for this purpose but the first heavy bomber squadron, No. 166, was still waiting for its first Handley Page V/1500. On 7 October, No. 27 Group was finally informed the second V/1500 prototype had undertaken a reasonably successful flight and after a few more modifications would be ready for delivery.[62] However, Major Mulock, commander of No. 27 Group, was reminded that early examples of the bomber would be makeshift affairs, suitable only for training. At the beginning of October, the operational debut of the Handley Page V/1500 was still some way off.[63]

Something else capable of reaching Berlin had to be found quickly. Groves' department hastily drew up a list of existing planes that might be capable of bombing Berlin before 1 November—the list was very short; it consisted of just two planes, the Vickers Vimy and the Short Shirl prototype. There was a degree of desperation about the Shirl suggestion. This large single-seater, designed to carry the huge 1,500-lb Mk VIII torpedo, had been at Martlesham undergoing trials since June. It had an endurance of six hours, but if the fuel load was doubled, the plane could just about carry a 336-lb bomb to Berlin.[64] It was extraordinary that sending a pilot on a twelve-hour mission in a prototype was even considered, but it gives some idea of the determination to deliver a blow against Berlin before it was too late. The Vickers Vimy, the first of which was just coming off the production lines, seemed a more practicable option. On 14 October, the day before Balfour put his scorched earth retaliation scheme to the cabinet, Weir wrote to Trenchard with his ideas about bombing Berlin. Vickers had claimed that a modified Vimy could reach Berlin from Britain, but Weir thought this was a little ambitious and suggested that the stretched Vimy be used from Trenchard's bases in France. The fuel load of the standard production model would be doubled and, with a 1,000-lb bomb load, the total weight of the plane would be at the very limit of the design's capability, but it should be able to make it to Berlin and back.[65] Trenchard approved, although he was anxious not to take any excessive risks and suggested that the plane only carry two 230-lb bombs rather than the four Vickers claimed it could manage.[66]

There was one plane that Groves had not considered: the Handley Page V/1500 prototype. The day after Weir wrote to Trenchard, Mulock happened to be in the Air Ministry. Sykes led him into Weir's office where he was told that because of the situation at the front, they were very anxious that a bombing mission deep inside Germany be carried out as soon as possible; although the first V/1500 bombers were only really suitable for training, they would be used to bomb Berlin. The first two would be available within twelve days, Mulock was told. The decision was taken without any reference to Trenchard, Mulock's immediate superior, which left him in the embarrassing position of having to ask his commander for formal permission to carry out the raid he had already been instructed to perform. Trenchard gave his approval, but warned Mulock not to carry out the mission if he believed it involved unacceptable risks.[67] It was ironic that not so long ago, the Air Ministry had suspected Trenchard of causing unnecessary losses by expecting his aircrews to fly overloaded bombers too far. With the Vimy and V/1500 Berlin operation, it was Trenchard who was preaching caution.

There would be little time for crews to familiarise themselves with the giant four-engine Handley Page. There would be just one nine-hour trial run before the mission. The plan was to fly north of Holland, hug the northern German coast as far as Hamburg, and then follow the Elbe towards Berlin. They would then follow the river until it veered to the right 60 miles short of Berlin and from there fly the rest of the way by compass. The return would probably have to depend on the fuel situation. If they did not have enough to return to England, they would fly to Independent Force airfields in eastern France.[68] Silhouettes of the Handley Page bomber were hurriedly issued to Allied units in the region to ensure no pot shots were taken at the unfamiliar plane. The Vickers Vimy was another bomber that front line troops in France might need to become familiar with. Some hasty recalculations suggested more fuel would be required, reducing the Vimy's bomb load to 672 lbs[69], but there was no time to install or test the modification in Britain; the plane was to fly to Paris, have the tanks fitted there, and then fly on to eastern France. Trenchard was told to expect the first Vimy to arrive in the first days of November.[70]

By early November, No. 27 Group had two V/1500s. These and the long-range Vimy were not much to start an offensive against the German capital, but time was running out. German resistance on the ground was weakening. Ludendorff had been sacked and the talk within Lloyd George's cabinet was of how the post-war peace talks would go.[71] At the front, evidence that the end was near was growing, the German retreat was becoming more disorganised and fighter-bombers were finding increasing numbers of targets among the retreating columns. There was no question of the Allies having air supremacy and German pilots were still fighting fiercely. The German air force did not have sufficient numbers to regain control of the skies, but they could prevent the Allied air forces dominating totally. The long periods of poor weather helped conserve their dwindling supplies of petrol and when the weather was fine, powerful German fighter formations roamed the skies, with the hapless D.H.9 squadrons suffering particularly heavy losses.

30 October was the heaviest day's air fighting of the entire war with forty-one RAF planes shot down. During the month, some 350 RAF machines had been

lost, and although not as heavy as September, it was the third heaviest monthly loss of the war. The RAF was able to perform any mission the Army required, but it was air superiority achieved by weight of numbers rather than technical quality. The disciplined retreat of the German Army in France, the continued effective presence of the fighter force and a little help from the weather ensured nothing on the scale of the Wadi El Far'a rout occurred on the Western Front. The Austrian Army, however, would not be so fortunate. In late October 1918, the Italian Army broke through the Austrian front and air superiority rapidly became air supremacy as Austrian airfields were overrun. The retreat became a rout with unopposed low-level strafing by the Italian air force, assisted by some RAF Camels and Bristol Fighters, inflicting carnage on a scale the RAF had inflicted on the Turkish Army the month before. Austria and Hungary formally separated on 30 October and sought peace terms from the Allies. On the same day, Turkey signed an armistice. Germany was now on her own.

In the confusion, yet more opportunities for the long-range bomber force were opening up. As the Austro-Hungarian Empire began to fragment, the peoples of its component parts began to proclaim their independence, and one of the first countries to emerge was Czechoslovakia. The country declared its independence on 28 October and seemed to have established control over its own self-proclaimed independent territories. Tiverton immediately saw the new Czechoslovakia as a means of getting RAF bombers much closer to their targets. Bases in Bohemia would bring cities like Berlin, Dresden and Leipzig well within range of existing RAF bombers. If bomber bases could be established in Bohemia and Austria, no German target would be more than 200 miles away. For the first time, there was a real opportunity of having a decisive effect on German morale, Tiverton enthused. No longer was Tiverton claiming a bomb dropped on Berlin was a wasted bomb.[72]

On 4 November, another British offensive made good progress against crumbling resistance. Germany was exploring the possibility of an armistice and there was a frantic rush to get the attack on Berlin started. Trenchard got the approval of Czech representatives in Paris to use their country as a base, and on 9 November he dispatched parties to Bohemia to investigate possible sites for airfields.[73] As soon as they could establish that Czech forces were in control of their country and suitable airfields existed, RAF squadrons would start to fly out. The plan was that British-based Handley Page V/1500s would bomb targets in Germany, fly on to Bohemia, refuel and rearm, and bomb targets as they returned to Britain. A racecourse outside Prague was identified as a likely base for the bombers[74] and was immediately set aside as an emergency landing strip for the first V/1500 Berlin mission. On 5 November, Groves instructed Middle East Command to prepare to transfer as many aircraft as possible to airfields in Austria and Bohemia to join the Independent Force in one final all-out strike against Germany.[75]

While RAF teams prepared to depart for Bohemia, No. 27 Group was instructed to get the Handley Page V/1500s ready for their raid on the German capital. In France, the sole long-range Vimy was on its way to Trenchard. Germany, however, was in turmoil. On 29 October, the German Fleet had mutinied, refusing to follow orders to engage the British fleet in one last pointless battle. Revolution was spreading through the country and there were demands for the Kaiser to abdicate. On the Western Front, the lack of supplies was becoming more of a hindrance to the Allied advance than the German Army. On 1 November, the Admiralty reported that there had been no ships lost to U-boat attacks since 24 October and German submarines in the Mediterranean appeared to be returning to port.[76] Berlin was reported to be in a state of panic.[77] The Kaiser seemed to have abdicated[78] and the end looked very near.

Wilson, even at this stage, had his doubts. On 7 November, he told the cabinet that despite the turmoil inside Germany, there was no military reason for Germany to surrender. Their Army was retreating in reasonably good order, it was holding a continuous front, and with winter approaching, there was no reason why they should not be able to establish a solid defensive line. There was still time for the RAF to inflict the *coup de grâce*. The War Cabinet officially approved the Air Ministry plan to transfer as many bombers as possible from the Middle East to Bohemia to attack industrial and 'moral targets', but the Foreign Office stopped short of sanctioning a raid on the capital.[79]

On 6 November, a delegation had been dispatched from Berlin with instructions to obtain a ceasefire at any price. On 8 November, they met Foch and were told the price was total surrender. The Germans requested an immediate temporary armistice while they considered the French demands; Foch refused and gave them three days to decide. A raid on Berlin by one plane might appear a mere gesture, but politically Balfour decided that it could send a very strong and direct message to Germany's leaders. Clearance was given for the RAF to bomb Berlin. The Handley Page V/1500 was to set off on 9 November and the Vimy in France was to follow as soon as it was ready. Poor weather forced the first V/1500 raid to be postponed for forty-eight hours. At dawn on 11 November, the crews prepared for another attempt, but before they could get into the air, news arrived that an armistice would come into effect later that day. There would be no opportunity to bomb Berlin—not in this war at least.

Conclusion

For the Air Ministry, it was an anti-climax and unsatisfactory conclusion to their strategic bombing campaign—the end of the war had come before the value of the strategic bomber could be proven. Indeed, far from being proven, doubts were growing about it having any significant military value. The optimism of midsummer had been replaced by a growing realisation that little physical damage was being inflicted on the German economy. The ability of the bomber to cripple German industry had been vastly exaggerated. The effect of the bombing on the German population had also been overestimated. Deaths as a result of any one raid rarely reached double figures and less than 1,000 German civilians died in bombing raids during the First World War. Tragic as each individual loss was, given the huge problems Germany faced and the horrendous scale of casualties at the front, the impact of bombing casualties on the population as a whole was slight. The deaths through air bombardment were dwarfed by the 400,000 German civilians who died in 1918 as a result of the flu pandemic.

The deprivations caused by the blockade, the onset of the flu pandemic, the surrender of Germany's allies and the general hopelessness of the military situation were far more significant factors in the decline of German morale. The scattering of a few bombs over Berlin in the last hours of the war might have added to the sense of hopelessness. Alternatively, the indignation such attacks caused might equally have helped unite a broken nation and stiffen resolve. Most likely of all, it would scarcely have been noticed in a country already racked by despair, disorder and internal dispute.

The war had ended with no evidence that a country could be intimidated into accepting defeat by the air weapon. Haig had apparently been proven right. The bombing of London, or any other city, could not change the course of the war. It was perhaps easier for Haig in France to make this judgement than the politicians and military sitting in London as the bombs fell around them. Haig's insistence that the Army should get priority over home air defence might seem cold and calculating, even callous, but he simply did not believe the compatriots of his stoic conscript Army would cave in so tamely under the threat of air attack. It is neither difficult nor surprising to find evidence that civilians find bombing extremely distressing, but it is hard to find evidence that it induces a desire to surrender. As well as causing grief, the killing and maiming of innocent civilians inspires resentment and anger. It does not take much, if any, manipulation by the government and media to exploit these emotions to stiffen the determination of a nation to fight on. As Mond had suggested in 1909, 'No nation would make peace because the enemy was killing its civilians'.

As a last resort, advocates of long-range bombing claimed that even if the bombers did not achieve decisive results, the effort that the enemy had been compelled to put into air defence was a victory for the bomber. The problem was that long-range bombers required far more resources to build and operate than the short-range interceptors that shot them down: ten Snipes could be built for the price of one Handley Page V/1500.[1] Fighters were also more versatile than huge long-range bombers. Interceptors were often the same machines as those operating over the front, but huge and cumbersome Handley Page V/1500 bombers would be as vulnerable as Zeppelins over the battlefield.

Perhaps the biggest error made by the pro-bombing lobby was that bombing was easy and preventing it difficult. By the end of the war it was becoming clear the opposite was far closer to the truth. The defences of both sides were improving quicker than the efficiency of the bomber forces. Even if the defences were overcome and targets found, planners were becoming aware of the countermeasures open to the country under attack. Cities could not be moved but industries could. As a last resort, dispersion and relocation of vulnerable industries was always possible. Tiverton's greatest fear had always been that a premature and unsuccessful offensive against any particular target would give the enemy time to relocate to a more distant part of Germany.

The German daylight raids on London had provoked a radical shift in British air policy. At the time, it seemed like the dawn of a new era in warfare, but even before the war ended a little more than a year later, there was growing evidence that this had been a massive over-reaction and misjudgement. Long-range bombing was fraught with far more problems than anyone had appreciated and the battle for resources in the last year of war demonstrated that Britain did not have the means to build a long-range bomber fleet and maintain an effective Army and Navy. By November 1918, it was the advocates of strategic bombing who were very much on the back foot, desperate to find last-minute proof, or even just a little evidence, that they might still be right.

Only the politicians seemed to have been won over. Many seemed to have been taken in by some of the extraordinary claims made for the destructive capabilities of very small numbers of bombers. As always, it was the politicians who tended to be most impressed by the morale argument. This is scarcely surprising; it is, after all, the politicians' responsibility to worry about civilian morale. Defending one's own civilians from aerial bombardment is a perfectly reasonable priority for any government. The ability to retaliate effectively made politicians feel more confident about securing the support of their own people and less vulnerable to threats from enemies. The political advantages and the military benefits of having an intimidating long-range bomber force would become increasingly muddled in the years ahead.

While the strategic use of air power had failed to make the expected impact, the tactical applications of air power had gone from strength to strength. Aerial reconnaissance and artillery direction developed very rapidly, achieving a degree of operational sophistication and efficiency that, even after four years of war, the long-range bombing advocates could not come close to matching. The problem of the air and artillery combination was that it worked so well: it stifled movement on the battlefield and deepened the stalemate. However, as the war progressed and new tactics began to break the tactical gridlock, air power was able to demonstrate its versatility.

In any sort of conflict, reconnaissance is crucial. If reconnaissance had been the only task aircraft were capable of performing in 1918, it would still have justified the resources poured into the development of military aviation; however, aircraft were capable of much more. Attacking ground targets began to produce significant results once it was appreciated that the more relevant they were to the immediate battle, the more difference they could make. By the end of the war, fighter-bombers were being employed and directed in exactly the same way as artillery. Ground attack was merely an extension of the artillery support an Army corps could expect. By 1918, close air support was not an innovation, it was normal. The expectation was that eventually even a platoon commander held up by an enemy strongpoint should be able to call for air support.[2] Techniques for supporting ground forces more normally associated with the Second World War had become established procedures in the First World War.

In defence, close air support had demonstrated its mobility and ability to deal with emergencies. In attack, it had in extreme circumstances demonstrated the ability to turn retreat into a rout. Most of the time, its impact was far less spectacular. It was just another useful tool available to Army commanders, but this capability alone was valuable enough to justify its existence and should have been enough to guarantee its future.

In 1918, the Army was developing along the right lines. The War Office was developing high-speed tanks that could do more than just crush barbed wire and support the infantry. Armoured close support planes and self-propelled artillery were being developed, which could support deep thrusts into the enemy rear. No longer would the infantry have to wait for the artillery to move into place before advancing.[3] The fast moving tanks still had to be developed and the tactics they would use formulated, but the air element was already in place. Britain had its blitzkrieg air force.

As valuable as the fighter-bomber had proven, the Army appreciated the first duty of the fighter was to establish air superiority. The struggle for air superiority was a battle that proved as crucial as any fought on land or sea. To win it required the right training, tactics, organisation and equipment. In the autumn of 1918, the Germans might have been losing the war, but with their excellent Fokker D.VII and 'Flying Circuses', they were ahead of the RAF in most of these respects.

No country could have been quicker than Britain to see the need for an efficient fighter, but developing the correct solution proved to be a very slow process. False analogies with naval warfare had led to an obsession with aerial battleships that could dominate huge areas of airspace. The realities of war eventually forced an acceptance that speed and agility were the key qualities, more important even than firepower. No other item of First World War military equipment had such a rapid turnover as the fighter. A new design might only dominate the skies for months before becoming obsolete. No item of military equipment was considered more important. The Fokker D.VII was considered such a vital element of the German war machine, it was the only item of military equipment specifically mentioned by name in the list of war material the Germans had to hand over as the price for an armistice.

The flying qualities required of an air superiority fighter are simple to list: ease of control; ability to turn tightly and change direction quickly; high horizontal, climbing and diving speeds; high acceleration; and high service ceiling. The problem is that many of these qualities are contradictory and one can only be achieved at the expense of another. The first Martinsyde F.3/4 fighters to reach the RAF would have found themselves opposed by the Fokker D.VIII. No two fighters could be more different than the light Fokker and the powerful Martinsyde. Each had its advantages and it would have been an interesting contest between the two.

Developing the correct fighter tactics had been a particularly hard struggle for the RFC and RAF, but theories about providing indirect protection by dominating the enemy rear had eventually given way to more focused fighter operations in the battle zone. Fighters had to operate where they were likely to encounter the enemy, not where theories dictated the battle ought to take place. If patrols flying low over the battle area needed higher level patrols to protect them, then an independent battle for air superiority between the opposing fighter forces might well emerge, but fighter resources could not be wasted looking for a battle that served no purpose. The first priority was to establish superiority in the immediate vicinity of friendly forces, whether they are troops in the front line or reconnaissance and bombing machines penetrating enemy airspace. Once this has been established, then it might well be profitable for fighters to patrol further afield. Trenchard's offensive patrols would have been an excellent way of extending and reinforcing air superiority already achieved over the battlefield, but they were not a way of achieving that air superiority.

Ironically, given that much air force strategy was based on naval practice, the Navy and RAF ended up making the same mistakes and having to learn the same lessons. The Navy began the war believing a broad offensive policy aimed at dominating the oceans would enable individual vessels to move freely. The policy had failed and been replaced by the more pragmatic approach of concentrating shipping in convoys that were protected by strong naval escorts. Exactly the same had happened in the air.

It was the expansion of the strategic bomber force, not the tactical air force, which was in most doubt when the war came to an end. If the war had continued into 1919, the RAF, with a large Army in the field to support, would undoubtedly have continued to develop as a powerful tactical force. The development of a powerful strategic bombing force would have been far more problematic. Britain did not have the resources to build a strategic and a tactical air force. If the war had continued, the huge expense of the strategic bomber, in terms of manpower and resources, and the needs of the Army and Navy, would probably have continued to restrict the development of the Air Ministry's independent bombing ambitions.

Much had happened in four years. In 1914, the British had committed a small professional Army supported by four RFC squadrons to a European conflict that was expected to be of limited duration. Instead, the war had lasted for more than four years and a huge conscript Army had been raised. Plans for the spring of 1919 envisaged fifty divisions of the British Army supported by a tactical air force with 400 day and night bombers, 400 low-level fighter-bombers, 300 two-seater fighter-reconnaissance planes and 700 armoured corps planes, all protected by 1,200 single-seater fighters. In 1919, the British soldier would not have lacked air support. It was a level of support that British soldiers fighting future battles in future wars would be denied. Why they did not get it is another story.

Endnotes

Chapter 1: Cities in the Frontline

1. Raleigh, *The War in the Air Vol. 1 (1969), pp. 29-31.*
2. Paris, *Winged Warfare* (1992), Chapter 2.
3. www.icrc.org/ihl/INTRO/160?OpenDocument.
4. Gollin, *The Impact of Air Power (1989), pp. 5, 13.*
5. Paris, *Winged Warfare* (1992), p. 210/Hankey, *Supreme Command* (1961), p. 76.
6. Hare, *Royal Aircraft Factory* (1990), pp. 14-17.
7. Ibid. p. 19/*The Times*, 17 October 1908.
8. Gollin, *The Impact of Air Power* (1989), p. 286.
9. AIR1/2100/207/28/1 (January 1909).
10. Ibid.
11. Gollin, *The Impact of Air Power* (1989), pp. 44-45.
12. Nicholson quoted in Gollin, *The Impact of Air Power* (1989), p. 116.
13. *Hansard*, 3 August 1909/Gollin, *The Impact of Air Power* (1989), pp. 3, 11, 19.
14. *Flight*, June 1910/Hare, *Royal Aircraft Factory* (1990), pp. 20-21/*Hansard*, 14 September 1909.
15. Quote by Col. Stone, *Flight*, 11 December 1909.
16. *Hansard*, 17 May 1909.
17. Gollin, *The Impact of Air Power* (1989), pp. 59-60.
18. *The Times*, 1 June 1909.
19. www.youtube.com/watch?v=d_6rWndnJCM.
20. *Hansard*, 3 August 1909.
21. Ibid.
22. AIR1/204/5/69 (15 November 1909).
23. AIR1/729/176/5/62 (1910).
24. Hankey, *The Supreme Command* (1961), p. 111.
25. Roskill, *The Naval Air Service Vol. 1* (1969), pp. 14-18.
26. Ibid. p. 23.
27. Mead, *The Eye in the Air* (1983), p. 37/Raleigh, *The War in the Air Vol. 1* (1969), p. 177.
28. Gollin, *The Impact of Air Power* (1989), p. 152.
29. *Flight*, 11 February 1911.
30. AIR1/1/4/1 (8 May 1919)/Roskill, *The Naval Air Service Vol. 1* (1969), pp. 25-26/Gollin, *The Impact of Air Power* (1989), pp. 164-167.
31. AIR1/729/176/5/63 (3 March 1911).

32. LHC, Brooke-Popham papers 1/4 (1913).
33. Barnes, *Bristol Aircraft since 1910* (1995), p. 47.
34. AIR1/762/204/4/174 (1 May, 31 August, 20 November, 19 December 1911).
35. AIR1/1609/204/85/1 (1 September 1911).
36. AIR1/1/4/1 (8 May 1919)/Raleigh, *The War in the Air Vol. 1 (1969), pp. 193-195.*
37. *Hansard*, 3 August 1909.
38. AIR1/731/176/5/102.
39. *Hansard, 11 July 1911.*
40. AIR1/731/176/5/102/Hare, The Royal Aircraft Factory (1990), pp. 36-42.
41. *Flight*, 20 May 1911.
42. Gollin, *The Impact of Air Power* (1989) pp. 171-172.
43. *Hansard*, 26 March 1913.
44. *Ibid*. 30 October 1911.
45. Bruce, *British Aeroplanes 1914–1918* (1957), p. 34.
46. *Flight*, 16 December 1913.
47. Gollin, *The Impact of Air Power (1989), pp. 197-198.*
48. Sykes, *From Many Angles* (1943) pp. 46-48, 80, 93, 107/Paris, *Winged Warfare* (1992), p. 189/*Flight*, 8 March 1913.
49. AIR1/21/15/1/110 (February 1912).
50. *Ibid*.
51. Macmillan, *Sefton Brancker* (1935), p. 6.
52. CAB14/1 (31 July 1912).
53. *Ibid*. (7 November 1912).
54. *Ibid*.
55. *Ibid*. (31 July 1912, 14 March 1913).
56. AIR1/724/76/2 (March 1912).
57. AIR1/626/17/88 (18 October 1912).
58. MacBean, Hogben, *Bombs Gone* (1990), p. 21.
59. Jones, *The Origins of Strategic Bombing* (1973), pp. 45-46.
60. AIR1/727/152/7 (post-war account of Sopwith planes).
61. Longmore, *From Sea to Sky* (1946), p. 36.
62. AIR1/626/17/47 (1913).
63. AIR1/2104/207/3 (4 July 1914).
64. AIR1/1284/204/11/19 (24 May 1912).
65. *Ibid*. (24 May-19 July 1912).
66. WO 32/7069 9 (14 June 1912).
67. *Ibid*. (20 June 1912).
68. Woodman, *Early Aircraft Armament* (1989), p.13.
69. WO 32/7069 (26 July 1912).
70. Hare, *The Royal Aircraft Factory* (1990), p. 44.
71. AIR1/21/15/1/110, AIR1/1608/204/85/383 (1 January 1912).
72. *Flight*, 17 August 1912.
73. AIR1/804/204/4/1180 (12 August 1913).
74. AIR1/731/176/5/102.
75. Jackson, *Avro Aircraft since 1908* (1965), p. 43.
76. WO 279/47 (1912).
77. WO 33/620 (1912).
78. *Flight*, 7 December 1912.
79. WO 279/47 (1912).
80. WO 33/620 (1912).
81. Paris, *Winged Warfare* (1992), pp. 210-211.

82. Sykes, *From Many Angles* (1943), p. 105.
83. LHC/Kiggel papers.
84. *Flight*, 8 March 1913.
85. *Ibid.*

Chapter 2: The Tactical Vision

1. WO 32/7069 (*September–November* 1912).
2. *Ibid.* (1 January 1913–6 March 1913).
3. *Ibid.* (20 March 1913).
4. AIR1/779/204/4/469 (June 1913).
5. Raleigh, *The War in the Air Vol. 1 (1969), p. 250.*
6. AIR1/774/204/4/355 (October–November 1913)/AIR1/774/204/4/353 (13, 15 July 1913).
7. AIR1/779/204/4/469 (June 1913).
8. AIR1/782/204/4/492 (14 April 1913).
9. *Ibid.*
10. Macmillan, *Sefton Brancker* (1935), p. 33.
11. *Ibid.* Chapter 3.
12. *Ibid.* p. 35.
13. Jones, *The War in the Air Vol. 2* (1968), pp. 257-258.
14. *Flight*, 14 March 1914.
15. Macmillan, *Sefton Brancker* (1935), p. 45.
16. *Hansard*, 19 March 1913.
17. AIR1/730/176/5/92.
18. AIR1/810/20/41208 (29 August 1913).
19. Macmillan, *Sefton Brancker* (1935), p. 51.
20. AIR1/810/204/4/1227 (August 1913).
21. AVIA 6/25702 (June 1913).
22. *Ibid.*/AVIA 6/25702 (June 1913)/AIR1/730/176/5/92 (14 November 1913).
23. AIR1/784/204/4/544 (1913).
24. AIR1/774/204/4/355 (November 1913).
25. AIR1/810/204/4/1210.
26. *The Times*, 29 September 1913/AIR1/775/204/4/384 (1913).
27. AIR1/782/204/4/499 (January 1914).
28. *Flight*, 14 February 1914.
29. AIR1/781/204/4/485 (30 April 1914).
30. *Ibid.*
31. *Flight*, 14 February 1914.
32. AIR1/798/204/4/1018 (May 1914).
33. AIR1/783/204/4/517 (July 1914).
34. AIR1/781/204/4/485 (30 April 1914).
35. *Ibid.* (30 April 1914).
36. *Ibid.* (30 April 1914).
37. *Ibid. (30 April 1914).*
38. AIR1/117/15/40/27/AIR1/774/204/4/353 (July 1913-May 1914).
39. Hare, *The Royal Aircraft Factory* (1990), p. 273.
40. AIR1/789/204/4/650.
41. AIR1/727/152/7.
42. AIR1/764/204/4/199 (13 June 1914).

43. *Hansard*, 24 March 1914.
44. Hare, *The Royal Aircraft Factory* (1990), p. 279.
45. Sopwith interview: www.fathom.com/course/10701016/session4.html.
46. Macmillan, *Sefton Brancker* (1935), p. 47.
47. *Ibid.* p. 55.
48. *Ibid.* pp. 54-55.
49. AIR1/764/204/4/199 (13 June 1914).
50. AIR1/2302/215/12.
51. Gollin, *The Impact of Air Power* (1989), p. 223.
52. *Ibid.* p. 243.
53. *Hansard*, 19 March 1913.
54. Cole, Cheesman, *The Air Defence of Britain 1914–1918* (1984) pp. 4-5.
55. Gollin, *The Impact of Air Power* (1989), p. 279.
56. *Ibid.* p. 285.
57. Hankey, *Supreme Command (1961), p. 150.*
58. AIR1/118/15/40/47 (October 1913)/Cole, Cheesman, The Air Defence of Britain 1914-1918 (1984), p. 4.
59. *Macmillan, Sefton Brancker (1935), p. 53.*
60. *Ibid.* pp. 55-57.
61. AIR1/789/204/4/651 (21 July 1914).
62. AIR1/812/204/4/1250 (29 July 1914).
63. Boyle, *Trenchard* (1962), p. 116.
64. *Ibid.* p. 117.

Chapter 3: Early Success and Stalemate

1. Gollin, *The Impact of Air Power* (1989), p. 296.
2. *The Times*, 6 August 1914.
3. Macmillan, *Sefton Brancker* (1935), p. 68.
4. Cole, Cheesman, *The Air Defence of Britain 1914–1918* (1984), pp. 6-7.
5. Gollin, *The Impact of Air Power* (1989), p. 318.
6. Macmillan, *Sefton Brancker* (1935), p. 76.
7. *Ibid.* p. 76.
8. Raleigh, *The War in the Air Vol. 1* (1969), p. 375.
9. Jones, *The War in the Air Vol. 3* (2002), p. 79.
10. Cole, Cheesman, *The Air Defence of Britain 1914–1918* (1984), p. 7.
11. *www.bcmh.org.uk/archive/articles/RNASAntwerpPollard.pdf.*
12. Raleigh, The War in the Air Vol. 1 (1969), pp. 395-400.
13. *Layman, Naval Aviation in the First World War* (1996), p. 68.
14. Paris, *Winged Warfare (1992), pp. 75-78.*
15. *Ibid.* p. 133/Cole, Cheesman, *The Air Defence of Britain 1914–1918 (1984), p. 18.*
16. Henshaw, *The Sky Their Battlefield* (1995), p. 19.
17. Raleigh, *The War in the Air Vol. 1* (1969), p. 300.
18. *Ibid.* pp. 295-316.
19. *Ibid.* p. 331.
20. Boyle, *Trenchard* (1962), pp. 125-126.
21. *Ibid.* p. 128.
22. Sykes, *From Many Angles* (1943), pp. 62-63.
23. Boyle, *Trenchard* (1962), pp. 125-126.
24. Jones, *The War in the Air Vol. 2* (1968), p. 101.

25. *Ibid.* p. 112.
26. AIR1/834/204/5/232 (24 October 1914).
27. Strange, *Recollections of an Airman* (1989), p. 75.
28. *Flight*, 4 December 1914.
29. AIR1/2413/303/11, (8, 21 December 1914).
30. Pugh, *The Magic of the Name (2000), Chapter 3.*
31. AIR1/2302/215/10/Jones, The War in the Air Vol. 2 (1968), Appendix 1.
32. *Jones, The War in the Air Vol. 2 (1968), pp. 89-91.*
33. *Ibid.* pp. 95-96.
34. *Ibid.* p. 112.
35. *Ibid.* pp. 123-124.
36. AIR1/921/204/5/889 (June 1915).
37. Strange, *Recollections of an Airman* (1989), p. 42.
38. Henshaw, *The Sky Their Battlefield* (1995), p. 21.
39. Strange, *Recollections of an Airman* (1989), p. 48.
40. Raleigh, *The War in the Air Vol. 1* (1969), p. 412.
41. Douglas, *Years of Combat* (1963), pp. 76-77.
42. Baring, *Flying Corps Headquarters 1914-1918* (1985), p. 113.
43. Bruce, *British Aeroplanes 1914-1918 (1957), p. 663.*
44. *AIR1/689/21/20/15 (April 1916).*
45. AIR1/731/176/6/12/Bruce, *Warplanes of the First World War: Fighters Vol. 2* (1968), pp. 36-37.
46. Bruce, *Warplanes of the First World War: Fighters Vol. 1* (1970), pp. 93-94/Vol. 2, p. 69.
47. *AIR1/713/27/19/11.*
48. *Strange, Recollections of an Airman (1989), pp. 116-117.*
49. Baker, *From Biplane to Spitfire* (2003), p. 66.
50. Andrews, Morgan, *Vickers Aircraft since 1908* (1989), p. 76.
51. AIR1/941/204/5/966 (4 July 1915).
52. *Ibid.* (9 July 1915)/AIR1/941/204/5/966 (1 August 1915)/AIR1/149/15/97 (7 October 1915)/AIR1/149/15/97 (5, 7 November 1915).
53. AIR1/1001/204/5/1260 (spring 1915).
54. AIR1/908/204/5/814 (29, 30 June 1915).
55. AIR1/920/204/5/885 (29 July 1915).
56. Ibid.
57. *Ibid.* (21 August 1915)/Macmillan, *Sefton Brancker* (1935), p. 99.
58. Bruce, *Warplanes of the First World War: Fighters Vol. 3* (1969), pp. 81-85, 91-93.
59. Barnes, *Bristol Aircraft since 1910* (1995), pp. 25, 101-102.
60. AIR1/1001/204/5/1260 (1915).
61. *Ibid.*

Chapter 4: Fading Promise and Fokkers

1. AIR1/1001/204/5/1260 (24 August 1915)/Raleigh, *The War in the Air Vol. 1 (1969), p. 448.*
2. *Jones, The War in the Air Vol. 2 (1968), p. 134.*
3. *Ibid.* p. 125.
4. *Ibid. p. 130.*
5. *See Milne's comments WO 32/2980 (15 November 1929).*

6. *AIR1/920/204/5/885 (29 July 1915).*
7. AIR1/404/15/231/45 (23 November 1915):
8. AIR1/404/15/231/45 (23, 24 November 1915).
9. Jones, The War in the Air Vol. 2 (1968), Appendix VI.
10. AIR1/1001/204/5/1260 (21 November 1915).
11. Hendon, 76/1/76 (December 1915)/AIR1/1001/204/5/1260 (25 November 1915).
12. AIR1/942/204/5/972 (18 December 1915).
13. Hare, The Royal Aircraft Factory (1990), p. 228.
14. AIR1/908/204/5/814 (8 December 1915).
15. Baring, *Flying Corps Headquarters 1914–1918* (1985)/Bruce, *Warplanes of the First World War: Fighters Vol. 5 (1972), p. 70.*
16. *AIR1/942/204/5/970 (26 December 1915).*
17. *Bruce, British Aeroplanes 1914–1918* (1957), p. 166.
18. AIR1/941/204/5/966 (spring 1916).
19. AIR1/138/15/40/281 (13 January 1916).
20. Boyle, *Trenchard* (1962), p. 162.
21. AIR1/941/204/5/966 (27 December 1915).
22. Baring, *Flying Corps Headquarters 1914–1918* (1985), p. 112.
23. AIR1/138/15/40/281 (13 January 1916).
24. Hendon, 76/1/5 (10 March 1916).
25. AIR1/716/27/19/27 (February 1916).
26. AIR1/731/176/5/102 (February 1916).
27. Hendon 76/1/5 10 (March 1916).
28. AIR1/689/21/20/15 (History of No. 15 Squadron).
29. AIR1/690 (February-June 1916).
30. AIR1/507/16/3/49 (23 March 1916).
31. *The Times* (23 March 1916).
32. Henshaw, *The Sky Their Battlefield* (1995), Appendix 1.
33. AIR1/1001/204/5/1260 (March 1916).
34. *Ibid.*

Chapter 5: Naval Help and Flying Dreadnoughts

1. Raleigh, *The War in the Air Vol. 1* (1969), pp. 473-475.
2. Bowyer, *Handley Page Bombers of the First World War (1992), p. 9.*
3. Roskill, The Naval Air Service Vol. 1 (1969), p. 310.
4. *Macmillan, Sefton Brancker* (1935), p. 123.
5. Cooper, *The Birth of Independent Air Power (1986), p. 49.*
6. Roskill, The Naval Air Service Vol. 1 (1969), p. 319.
7. Hare, The Royal Aircraft Factory (1990), p. 260.
8. *AIR1/1149/204/5/2380 (27, 29 January 1916)/Bruce, British Aeroplanes 1914–1918* (1957), pp. 399, 549.
9. Roskill, *The Naval Air Service Vol. 1* (1969), p. 333.
10. *Ibid.* p. 216.
11. *Ibid.* p. 288.
12. *Ibid. p. 310.*
13. AIR1/2251/209/54/24 (28 March 1916).
14. Hendon, 76/1/76 (March 1916).
15. AIR1/716/27/19/27 (9 March 1916).
16. Hendon, 76/1/76 (March 1916).

17. AIR1/1087/204/5/1741 (17 April 1916).
18. AIR1/1088/204/5/1742 (June 1916).
19. Hendon, 76/1/76 (March 1916).
20. AIR1/2251/209/54/24, (29 March 1916).
21. Hendon, 76/1/76 (March 1916).
22. AIR1/2623 (15 May 1916).
23. AIR1/507/16/3/49 (21 March 1916)/Hendon 76/1/5 (10 March 1916).
24. AIR6/1 (13 June 1916).
25. Bruce, British Aeroplanes 1914–1918 (1957), p. 122.
26. AIR6/1 20 (June 1916).
27. AIR1/908/204/5/8155 (June, 29 July, 11 August 1916).
28. Bruce, British Aeroplanes 1914–1918 (1957), p. 123/AIR1/908/204/5/815.
29. AIR1/907/204/5/811 (July 1916).
30. AIR1/716/27/19/27 (24 April 1916).
31. Baring, *Flying Corps Headquarters 1914–1918* (1985), p. 132.
32. Douglas, *Years of Combat* (1963), p. 134.
33. AIR1/521/16/12/2 (14, 20 June 1916).
34. Hare, *The Royal Aircraft Factory* (1990), pp. 222-225.
35. AIR1/1001/204/5/1260 (March 1916).
36. *Ibid.* (15 June 1916).
37. AIR1/815/204/4/1277 (29 May 1916).
38. AIR1/668/17/122/768 (22 June 1916).
39. AIR1/713/27/19/11 (undated: spring 1916).
40. *Ibid.* (13 April 1916).
41. AIR1/815/204/4/1277 (29 May 1916).
42. Hendon, 76/1/76 31 (May 1916).
43. AIR1/920/204/5/885 (June 1916).
44. Bruce, *Warplanes of the First World War: Fighters Vol. 2* (1968), p. 24.
45. Lewis, *Sagittarius Rising* (2003), p. 54.

Chapter 6: Ascendancy and the Seeds of Disaster

1. AIR1/1303/204/11/169 (15 May 1916).
2. *Ibid.* (7 May 1916).
3. Henshaw, *The Sky Their Battlefield* (1995), Appendix 1.
4. AIR1/690 (June 1916).
5. Jones, *The War in the Air Vol. 2 (1968)*, Appendix 4.
6. *Ibid.* p. 175/Lewis, *Sagittarius Rising (2003)*, pp. 82-83.
7. Jones, *The War in the Air Vol. 2 (1968)*, pp. 200, 215-217, 221.
8. Henshaw, *The Sky Their Battlefield* (1995), p. 575.
9. AIR1/690 (July 1960).
10. Jones, *The War in the Air Vol. 2 (1968)*, p. 324.
11. Lewis, *Sagittarius Rising* (2003), pp. 107-108.
12. Boyle, *Trenchard* (1962), p. 184.
13. AIR2/2964 (22 June 1938).
14. Cooper, *The Birth of Independent Air Power* (1986), p. 78.
15. AIR1/920/204/5/885 (15 August 1916).
16. *Ibid.* (13,15 August 1916).
17. AIR1/689/21/20/15 (April 1916).
18. AIR1/920/204/5/885 (15 August 1916).

Endnotes

19. AIR1/903/204/774 (8 July 1916).
20. *Ibid. (23 July 1916).*
21. *AIR1/1001/204/5/1260 (5 August 1916).*
22. *AIR1/129/15/40/191 (30 August 1916).*
23. Scott, Sixty Squadron (2003), pp. 6-7/Bruce, *Warplanes of the First World War: Fighters Vol. 5 (1972) p. 68.*
24. AIR1/129/15/40/191 (19 October 1916).

Chapter 7: RFC in Crisis

1. Henshaw, *The Sky Their Battlefield* (1995), Appendix 2.
2. Hendon, 76/1/76 (21 September 1916).
3. Hendon, 76/1/76 (21 September 1916)/Jones, *The War in the Air Vol. 2* (1968), p. 297.
4. AIR1/1088/204/5/1742 (6 October 1916).
5. AIR1/903/204/774 (3 October 1916).
6. AIR1/1088/204/5/1742 (15, 22 October 1916).
7. AIR1/907/204/5/810 (18, 19 September 1916).
8. AIR1/1068/204/5/1625 (23 September 1916).
9. *Ibid.* (September-November 1916).
10. Hendon, 76/1/76 (1 October 1916).
11. AIR1/920/204/5/885 (15 August 1916).
12. AIR1/129/15/40/191 (19 October 1916).
13. Jones, *The War in the Air Vol. 2* (1968), p. 316.
14. AIR1/920/204/5/885 (11 October 1916).
15. Jones, *The War in the Air Vol. 3* (2002), Appendices 10 and 11.
16. Douglas, *Years of Combat* (1963), pp. 246-247.
17. Jones, *The War in the Air Vol. 3* (2002), pp. 307-310.
18. Hendon, 76/1/76 (13 November 1916).
19. AIR6/4 (4 January 1917).
20. McCudden, *Flying Fury* (2000), p. 168.
21. Bruce, *British Aeroplanes 1914–1918* (1957), p. 455.
22. *AIR6/4 (31 January 1917).*
23. *AIR6/6 (7, 12 March 1917).*
24. *AIR1/1150/204/5/2385 (17 January 1917).*
25. Ibid. (16 October 1916)/Hendon, 76/1/9.
26. *Hendon, 76/1/9 (6 January 1917).*
27. *Ibid. (8 January 1917).*
28. AIR6/11 (12 December 1917).
29. AIR6/3 (11 December 1916).
30. Ibid.
31. Ibid.
32. Roskill, The Naval Air Service Vol. 1 (1969), p. 410.
33. *Jones, The War in the Air Appendices* (2002), Appendix 37.
34. Hendon, 76/1/76 (12 February 1917).
35. *Ibid. (5, 7, 9 March 1917).*
36. *Ibid. (19 March 1917).*
37. *AIR6/5 (3 February 1917).*
38. *AIR1/503/16/3/17 (13 February 1917).*
39. *AIR1/503/16/3/17/AIR1/878/204/5/586 (November 1916).*

40. Bruce, *Warplanes of the First World War: Fighters Vol. 2* (1968), p. 58/Cooper, *The Birth of Independent Air Power (1986)*, pp. 57-58.
41. Henshaw, The Sky Their Battlefield (1995), Appendix II.
42. Hendon, 76/1/10, 6 (7 February)/AIR6/6, 21 (March 1917).
43. Ibid. 76/1/10, (8, 9 March 1917).
44. Ibid. 76/1/10 (9 February 1917).
45. Ibid. 76/1/10 (8 March 1917).
46. AIR6/6, (12, 21 March 1917).
47. Hendon, 76/1/10 (13 February 1917).
48. Jones, *The War in the Air Vol. 3* (2002), p. 346.
49. Scott, *Sixty Squadron* (2003), p. 42.
50. Hendon, 76/1/9 (15 January 1917).
51. AIR1/876/204/5/575 (6 January 1917).
52. Jones, *The War in the Air Vol. 3* (2002), Appendix 11.
53. Hendon, 76/1/9 (8 January 1917).
54. AIR1/1/4/19 (undated, summer 1917).
55. AIR1/1088/204/5/1742 (10 January 1917).
56. Ibid. (5 May 1917).
57. AIR6/4, (26, 28 February 1917).
58. Lewis, *Sagittarius Rising* (2003), p. 197.
59. Hendon, 76/1/76 (9 April 1917).
60. AIR6/7 (13 April 1917).
61. Franks, Guest, Bailey, *Bloody April ... Black September* (1995), p. 113.
62. Ibid. pp. 17-28.
63. AIR1/477/15/312/225 (8 April 1917).
64. Hendon, 76/1/76 (1 April 1917).
65. Ibid. (6 April 1917)/AIR1/477/15/312/225 (6 April 1917).
66. Boyle, *Trenchard* (1962), p. 215.
67. AIR1/920/204/5/885 (24 April 1917).
68. Ibid. (30 April 1917).
69. Hallion, *Rise of the Fighter Aircraft 1914–1918* (1984), p. 79.
70. Hendon, 76/1/76, 1 (30 April 1917).
71. Hendon, 76/1/76 (30 April 1917).
72. Lewis, *Sagittarius Rising* (2003), p. 168.
73. Jones, *The War in the Air Appendices* (2002), p. 161.
74. Henshaw, *The Sky Their Battlefield* (1995), Appendix II.
75. Franks, Guest, Bailey, *Bloody April ... Black September* (1995), p. 114.

Chapter 8: The Brave New World of Strategic Bombing

1. AIR1/665/17/122/706 (November 1915)/Barnes, Short Aircraft since 1900 (1989), pp. 123-125.
2. *Jones, The Origins of Strategic Bombing* (1973) p. 113.
3. Cole, Cheesman, *The Air Defence of Britain 1914–1918* (1984), p. 31.
4. Ibid. pp. 56-57.
5. Ibid. pp. 73, 83.
6. Paris, *Winged Warfare* (1992), p. 77.
7. *The Times*, 28 March 1916.
8. Roskill, *The Naval Air Service Vol. 1 (1969), p. 230*.
9. Ibid. p. 297.

Endnotes

10. AIR6/1 (13 June 1916).
11. Roskill, *The Naval Air Service Vol. 1* (1969), p. 335.
12. *Ibid.* p. 342.
13. *Ibid.* p. 344.
14. *Ibid. p. 335.*
15. AIR6/1 (5 June 1916).
16. AIR6/1 (13 June 1916).
17. Roskill, *The Naval Air Service Vol. 1* (1969), p. 344.
18. *Ibid.* p. 364.
19. *Ibid. p. 364.*
20. Jones, The Origins of Strategic Bombing (1973) p. 104.
21. AIR6/3 (24 October 1916).
22. Roskill, *The Naval Air Service Vol. 1* (1969), p. 405.
23. *Ibid.* p. 418.
24. Cole, Cheesman, *The Air Defence of Britain 1914–1918* (1984), p. 106.
25. *Ibid. pp. 151-152.*
26. Roskill, *The Naval Air Service Vol. 1* (1969), p. 418.
27. *Ibid. p. 408.*
28. AIR6/3 (11 December 1916).
29. Roskill, *The Naval Air Service Vol. 1* (1969), p. 389, p. 423.
30. Jones, *The Origins of Strategic Bombing* (1973), p. 121.
31. *Ibid.* p. 108.
32. Jones, *The War in the Air Vol. 2* (1968), pp. 452-453.
33. Jones, *The Origins of Strategic Bombing* (1973), pp. 116-118.
34. Cooper, *The Birth of Independent Air Power (1986), p. 85.*
35. Roskill, The Naval Air Service Vol. 1 (1969), p. 209.
36. Jones, The War in the Air Vol. 2 (1968), pp. 404-410.
37. Roskill, *The Naval Air Service Vol. 1* (1969), pp. 460, 471.
38. *Ibid.* p. 473.
39. Chickering, Forster, *Great War, Total War* (2000), p. 212/Jones, *The War in the Air Vol. 6 (1998), p. 121.*
40. AIR6/4 (4 January 1917).
41. Gunston, Rolls-Royce Aero Engines (1989), pp. 20-21, 34.
42. *Jones, The War in the Air Vol. 5* (1998), p. 49/Jones, *The War in the Air Appendices (2002), p. 157.*
43. CAB23/2 *(14 June 1917).*
44. *Ibid.* (14 June 1917).
45. *Ibid.* (30 May 1917).
46. *Ibid.* (5 June 1917).
47. *Ibid.* (5 June 1917).
48. AIR6/8 (6 June 1917).
49. CAB23/2 (14 June 1917).
50. AIR6/8, 15 (15, 20 June, 2 July 1917).
51. CAB23/2, AIR6/8.
52. AIR6/8 (27 June 1917).
53. CAB23/2 (2 July 1917).
54. *Ibid.* (7 July 1917).
55. *Ibid.* (7 July 1917).
56. *Ibid.* (7 July 1917).
57. Jones, *The War in the Air Vol. 6* (1998), pp. 2-4.
58. Jones, *The War in the Air Appendices (2002), Appendix 3.*

59. Roskill, *The Naval Air Service Vol. 1* (1969), p. 501.
60. *Ibid.* p. 499.
61. *Ibid.* p. 520.
62. *Ibid.* p. 495.
63. Jones, *The War in the Air Vol. 6* (1998), p. 42.
64. AIR6/10 (14 September 1917).
65. *Ibid.* (16 October 1917).
66. Jones, *The Origins of Strategic Bombing* (1973), p. 143.
67. *Ibid.* pp. 144-147.
68. AIR6/8 (30 July, 10 August 1917).
69. *Ibid.* (23 July 1917).
70. *Ibid.* (23, 30 July, 3, 8 August 1917).
71. Jackson, Bramall, *The Chiefs* (1992), p. 94.

Chapter 9: A Modern Tactical Air Force

1. Hendon, 76/1/76/AIR6/8 (7 May 1917).
2. AIR6/8 (21 May 1917).
3. AIR1/694/21/20/70.
4. AIR1/1149/204/5/2378 (16 June 1917)/AIR1/878/204/5/586, (June 1917).
5. Lewis, *Sagittarius Rising* (2003), p. 182.
6. AIR1/1158/204/5/2486 (June 1917).
7. Hendon, 76/1/1414 (June 1917).
8. AIR6/8 (2 July 1917).
9. *Ibid.* (23 May 1917).
10. AIR1/69/15/9/113 (19 April 1917).
11. Hallion, *Rise of the Fighter Aircraft 1914–1918* (1984), pp. 114-116.
12. AIR6/10 (7 September 1917)/ AIR1/1/4/17 (September 1917).
13. *Ibid.* (31 October 1917).
14. *Ibid.* (10 September 1917).
15. AIR1/1149/204/5/2378 (21 August 1917)/AIR10/1026 (November 1917).
16. AIR6/10 (10 September 1917).
17. AIR10/1026/AIR6/10 (6 September 1917, 24 October 1917).
18. AIR6/7 (8 June 1917).
19. AIR1/1075/204/5/1672 (13 June 1917).
20. AIR1/69/15/9/113 (19 April 1917).
21. AIR1/716/27/19/27 (31 March 1917).
22. AIR1/69/15/9/113 (19 April 1917).
23. Hendon, 76/1/10 (22, 24 April 1917).
24. Bruce, *Warplanes of the First World War: Fighters Vol. 1* (1970), pp. 168-170.
25. AIR6/8 (4 July 1917).
26. AIR6/10 (24 October 1917).
27. AIR6/11 (19 November 1917).
28. Bruce, *Warplanes of the First World War: Fighters Vol. 1* (1970), p. 178.
29. AIR6/11 (19 November 1917).
30. *Ibid.* (19 November 1917).
31. *Ibid.* (19 November 1917).
32. *Ibid.* (19 November 1917).
33. AIR1/69/4/38 (31 December 1917).
34. AIR6/11 (19 November 1917).

35. Jones, *The War in the Air Vol. 4* (2002), pp. 114-115.
36. *Ibid. pp. 167-168.*
37. *Jones, The War in the Air Vol. 3* (2002), pp. 119-120/*Vol. 4 (2009), pp. 115-117, 119-120.*
38. AIR1/129/15/40/191 (18 December 1917).
39. Jones, The War in the Air Vol. 2 (1968), p. 333/AIR1/678/21/13/2137.
40. AIR1/694/21/20/100.
41. Ibid.
42. *Ibid.*/Bruce, *British Aeroplanes 1914–1918 (1957), p. 396.*
43. *Jones, The War in the Air Vol. 3* (2002), pp. 399-400.
44. *Ibid.* p. 378.
45. Jones, *The War in the Air Vol. 4* (2002), pp. 129-130.
46. *Ibid.* pp. 163-166.
47. *Ibid.* pp. 163-167.
48. *Ibid.* p. 177.
49. Douglas, *Years of Combat* (1963), p. 277.
50. Jones, *The War in the Air Vol. 4* (2002), p. 136.
51. AIR1/129/15/40/191 (18 December 1917).
52. AIR1/2313/221/53 (20 November 1917).

Chapter 10: The Government Opts for the Bomber

1. Jones, *The War in the Air Vol. 6* (1998), p. 40-41.
2. Jones, *The Origins of Strategic Bombing* (1973), p. 152.
3. Cole, Cheesman, *The Air Defence of Britain 1914–1918* (1984), p. 302.
4. *Ibid.* pp. 308, 336.
5. AIR1/477/15/312/225 (23 November 1917).
6. AIR1/2313/221/53 (14 November 1917).
7. Jones, *The War in the Air Vol. 6* (1998), p. 126.
8. *AIR1/1978/204/273/67 (September–October 1917).*
9. *AIR1/2302/215/12 (November 1917).*
10. *AIR1/1978/204/273/67 (June 1918)/*Bowyer, *Handley Page Bombers of the First World War* (1992), p. 122/Meekcoms, Morgan, *The British Aircraft Specifications File (1994), p. 17.*
11. *AIR2/1030, (9, 16 October 1917).*
12. *Ibid.* (7 December 1917).
13. *Ibid.* (30 January 1918).
14. *Ibid.* (15 March 1918).
15. Jones, *The War in the Air Vol. 6 (1998), pp. 32-35.*
16. Jones, The War in the Air Vol. 6 (1998), pp. 37-38/AIR1/1/4/17 (13 September 1917).
17. *AIR2/56 (26 October 1917).*
18. *AIR1/477/15/312/225 (23 November 1917).*
19. *AIR6/1 (12 February 1918).*
20. *Jones, The War in the Air Vol. 5* (1998), p. 16.
21. AIR6/10 (16 October 1917).
22. Jones, *The Origins of Strategic Bombing* (1973), p. 152.
23. Macmillan, *Sefton Brancker* (1935), pp. 168-170.
24. Cole, Cheesman, *The Air Defence of Britain 1914–1918* (1984), *p. 359.*
25. Scarth, *Echoes from the Sky* (1999), pp. 11-14, 24-25/Cole, Cheesman, *The Air Defence of Britain 1914–1918* (1984), p. 436.

26. Cole Cheesman, *The Air Defence of Britain 1914–1918* (1984), pp. 343-350.
27. *Ibid.* pp. 387-388.
28. AIR8/167, 1934.
29. AIR1/477/15/312/225 (23 November 1917).

Chapter 11: New Options on the Battlefield

1. Jones, *The War in the Air Vol. 2* (1968), pp. 290-291.
2. Jones, *The War in the Air Vol. 4* (2002), p. 230.
3. *Ibid.* pp. 230-231.
4. Henshaw, *The Sky Their Battlefield* (1995), p. 253.
5. Jones, *The War in the Air Vol. 4* (2002), p 241.
6. *Ibid.* pp. 245-247.
7. Henshaw, *The Sky Their Battlefield* (1995), pp. 255-256.
8. Jones, *The War in the Air Vol. 4* (2002), pp. 250-259.
9. AIR1/477/15/312/225 (16 January 1918).
10. *Ibid.* (16 January 1918)

Chapter 12: Tactical Air Support Comes of Age

1. Hendon, 76/1/92 (13 February 1918).
2. Macmillan, *Sefton Brancker* (1935), pp. 175, 179.
3. Slessor, *The Central Blue* (1956), p. 31.
4. AIR6/12 (Air Council meetings January-March 1918).
5. Roskill, *The Naval Air Service Vol. 1* (1969), p. 562.
6. Jones, *The War in the Air Vol. 6* (1998), p. 340.
7. AIR1/17/15/1/85 (18 July 1918).
8. AIR8/167 (1934).
9. Bruce, *British Aeroplanes 1914–1918* (1957), pp. 454, 591, 605.
10. *AIR1/6A/4/36, (25, 28 January 1918).*
11. *AIR1/6A (3 March 1918).*
12. *AIR1/1/4/11 (17 August 1917).*
13. *AIR6/11 (21 November 1917).*
14. *AIR6/12 (12 March 1918).*
15. *AIR1/6A/4/36 (25, 28 January 1918).*
16. *AIR1/1150/204/5/2387 (March 1918).*
17. AIR2/1029/AIR2/57/A.B.279/74/AIR1/970/204/5/1106 (12 March 1918).
18. AIR1/1150/204/5/2384 (11 March 1918)/AIR1/970/204/5/1106 (13 March 1918).
19. *AIR2/1029 (March 1918).*
20. Jones, *The War in the Air Vol. 4* (2002), pp. 287-289, 291.
21. *Ibid.* pp. 294-301.
22. Henshaw, *The Sky Their Battlefield* (1955) pp. 284-285/Jones, *The War in the Air Vol. 4 (2002), pp. 297-298.*
23. Pitt, *1918—The Last Act* (2003), p. 83.
24. AIR1/677/21/13/1887 (30 July 1918).
25. Jones, *The War in the Air Vol. 4* (2002), p. 306.
26. Henshaw, *The Sky Their Battlefield* (1995), p. 286/Jones, *The War in the Air Vol. 4 (2002), p. 313.*

Endnotes

27. Jones, *The War in the Air Vol. 4* (2002), p. 311.
28. *Ibid.* p. 336.
29. *Ibid.* p. 348.
30. AIR1/970/204/5/1106 (22 April 1918).

Chapter 13: A Glimpse into the Future

1. AIR1/1074 (18 January 1918)/AIR1/725/97/10 (post-war report by Ludlow Hewitt).
2. AIR1/725/97/10 (post-war report by Ludlow Hewitt).
3. AIR1/1074 (25 May 1918).
4. AIR1/677/21/13/1887 (report on air operations on Western Front May-November 1918).
5. AIR1/677/21/13/1887.
6. Jones, *The War in the Air Vol. 6* (1998), pp. 441-451.
7. AIR1/1074.
8. *Ibid.* (14 August 1918).
9. AIR1/677/AIR1/677/21/13/1887 (22 August 1918).
10. CAB23/8 (20 August 1918).
11. AIR1/2025/204/324/1 (15 August 1918).
12. CAB23/8 (20 August 1918)/AIR2/1027.
13. AIR1/677/21/13/1887.
14. AIR1/1074.
15. AIR1/725/97/10 (post-war report by Ludlow Hewitt).
16. AIR1/677/21/13/1887 (report on air operations on Western Front May-November 1918).
17. *Ibid.*
18. Henshaw, *The Sky Their Battlefield* (1995), p. 392.
19. *Ibid.* p. 400.
20. AIR1/677/21/13/1887 (report on air operations on Western Front May-November 1918).
21. *Ibid.*
22. Henshaw, *The Sky Their Battlefield* (1995), p. 394.
23. *Ibid.* p. 576.
24. AIR1/1150/204/5/2387.
25. Ibid. p. 66.
26. Jones, *The War in the Air Vol. 6* (1998), p. 525.
27. *Ibid.* p. 520.
28. *Ibid.* pp. 224-226.
29. *Ibid.* pp. 294-313.
30. AIR1/1074 (13 October 1918).

Chapter 14: Strategic Bombing in Retreat

1. Jones, *The War in the Air Appendices* (2002), Appendix 5.
2. Jones, *The Origins of British Strategic Bombing* (1973), pp. 154-156.
3. AIR1/30/15/1/155 1-3 (15 January 1918).
4. *Ibid.* (10 January 1918).

5. Jones, *The War in the Air Vol. 6* (1998), p. 101.
6. *Ibid.* p. 134.
7. AIR1/2422/305/18/17 (25 March 1918).
8. *Ibid.*
9. Boyle, *Trenchard* (1962), pp. 261-262.
10. Cooper, *The Birth of Independent Air Power* (1986), p. 114.
11. Boyle, *Trenchard* (1962), pp. 269, 279.
12. Cooper, *The Birth of Independent Air Power* (1986), p. 123.
13. Boyle, *Trenchard* (1962), p. 277.
14. Ash, *Sir Frederick Sykes and the Air Revolution 1912–1918* (1999), Chapter 5.
15. Sykes, *From Many Angles* (1943), p. 227.
16. Cooper, *The Birth of Independent Air Power* (1986), p. 124.
17. Jones, *The War in the Air Vol. 5* (1998), pp. 173-176.
18. IWM 69/34/1 (17 November 1917).
19. AIR1/30/15/1/155 1-3 (14 May 1918).
20. AIR1/460/15/312/101 (April 1918).
21. AIR1/2418/305/6 (23 May 1918).
22. *Ibid.* (25 May 1918).
23. *Ibid.* (23 May 1918).
24. AIR1/461/15/312/107 (22 June 1918).
25. Hendon, 77/13/53 (13 May 1918).
26. AIR1/30/15/1/155 1-3 (14 May 1918).
27. Reader, *Architect of Air Power* (1968), pp. 73-74.
28. Boyle, *Trenchard* (1962), p. 288.
29. AIR2/76 (3 June 1918).
30. *Ibid.* (13 June 1918).
31. AIR1/1978/204/273/67 (June 1918)/AIR2/76 (29 August 1918).
32. AIR1/2302/215/11 (8 July 1918)/Bowyer, Handley Page Bombers of the First World War (1992), pp. 122-123.
33. AIR2/1030 (26 March 1918).
34. Ibid. (22 March 1918).
35. IWM 69/34/1 (27 August 1918): Geoffrey Salmond was John Salmond's brother.
36. AIR1/460/15/312/99 (22 May 1918).
37. AIR1/30/15/1/1255 1-3 (13 May 1918).
38. Jones, The War in the Air Vol. 6 (1998), pp. 104-105/Hendon, 77/13/53 (3 June 1918).
39. Boyle, Trenchard (1962), pp. 290-291.
40. *Boyle, Trenchard* (1962), p. 293/Jones, *The War in the Air Vol. 6* (1998), pp. 103-104.
41. AIR1/678/21/13/2100/Jones, *The War in the Air Vol. 6* (1998), pp. 105-106/ Boyle, *Trenchard* (1962), *p. 293*.
42. *Hendon, 77/13/53 (23 July 1918).*
43. *Hendon, 76/1/94 (27 June 1918).*
44. *Hendon, 77/13/53 (1 June 1918).*
45. *Ibid.* (17 June 1918).
46. AIR1/30/15/1/155 1-3 (28 June, 7 August 1918).
47. Hendon, 77/13/53 (23 July 1918).
48. AIR1/30/15/1/155 1-3 (7 August 1918).
49. Hendon, 77/13/53 (17 June 1918).
50. AIR1/30/15/1/155 1-3 (7 August 1918).
51. Hendon, 77/13/53 (17 June 1918).

Endnotes

52. Hendon, 76/1/94 (29 June 1918).
53. Hendon, 77/13/53 (23 July 1918).
54. AIR1/20/15/1/155 (14 May 1918).
55. Jones, *The War in the Air Appendices* (2002), Appendix 8.
56. Boyle, *Trenchard* (1962), p. 295.
57. Hendon, 76/1/94 (18 August 1918).
58. *Ibid.* (22 August 1918).
59. Jones, *The War in the Air Appendices (2002), Appendix 10.*
60. *AIR1/460/15/312/101 (undated, summer 1918).*
61. *AIR1/30/15/1/155 1-3 (8 August 1918).*
62. *AIR1/17/15/1/85 (15 June 1918).*
63. Roskill, *The Naval Air Service Vol. 1* (1969), p. 680.
64. Jones, *The War in the Air Vol. 6* (1998), p. 171/AIR1/17/15/1/85 (5 June 1918).
65. Jones, *The War in the Air Vol. 6 (1998), p. 89/AIR1/17/15/1/85.*
66. Jones, *The War in the Air Vol. 6* (1998), p. 171.
67. AIR1/17/15/1/85.
68. AIR6/12/AIR1/17/15/1/85 (July–August 1918).
69. AIR1/17/15 /1/85 (July 1918).
70. *Ibid.*
71. *Ibid.*
72. AIR1/1/4/11 (17 August 1918).
73. AIR1/17/15/1/85 (18 July 1918).
74. *Ibid.* (June/July 1918).
75. *Ibid.*
76. *Ibid.* (28 June 1918).
77. *Ibid. (15 July 1918).*
78. Ibid./AIR6/17, AIR6/12 (15 July 1918).
79. *Jones, The War in the Air Vol. 6 (1998), p. 172/Boyle, Trenchard (1962), p. 298.*
80. *AIR1/17/15/1/85 (14 July 1918).*
81. AIR2/948 (13 March 1918)/AIR1/2422/305/18/17 (25 March 1918).
82. *AIR1/17/15/1/85 (31 July 1918).*
83. *Ibid.* (27 July 1918).
84. *Ibid.* (August 1918).
85. *Ibid. (13 August 1918).*
86. Cole, Cheesman, The Air Defence of Britain 1914–1918 (1984), pp. 423-436.
87. *Ibid.* pp. 436-445.
88. *Ibid.* p. 365.
89. *Ibid.* pp. 421, 436, 456.
90. *Ibid.* pp. 456-457.
91. AIR1/17/15/1/85 (5 September 1918).
92. Boyle, *Trenchard* (1962), p. 308.
93. AIR1/463/15/312/137.
94. AIR1/17/15/1/85 (5 September 1918).
95. *Ibid.* (September 1918).
96. Jones, *The War in the Air Vol. 6* (1998), p. 343.
97. AIR1/17/15/1/85 (September 1918).
98. *Ibid.* (5 September 1918).
99. *Ibid.* (5 September 1918).

Chapter 15: Last Gasp for the Long-Range Bomber

1. AIR1/461/15/312/112 (25 September 1918).
2. Ibid.
3. AIR1/20/15/1/155 1-3 (14 May 1918).
4. Henshaw, *The Sky Their Battlefield* (1995), p. 363.
5. AIR1/460/15/312/100 (4 August 1918).
6. Ibid.
7. Ibid.
8. AIR1/2422/305/18/17 (3 August 1918).
9. AIR2/56 (21 October 1918).
10. AIR1/460/15/312/100 (8 August 1918).
11. Ibid.
12. Ibid.
13. Jones, *The War in the Air Vol. 6* (1998), pp. 142-146.
14. Hendon, 76/1/94 (27 August 1918).
15. AIR1 2301/215/8 (January 1918).
16. Ibid.
17. *AIR1/457/15/312/61 (16 October 1918).*
18. Hendon, 76/1/94 (10 September 1918)/Boyle, Trenchard (1962), p. 312.
19. *Jones, The War in the Air Vol. 6* (1998), p. 161.
20. AIR1/30/15/1/155 1-3 (11 August 1918).
21. Ibid. (24 August 1918).
22. AIR1/451/15/312/19.
23. Jones, *The War in the Air Appendices (2002), Appendix 8.*
24. *AIR1/460/15/312/99 (11 July 1918).*
25. *AIR1/461/15/312/107 (12 September 1918).*
26. Cooper, The Birth of Independent Air Power (1986), p.134/ AIR1/460/15/312/97 (11 September 1918).
27. Hendon, 76/1/94 (17 September 1918).
28. Ibid.
29. AIR1/461/15/312/107/Ibid. (20 September 1918).
30. AIR10/1214 (August 1918).
31. Hendon, 76/1/94 (29 June 1918).
32. *Henshaw, The Sky Their Battlefield* (1995), pp. 383, 396/Jones, *The War in the Air Appendices (2002), Appendix 13.*
33. Jones, The War in the Air Appendices (2002), Appendix 13.
34. AIR1/1150/204/5/2387.
35. *Henshaw, The Sky Their Battlefield* (1995), pp. 411-412/Jones, *The War in the Air Appendices (2002), Appendix 13.*
36. *AIR1/461/15/312/107 (15, 17 October 1918).*
37. Ibid. (15 October 1918).
38. AIR1/461/15/312/107 (10 October 1918).
39. Boyle, *Trenchard (1962), p. 300.*
40. Ibid. p. 312-313/Jones, *The War in the Air Vol. 6 (1998), p. 149.*
41. AIR1/30/15/1/155 1-3 (24 September 1918).
42. AIR1/460/15/312/99 (2 October 1918)/AIR1/2131/207/114/1 (2 October 1918).
43. Ibid. (4 October 1918).
44. AIR10/1214 (October 1918).
45. AIR1/30/15/1/155 1-3 (3 October 1918).
46. AIR1/2418/305/6 (October 1918).

47. AIR6/12 (3 October 1918).
48. AIR1/461/15/312/107 (11 June 1918).
49. AIR1/1978/204/273/68 (25 September 1918).
50. AIR1/461/15/312/107.
51. CAB23/8 (15 October 1918).
52. *Ibid.*
53. AIR1/460/15/312/95 (3 October 1918).
54. Ash, *Sir Frederick Sykes and the Air Revolution 1912–1918 (1999), p. 169.*
55. AIR1/2418/305/6/CAB23/8 (15 October 1918).
56. AIR1/460/15/312/101 (12 October 1918).
57. Ibid./AIR1/2418/305/6 (14 October 1918).
58. *CAB23/8 (15 October 1918).*
59. *Ibid.* (16 October 1918).
60. Ash, *Sir Frederick Sykes and the Air Revolution 1912–1918* (1999), p. 168.
61. AIR1/461/15/312/107 (15 October 1918).
62. AIR1/1978/204/273/68 (7 October 1918).
63. AIR1/1978/204/273/67 (June 1918).
64. AIR1/461/15/312/107 (17 October 1918).
65. AIR1/1978/204/273/67 (June 1918).
66. Hendon, 76/1/94 (17 October 1918).
67. AIR1/974/204/273/8 (17 October 1918).
68. *Ibid.*
69. AIR1/1978/204/273/67 (19 October 1918).
70. *Ibid.* (24, 31 October 1918).
71. CAB23/8 (24, 29 October 1918).
72. AIR1/460/15/312/101 (4 November 1918).
73. AIR1/460/15/312/96 (9 November 1918).
74. Hendon, B 405.
75. AIR1/406/15/312/101 (5 November 1918).
76. CAB23/8, 24 (1 November 1918).
77. *Ibid.* (29 October 1918).
78. *The Times*, 4 November 1918.
79. CAB23/8, (7, 24 November 1918).

Conclusion

1. Jones, *The War in the Air Appendices* (2002), Appendix 23.
2. AIR1/677/21/13/1887, p. 81.
3. AIR1/923/204/5/899 (26 November 1918).

Sources and Bibliography

Details of air operations have mostly come from published sources such as *The Air Defence of Britain*, *Bloody April ... Black September*, *The Sky Their Battlefield* and *The War in the Air* series. Policy issues are based on AIR, AVIA, CAB and WO archives held by the National Archives, the RAF Museum (Hendon), and to a lesser extent documents held by the Imperial War Museum (IWM) and the Liddell Hart Centre (LHC).

Editor's note: publication dates are of editions used.

Air of Authority: www.rafweb.org
Andrews, C. F. and C. B. Morgan, *Vickers Aircraft since 1908* (London: Putnam, 1989)
Ash, E., *Sir Frederick Sykes and the Air Revolution 1912–1918* (London: Frank Cass, 1999)
Baker, A., *From Biplane to Spitfire* (Barnsley: Leo Cooper, 2003)
Baring, M., *Flying Corps Headquarters 1914–1918* (London: Buchan & Enright, 1985)
Barker, R., *The Royal Flying Corps in World War One* (London: Robinson, 2002)
Barnes, C. H., *Bristol Aircraft since 1910* (London: Putnam, 1995)
Barnes, C. H., *Short Aircraft since 1900* (London: Putnam, 1989)
Benbow, T., *British Naval Aviation* (Farnham: Ashgate, 2011)
Biddle, T. D., *Rhetoric and Reality in Air Warfare* (Princeton: Princeton University Press, 2002)
Bishop, W. A., *Winged Warfare* (Manchester: Crecy Publishing, 1990)
Bowyer, C., *Handley Page Bombers of the First World War* (Bourne End: Aston Publications, 1992)
Boyle, A., *Trenchard* (London: Collins, 1962)
Brookes, A. J., *Photo Reconnaissance* (Shepperton: Ian Allen, 1975)
Bruce, J. M., *British Aeroplanes 1914–1918* (New York: Funk & Wagnalls, 1957)
Bruce, J. M., *Britain's First Warplanes* (Poole: Arms and Armour, 1987)
Bruce, J. M., *Warplanes of the First World War: Fighters Vol. 1-5* (London: Macdonald, 1970, 1968, 1969, 1972, 1972 respectively)
Carradice, P., *First World War in the Air* (Stroud: Amberley Publishing, 2012)
Chickering, R. and S. Forster, *Great War, Total War* (Cambridge: Cambridge University Press, 2000)
Clarke, A., *Aces High* (London: Fontana, 1974)
Cole, C. and E. F. Cheesman, *The Air Defence of Britain 1914–1918* (London: Putnam, 1984)
Cooper, M., *The Birth of Independent Air Power* (London: Allen & Unwin, 1986)
Divine, D., *The Broken Wing* (London: Hutchinson, 1966)
Douglas, W., *Years of Combat* (London: Collins, 1963)

Sources and Bibliography

Franks, N. R., Guest, F. Bailey, *Bloody April ... Black September* (London: Grub Street, 1995)
Gollin, A., *The Impact of Air Power* (London: Macmillan, 1989)
Gunston, B., *Rolls-Royce Aero Engines* (Patrick Stevens, 1989)
Hallion, R. P., *Rise of the Fighter Aircraft 1914–1918* (Maryland: The Nautical & Aviation Publishing Company, 1984)
Hankey, M., *Supreme Command* (London: George Allen & Unwin Ltd, 1961)
Hare, P. R., *The Royal Aircraft Factory* (London: Putnam, 1990)
Hart, L., *History of the First World War* (London: Pan Books, 1972)
Henshaw, T., *The Sky Their Battlefield* (London: Grub Street, 1995)
Hooton, E. R., *War over the Trenches* (Hersham: Midland Publishing, 2010)
Imrie, A., *Pictorial History of the German Air Service* (London: Ian Allan, 1971)
Jackson, A. J., *Avro Aircraft since 1908* (London: Putnam, 1965)
Jackson, B. and D. Bramall, *The Chiefs* (London: Brassey's, 1992)
James, J., *The Paladins* (London: Futura Publications, 1990)
Jones, H. A., *The War in the Air Appendices* (Uckfield: The Naval & History Press, 2002)
Jones, H. A., *The War in the Air Vol. 2* (London: Hamish Hamilton, 1968)
Jones, H. A., *The War in the Air Vol. 3* (Uckfield: The Naval & History Press, 2002)
Jones, H. A., *The War in the Air Vol. 4* (Uckfield: The Naval & History Press, 2002)
Jones, H. A., *The War in the Air Vol. 5* (Nashville: Battery Press, 1998)
Jones, H. A., *The War in the Air Vol. 6* (Nashville: Battery Press, 1998)
Jones, N., *The Origins of Strategic Bombing* (London: William Kimber, 1973)
Laffin, J., *Swifter than Eagles* (Edinburgh: William Blackwood and Sons, 1964)
Layman, R. D., *Naval Aviation in the First World War* (London: Chatham Publishing, 1996)
Lewis, C., *Sagittarius Rising* (London: Greenhill Books, 2003)
Longmore, A., *From Sea to Sky* (London: Geoffrey Bles, 1946)
MacBean, J. A. and A. S. Hogben, *Bombs Gone* (Wellingborough: Patrick Stevens, 1990)
Macmillan, N., *Sefton Brancker* (London: Heinemann, 1935)
McCudden, J., *Flying Fury* (Barton-under-Needwood: Wren's Park Publishing, 2000)
Mead, P., *The Eye in the Air* (London: HMSO, 1983)
Meekcoms, K. J. and E. B. Morgan, *The British Aircraft Specifications File* (Tonbridge: Air Britain Publication, 1994)
Morrow, J. H., *The Great War in the Air* (Shrewsbury: Airlife Publishing, 1993)
Neumann, G. P., *The German Air Force in the Great War* (Hong Kong: Forgotten Books, 2010)
Paris, M., *Winged Warfare* (Manchester: Manchester University Press, 1992)
Pitt, B., *1918—The Last Act* (Barnsley: Pen and Sword, 2003)
Probert, H., *High Commanders of the Royal Air Force* (London: HMSO, 1991)
Pugh, P., *The Magic of the Name* (Duxford: Icon Books, 2000)
Raleigh, W., *The War in the Air Vol. 1* (London: Hamish Hamilton, 1969)
Reader, W. J., *Architect of Air Power* (London: Collins, 1968)
Roskill, S., *Hankey: Man of Secrets Vol. 1* (London: Collins, 1970)
Roskill, S., *The Naval Air Service Vol. 1* (The Navy Records Society, 1969)
Scarth, R. N., *Echoes from the Sky* (Hythe: Hythe Civic Society, 1999)
Scott, J. L., *Sixty Squadron* (Uckfield: The Naval and Military Press Ltd, 2003)
Slessor, J., *The Central Blue* (London: Cassell, 1956)
Strange, L. A., *Recollections of an Airman* (London: Greenhill Books, 1989)
Sykes, F., *From Many Angles* (London: George G. Harrap, 1943)
Whitford, R., *The Fundamentals of Fighter Design* (Marlborough: Crowood Press, 2004)
Woodman, H., *Early Aircraft Armament* (London: Arms and Armour, 1989)

Index

ABC Dragonfly, 168-169, 187, 203-204; Wasp, 168-169
Admiralty, 17, 21, 25, 35, 44, 49-50, 79-82, 167, 202; dispute with War Office, 24-25, 46-47, 79-82, 105, 119-123; strategic bombing, 25, 51, 80-81, 105, 117, 120-122, 126-127; war strategy, 46-47, 80-81, 117, 121, 125-126; U-boat menace, 51, 105, 121, 126- 127, 136-7, 167, 208; Fifth Sea Lord, 124-125, 155-156; Dispute with Air Ministry, see Air Ministry
Air Battalion, 18, 22-24
Air Board, First (Curzon), 120-124
Air Board, Second (Cowdray), 126-127, 130-131, 134-136, 141-143, 153-155, 191
Air Committee, 24, 46, 119
Air Council, 155, 158, 166-167, 192-193, 197
Air defence (UK), 44-50, 118-119, 122-123, 128-133, 151, 157, 204, 206-207
Air Department (War Office), 24, 27, 32, 34
Air Ministry, proposed, 24, 119, 127, 133-134; creation, 134-135, 155; dispute with Admiralty, 195-196, 204, 208-209; dispute with French, 198-199, 201, 218-219; dispute with War Office, 204-205, 208
Airco D.H.1, 64: D.H.2, 64-65, 76-77, 82, 87, 96, 107, 139; D.H.3, 64, 73; D.H.4, 103-104, 114, 136, 145, 154, 217; D.H.5, 102, 109, 138, 148; D.H.6, 131; D.H.9, 136, 154; D.H.9a, 187, 212, 214, 217; D.H.10, 152
Aircraft/engine production (British), 34, 36-37, 43, 46, 56-7, 66, 127-128, 130-131, 135, 154-155, 167
Albatros D series, 96-99, 104-107, 109-111, 113, 115, 138, 139-140
Armstrong Whitworth F.K.8, 103-104, 107-108; F.K.9 Quadruplane, 104, 109
Army manoeuvres (1912), 29-30
Ashmore, Maj. Gen., 133, 207
Asquith H, 21, 23-24, 43, 46, 49, 125
Aviatik C, 64
Avro 500, 22, 28, 34, 37; Avro 504, 37, 42-43
Baird, Major, 114, 120, 143, 166
Balfour, A., 81, 120, 125, 220-223, 226
Bannerman, Maj., 18-20, 22-23
Bares, Col., 98, 121-122, 124, 152
Baring, M. 72, 74, 84
Barnwell, F., 41-42, 65, 85, 103
Battles, Marne, 53-54; Neuve Chapelle, 57-59; Aubers Ridge, 58-59; Loos, 68-69; Jutland, 125; Somme, 89-93; Arras (1917), 110-115; Ypres (1917), 137, 144, 147-149; Cambrai, 160-164; German offensive 1918, 170-176; Amiens, 179-182; Allied offensives 1918, 184-189, 220
Beatty, Adml, 125, 135, 167
Bentley BR2, 142-143, 168-169
BHP engine, 103, 128, 136, 153-154
Bleriot, L., 16; planes, 16, 20-21
Boelcke, Lt., 73, 88, 93, 95-97
Brancker, Maj.-Gen., 24, 34-37, 39, 42-43, 46-47, 49, 56, 65-69, 71-72, 77-79, 82-84, 93-94, 99, 101-102,

Index

104-109, 120, 131-132, 140-141, 156, 166-167, 194; relationship with Trenchard, see Trenchard
Bristol Boxkite, 19, 24; Scout, 41-42, 61-62, 65-66, 72, 75, 83-84; TTA, 65, 84-85; Bristol Fighter, 103-105, 108, 111, 139-140, 142, 186-187, 205
Brooke-Popham, Col., 37, 46, 64, 140, 204
Capper, Col., 13-15
Churchill, W., 21- 23, 25, 44-45, 47, 49, 51, 81, 119, 132
Clemenceau, G., 198, 201, 218-219
Clerget rotary, 85, 99, 101, 104, 140-142
Cody, S., 13-15, 27-28
Cowdray, Lord, 126, 130-132, 155
Curzon, Lord, 119-125, 129, 132
De Havilland, G., 12, 20, 42, 64-65, 73, 76, 102, 153
Derby, Lord, 82-83, 120, 131-132
Directorate of Military Aeronautics, 34-37, 43, 61, 69, 71, 85, 104, 124, 143, 155-156
Dowding, Col., 85-86, 89, 91-92
Dunne, J., 12-15
Duval, Col., 198-199, 201
Ellington, Maj-Gen., 24, 35, 156-157, 194-195, 205
Esher CID subcommittee (1908), 14, 17-18
Farman, 20, 37, 43; Maurice, 58; Henri, 27, 37-38, 40, 46, 60
Foch, Marshall, 177, 179, 183-184, 190, 196, 198-199, 201-202, 204, 208, 218-219, 222, 226
Fokker E series, 63-66, 68, 73-8, 80, 82-83, 85, 87-88, 96, 143; D.II/III, 96; Dr 1, 111, 140, 171; D.VII, 143, 178-181, 185-189, 204, 209, 211, 216, 230; D.VIII, 230
Folland, H., 42
French, Field Marshall, 26, 30, 53, 56, 69, 131-133
Garros, R., 63, 65
Geddes, E., 135
Gotha GIV, 128; raids on UK, (day) 128-133; (night), 150-151, 157-159, 206-207
Grahame-White, C., 12, 21, 40
Grierson, Gen., 29, 32
Groves, Gen., 194-195, 197, 210-211, 215, 217, 219, 222-223, 225

Hague Peace Conference, 12-14, 46
Haig, Field Marshall, 24, 29-30, 54, 68-69, 101, 106, 115-116, 121-122, 126, 132, 137, 149, 153, 157, 159, 161, 163, 170, 173-174, 181-182, 190, 194, 196, 202, 208: views on strategic bombing, 122, 130, 134-135, 228
Halberstadt D II, 96-97, 99
Haldane, R., 14-16, 20, 21, 27, 29
Handley Page H.P. O/100, 80, 117, 126; H.P. O/400, 135-36, 151, 199, 212-213, 223; H.P. V/1500, 153, 196-197, 202-203, 210, 213, 220, 223-226, 228
Hankey, M, 17-18, 23, 46, 119
Hawker L., 63-64, 67-68, 74, 76, 89, 95, 99
Henderson, Lt.-Gen., 22-28, 32-36, 42-43, 46-47, 54-55, 60, 63, 65-72, 75, 77-78, 80, 82-84, 86, 101, 104-106, 112, 120, 131-133, 136, 152, 155-156, 166-167, 194; relationship with Trenchard, see Trenchard
Hispano-Suiza, 102, 105, 140-141, 154, 168; HS 8A (150-hp), 85, 99; HS 8B (200-hp), 110, 139-140; HS 8F (300-hp), 143, 169, 168-169, 187
Immelmann, Lt., 73, 88
Independent Force, 196-219, 222-225
Jellicoe, Adml, 125, 136
Joint War Air Committee, 82, 119-120, 156
Kerr, Rear Adml., 132, 135, 151, 155, 158-159, 166-167, 191, 194
Kitchener, Lord, 49-50, 54, 56, 67, 71
Lana, F., 11
Leigh-Mallory, Maj. 179, 182, 184
Liberty engine, 153-154, 187, 212, 214, 217
Lloyd George, D., 14, 116, 125-126, 129, 132, 137-138, 149, 155, 158, 167, 191, 194, 224
Martin, R., 12
Martinsyde S.1, 61; G.100, 72, 89, 93, 97; F.3/4, 142-143, 168-169, 187, 212, 230
Maxim, Sir Hiram, 14
Mayfly, 15, 21-22, 24
McKenna, R., 14, 21
Military aeroplane competition (1912), 22, 27-29

Mond, A., 16-17, 228
Montagu, Lord, 15, 119-120
Morane-Saulnier Parasol, 62-63, 65, 87; BB Biplane, 75, 83, 87; Type N, 63, 72, 74-75, 77, 86-87, 92-93, 95
Musgrave, Maj., 32-33, 38-41
Newall, Lt. Col., 152, 159, 191-192, 195, 197, 215
Nicholson, Field Marshall, 13-14, 17, 26
Nieuport, 75, 77, 81-84, 86-87, 98-99, 104, 108, 140, 147; N.10, 72-73, 83; N.11, 72; N. 12, 94, 98; N. 16, 82, 89, 95; N. 17, 82, 109, 111, 113, 138
Norman, H., 192, 194, 204
Northcliffe, Lord, 12-13, 16, 155
O'Gorman, M., 15, 20-23, 26-28, 32-34, 36-37, 42-44, 72
Ottley, Rear Adml, 17-18, 23
Paine, Maj.-Gen., 24, 30, 125-126, 131-132, 136, 142, 166
Pemberton-Billing, N, 52, 77, 118
Peuty, du, Commandant, 88, 91, 177
R.A.F. B.E.1, 20, 27; B.E.2a/b, 27-28, 33-34, 42; B.E.2c, 36-37, 43, 63, 77; used as bomber, 56, 90-91, 97, 100, 110-111, 113-114, 145; night fighter, 122-123; B.E.8, 36-37; B.E.12, 72, 84, 86, 93, 96-97
R.A.F. B.S.1, 26, 41
R.A.F. F.E.1, 20; F.E.2, 27, 32; F.E.2a, 38, 61; F.E.2b, 61, 76, 80, 87, 94, 97; F.E.2d, 79, 98, 104; used as bomber, 145-146, 152, 173, 185; F.E.3, 37-38; F.E.4, 38, 63-64, 73, 76, 79, 84-85, 152; F.E.5, 38, 63, 73, 76, 79, 85; F.E.6, 38, 63; F.E.7, 38, 63; F.E.8, 65, 72, 86, 93, 95, 106-107, 139; F.E.9, 86, 104, 157
R.A.F. N.E.1, 157
R.A.F. R.E.1, 36; R.E.4, 29; R.E.5, 36-37, 39, 41; R.E.7, 29, 39, 73, 84-85; R.E.8, 80, 94, 103, 107-108, 111, 113, 145, 174
R.A.F. S.E.1, 20; S.E.2, 41, 61; S.E.4, 42, 63; S.E.4a, 63; S.E.5, 86, 102, 104, 110, 115, 138; S.E.5a, 41, 139-141, 149, 161, 163, 168-169, 171
RFC formation, 23-24; aircraft types required, 18-19, 22, 44, 65, 141; role, 19, 22, 26-27, 36, 46, 52, 164-165, 170; expansion plans, 24, 34, 67, 69, 78, 104-105, 131, 135, 149-150; relationship with Army, 35, 100-101, 144
Richthofen, M. von, 99-100, 107, 111, 113, 140, 146, 163
RNAS, formation, 25; aircraft types required, 25-26, 62, 79, 80, 167; role, 25-26, 125-126; expansion plans, 167, 202; 3rd Wing, 124-126, 130
Robertson, Field Marshall, 129, 131, 134
Rolls, C., 14
Rolls-Royce, 43; Falcon, 57, 105, 127, 139, 142-143, 153, 168-169; Eagle, 57, 79, 84-86, 98, 103, 105, 127-128, 136, 142, 153-154, 197
Rothermere, Lord, 155, 166-167, 191-194
Royal Air Force, separate service proposed, 119, 127, 134; formation, 155, 166; role, 155, 192, 195; expansion, 202-203, 206
Royal Aircraft Factory (previously Balloon Factory) 20-21, 24-29, 32-34, 36-44, 60, 63-65, 72-73, 75, 77, 81, 84, 86, 102-104, 157, 169, 197
Salmond, Maj. Gen., 156-157, 168-170, 173-174, 178, 193, 196, 200, 204-206, 208, 211
Samson, Lt., 21, 23-26, 51
Seely, J., 20-24, 28-29, 34, 36, 42-44, 46
Short 184, 26, 80; Short Bomber, 80, 117, 126
Smuts, J., 129, 132-134, 149-151, 156-157, 203
Smythies, Maj., 185, 188
Sopwith Tabloid, 41-42, 52, 60-61; Strutter, 80, 82-84, 94, 96, 98, 106, 113-114, 117, 147; Pup, 84-86, 95, 98, 102, 109, 129, 140, 147; Camel, 102-103, 129, 138-140, 147-148, 157-158, 168, 179, 186-187; TF1, 169, 183; Triplane, 85, 102, 109-111, 140; Snipe, 142, 168-170, 186-187, 212, 217, 228; Salamander TF2, 169-170, 183; Dolphin, 139-141, 155, 168-171, 186
Sopwith, T., 42
Spad S.7, 85-86, 97-98, 109-110, 147; S.13, 110, 140
Stone, Col., 23
Strange, Lt., 55-56, 60, 62, 67

Strategic bombing, 9, 25-26, 44, 51-52, 69-70, 80-81, 105, 117-134, 152-153, 166-167, 190, 194-204, 210- 229, 231; public reaction, 12, 15-16, 44, 49, 128, 130; bombing Berlin, 16, 152-153, 195, 197, 206, 210, 222-226; RFC/RAF 41st Wing, 152, 159, 191; retaliation, 44, 118-120, 126, 128, 130, (see also RNAS 3rd Wing, Gotha raids, Zeppelin raids, Independent Force)

Sueter, Capt., 24-25, 80, 105, 119-120, 125, 132

Sunbeam, 43; Arab, 128, 153-154

Sydenham, Lord, 119-120

Sykes, Maj.-Gen., 23, 30-33, 38-39, 43, 47, 54-55, 194, 198-207, 210-211, 218-219, 222-223

Tactical air combat, single-seater fighter, 23, 61-62, 71-72, 83-84, 93-94, 97-98; two-seater fighter, 22, 26-27, 37-38, 62-63, 85, 93-95, 108-109, 113-114; multi-seater fighter, 22, 38, 62-63, 73, 84-85, 152, 211; tactics, 38-40, 60, 66, 73-76, 88-94, 100, 144-145, 148, 163, 170, 176-178, 230; deflector system, 63-65, 72, 74-75; synchronisation system, 63, 75, 77, 82-83, 85-86, 94-95

Tactical bombing; interdiction, 39-41, 58-60, 68, 176, 180-182; nocturnal, 40, 145-146, 173; close air support, 55-6, 146-148, 161-165, 183, 185, 188-189, 229; air/tank cooperation, 160, 179, 182, 184-185; Wadi El Far'a, 189-190

Tactical reconnaissance, 11, 22, 29, 53-55; directing artillery fire, 18, 41, 55, 58-59, 92, 148-149, 173; photo-reconnaissance, 33, 41, 55, 68, 108; contact patrols, 58, 69, 91; trench patrols, 91

Tank. 160-164, 179-180, 182, 184-185, 190

Tarrant Tabor, 153, 197

Tiverton, Lord, 135, 191, 195-197, 202, 204, 219, 225

Trenchard, Maj.-Gen., 30-31; 1st Wing, 54-55; GOC RFC, 66-67; CAS, 156-157, 166-167; GOC Independent Force, 196-197; relationship with Sykes, 47, 54; aircraft types required, 71-76, 82-85, 93, 97-99, 101- 104, 141, 152, 154; offensive fighter patrols, 88-93, 99-100, 110, 112-114, 143-145, 230; views on strategic bombing, 151-152, 159, 201, 205-206, 218; relationship with Brancker/Henderson, 101, 106,

Tudor, Rear Adml., 120-121, 123-124

Vaughan-Lee, Rear Adml. 105, 119-121, 123, 125-126

Vickers Gunbus, 38, 44, 46, 61-62, 68, 71, 74, 94; E.F.B.7, 63, 65, 73, 85, 152; E.F.B.8, 68, 73, 85; F.B.12, 104; Vimy, 136, 152, 206, 223-224, 226

War Office, 13, 17-18, 22, 24-26, 31, 34-36, 38-39, 42, 44-46, 49, 63, 66, 68, 71, 79, 105, 119, 134, 154-157, 167; dispute with Admiralty, see Admiralty; dispute with Air Ministry, see Air Ministry

Weir, W., 108, 127-128, 130-132, 135-136, 139-143, 150-155, 166-169, 170, 194-201, 204-210, 213-216, 218-220, 222-223

Wells., H. G., 16

Wilson, Gen., 46, 220, 222, 226

Wireless, 25, 29, 41, 55, 58, 68, 179, 183-184, 207

Wright Brothers, 12

Zeppelin, 12-13, 44-49, 151; threat to London, 14-17, 44-50; bases bombed, 51; factory bombed, 52; raids, 117-118, 158, 207-207

Zeppelin-Staaken R, 151, raids, 158, 206